MW01122114

MUSIC THERAPY EDUCATION AND TRAINING

MUSIC THERAPY EDUCATION AND TRAINING

From Theory to Practice

By

KAREN D. GOODMAN

Professor, Music Therapy

CHARLES C THOMAS • PUBLISHER, LTD.
Springfield • Illinois • U.S.A.

Published and Distributed Throughout the World by

CHARLES C THOMAS • PUBLISHER, LTD.
2600 South First Street
Springfield, Illinois 62794-9265

© 2011 by CHARLES C THOMAS • PUBLISHER, LTD.

ISBN 978-0-398-08609-1 (hard)
ISBN 978-0-398-08610-7 (paper)
ISBN 978-0-398-08611-4 (ebook)

Library of Congress Catalog Card Number: 2010033007

With THOMAS BOOKS *careful attention is given to all details of manufacturing
and design. It is the Publisher's desire to present books that are satisfactory as to their
physical qualities and artistic possibilities and appropriate for their particular use.*
THOMAS BOOKS *will be true to those laws of quality that assure a good name
and good will.*

*Printed in the United States of America
MM-R-3*

Library of Congress Cataloging in Publication Data

Goodman, Karen D.
 Music therapy education and training : from theory to practice / by Karen
D. Goodman.
  p. cm.
 Includes biographical references and index.
 ISBN 978-0-398-08609-1 (hard)–ISBN 978-0-398-08610-7 (pbk.)
 1. Music therapy–Instruction and study. 2. Music therapy. I. Title.

ML3920.G655 2011
615.8'5154–dc22   2010033007

For Jonathan, Sara and Adam

FOREWORD

Professor Karen Goodman's text on the education and training of music therapists should find its home on every academic bookshelf in music therapy departments across the globe. As an educator of music therapists, I appreciate Professor Goodman's ability to frame the competencies that board-certified music therapists must practice within the rich context of history of the profession, theories of learning and teaching, and the research behind educational and clinical training standards and methodology. The text opens with Martin Heidegger's quote that the "real teacher . . . lets nothing else be learned than learning." This is what Goodman does in her comprehensive treatment of education and training in music therapy. She provides the background and teaching tools, and lets the learning begin.

Historical perspective is important in considering the current state of the art of any science. In the first part of the book, we learn how the music therapy curriculum began and evolved in the United States. The research on music therapy education is punctuated by personal commentary based on the author's experience with her own students. Each competency declared as a necessary skill by the American Music Therapy Association is listed and reviewed. Goodman comments on how these are covered in various music therapy curricula, while she poses significant questions, such as "What is the therapist doing with the client(s) in response to the perceived needs of the client and the perceived or stated goals/objectives for the session?" and "What is the theoretical basis for the decisions the therapist is making in terms of methods, techniques and materials?" I found the semantic issues, such as the distinctions between methods and techniques, very interesting.

As she lays out her critical analysis of the competency-based music therapy curriculum, Goodman challenges every educator to integrate knowledge from multiple disciplines, whether it is from applications of music history or the reproduction and transcription of the musical responses of clients. She points out how problems in music theory raise questions of music cognition and perception. Goodman also explores the nature of performance skills and their "need to transcend the concert stage." She offers the thoughtful questioning of a seasoned clinician and experienced educator. The author confronts the many challenges of the music therapy educator, including such areas as translating keyboard ability into the clinical context, and transferring improvisation skills to meet the needs of the exceptional learner.

Goodman reminds us about the rich texture of clinical training for future music therapists. She emphasizes the structure, support and supervision inherent in practica and internships, that enable music therapy students to practice what they are learning in the classroom. Using music in supervision is one of many excellent suggestions. As the reader is introduced to the developmental stages of internship, it is clear that this perspective can inform supervisors of the needs of interns as they begin, continue, and terminate their internship experiences. Discussion of problematic phase development is extremely useful for supervisors who encounter resistance and parallel processes in the interpersonal dynamics between supervisor and student. I value Goodman's suggestions regarding the selective use of a journal as a concomitant during clinical training, and plan to incorporate these recommendations with my students.

Advanced practice is addressed by Goodman in a tour and comparison of masters' standards and advanced competencies. As I read Goodman's extensive list of expectations for the music therapist, I was impressed with the depth and breadth of the music therapy teaching agenda as compared with other healthcare curricula. In addition to learning clinical strategies and the complex needs and goals of a wide variety of clinical populations across the life cycle, the music therapist must also master the art of music and music engagement. These multiple talents constitute a tall order for any training program.

As an educator, I noted the various learning theories and taxonomies that underlie and guide teachers of prospective music therapists. Every educator may learn from these approaches. Goodman's presentation of developmental levels of engagement informs us about the experience of students relative to their readiness and ability to learn. This is certainly a significant indicator of success.

Particularly intriguing is the think-pair-share model that allows students to collaborate, learn from one another, and articulate the answer to a problem. Goodman offers a compendium of methods for teaching content of all kinds. Throughout training, ongoing assessment is critical. Goodman offers sample assessments, learning tasks and rubrics. An overview of international models of music therapy training offers a generous sampling of training programs. Goodman synthesizes common points of view and definitions from around the world. Appendices include major websites, books and monographs, and a useful bibliography—all great resources!

Karen Goodman has succeeded in offering educators and supervisors a pragmatic resource that reminds us of our history, emphasizes the diversity of competencies expected of a music therapist, and guides us with underlying theories, research, and methodologies for preparing the expert music therapist.

Suzanne B. Hanser, Ed.D, MT-BC
Chair, Music Therapy Department, Berklee College of Music
Past President, National Association for Music Therapy &
World Federation of Music Therapy

PREFACE

As a full-time tenure track professor at Montclair State University in the late 1970s, I experienced the various challenges of teaching in a fledgling specialty. Now, three decades later, having taught 31 undergraduate and graduate courses, I write this book with a sense of pride that I am privileged to be part of a profession which has grown so significantly. As the literature has burgeoned, so have the competencies for practicing effectively in the field. Once confined to education and training in the midwestern states of the United States in the late forties and early fifties, music therapy is now offered as a unique and known major discipline of study at undergraduate and graduate levels throughout the United States and around the globe.

As a singular resource on education and training of the music therapist, this book is written for multiple audiences: prospective and current music therapy students, prospective and current clinical supervisors, prospective and current educators and career advisors for students considering a future in music therapy. Although I write from the perspective of an educator from the United States, I trust that audiences around the globe will find information that is useful.

Students of music therapy deserve an understanding of how skills taught and developed in music therapy relate to clinical practice and the therapist's professional development. Further, students may benefit from understanding the various ways in which music therapy training programs can be organized and taught in order to select the training course best suited to them.

Clinical supervisors may profit from an overview of the academic process and the critical role that practicum and internship (see Chapter 3) play in this.

Educators entering or looking forward to enter music therapy pedagogy may benefit from this book on many levels by considering the who, what, and why of education and training in music therapy. Who are we training? What skills and toward what ends are we training? Why are we training students? We are training talented musicians who possess interpersonal skills and motivation so that they may apply music therapy skills and knowledge in helping others. In order to do this, we need to provide the student with a graduated sense of learning music therapy, a critical review of literature and a means of integrating information and skills.

Seasoned educators of music therapy may profit from a sense of looking back as well as forward in their teaching careers in order to reflect and improve upon their own goals, methods and evaluation in teaching. I know I have.

Finally, academic advisors, on the high school and college levels, may benefit from learning about the content and scope of education and training in the music therapy profession and what kind of student would profit from this.

The voice of the book, alternatively using the personal pronouns of *I* and *We* reflects a conscious effort to reach out to my reading audience of students and educators. Despite the absence of a currently published book on education and training in music therapy, the search for related material from the years 1964–2009 led to over 500 periodic references. Based on this search, I conclude that topics related to education and training in our field are vital.

In my writing, I reflect on the current literature, suggest new perspectives on education and training and profit from my years of teaching so as to provide the reader with multiple vignettes and advice. Since the majority of students train on bachelor and masters levels, my writing refers primarily to these levels of training. Education is the acquisition of skills and knowledge, originating in the classroom; training is the application of such skills and knowledge, arrived at through preprofessional clinical practice. How can we consider skills and knowledge not as isolated but within the context of music therapy? Further, how can we consider clinical training as a reflection of past-learned skills and knowledge?

Chapter 1, "Music Therapy Education and Training in the United States," provides an overview of how music therapy training programs in the United States are structured. Beginning with historical perspectives on the subject, we review academic standards defined by both the National Association of Schools of Music (NASM) and the American Music Therapy Association (AMTA), faculty qualifications, levels of practice suggested by levels of educational programming, post-graduate training and distance learning.

Chapter 2, "Competency-Based Education and Training," details how the competencies that guide entry-level education and training were composed. In discussing the competencies in depth, I share my perspectives regarding the need to incorporate, contextualize and extend music foundations and clinical foundations into music therapy coursework, teach music therapy foundations at successive levels of depth across clinical populations and foreshadow music therapy practice competencies through instructor demonstration and experiential role-playing in class.

Chapter 3, "Preprofessional Clinical Training," details suggestions for training the student in practice competencies both in practicum and internship that not only demonstrate theory to practice but, conversely, practice to theory.

Chapter 4, "Advanced Competencies," reviews the history of how the competencies for advanced practice were composed and how revised standards will play a part in the development of masters programs in the United States. Coursework in 32 graduate programs across the United States is analyzed in order to demonstrate the nature of the masters as immersion learning experience and survey the current use of coursework to meet competency areas.

Chapter 5, "Theories of Teaching and Learning," reflects on the ways in which students take in information. We review relevant learning theory, learning styles and developmental phases of the college student in order to integrate this information within the scope of music therapy pedagogy and evaluation.

Chapter 6, "Music Therapy Pedagogy," presents information related to admissions, advisement, retention, and teaching and evaluation techniques in music therapy university programs. Further, we take a look at the sixty-year history of music therapy books published in English and consider the basis on which we select reading for our students.

Chapter 7, "Around the Globe," considers training models in 30 countries spanning all continents and closes with a discussion of common themes and issues in the development of education and training.

The book concludes with a positive appreciation for all the educational advances we have made throughout the world and encouragement for prospective and current students and prospective and current educators.

Since I have written the book for different audiences, readers should feel free to refer to chapters most pertinent to their interests and levels of experience.

I am grateful for the past, current and future opportunities in my personal and professional life to learn and teach.

Karen D. Goodman, June 2010
Montclair, New Jersey

ACKNOWLEDGMENTS

I acknowledge the support of many individuals and groups who have supported my efforts in writing this book.

- To my parents, Daniel and Ruth Goodman, for their love and encouragement.
- To my mother, Ruth Miller Goodman, for being an inspirational teacher.
- To my husband, Jonathan Lautman, for his love, editing suggestions, and encouragement.
- To my children, Sara and Adam Lautman for their love, thoughtful conversation about the college experience and encouragement.
- To my brother, Dr. Harold Goodman, for our many inspiring conversations about alternative medicine, writing and learning.
- To Ronald Sharps, Associate Dean, College of the Arts, Montclair State University, for his suggestions regarding my sabbatical application.
- To the Research Academy for University Learning and the Service Learning Programs at Montclair State University for opening up new areas of inquiry
- To Montclair State University for providing the necessary release time and sabbatical to write this book.
- To music therapy colleagues from this country and abroad who very kindly responded to my inquiries for most recent information: Jane Creagan, Kenneth Bruscia, Kate Gfeller, Shannon de L'Etoile, Jayne Standley, Peggy Codding, Sr. Miriam Pfeifer, Suzanne Sorel, Denise Grocke, Louise Steele, Thomas Wosch, Monika Nöcker-Ribaupierre, Paul Nolan, Elaine Streeter, Colin Lee, Cynthia Briggs, Gabriela Wagner, Cochavit Elefant, Chava Sekeles, Hyun Ju Chong, Astrid Lorz-Zitzmann, Francois-Xavier Vrait, Simon Gilbertson, Eric Miller, Heidi Fauch, Edith Lecourt, Annemiek Vink, Henk Smeijsters, Marilyn Sandness, Clive Robbins, Alan Turry, and Tian Gao.
- To Grietje Wijbenga, Cristina Zamani, Robert Glick and You-ri Lee for their generous help in translations of websites.

- To Donna Chadwick for her critical and supportive listening.
- To Suzanne Hanser for graciously lending her experience and expertise in preparing the Foreword.
- To Michael Thomas, Charles C Thomas, Publisher, for his efforts in publishing this book.
- To my students, current and former, at Montclair State University, who have inspired me to write this book.

CONTENTS

MUSIC THERAPY EDUCATION
AND TRAINING

Chapter 1

MUSIC THERAPY EDUCATION AND TRAINING IN THE UNITED STATES

Teaching is more difficult than learning because what teaching calls for is this: to let learn. The real teacher, in fact, lets nothing else be learned than learning. His (Her) conduct, therefore, often produces the impression that we properly learn nothing from him, if by "learning" we now suddenly understand merely the procurement of useful information.

Martin Heidegger

INTRODUCTION

All of us have had the experience of attending a social occasion and, as a matter of small talk or genuine curiosity, being asked what we do for a living. When you reply, "I am a music therapist," the response may frequently be, "Oh, how interesting. I think I have heard about that. What is it . . . listening to a CD?" As a polite person, you provide your own informal definition or a formal definition such as the following: "Music Therapy is the clinical and evidence-based use of music interventions to accomplish individualized goals within a therapeutic relationship by a credentialed professional who has completed an approved music therapy program" (AMTA, 2010). Yet, for some strange reason, which I have yet to figure out, that answer does not seem to suffice. You are drawn into a discussion of how music therapy might work, with whom, how, and so forth.

However perplexing this scenario may be, it is true that we feel, on one hand, compelled to relay the complexity of our work and education and training or, on the other hand, annoyed that we have to explain this! Why does the work as well as the education and training of the music therapist seem difficult to grasp? Perhaps, it is the interdisciplinary and transdisciplinary nature of the craft itself, a craft that requires musicianship, interpersonal ability, knowledge of disability, creativity and the ability to extend what we call theory to practice, true learning which is implied by the Heidegger quote.

In this chapter, I review the history of education and training in the United States and describe how the American Music Therapy Association (AMTA) and The National Association of Schools of Music (NASM) structure training programs, both undergraduate and graduate.

Music therapy education and training at the university level, originating in the United States in 1944, has, like the world and people it affects, changed and grown throughout the decades. In the United States, music therapy is currently offered at universities located across seven geographical regions (New England, Mid-Atlantic, Midwest, Great Lakes, Southeastern, Southwestern and Western) and 31 states, with 38 universities offering programs at the undergraduate level, 30 universities offering both undergraduate and graduate programs, two universities offering only the masters and eight universities offering doctoral level work (within the context of creative arts therapy, music therapy or music education with emphasis in music therapy). Over two decades ago (Maranto & Bruscia, 1988), 52 universities offered programs at the undergraduate level, 21 universities offered both undergraduate and/or graduate programs and eight universities offered doctoral level work (primarily within the context of music education with emphasis in music therapy). Today, the numbers indicate a 33 percent growth in the number of masters level programs over the last two decades, a 28 percent decrease in the number of undergraduate programs, and no overall growth in the number of doctoral programs. For the academic year, 2008–2009, there was an average program enrollment of 29 students in 4.5-year undergraduate programs and 20 students in 2–3-year graduate programs (Creagan, 2010); this indicates a proportionately higher number of students enrolled in graduate programs.

At this time in history, music therapy is a profession with a proliferating literature base, scientific data to support clinical gains and expansive areas of clinical expertise. Music therapy education and research reflects interdisciplinary as well as transdisciplinary connections with the academic literature in many social sciences and natural sciences while its application crosses a plethora of other helping professions. All university training programs receive applications from musicians who wish to use their talents in a helping profession.

Consider the following:

1. Where, when and how did music therapy education and training begin in the United States?

2. What guidelines structure university programs in the United States?
3. How are levels of practice in the United States related to educational content and structure?

THE DEVELOPMENT OF UNIVERSITY PROGRAMS

Historical Perspectives

Several fine historical research publications document the beginnings of music therapy in the United States. They include discussion regarding music therapy practice in nineteenth century America (Davis, 1987), biographical sketches of music therapy pioneers (Davis, 1993), practice in New York City in the thirties (Davis, 1997), the historical formation of the National Association for Music Therapy (Boxberger, 1962), the initial journal literature of the *Journal of Music Therapy* (Solomon, 1993) and, most relevant to this chapter, a comprehensive overview of what led to the formation of music therapy education and training programs in the fifties (de L'Etoile, 2000).

Music therapy education began in the United States as single courses, the first of which was conducted in 1919 at Columbia University and developed into a series of courses by 1926. The development of the first university programs, at Michigan State in 1944, the College of the Pacific, California in 1947, the University of Kansas in 1948, and Alverno College, Wisconsin in 1948 led to an established NAMT curriculum in 1952. What was the character of this early training?

Musicians Margaret Anderson and then Isa Maud Ilsen, who had used music in the treatment of Canadian soldiers afflicted with what we would probably consider today as post-traumatic stress disorder, taught the initial 1919 coursework at Columbia University in New York City. These courses focused on understanding psychophysiological reactions to music in order to apply this information in delivering music to hospital patients.

Subsequent music therapy education proceeded in the 1940s, largely in response to train hospital volunteers who were using music with war veterans. These educational efforts developed through courses in colleges, courses in hospitals and courses under the auspices of relevant musical organizations.

For example, college lectures and practicum entitled "The Principals and Practices of Music Therapy in the Neuropsychiatric Hospital" were offered at Westminster College in Princeton, New Jersey in order to support the training of hospital music volunteers planning and presenting musical programs at the nearby Veterans Administration Hospital in Lyons, New Jersey. Similarly, state hospitals such as the one located in Mount Pleasant, Iowa and Agnew, California provided coursework (i.e., psychopathology, psychiatry, psychotherapy, specialized therapies for psychiatric patients) for music volunteers in order to conduct musical ensemble and instruct patients in music appreciation, music theory and vocal and instrumental techniques.

Organizational Support

Organizations such as Musical Guidance, headed by Arthur Flagler Fultz and The National Foundation of Music Therapy, headed by Harriet Seymour, also provided training courses. Fultz taught at the Boston School of Occupational Therapy in 1948 and Seymour taught at Steinway Hall in New York City, 1941–1944, using her text, *An Instruction Course in the Use and Practice of Music Therapy* (Davis, 1996), published in 1944.

In addition to these latter organizations, other organizations began to discuss the importance of training: the Music Teachers' National Association (MTNA), the National Association of Schools of Music (NASM), and the Music Educators' National Conference (MENC). In 1946, both MTNA and MENC formed cooperative subcommittees, namely the Committee of Functional Aspects of Music in Hospitals (MENC) and the Committee on Music in Therapy (MTNA), headed by Roy Underwood who had started the music therapy program at Michigan State two years before. The preliminary role of musicians in hospitals as entertainers began to change as an "increased awareness of the effectiveness of music in altering mood states and affecting behavioral change" (de L'Etoile, 2000, p. 63) began to develop.

The development of the first university programs in the late forties and early fifties was interdisciplinary, encouraged by figures such as Dr. Rudolf Dreikurs, the Austrian psychiatrist, Dr. Ira Altschuler, the American psychiatrist, Dr. Karl Menninger, the director of the well-known Menninger Foundation, and Dr. E. Thayer Gaston, the music educator and educational psychologist. As pioneers in the field, music therapy faculties were trained in other professions, generally music education or performance.

Initial University Programs

The first music therapy program in the United States was established at Michigan State University in 1944 under Roy Underwood. Others followed. The undergraduate program at Alverno College in Milwaukee, Wisconsin, established in 1948 under the direction of Sister Xaveria, included three semesters of Theory of Music Therapy and closed with a nine-month training period. The undergraduate program at the Chicago Musical College, headed by Esther Goetz Gillanland, unlike other programs, called for the student to look "into one's own personality problems" as a source of "therapeutic effectiveness" (de L'Etoile, 2000, p. 61). This training included psychology of music, the influence of music on behavior and the theory and practice of music therapy in addition to a broad general education.

Early university programs were conducted at the undergraduate level, with the exception of the academic program at University of Kansas, under the direction of Dr. E. Thayer Gaston. This program started with graduate level courses in the Psychology of Music and The Influence of Music on Behavior, courses that remained the core of the approved NAMT undergraduate curriculum in 1952 and proceeded into the seventies.

The University of Kansas degree program was offered in 1948 as a 27 credit graduate program, Master of Music Education in Functional Music, which also included studies in Organization of School Music, Music in Society and Abnormal Psychology. Students at KU completed a six-month internship at the Winter Veteran's Administration Hospital in Topeka, Kansas, under the clinical direction of Donald E. Michel and administrative oversight of Dr. Karl Menninger. Undergraduate applicants to this program had a degree in music with additional prerequisites in biological sciences, sociology and general psychology. Gaston, a leading figure in music therapy education in the fifties, teaching at the University of Kansas, was a musician as well as an educational psychologist and his early writings present principles of music therapy which remain true to this day (1968), forecasting current writings on the role of music in the context of neurobiology, multiculturalism and aesthetics (Gaston, 1964a).

Wanda Lathom, who had been trained at the University of Kansas, organized the first program in the northeast in 1970 at Montclair State College (now Montclair State University), Montclair, New Jersey. Montclair State proved a perfect home for music therapy, welcoming students to an academically strong college community with an exceptionally gifted music faculty from neighboring New York City. Nearby hospital, school and nursing home affiliations for clinical work included Overlook Hospital, now Essex County Hospital Center, then known as one of the most progressive therapeutic communities in the United States.

De l'Etoile (2000) identifies three primary concerns shared by pioneering university music therapy educators: (1) the compatibility of academic standards and health care trends; (2) the question of standardizing the undergraduate curriculum; and (3) identification of the most suitable candidates for music therapy training.

Initial Curriculum in Music Therapy

With the formation of the National Association for Music Therapy in June 1950, an Education Committee was formed to recommend standards in education and training. Roy Underwood, the chair of this committee as well as the President-elect of the aforementioned Music Teachers National Association and the director of the first music therapy program at Michigan State, worked with Dr. E. Thayor Gaston as well as John Anderson, M.D., Superintendent of the Topeka State Hospital, to design an initial curriculum for NAMT approved schools (de L'Etoile, 2000).

The first core undergraduate curriculum in music therapy, approved by the education committee in 1952 for the National Association for Music Therapy, which was established in 1950, included the following:

1. General Education, 30 s.h., to include such subjects as English, Speech, Biology, Physiology and the Humanities.
2. Physical Education, 4 s.h., to include dancing such as folk, square, tap and creative dance.
3. Music, 60 s.h., to include two years of music theory, one year of music history, piano skills (i.e., encompassing sight-reading, accompanying, transposition, improvised accompaniments and piano literature), vocal methods, organ, class instruments (brass, woodwind and strings required; percussion recommended), conducting, arranging (instrumental and vocal arranging and adapting for small vocal/instrumental combinations) and recreational music (i.e., rhythm band, musical games, community song).
4. Social sciences to include Principles of Sociology, Delinquent and Normal Behavior, Mental Hygiene, The Family.
5. Psychology to include General Psychology, Child or Adolescent Psychology, Abnormal Psychology, Clinical and Experimental Psychology recommended, Psychology of Music and Influence of Music on Behavior.
6. General hospital orientation.
7. General electives.
8. Clinical training of six months in a neuropsychiatric hospital (note: the requirement of working in a neuropsychiatric hospital did not change until 1971) in addition to 128 hours of preinternship and two additional months in another facility for those students wishing to practice music therapy with children.

It is striking to note that only Psychology of Music, Influence of Music on Behavior and General Hospital Orientation constituted what was then considered music therapy coursework. This collection of three courses stands in sharp contrast to the many music therapy courses developed in current university curriculums.

Yet only two years after the initial curriculum was approved, in 1954 educators and clinicians began to call for more uniform standards and educational foundations of music therapy. In 1960, Charles Braswell, Director of Music Therapy at Loyola University, called for a reexamination of education and training, citing concerns regarding the development of specific skills, historical and theoretical knowledge, professional growth and development and research. These concerns also recognized that the curriculum was weighty due to demands from the university and NASM, an issue we live with today.

In 1961, Braswell suggested a five-year music therapy curriculum that would allow students sufficient time to develop musical skills as well as background courses in sociology and what we know today as group dynamics. These latter social science courses were developed in anticipation of the social restructuring of psychiatric institutions and perceived needs in clinical practice.

Today, as it was in the past, changes in mental health; social service and educational agencies serve to forecast different demands in clinical practice and, subsequently, needs in music therapy education and training.

Music Therapy Organizations

The development of music therapy programs proceeded under the umbrellas of two independent music therapy organizations, The National Association for Music Therapy (inception, 1950) and The American Association for Music Therapy (inception, 1971). At the time of the AAMT inception, many music therapists seemed to associate the two different organizations with varying clinical perspectives, NAMT as behavioral and AAMT as humanistic. However, organizations are composed of clinicians with multiple perspectives, some of whom belonged to and were active in both organizations. As the years passed, many realized that we were all closer in spirit than previously realized. As a relatively small profession, we began to draw closer together, a move that would ultimately standardize the seven educational programs of AAMT under the same umbrella as the 66 programs of NAMT. In 1989, 16 educators from both AAMT and NAMT met at The California Symposium on Music Therapy Education and Training to discuss types of clinical practice as well as needs in education and training (Maranto, 1989a). Stated concerns in education and training included the following:

1. Identification of entry level competencies.
2. Availability of clinical specialization for students.
3. Greater emphasis on music therapy methods and clinical applications, as opposed to theory and research, needed in the undergraduate curriculum.
4. Functional music examinations for prospective interns (voice, keyboard, guitar, improvisation, group ensemble, adapted methods).

5. Mechanisms for screening students at academic and clinical sites.
6. Consideration of student learning styles in designing education and training program.
7. Encouraging students to experience personal therapy.

In 1998 the two organizations, NAMT and AAMT, merged to form the American Music Therapy Association. As a result of the merger, guidelines for program approval as well as internship were jointly refined and presented to the membership.

AMTA GUIDELINES FOR APPROVED PROGRAMS

Formed in 2002, under the AMTA, the Education and Training Advisory Board was charged with the responsibility to analyze "the relationship of standards and competencies to advanced degrees, education and training requirements, levels of practice, professional titles and designations, and various state licenses" (AMTA, 2005).

The *Standards for Education and Clinical Training*, in tandem with the *AMTA Professional Competencies* (for undergraduate and equivalency studies) and *AMTA Advanced Competencies* (for masters level study) *continue* to be reviewed and revised, most recently in November 2009 (AMTA, 2009). These documents are three of several (see *AMTA Standards of Clinical Practice, AMTA Code of Ethics*) which uphold professional standards for music therapists, including standards for clinical interventions and ethical conduct.

Bachelors Degree

Coursework

The standard Bachelors degree in music therapy, in compliance with the standards of NASM (NASM, 1985) and AMTA (AMTA, 2009, p. 5) includes 45 percent of coursework in Musical Foundations, 15 percent in Clinical Foundations, 15 percent in Music Therapy and 20–25 percent in General Education with 5 percent Electives. There may be variation in this formula dependent upon the nature of the Bachelors degree (i.e., Bachelor of Arts, Bachelor of Music, Bachelor of Science). Professional competency-based standards established by AMTA in 1994 (*AMTA Professional Competencies*) are the basis of undergraduate coursework in approved music therapy programs, education and training which includes both classroom, practicum and internship experience. By definition, therefore, a program with 120 credits would include at least 18 credits in music therapy core courses. The reality is that most programs are much larger than 120 credits, typically taking 4.5 years to complete, and the requirement to include competency-based skills in coursework results in an intensive and demanding program of study. Music therapy courses at the undergraduate level incorporate theory and practice within the context of the therapeutic process for a variety of client groups and ages. Beginning research training is introduced.

Bachelors programs in music therapy are composed of students entering college from high school or transferring from other collegiate programs. In order for them to remain competitive for music auditions, they are well advised to start professional training on their primary instrument early in schooling and, in conjunction with that training, study music theory. Most programs audition classical musicians; an increasing number are also auditioning jazz musicians. Students who have completed their studies at the undergraduate level will typically take time to practice clinically before considering graduate school. Some graduates choose to continue music therapy degree work while others may supplement their training and credentials with masters' degrees in social work, special education, speech pathology, physical therapy, psychology, and other helping professions.

Clinical Training Component

The undergraduate requirement for the clinical training component of the degree includes a system of 1200 hours of clinical training (AMTA, 2009, p. 7). The typical breakdown of the hours is 200 for practicum and 1000 for internship. The student is qualified to begin internship after successful completion of undergraduate coursework.

The music therapy educator/advisor is responsible for arranging both pre-internship and internship affiliations. These experiences provide a successive deepening of clinical experiences and related seminars.

According to AMTA, "The academic institution shall develop an individualized training plan with each student for completion of all facets of clinical training, based on the AMTA competencies, student's needs, student's competencies, and life circumstances. . . . A written internship agreement will also be made between the student, internship supervisor, and the academic faculty to describe the student's level of performance at the initiation of the internship and the expected student's level of performance in demonstrating the required exit-level competencies at the conclusion of the internship. . . . This internship agreement is required for both the university affiliated and AMTA national roster internship programs" (AMTA, 2009, p. 6). Such agreements, if properly executed, consider the internship as the final step of course mastery with associated competencies.

Prior to the merger of NAMT and AAMT, there were no university affiliation agreements for internship. It is likely that guidelines for university affiliation will be further detailed in the near future as these options become more popular (AMTA, 2009). The structure and considerations for both practicum and internship are described at length in Chapter 3 of this book.

Equivalency

It is commonplace for students with degrees in fields other than music therapy to take what is referred to as the *Equivalency* program, essentially taking all those courses required of the undergraduate music therapy student in order to prepare for the board certification exam. Generally speaking, students who have a degree in a field unrelated to music will be responsible for taking the undergraduate equivalent of a degree in music therapy without the general education requirements. Students who have a degree in a field related to music will be responsible for taking the undergraduate music therapy courses. Equivalency programs do not grant degrees but will, in many cases, be considered linked to forthcoming study on the Masters level. In such cases, prospective students will be well advised to insure that programs are offering coursework incorporating the *AMTA Professional Competencies* as prerequisite to coursework incorporating the *AMTA Advanced Competencies*. Most universities recognize the entry level content as content housed in undergraduate courses, or prerequisites to graduate courses while a few universities consider all coursework, entry level or not, as masters' degree coursework.

Students who hold the undergraduate degree in music therapy and have attained a professional credential do not, generally, have to take prerequisite courses prior to applying to and entering a masters' program in music therapy.

Masters Degree

Coursework

NASM requirements for Masters degrees are dependent upon the nature of the degree title (AMTA, 2009). The Master of Music, placing advanced music therapy studies within the musical context, includes 40 percent music therapy, 30 percent music and 30 percent electives in related areas. The Master of Music Therapy, placing advanced music therapy studies within a context of theory, research and practice in music therapy, includes 50 percent music therapy and 50 percent electives (i.e., supportive studies in areas related to music therapy). The Master of Arts or Master of Music Education degree, placing advanced music therapy studies within a context of creative arts therapy, expressive therapies, psychology, counseling, social sciences, education arts, and/or humanities, includes 40 percent music therapy, 30 percent specialization field and 30 percent electives (i.e., supportive studies in areas related to music therapy). Lastly, the Master of Science degree, placing advanced music therapy studies within a context of medicine, allied health and other physical sciences, includes 40 percent music therapy, 30 percent science specialization and 30 percent electives (i.e., supportive studies in areas related to music therapy). It is noteworthy that there is only one music therapy graduate program in the United States granting a Master of Science degree at this time. With the development of research in neurology and music processing, it is hopeful that more programs of this type will emerge in the near future.

With 40–50 percent of masters level coursework in the area of music therapy and an additional percentage in related electives, the bulk of graduate study, which may span 30–48 credits (48 credits required at Masters level for the New York State License in Creative Arts Therapy) is primarily devoted to a more intensive study of and experience with theory, advanced music therapy, supervision and research.

According to the recently updated *AMTA Standards for Education and Clinical Training* (2009), students in the master's degree are expected to acquire in-depth knowledge and competence in music therapy theory (e.g., principles, foundations, current theories of music therapy practice, supervision, education, implications for research) (AMTA, 2009, p. 8), advanced clinical skills (e.g., in-depth understanding of the clinical and supervisory roles and responsibilities of a music therapist acquired through a supervised clinical component), and knowledge and competence in one or more of the following areas: research, musical development and personal growth and/or clinical administration. Programs are expected to be a minimum of 30 semester hours with a minimum of 12 semester hours in music therapy. Culminating projects include suggested options of thesis, clinical paper or project.

Beyond the NASM guidelines, AMTA suggests the formulation of different types of curricular structures:

- *Practice Oriented:* focus on advanced clinical practice.
- *Research Oriented:* focus on "scholars and researchers in music therapy, preparing graduates for doctoral study" (AMTA, 2009, p. 8).
- *Research and Practice Orientations:* simultaneous development of student ability to produce research "and utilize, combine or integrate these findings within the practice of music therapy" (AMTA, 2009, p. 8).

AMTA suggestions encourage the development of specialization areas incorporating advanced topics based on faculty expertise and institutional resources. The *AMTA Advanced Professional Competencies* are described at length in Chapter 4 of this book. Of note is the proviso that all master's degree in music therapy "must include a supervised clinical component beyond the completion of the 1200 hours of clinical training required for acquisition of the *AMTA Professional Competencies* and concurrently with or following completion of graduate music therapy courses" (AMTA, 2009, p. 8) in concert with supervision.

Prospective students for masters' programs in music therapy, depending on individual academic needs, will profit from considering the nature and breadth of the curriculum in terms of music therapy specializations, research training, opportunities for clinical training and supervision, thesis support and the clinical backgrounds of the faculty.

With completion of the Masters' degree, graduates will do well to continue to refine their clinical practice and related research.

Doctoral Degree

Coursework

There are eight doctoral programs in the United States that are of greatest relevance to music therapy: five grant a doctoral degree in Music Education with emphasis in music therapy, two grant a doctoral degree in Expressive Therapies (or Creative Arts Therapy) and one grants a doctoral degree in Music Therapy. Two of the eight programs were developed since 2008. Program content is largely individualized: credits, including coursework and dissertation, range from 45 to 72 beyond the Masters and while prerequisites vary widely by program, all currently require a minimum of either three or five years of employment as a professional music therapist, conforming to the AMTA standards for full-time music therapy faculty teaching at the undergraduate or graduate level.

Prospective students, depending upon their individual needs, will have to consider the degree of breadth given to music therapy as a major discipline within each program, the academic strength and availability of elective courses in departments related to music therapy, the rigor of training in research and the nature of and institutional commitment to dissertation supervision. In cases where music therapists pursue a doctorate and the subject matter is possibly related to music therapy (i.e., music education, psychology, ethnomusicology, etc.) but does not provide the option of emphasis in music therapy, it is, of course, incumbent upon the student to achieve a new level of integration independently, possibly through the dissertation.

The doctoral degree "shall impart advanced competence in research, theory development, clinical practice, supervision, college teaching and/or clinical administration, depending on the title and purpose of the program" (AMTA, 2009, p. 10). AMTA also states," AMTA and NASM will work together in the delineation of the doctoral degree in music therapy" (AMTA, 2009, p. 10).

Faculty and Clinical Supervisor Qualifications, AMTA

According to AMTA, undergraduate and graduate faculty with teaching and/or administrative responsibilities at the undergraduate level should hold an appropriate professional credential, a masters degree in music therapy or a related area (with a minimum of 12 semester hours in graduate music therapy) and have a minimum of three years of full-time (or its equivalent in part-time work) clinical experience if teaching at the undergraduate level and five years of full-time (or its equivalent in part-time work) clinical experience if teaching at the graduate level. Both undergraduate and graduate faculty should pursue continuing education relevant to teaching and demonstrate mastery of entry and selected advanced competencies as well as effectiveness as a clinician (in at least one area of practice for undergraduate faculty and two areas of practice for graduate faculty), teacher, supervisor and administrator (AMTA, 2009).

Academic programs are required to have one full-time faculty position in music therapy for each degree program offered. Adjunct faculty is to be determined in line with student enrollment and teaching loads. The interrelationship of the undergraduate program and the graduate program frequently necessitate graduate students taking undergraduate coursework prior to or in conjunction with certain graduate courses. It is of benefit to academic programs offering both undergraduate and graduate coursework to have faculty teaching at both levels in order to offer different clinical perspectives and teaching approaches for students. This crossover benefits from cooperative and regular planning on the part of faculty in the program.

Adjunct faculty with teaching responsibility should have an appropriate professional credential, a bachelor's degree or equivalent in music therapy, at least two years of full-time clinical experience (or its equivalent), pursue continuing education relevant to teaching and demonstrate competencies appropriate to the teaching assignment (AMTA, 2009).

Clinical supervisors in the preinternship or practicum phase of training should hold an appropriate professional credential, a bachelor's degree or equivalent in music therapy, at least one year of full-time clinical experience (or its equivalent), pursue continuing education relevant to teaching, demonstrate entry level competencies, and demonstrate effectiveness as a clinician (in at least one area of practice) and beginning supervisor (AMTA, 2009).

Internship supervisors should hold an appropriate professional credential, a bachelor's degree or equivalent in music therapy, at least two years of full-time clinical experience (or its equivalent), experience working in the internship setting, pursue continuing education relevant to teaching, demonstrate entry level competencies, and demonstrate effectiveness as a clinician (in at least one area of practice) and senior level supervisor (AMTA, 2009).

Academic Approval Process, AMTA

The academic approval process for Bachelors and Masters programs is required every ten years. Ideally this is scheduled concurrently with the NASM review for academic accreditation. On the undergraduate level, music requirements dictated by NASM (emphasizing classical music training), coursework based on music therapy competencies and, finally, university general education requirements create a juggling act for educators and students. It may be that the issue of NASM accreditation as a formal prerequisite for AMTA academic approval should be reevaluated in the near future, especially if a need for more popular and contemporary training in music is important to the profession.

Technically, the Academic Program Approval Committee (APAC), may recommend the following: (1) approval; (2) defer approval until necessary changes are documented; (3) conditional approval pending NASM accreditation; and (4) not approve. Reviews of competency-related coursework, faculty resumes and questions that reflect in-depth curricular review examination are completed during the academic approval process.

Distance Education

The lure of online learning beckons. As a convenient means of accessing education for the consumer and therefore a possible lucrative source of income for the university, distance learning is quickly gaining in popularity among students and university. Yet, with music therapy training known as an entity that revels in experiential learning and the use of active music making, how is educating students in music therapy by means of the computer successfully realized?

In my review of masters programs throughout the United States, I found five programs that were online. I found no mention of online learning outside of the United States although information may have changed since this book was published.

In their most recent guidelines, AMTA (2009) cites an unpublished study conducted by Keith and Vega in 2006 which defines distance learning as "programs in which more than 40 percent of the requirements are fulfilled through distance learning" (AMTA, 2009, p. 13) and, concludes that "technology beyond the posting of syllabi, course outlines, and use as a communication device, is currently being used in 50 percent of music therapy undergraduate programs, 45 percent of which use technology only for discussions and online assignments . . . 58 percent of graduate programs in the United States reportedly rely on distance learning" (AMTA, 2009, p. 13).

The American Music Therapy Association, in conjunction with NASM, has, in light of the Keith and Vega study as well as frequent inquiry on the part of prospective students and prospective distance learning programs (AMTA, 2009, pp. 12–16), instituted guidelines for distance learning in order to insure that students continue to be properly trained. The gist of these guidelines is the underlying concern that students receive online education that is equivalent to what would have been received in a program in residence. This includes virtual office hours, admission in compliance with typical university admission policies for music therapy programs, coursework which meets curricular structures and competencies as outlined in AMTA *Standards for Education and Clinical Training* (AMTA, 2009), evaluation of music competencies prior to acceptance into a distance–learning program, establishing clinical experiences in accordance with AMTA standards for clinical training, site visits by academic faculty and audio-video recordings acceptable for evaluation of clinical competency. Preliminary research (Gregory, 2009b) suggests that selecting and coding written self-reports of on-site (i.e., clinical practice) task behaviors provides a means of evaluating effective online instruction.

CREDENTIALING OF MUSIC THERAPISTS IN THE UNITED STATES

Prior to 1998, the entry level professional certification was achieved through the completion of the academic program, a program either accredited by the National Association for Music Therapy, which granted the Registered Music Therapist (RMT) credential or the American Association for Music Therapy, which granted the Certified Music Therapist (CMT) or Advanced Certified Music Therapist (ACMT) credential. These former credentials are and will continue to be maintained through the National Music Therapy Registry through the year 2020 as professional credentials for the practice and teaching of music therapy.

Originating in 1983, at which time all registry applicants were offered a waiver of the CBMT exam in order to become board certified, the Certification Board of Music Therapy serves as an outside body to evaluate the education and training of the music therapy applicant for the purposes of awarding board certification. Applicants for these exams have completed an AMTA accredited and approved program of training (accredited by NASM and approved by AMTA subject to the academic approval process), which bases coursework on the published AMTA competencies. The questions on the CBMT exam are based on reported entry-level knowledge and skills of the professional music therapist, information that is updated every five years. In order to maintain board certification, the Board Certified music therapist (MT-BC) must accrue a certain number of training points over a five-year cycle. The credential of MT-BC became the only professional credential available for new professionals in the United States in 1998 when the American Music Therapy Association was formed.

INFORMATION RELATED TO EDUCATION AND TRAINING

Multiple Credentials in Music Therapy Education and Training

Universities are in a state of ongoing change. Music therapists, responding to the needs of the workplace as well as the desire to augment their education complement their credentials with additional degrees, certifications and/ or licenses, as appropriate to various fields such as counseling, music education, special education and creative arts therapy.

Currently, one of the results of real (New York State License in Creative Arts Therapists, necessitating a 48 credit Masters) or perceived pressures in the marketplace is the packaging of music therapy education. For example, one-quarter of current graduate programs include coursework leading to other credentials in counseling, special education or creative arts therapy. With music therapy education already a pressure cooker for many of our students, we will have to continue to consider how additional training, albeit related and valuable, impacts our students and their delivery of music therapy services.

Post-Graduate Training Credentials

Prospective students entering the field of music therapy may be confused with the array of letters following the names of many practitioners in the field. What do they mean? With the development of specialty approaches, post-graduate training (training generally following the Masters level) in specific music therapy approaches has led to the following credentials, more of which may follow in the coming decades:

- *AMT:* Analytical Music Therapist. A practice which originated with the work of Mary Priestley in London (Priestley, 1975), AMT is described as a selective postmasters training, usually two years, which entails clinical training in AMT techniques and strategies, review of case studies, self-therapy in AMT, and individual and group supervision based on one's AMT clinical work.
- *FAMI:* Fellow of the Association for Music and Imagery. Trained in Bonny Method of Guided Imagery (BMGIM) programs endorsed by the Association for Music and Imagery (http://www.ami-bonny method.org/faq.asp) exist not only in the United States but also in Australia, the United Kingdom, Canada, Germany, Denmark, Italy, and Sweden.
- *HPMT:* Hospital and Palliative Care Music Therapy Certificate. The Center for Music Therapy in End of Life Care, partnering with Seasons Hospice and Palliative Care (http://www.hospicemusicthera py.org/index.html) was established by Russell Hilliard and offers a series of three courses (i.e., Hospice & Palliative Care Music Therapy Institute, Grief and Loss Music Therapy Institute, Death and Dying Course or Counseling Skills Course) for completion of this certificate.
- *NICU-MT:* Neonatal Intensive Care Unit Music Therapist. The National Institute for Infant and Child Medical Music Therapy, formally established by Jayne Standley of The Florida State University in 2005, is approved by the Certification Board for Music Therapy to offer 30 continuing education credits for NICU-MT. (http://www.music.fsu .edu/Areas-of-Study/Music-Therapy/Certifications/NICU-MT)
- *NMT:* Neurologic Music Therapy. Michael Thaut established the Academy of the Neurologic Society of Music Therapy at Colorado State University in 2002. Initial and advanced training will qualify a post-graduate student to be considered at NMT (http://www.colostate .edu/dept/cbrm/academymissionstatement.html). Members of the International Society for Clinical Neuromusicology and Members of the World Federation for Neurologic Rehabilitation provide instruction.
- *NRMT:* Nordoff Robbins Music Therapist. Nordoff-Robbins centers for post-graduate training in creative music therapy offer training in the United States (New York City), the United Kingdom (London), and Australia (Sydney). Three levels of certification include the following: (1) Level One: focusing on the clinical practice of Nordoff-Robbins music therapy; (2) Level Two: building upon Nordoff-Robbins therapist's clinical skills, facilitates supervisory ability with opportunities to train a fieldwork student or participate as a co-therapist with an Intern or Certification Candidate; and (3) Level Three: developing effective trainers of the approach, helping the candidate to

achieve the skills to teach the full range of course material offered in Level One Certification and also presenting and/or publishing work relevant to Nordoff-Robbins philosophy or practice. (http://steinhardt .nyu.edu/music/nordoff/training/level3)

LEVELS OF PROFESSIONAL PRACTICE

Levels of practice (Wheeler, 1983; Standley, 1989; Bruscia, 1988, 1989) as well as the related issue of levels of certifications (Scartelli, 1989) have been an ongoing concern, discussed in the literature by music therapy educators who suggested or implied a logical link between levels of education and levels of practice.

These connections had already been suggested by The Commission on Education and Clinical Training (AMTA, 1999) with the Bachelors level training considered "Professional," the Masters level training subsuming "Advanced Professional" and the doctoral degree focusing on research, teaching and supervision as well as possible specialization areas in music therapy.

Education and Training Advisory Board

Subsequently the Education and Training Advisory Board issued an advisory in 2005 regarding levels of practice, which presented the basic tenets of the *Advanced Competencies,* which were to follow, and included the following statement:

A music therapist at an Advanced Level of Practice has a Bachelor's degree or its equivalent in music therapy, a current professional designation or credential in music therapy (i.e., ACMT, CMT, MT-BC, or RMT), professional experience, and further education and/or training (e.g., continuing education, a master's degree, a doctoral degree, or in-depth training in areas of specialization such as AMT, BMGIM, or NRMT). It is anticipated that in the future music therapists at the Advanced Level of Practice will hold at least a Master's degree in music therapy that includes advanced clinical education. The advanced music therapist demonstrates comprehensive understanding of foundations and principles of music, music therapy, treatment, and management in clinical, educational, research, and/or administrative settings. (AMTA, 2005)

Relationship of Levels of Practice to Psychotherapeutic Practice

In 2005, the AMTA definition of advanced level of practice suggested graduate education and/or post-graduate specialty music therapy training along with professional experience. Today's advanced competencies presume a masters level training.

Related to these preliminary guidelines is the discussion of psychotherapeutic levels (Wolberg, 1977) in the context of music therapy (Wheeler, 1983, 1987), which may be considered as related to entry level and advanced practice training. The original psychotherapeutic levels defined by Wolberg (1977) included the following: (1) Supportive therapy, intended for those clients who need only brief therapy in order to restore them to normal functioning or, on the other hand, people whose best prognosis is symptom alleviation, enabling a more comfortable way of living; (2) Reeducative therapy, intended to change behavior through positive and negative reinforcers and/or interpersonal relationships, hopefully leading to greater self-growth; and (3) Reconstructive therapy, intended for alteration of the structure of the personality, intended for those whose ego is strong enough to change, motivated and able to devote extensive time to change.

Wheeler contextualized these three levels in music therapy to suggest the following: (1) Activity therapy; (2) Insight therapy with reeducative goals; and (3) Insight therapy with reconstructive goals. Subsequently AMTA has suggested, as *issues for future consideration* (AMTA, 2009, p. 16) these levels of therapy as aligned to levels of practice and education and training. See below.

Entry Practice Level

We may consider (AMTA, 2009) that the Bachelors level of practice be used primarily as "an activity therapy, focused on bringing about changes in behavior, as a supportive therapy to enhance the clients overall function, or as an adjunctive therapy, focused on using music to supplement other types of treatments" (AMTA, 2009, p. 16).

Advanced Practice Levels

We may consider (AMTA, 2009) that the master's degree can prepare students for practice at a reeducative level of psychotherapy which leads to insight and improved functioning for clients across a broad spectrum of needs (i.e., physical rehabilitation, music medicine, palliative care and other areas). In this way, the music therapist takes a "more central and independent role in client treatment plans and, as a result, induces significant changes in the client's current situation" (AMTA, 2009, p. 16).

Finally, we may consider that "advanced professional designations such as Nordoff-Robbins Music Therapist (NRMT), or Fellow of the Association for Music and Imagery (FAMI) and additional clinically-based education/training (i.e., doctoral level studies in music therapy) may lead to the use of music for the following purposes: (a) achieve reconstructive goals in psychotherapy, eliciting unconscious material and working with that to promote reorganization of the personality, (b) achieve primary goals in physical rehabilitation, music medicine, palliative care, and various other areas of music therapy practice, (c) establish treatment goals independently, and (d) work as the primary therapist responsible for inducing pervasive changes in the client's health" (AMTA, 2009, p. 16).

These guidelines for "future consideration" on the part of AMTA are instructive for training purposes at different levels and provoke interesting dialogue. Can we so ascribe degrees and specific certifications to therapist roles? Have we strayed from the original definitions of psychotherapeutic levels of therapy (Wolberg, 1977) and their context in music therapy (Wheeler, 1983)? I believe we have.

CONCLUSION

In the beginning, music therapy educators in the United States were challenged to begin music therapy programs based not on music therapy backgrounds, but rather, on backgrounds in music education, music performance, psychology, psychiatry and experience working in hospitals after the first and second World Wars.

While undergraduate music therapy programs started with only a few courses, they rapidly expanded to four and a half to five-year training programs by the sixties. With the proliferation of music therapy literature, graduate programs became commonplace in the United States by the eighties. All were formalized through agreement with either NAMT or AAMT and, since 1998, through AMTA.

Levels of therapy conducted through music therapy are described simply as entry level or advanced, with further delineation based on levels of psychotherapeutic practice that may be associated with varying degrees of education. Post-graduate specialty credentials, continuing education and distance learning have become part of the current educational practice; as have various packages for education leading to multiple credentials in counseling, school certifications and creative arts therapy.

As clinicians and educators in the United States, we continue to build a broad network amongst ourselves and throughout the world. Faced with continuing changes in healthcare and education, we may have to adapt clinical practice and, along with those adaptations, changes in education and training. We now move on to Chapter 2 in order to carefully consider how entry-level competencies, approved by AMTA, impact the organization and delivery of information in undergraduate programs. Although these were composed for university programs in the United States, they may be useful as guidelines for entry-level curriculum in other countries as well.

Chapter 2

COMPETENCY-BASED EDUCATION
AND TRAINING

*The principal goal of education is to create men who are capable of doing
new things, not simply of repeating what other generations have done.*

Jean Piaget

INTRODUCTION

Several years ago, I took on the task of reviewing our undergraduate curriculum at the University (Goodman, 2001a) to see how the *AMTA Professional Competencies* were addressed in our courses. I concluded that we had some deficit areas to cover and I adapted the curriculum to meet those needs. I must admit, however, that I was somewhat overwhelmed by the sheer volume of the competencies. What were the purposes of the competencies? How were these competencies determined? What true relevance did they have to do with the work of music therapy? Was it really realistic for educators to assume that students would master all these skill areas within the undergraduate program? What did mastery mean? In our administrative zest to organize levels of information, did we compartmentalize skills and knowledge? I hope that in reviewing the *AMTA Professional Competencies* with you, we may consider them in a new light, in accordance with Piaget's sentiment to create knowledge anew from the minds of both men and women.

In this chapter, current and prospective students and educators will profit from discussion and considerations for the delivery of the *AMTA Professional Competencies,* which spans classroom education and clinical preprofessional training.

Consider:

1. What was the process that shaped the *AMTA Professional Competencies* in the two organizations fostering music therapy in the United States, the National Association for Music Therapy (1950–1998) and the American Association for Music Therapy (1971–1998), now merged as the American Music Therapy Association?
2. What is the difference, if any, between education and training?
3. How can we consider presentation of the *AMTA Professional Competencies* as interrelated and successive learning experiences in music, psychology, music therapy courses and preprofessional clinical training experiences (practica and internship) which move from theory to practice?
4. Conversely, how can we consider practice of music therapy (i.e., preprofessional clinical work) in the spirit of reflecting on skills and theory already learned but not necessarily integrated or mastered?
5. Therefore, what are the teaching challenges for the music therapy educator in presenting the competencies?

DEVELOPMENT OF PROFESSIONAL COMPETENCIES

Both the National Association for Music Therapy and the American Association for Music Therapy as well as the universities themselves, were, in the last decades, rightfully concerned with identifying coursework and related competencies in order to provide the best outcomes in training music therapists.

Historical Perspective

Development of Competencies, American Association for Music Therapy

Competency requirements, to be used as criteria for entry level into a profession as well as guidelines for education and training (Bruscia, Hesser, & Boxill, 1981), originally appeared in the AAMT manual on education and training in 1975 and were revised for AAMT in 1981. In developing the competencies, the authors (Bruscia, Hesser, & Boxill, 1981) reportedly analyzed the common learning objectives of music therapy curricula, surveyed job descriptions, task analyzed basic steps in the therapeutic process, formulated and grouped competencies into areas and evaluated each area for its completeness as well as possible redundancy. The final list of competencies was selected according to four criteria:

1. Essential rather than peripheral
2. Entry level rather than advanced
3. Universal rather than population-specific
4. Professional rather than personal

Related Literature: The Development of Competencies

Taylor (1987) described how professions identify competencies, typically by two basic procedures: expert consensus and job task analysis. Apparently, the music therapy profession proceeded along both these paths. As already described, expert consensus had provided basic music therapy competencies in conjunction with analysis of job tasks for the *AAMT Professional Competencies.* Subsequently, the *NAMT Professional Competencies* were also composed with expert consensus and further influenced by job task analysis. Prior to the completion of the NAMT competencies, a number of influential studies provided relevant information.

McGinty (1980, pp. 164–165) reported on a survey with 127 music therapists responding to self-perceived duties and responsibilities on the job which included the following: (1) devising and evaluating treatment plans; (2) designing music therapy sessions; (3) observing, measuring, reporting and evaluating client response; (4) knowledge of physiological effects of drugs; (5) proficiency on accompanying instruments; (6) pedagogy skills in piano, guitar, percussion and voice; (7) movement and dance skills; (8) knowledge of related activity and recreation therapists; (9) research design and implementation; (10) role of primary therapist; (11) equipment procurement, maintenance and repair; and (12) public relations skills.

Lathom (1982) surveyed 466 music therapists on a total of 157 items including demographics, task performance, program goals and program preparation/planning tasks. In the evaluation of 29 tasks, for example, music therapists rated the following five as high frequency: implementing group music therapy, conducting self-education, planning music therapy programs, implementing programs and preparing music therapy goals as well as outcomes for written treatment plans (Lathom, 1982, p. 9). Low frequency tasks included attending family conferences, supervising music therapy staff, facility travel, receiving supervision and training volunteers.

The Certification Board for Music Therapy, a separate credentialing agency formed in 1983, sought information from entry-level therapists based on their knowledge and skills statements sent forward every five years (i.e., CBMT, 1983, 1989). The development of the NAMT competencies was further influenced by clinician, educator and intern response to entry-level competencies through a series of surveys (Braswell, Decuir, & Maranto, 1980; Taylor, 1987; Maranto & Bruscia, 1988; Petrie, 1989), each developed and administered differently.

Braswell, Maranto, & Decuir (1980), listed 131 entry-level skills (67 music therapy and clinical behaviors and 64 music skills) to be rated on a 9-point scale of priority. The entry level skills were based on coursework objectives at Loyola University and the survey received 48 responses, primarily from graduates of Loyola, in response to the survey.

Taylor (1987) organized 150 competencies based on previously published materials (*AAMT Professional Competencies,* the Braswell et al. survey, training objectives used by NAMT clinical training sites, *NAMT Standards of Clinical Practice* and curricular objectives published from some NAMT approved academic programs). Distributed to 1,907 music therapists, obviously the largest sample size to date, the Taylor survey involved the prioritization of competencies; items that seemed inconsistently rated were modified and resubmitted to another random sample.

Based, in part, on the format developed by Taylor (1987) and Lathom (1982), Petrie (1989) organized 130 intended learning outcomes (Petrie, 1989, p. 125) encompassing music therapy, clinical theories and techniques and musical skills. Subject to the perceptions of 211 professional music therapists, the results of the survey led to the identification of 85 intended learning outcomes. Feedback from the respondents focused on the need for the student to function more effectively and efficiently in the clinical setting, suggesting the need to decrease emphasis on research in the entry level curriculum and increase an understanding of exceptionality and increased mastery of functional music skills.

The most exhaustive survey investigating teaching of prospective competencies (Maranto & Bruscia, 1988), a two-year project supported by a grant from Temple University, used the AAMT competencies as well as the knowledge and skill statements (K/Ss) that had been composed by the Certification Board for Music Therapy (1983) to survey job task analysis and the knowledge, skills, and abilities related to such tasks. Maranto and Bruscia included a list of 42 competency areas in a survey receiving response from 83 clinical training directors, 1,323 clinicians and 37 directors of NAMT-approved university programs. For purposes of this book, the Maranto and Bruscia (1988) study, although dated and limited insofar as the number of university director respondents, is instructive because it provides perspective on the context (classroom, practicum, internship, on the job) in which certain skills have been taught, how they have been taught (i.e., methods and materials), the breadth and depth with which they have been taught (i.e., rated 1 to 5), methods of student evaluation, admission and retention practices and educational philosophies and attitudes of faculty and supervisors.

In this study, educators and clinical training directors agreed that undergraduate courses were the most efficient context for learning all music competencies (i.e., music theory, music history, performance on primary instrument, functional music skills), three of eight clinical foundation areas (i.e., human development, models of psychotherapy, psychopharmacology) and six (i.e., ethics, improvisation, movement/dance, theoretical foundations, psychology of music, music education principles) of 18 music therapy areas. Practicum and internship were deemed the desirable context for learning two (i.e., verbal therapy techniques, group therapy techniques) of the eight clinical foundation areas and nine (i.e., communicating with client, client assessment, therapeutic relationship, treatment planning, implementing therapy, treatment evaluation, therapy closure, interdisciplinary skills, clinical administration) of the 18 music therapy areas. Educators and clinical training directors recommended that family therapy and research be taught in graduate coursework. Clinicians were in agreement with educators and clinical training directors in all of these respects.

However, clinicians, unlike educators, felt that there were seven areas of competencies that had been learned on the job rather than in training. These areas included the following: psychopharmacology, client assessment, therapeutic relationship, interdisciplinary skills, clinical administration, music therapy approaches and miscellaneous techniques.

It is possible that the response from these surveys, the aforementioned job surveys of knowledge and skills vital to the music therapy profession (CBMT, 1983, 1988) and the Jensen and McKinney (1990) analysis of discrepancies between curriculums from 66 university programs and competency areas suggested by Maranto and Bruscia (1988) further helped objectify the process of formulating the competencies approved in 1993.

It appears that both organizations proceeded independently until The California Symposium on Clinical Practices in 1989 when representatives of both NAMT and AAMT met to discuss, among other areas pertinent to education and training, the competencies (Maranto, 1989a, 1989b).

Development of Competencies: National Association for Music Therapy

In 1993, a finely tuned version of the NAMT Professional Competencies was initially adopted. In the fall of 1994, music therapy educators were asked to incorporate these competencies into coursework.

American Music Therapy Association: Professional Competencies

When NAMT and AAMT passed a unification agreement in 1996, a two-year unification period provided the time for a designated transition group to draft recommendations encompassing education and training models from both organizations. The report of this Education and Clinical Training

Commission was issued as a draft in November, 1998. Draft recommendations suggested outcome/competency-based standards for education and
training versus curricular/course-based standards with the responsibility for
quality control at the local level, with schools and training sites (Crowe &
Bruscia, 1999). With the founding of the American Music Therapy Association in 1998, a further revised set of competencies was put forth in 1999
as a result of the Education and Clinical Training commission. Minor revi-
sions, including the most recent in 2009 (AMTA, 2009) followed.

Initial Educator Response to Competency-Based Education

A survey presented to educators in 1998 (Groene & Pembrook, 2000) represented the opinions of 58 respondents regarding the competencies.The
first part of the survey included questions regarding the importance of training in various areas. In terms of adding technology courses, respondents considered musical technology most important (42%) followed by medical technology (32%) and educational technology (20%); 57 percent of the respondents had already added new classes in music technology. In terms of delet-
ing courses, respondents suggested that, given the option, they would reduce
music theory (12), music history (12), general studies (8), ensembles (6),
applied lessons (5), techniques courses (6) and music education methods (2).
In terms of adding classes, respondents suggested that, given the option, they
would add more functional keyboard (13), functional guitar (13), improvisation skills (13), more psychology (10), music therapy classes (9), and clinical/
practicum experience (6).

The second part of the survey polled music therapy faculty on their agreement regarding competency-based mastery for degree completion. Sixty-six
percent of faculty approved of this system with 22 percent remaining impar-
tial and 12 percent preferring a course completion system. Outcome specific approach was considered to be an improved way of monitoring student
skill and knowledge (78%) as well as the quality of future music therapists
(68%). Despite this apparent vote of approval, there were significant reser-
vations voiced about whether faculty, internship supervisors and students
would be able to agree on how to define quality outcomes (48%), AMTA's
ability to develop standardized evaluation tests for competency testing (43%)
and a possible problem with national accreditation (38%).

The final area of the survey, concerned with clinical sites, demonstrated
educator concern with the number of quality sites (55%), number of quality
supervisors (45%), student music preparation before clinical training (45%),
supervision by the on-site music therapist during clinical training (26%), clinical experience before clinical training (21%), and supervision by university
faculty during clinical training (16%).

Summary, Expectation and Possible Issues at This Time

It is interesting to note that essentially the same groups of competencies that existed in 1981, with the exception of research competencies (now included), remain today in 2010. Further, the concept of establishing student competencies as a means of diagnostic, individualized evaluation for each student (Alley, 1978) over 30 years ago at Florida State University is one supported today by the Academic Program Approval Committee of the American Music Therapy Association.

In reviewing the competencies and considering the responsibility of the institution to individually track student mastery of the competencies, questions come to mind.

How does the institution track the delivery and completion of the undergraduate competencies? Although the educator will include certain course competencies, most likely at successive levels of mastery, passing the course(s) does not necessarily mean the student has achieved each competency. Is it then incumbent upon the educator to provide remedial training prior to creating an individual education plan as a piece of the internship training agreement and/or pass on this responsibility as part of the clinical training agreement?

In terms of understanding the *transfer of skills and theory to clinical practice,* can we determine which undergraduate competencies in the areas of music foundations, clinical foundations and foundations of music therapy seem to be the most difficult for students to transfer to their clinical work and why? What can we do to help students achieve that which we all aspire to, namely help students integrate skills and information toward clinical gains?

I suspect that these questions, unlike some of the earlier questions posed in surveys, cannot be finitely answered. Rather, they must be considered as an ongoing concern.

In considering our teaching of the undergraduate competencies, let us reflect, beyond mastery of skills, on the *ways in which skills and areas of information can best be incorporated toward the goal of effective clinical practice.*

CONSIDERATIONS IN TEACHING THE PROFESSIONAL COMPETENCIES

Premise

Let us consider *education as the initial introduction of skills and knowledge in the classroom and training as the application of skills and knowledge in the clinical realm,* preprofessional practica and internship.

The *AMTA Professional Competencies* (AMTA, 1999), considered as entry level to the profession, are delineated into the following core areas of study:

1. Music Foundations (36 skills)
2. Clinical Foundations (11 skills)
3. Music Therapy (105 skills)

I will consider them as follows:

Music Foundations

Music foundation competencies (1–11) are knowledge and skills primarily taught in music classes (with the exception of *nonsymphonic instrumental skills* and *improvisation skills*) and then contextualized in music therapy classes to serve as skills and knowledge for clinical practice. These will be considered in this chapter.

Clinical Foundations

Similarly, clinical foundation competencies (12–14) are knowledge and skills primarily taught in psychology classes (with the exception of *therapeutic relationship*) and then contextualized in music therapy classes to serve as skills and knowledge for clinical practice. These will be considered in this chapter.

Music Therapy Skills

The first segment of music therapy knowledge competencies, namely *Foundations and Principles* (15), is typically introduced in music therapy classes successively across varying clinical populations and contexts with readings and discussion (see Chapter 6). These competencies must be demonstrated and practiced, *incorporating music and clinical foundations,* in order to reaffirm conceptual understanding. Music therapy *Foundations and Skills* (15) will be considered in this chapter. More specific discussion of their realization in practice continues in Chapter 3.

The second segment of music therapy skills (16–25) incorporates music foundations, clinical foundations and music therapy foundations and principles through the *practice* of music therapy, at successive levels, through practicum and through internship. At the end point of internship the student should demonstrate an acceptable mastery of all the practice competencies that subsume the core music, clinical and music therapy competencies.

Therefore I will consider skills 16–25 as *Practice Music Therapy Competencies* in Chapter 3, "Preprofessional Clinical Training."

Challenges in Presenting the AMTA Professional Competencies

The unique challenge for the music therapy educator, within the context of music therapy courses, is threefold:

1. To introduce, conceptually, the foundations and principles of the music therapy process, across successive clinical populations.
2. To demonstrate and experience the components of the music therapy process, to *transfer, extend* (in ways that may not be apparent from the stated competencies) *and integrate the ongoing development of music foundation skills and clinical foundation skills with those of music therapy foundations and principles, thereby creating a new level of integration toward music therapy practice competencies.*
3. To initiate opportunities for the student to use music therapy practice competencies (i.e., in practicum for 4–6 semesters) at the same time students are processing their experiences through classroom assignments and supervision (see Chapter 3).

Therefore, let us take a closer look at the relevant literature regarding the competency areas typically presented in music, psychology and music therapy courses in order to *stimulate our thinking about the importance and scope of these competencies and the ways in which they can be transferred, extended and integrated toward the practice of music therapy.* My own suggestions and thoughts are certainly not inclusive but, rather, intended to spark your own spirit of integrative thinking, discussion and practice. Discussion follows each subsection of the competencies.

Music Foundations: Areas of Study and Related Discussion

Music History and Theory

1.1 Recognize standard works in the literature.
1.2 Identify the elemental, structural, and stylistic characteristics of music from various periods and cultures.
1.3 Sight-sing melodies of both diatonic and chromatic makeup.
1.4 Take aural dictation of melodies, rhythms, and chord progressions.
1.5 Transpose simple compositions.

Discussion, Music History Skills

Educators, clinicians and clinical training directors in the United States have reported that competencies in music history courses, taught primarily by music faculty, have been presented through a combination of group instruction and limited discussion (Maranto & Bruscia, 1988). Materials used have included assigned readings, scores and audio recordings. There is no record of crossover to the music therapy courses.

Yet it is important that the skills acquired in music history also be generalized and practiced within the context of music therapy. Madsen (1965) actually suggested a limit of one-year training in both music theory and music history, presumably because expanded courses of study in both these areas were not successfully being applied to clinical application. Perhaps the majority of the 37 educators responding to the Maranto and Bruscia survey (1988) who suggested decreasing music theory and music history requirements were thinking along the same lines.

How can music history training in isolation transfer to clinical application discussed within music therapy classes and practicum? As music history traces through the periods of music literature (i.e., medieval, renaissance, baroque, classical, romantic, 20th century), the student may gain a familiarity and love for repertory that clients will either choose to hear or play. The precursor to guided imagery through music, a larger sense of all that came before us in this world of music, is vital to helping a client select and choose that which will stir the emotions and hold a therapeutic sense of resolve. The *Advanced Competencies* (7.6) suggest that the clinician will design music listening programs for therapeutic purpose; I am proposing that this responsibility often falls within the entry-level job description as well.

When the student is listening to any piece of music, whether it is in music history class or in music therapy class, the listening will be both conscious (i.e., as in theoretical analysis) and subconscious or unconscious (i.e., as in framing a musical daydream). This important awareness helps the student begin to consider how a client may profit from listening to works of music.

In the clinical setting, there are many possibilities for the student to prepare. Can students working in a gerontology or rehabilitation setting with higher functioning clients introduce music appreciation classes in order to promote cognition and social skills? My colleague, Donna Chadwick, recalls working with a patient challenged by Broca's aphasia who had been a member of the Yale choir and would "sob and sing" throughout the Mozart Requiem (Chadwick, 2010) not only as a thankful expression of meaning but also as a means of reviving speech. Can students working with lower functioning clients recognize a well-known tune from an orchestral piece based on a few pitches from the client? Can students identify classical music that will be appropriate for a client to learn, orchestrate and purposefully listen to? Can compositional techniques studied in early, romantic, classical and twentieth century literature be introduced to higher functioning clients? To answer the question, "What can we learn from classical music about the possibilities for improvisational music making?" listen to the inspirational lectures of Paul Nordoff (Robbins & Robbins, 1998), lectures my graduate music therapy students use to spark their own ideas about keyboard improvisation. In a larger sense, students of music history learn to contextualize music as it fits into society and the life of the composer. Music and its reception are shaped by culture, not the other way around. This can have important implication for music therapy as we observe subcultures of our society creating and identifying with music that plays a larger part in the development of their thinking and acting.

Therefore, I suggest that music history not remain compartmentalized in the music history class, but filter into the music therapy courses and practicum seminars as well with experiences that help students become aware of their own love of various genres and periods of music, their psychological/physiological reactions to these pieces and how this personal knowledge can be transmitted to clinical use.

Discussion, Music Theory Skills

Educators, clinicians and clinical training directors in the United States have reported (Maranto & Bruscia, 1988) that skills in music theory courses have been overwhelmingly presented through a combination of group instruction, lecture and unspecified other formats with testing through written examinations, performance or class recitation. Similar to music history, there is no record of crossover to the music therapy discipline.

Sight-singing, aural notation and transposition seem straightforward enough skills but how are they utilized in the clinical setting? The entry-level competencies do not specifically provide this information. In the *Advanced Competencies,* we see mention of "reproduce, notate and transcribe musical responses of clients" (7.1); I am questioning why we need to wait until graduate studies to apply theory skills in this way. In conjunction with their four semesters of theory, are students able to identify and notate the pitch range of a client? Notate the vocal and/or instrumental melody the client has improvised in a session? Transpose on demand in response to a client's pitch range? Sight-sing a melody that a client has brought in or requested? In order to effectively evaluate the ability of a student to integrate music skills into the practice of music therapy, classes as well as practicum in music therapy must present opportunities for practice of these skills. More sophisticated skills such as graphic notation (Bergstrom-Nielsen, 1993); microtonal notation or theoretical analysis of client-therapist improvisation (Lee, 2000; Aigen, 2009) may be considered under advanced competencies discussed in Chapter 4.

It is also useful to consider music theory (i.e., sight-singing, aural notation and transposition) in the context of courses like Psychology of Music and Piano Improvisation. At times the traditional instruction of music theory may seem to contraindicate some of the unorthodox practices we see, for example, in the piano improvisation techniques of Paul Nordoff (Robbins & Robbins, 1998). However, even the contradictions are fuel for discussion in music therapy classes and possibly music theory classes. Why would we use parallel fifths in improvisation with clients? What are the stimulative and sedative effects of certain harmonies? What is the effect of musical mode on emotional state (DiGiacomo & Kirby, 2006)? What is the nature of each interval as discussed in anthroposophical writings (Steiner, 1983), which are expounded upon in the Nordoff lectures (Robbins & Robbins, 1998)?

Composition and Arranging Skills

2.1   Compose songs with simple accompaniment.
2.2   Adapt, arrange, transpose, and simplify music compositions for small vocal and nonsymphonic instrumental ensembles.

Discussion, Composition and Arranging Skills

As with theory and music history, many students study composition and arranging in classes with theorists who are not music therapists. Therefore, it is necessary to incorporate these skills into music therapy applications in both classes and practicum. Have the students carry out exercises where they are composing for clients. Encourage them to study and practice published music therapy orchestrated compositions (Nordoff & Robbins, 1964a, 1964b, 1969; Nordoff, 1972, 1977, 1979; Levin, 1998) for nonsymphonic instruments and then adapt compositions for simple nonorchestral arrangements with similar techniques suggested by music therapy literature (Nordoff & Robbins, 1983; Goodman, 2007). While competency 2.1 does not suggest composing songs in various genres (*Advanced Competencies* include composing songs "in various styles to meet specific therapeutic objectives" [7.2]), I suggest that it is possible for the entry-level therapy to compose music to appeal to many types of clients, foreshadowing the introduction of the song-writing process with clients. Likewise compositions for ensemble should be composed across musical genres and for different populations. In these ways, the use of musical skills is incorporated in all aspects of programming.

Arranging, traditionally taught in orchestration classes, may be more appropriately transferred to training in computer-based software such as Garage Band, so commonly used today. This information could be offered within the context of the music technology course or in music therapy methods courses.

Major Performance Medium Skills

3.1   Perform appropriate undergraduate repertoire; demonstrate musicianship, technical proficiency, and interpretive understanding on a principal instrument/voice.
3.2   Perform in small and large ensembles.

Discussion, Major Performance Skills

The perceived importance of the major performing instrument to clinical work has been an ongoing topic of discussion. Madsen (1965) suggested that music performance be delimited to one year of study, concerned about its priority in the education and training of the music therapist. Reportedly (Maranto & Bruscia, 1988), the music performance competencies have been taught in courses by music faculty through individualized instruction, experiential training and lecture all of which have incorporated musical instruments, scores and readings.

The results of McGuire's reported survey (Cohen, Hadsell, & Williams, 1997), sent to clinical training directors in 1994 in order to prioritize training skills, indicated that apart from vocal skills, which rated fifth out of 24 competency areas, performance on the primary instrument was considered only somewhat important, twentieth out of 24 competency areas. Taylor's survey (1987), directed to professional music therapists, yielded similar consensus. Educators themselves suggested (Petrie, 1989) that musical instruction for the student should focus on functional and improvisational music skills. It is possible that this concern is linked to the failure of students to transfer their performing abilities effectively into the clinical setting (Jensen & McKinney, 1990) as well as an inconsistent mastery of functional music skills.

A study designed to solicit information from both clinicians (250) and students regarding the importance of their primary instrumental training and its application to clinical work (Cohen, Hadsell, & Williams, 1997) found the following order of prevalence on the primary instrument: voice, piano, woodwind, string, brass, percussion. The majority of respondents reported that study on the primary instrument was vital and that the primary instrument was used in clinical practice. The authors point out that voice and piano, the most prevalent primary instruments, are a major part of the music therapist's functional music skills. Additional benefits to performance study are pin-pointed:

> It is not only the technical skills inherent in applied instrumental study that benefit the future music therapist, but also the growth in the secondary skills, such as leadership, nonverbal interaction, musicianship and confidence, which need to be emphasized and transferred to the clinical setting. (Cohen, Hadsell, & Williams, 1997, p. 71)

This conclusion was relevant not only for individual lessons but also for both solo and ensemble performance.

It is certainly true that while performing skills are of major importance for development of one's talents and self-esteem, they also need to transcend the concert stage and be used in constructive ways for the benefit of the clients we work with. When students study repertoire for performance, they ,as well as their instructors, often fail to make links to the study of music therapy. These skills go beyond the competencies but bear mention here.

What is the relationship between self-actualization and mastering an instrument? How does this relationship relate to helping clients through similar processes? I recall my own experiences in providing music therapy for clients with challenges such as borderline personality disorder, bipolar disorder and schizophrenia at The Creative Arts Rehabilitation Center in New York during the 1980s. The highlight of the year for many of these clients was the chance to perform at a Musicale in the auditorium of the Turtle Bay Music School. Before each client performed, each would volunteer a few words about what the music meant to them and what the experience of rehearsing, subsequent self-awareness and then the opportunity to perform meant. Perhaps we should encourage this same performance technique ourselves. Mary Priestley, in her interview with Leslie Bunt (2004) remarks:

> When I was at St. Bernard's, Peter Wright insisted that we should keep up our musical side and he had us every now and then having to play a concerto or a movement of a concerto in a concert in the church. This made us keep up our musical skills and this I think is important. That the music therapist should be doing some live music themselves.

Further, how is the student going to make functional use of their performance and/or technical proficiency on their instrument in music therapy? Is this training applicable to using the instrument (i.e., be it voice, piano, guitar) in therapy? One issue may be the student tendency to compartmentalize their performance playing and their playing for clients. I recall a student who sang brilliantly in his concert and then, in leading a music therapy group, could barely provide vocal support. When I asked him about this discrepancy, he replied "Oh, that other voice is for performing and this voice is for music therapy."

Another issue may be the narrow scope of training students encounter in their choice of classical, jazz or popular music pedagogy. Kennedy (2001) found that 80 percent of 41 programs offered guitar as a primary instrument either as a classical instrument (31%) or with options to study classical, jazz, country/western and folk (69%). This is heartening news.

The issue of functional use of the primary instrument becomes even more important when the primary instrument is not keyboard, voice or guitar, the most commonly used instruments in music therapy. Although pioneers in the field of music therapy used their string instruments in clinical practice (Mary Priestley and Helen Bonny, violinists; Juliette Alvin, cellist), toward "therapeutic music teaching" (Priestly, 1975; Alvin, 1976), this technique is little celebrated or represented in music therapy curriculum. Likewise, listening to orchestral instruments for auditory, visual and tactile perception (Alvin, 1976) deserves more attention in education and training as does the value of therapeutic chamber music ensemble (Lewis, 1964).

Voyajolu (2009) surveyed 250 respondents concerning the use of their primary instrument in clinical practice. The majority of her respondents stated that voice (27.6%), piano (26.4%) or woodwinds (24.8%) was the primary instrument followed by guitar (7.2%), strings (5.6%), brass (5.2%) and percussion (3.2%). Overall, 72.4 percent of the respondents reported using their primary instrument within the last year with voice, guitar, percussion and piano used more in clinical practice than woodwinds, strings and brass.

The clinical usage of the voice, guitar, percussion and piano are further detailed in the relevant competencies regarding those instruments. Although there has been no survey comparing the clinical usage of these instruments in clinicians who have had primary performing study on these instruments versus those who have not, it is probable that the primary instrumentalist will use their instrument with more facility and imagination in the clinical setting, therefore exceeding the minimal requirements detailed for keyboard, guitar, percussion and voice.

Fewer than 50 percent of the respondents in the Voyajolu study (2009) with primary instruments of strings, woodwinds or brass used their instruments for clinical purpose. However, those that did use their primary instruments did so in imaginative ways. For example, 23 of the 62 woodwind majors reported using their instruments in clinical practice for the following purposes: improvisation, playing for clients, using the instrument to aid in breathing/speech, communication, song identification, reminiscence, environmental needs, emotional/spiritual well-being, sensory input, accompaniment and as a novelty in sessions (Voyajolu, 2009, p. 77). Six of the 14 string majors reported using their instruments in clinical practice for the following purposes: relaxation, improvisation, teaching, songwriting, hospice interventions, playing with other clients, playing for clients and targeting cognitive needs (Voyajolu, 2009, p. 85). Finally, three of the 13 clinicians who were brass majors in this study (Voyajolu, 2009) used their instruments for therapeutic teaching (i.e., which particularly helped a client with breath control); as accompaniment to help strengthen arms, improve fine motor coordination and increase breath control; and for music appreciation; listening, and name that tune (Voyajolu, 2009, p. 92).

It is important for us, as music therapy educators, to support all instrumentalists emotionally and pedagogically to utilize their primary instrument for awareness of the therapeutic music-making process and, further, for imaginative use in clinical work.

Keyboard Skills

4.1 Accompany self and ensembles proficiently.
4.2 Play basic chord progressions (I-IV-V-I) in several keys.
4.3 Sight-read simple compositions and song accompaniments.
4.4 Play a basic repertoire of traditional, folk, and popular songs with or without printed music.
4.5 Harmonize and transpose simple compositions.

Discussion, Keyboard Skills

Functional music skills (presumably nonprimary performance on guitar, piano and voice) have been ((Maranto & Bruscia, 1988) taught by both music faculty (59%) and music therapy faculty (39%) through undergraduate courses (72%) and practicum or internships (32%). Skills have been taught through experiential training (52%), group instruction (30%) and individual instruction (16%). Clinicians have reported (Maranto & Bruscia, 1988) learning functional music skills on the job (12%) and with additional training outside of university or job setting (11%).

Cassity (1987), reported data from 100 clinical training directors in reference to keyboard skills. His questionnaire included 74 piano skills arranged under the areas of chord progressions, transposition, reading piano music, harmonization, improvisation and general performance skills. The results of the survey indicated the following in regards to intern performance of functional keyboard skills:

1. Mediocre performance on five of the chord progression skills and performance with difficulty on the other two; all chord progressions were

considered important with the ability to play 1-IV-V chords in major and minor skills as most essential.

2. Performance with difficulty on eight of nine transposition tasks.
3. Mediocre performance on six of the eight skills for music reading with one-part melody receiving the only superior rating.
4. Mediocre performance in eight of 15 harmonization skills and difficulty with the remaining seven. Midpoint ratings in using major chords and whole note triads in harmony.
5. Thirteen of 14 improvisation skills demonstrated with difficulty.

Upon review, the keyboard proficiencies in the Cassity study appear entirely reasonable and it is distressing that interns showed such poor performance as reported by their supervisors.

From my experience, I believe that these reported types of weaknesses result from one or a combination of the following issues: weak, inconsistent standards in secondary piano instruction; students being passed out of secondary piano instruction with unsatisfactory skills and/or students studying to pass secondary piano exams and not continuing to utilize skills in music therapy class demonstration and practica. The issue of piano improvisation will be discussed under improvisation in this chapter. Also note that the survey did not cover the issue of interns developing "a basic repertoire of traditional, folk, and popular songs with or without printed music" (4.4). I would suggest that this minimally be expedited with each student mastering a required number of songs for each practicum, practica presumably serving clients of different ages, ethnicity and musical interest. As the literature in music therapy increases, a need for listings of most commonly used repertoire with patient populations is helpful such as the information offered by VanWeelden and Cevasco (2007).

It is also interesting to note here that the simple attainment of the AMTA keyboard skills does not necessarily translate into successful use of these skills in the clinical context. Therefore, in going beyond the stated skills in keyboard, it is important for the student to have the opportunity to practice, in music therapy courses and practicum, skills that are particular to music therapy:

1. Singing and playing at the same time.
2. Singing, playing and maintaining eye contact with the client(s).
3. Singing, playing, maintaining eye contact with client(s) and possibly pausing to demonstrate use of another instrument, conduct or physically cue a client.
4. Playing while singing movement lyrics.

5. Playing while accompanying instrumental play.
6. Playing while talking to elicit guided imagery and relaxation.

Further, the awareness of different accompaniment styles and their effect on clients is important information that may be observed in practicum situations as well as practiced with simulated role-play in the music therapy courses. For these purposes, I teach a course entitled Piano Accompaniment for Music Therapy which includes accompaniment to singing, moving, guided relaxation, and clinical orchestration with simulated client experiences of varying ages, backgrounds and challenges.

Guitar Skills

5.1   Accompany self and ensembles proficiently.
5.2   Employ simple strumming and finger-picking techniques.
5.3   Tune guitar using standard and other tunings.
5.4   Perform a basic repertoire of traditional, folk, and popular songs with or without printed music.
5.5   Harmonize and transpose simple compositions in several keys.

Discussion, Guitar Skills

The discussion of teaching guitar skills has received a fair amount of attention in the music therapy literature. The number of semesters of secondary guitar classes and the content of these classes varies from one university program to another. In a 2001 survey completed by 48 program directors, Kennedy (2001) found that just over two-thirds of the university educators responding to his survey offered one semester of secondary guitar. The instructor of these secondary guitar courses was not specified. Generally speaking, secondary guitar is offered by music faculty who would benefit, in my opinion, with counsel from music therapy faculty. However, 16.6 percent of the respondents' programs in the Kennedy survey offered alternative or additional guitar classes including pop arranging, transcription and study of alternative tunings. The popularity of the guitar in clinical work was attributed, in great work, to its portability.

In order to further delineate and supplement the AMTA guitar competencies, Krout (2003b) suggests the following: (1) open chord in various positions for voice leading; (2) barre chords; (3) interesting strumming patterns with rhythmic emphasis (i.e., cinquillo rhythm); (4) varied fingerpicking patterns; (5) major and minor pentatonic scales for improvising; (6) familiarity with guitars of various types; (7) blues/rock/jazz chord extensions and progressions; (8) use of right-strum hand rhythms; (9) use of nonchord tones;

and (10) use of chord embellishment/left chording hand techniques.

The need to surpass basic competencies for the guitar also includes the ability to adapt the guitar for clinical use or learn particular methods that are helpful in clinical practice. For example, Cassity (1977) suggests a nontraditional tuning (see relevance for this in competency 5.3 above) which involves placing the open strings and placing an index finger across the neck as a bar position on the fifth and seventh frets to help clients play simply. Krout (1995) recommends the use of 12 bar blues as a mechanism for creating songs. In a limited but significant study, Groene (2001) points out the positive effect of more rhythmically and harmonically complex live guitar accompaniment styles on the response levels of patients with dementia, suggesting that redundant music background, while calming, may not be sufficiently stimulative. Interestingly, Groene suggests there are not enough studies of this type in the music therapy literature. This information suggests the importance of students not only being able to play varied accompaniment styles but also, as with any instrument, being aware of the effects of varying accompaniment styles and, therefore, choosing to use accompaniment styles strategically.

Teaching methods in the college-level beginning guitar class will vary (Gooding, 2009) but the use of guitar skills must be contextualized in music therapy courses and practica. Gregory and Belgrave (2009) document the presence or lack of presence of specific skills important for music therapy guitar accompaniment, pointing out that the skills such as eye contact with clients and consistent sound quality in accompaniment be included at the beginning of instruction and going forward. This, by the way, is an excellent principle for learning music on any instrument. The addition of relaxation and auditory discrimination activities are suggested (Gregory & Belgrave, 2009) in order to promote finger strength, independent finger movement and self-correction.

Voice Skills

6.1   Lead group singing by voice.
6.2   Communicate vocally with adequate volume (loudness).
6.3   Sing a basic repertoire of traditional, folk, and popular songs in tune with a pleasing quality.

Discussion, Voice Skills

Although there has been a great deal of music therapy literature devoted to use of the voice in music psychotherapy (Austin, 2009), there is, apparently, no discussion of functional secondary voice skills. It is possible, as we all know, that an otherwise talented musician may have difficulty using the voice effectively in therapy. Since the voice is such an essential component of conducting clinical work, it is important that baseline abilities in this area be screened, either in the audition process or upon entry to the program. Should the student take a secondary voice class, these skills should be carried over to the clinical arena both in classroom-simulated situations and in practica where the voice is used a cappella as well as with guitar and/or piano accompaniment and students begin to develop appropriate repertoire for the various clinical populations. It should be emphasized that the development of repertoire is ongoing and of essential concern for the music therapist. Logically, the content of age-appropriate repertoire will change depending upon generational shifts and preferences. For example, what was popular music for the grandparents of baby boomers is not going to be popular music for baby boomer grandparents. For these reasons, ongoing review of age and thematic repertoire is also critical, such as the analysis of songbook series for older adult populations (Cevasco & Vanweelden, 2010).

It is important for the student to learn how to vocally warm-up a group and determine an appropriate vocal range, skills which may be implied in the competencies but are not stated. There can be no self-consciousness in using the voice as a therapist and it is important to freely model the use of the singing voice in class.

Percussion Skills

7.1   Accompany self and ensembles proficiently.
7.2   Utilize basic techniques on several standard and ethnic instruments.
7.3   Lead rhythm-based ensembles proficiently.

Discussion, Percussion Skills

Percussion skills and the use of drum circles have become increasingly popular and clinically useful in music therapy. Typical classes in percussion, however, do not introduce ethnic percussion used in music therapy and as part of community drum circles. Therefore, instruction in ethnic percussion and drum circles may be facilitated by specialized readings within a music therapy course (i.e., Reuer, et al., 2007) or workshop training, a good example of which is the training provided by Remo (http://www.remo.com/por tal /hr/index.html) in the research protocol developed by Bittman and his associates (2001) for the reduction of stress and possible strengthening of the immune system.

Nonsymphonic Instrumental Skills

8.1   Care for and maintain nonsymphonic and ethnic instruments.
8.2   Play autoharp or equivalent with same competence specified for guitar.
8.3   Utilize electronic musical instruments.

Discussion, Nonsymphonic Instrumental Skills

The autoharp and the Q-chord are examples of nonsymphonic instruments commonly used in music therapy sessions and can be functionally used in music therapy classes and practicum. Although there is limited literature on the use of the autoharp, it is successfully used for accompaniment (Moore, Straum, & Brotons, 1992) and it's therapeutic use includes placing it on the laps of therapist and client facing each other while seated in order to promote shared use and eye contact. The same strategy can be used with the Q-chord, which takes minimal effort for the client to strum.

The use of ethnic instruments, which also introduce nonwestern scales to the ear, deserves more prominence in the music therapy literature. After my students and I experienced the chanting workshop led by Silvia Nakkach, I was struck by how much the harmonium, for example, can be used to advantage as a calming backdrop (Sundar, 2009) for vocal toning. Likewise the value of the gamelan for group improvisation, which Loth (2006) beautifully describes in her writing about a short teaching module of multicultural improvisation at Anglia Ruskin University in Cambridge, UK.

Improvisation Skills

9.1   Improvise on percussion instruments.
9.2   Develop original melodies, simple accompaniments, and short pieces extemporaneously in a variety of moods and styles, vocally and instrumentally.
9.3   Improvise in small ensembles.

Discussion, Improvisation Skills

In the past, most educators (60%) and clinical training directors (40%) reported (Maranto & Bruscia, 1988) that improvisation techniques were best learned in undergraduate courses, including practicum or internships (20% and 30% respectively) as did clinicians. Educators reported (Maranto & Bruscia, 1988) that the task of teaching improvisation was largely assigned to music faculty (51%) and then to music therapy faculty (37%), using experiential training, lecture, individual instruction and practicum. The materials used most frequently were readings (48%) as opposed to musical instruments (21%) and scores (12%) even though the method of evaluation in almost half the cases (42%) was through musical performance.

Currently, it seems entirely reasonable for music therapy faculty to teach improvisation skills in a manner that makes them most relevant to the practice of music therapy. How can a music therapy student know how to transfer the use of improvisation skills into the clinical setting unless a music therapist, comfortable teaching and using these skills, instructs them?

The possibilities of studying improvisation in the music therapy curriculum can seem endlessly invigorating. Where do we start?

Curiously enough, with the exception of percussion instruments, competency 9.2 above does not detail which instruments we can use to improvise with other than the free-ranging words, "vocally and instrumentally." Nor does the competency detail at what level of sophistication or within what theoretical context the beginning professional will improvise.

Are we to focus on the piano, guitar, and voice, or all of these? Even though the music therapy literature and training seems to focus on piano improvisation, it would probably be realistic to have each student develop improvisational skills to the greatest degree possible on their instrument of comfort, their primary instrument.

Furthermore, the option to develop "in a variety of moods and styles (9:2)" opens up an entire world of music which, of course, includes popular and jazz (Aigen, 2001), all styles related to western classical music (i.e., church modes, organum, baroque, romantic, 20th century whole-tone scales) and music of other lands (i.e., Middle eastern scales, Spanish scales, pentatonic scales characterizing music of Japan and China), each with their own sense of therapeutic strategy. Again, a beginning comfort level of improvisation with exposure to different types of moods and styles appears to meet an acceptable level of competency at the entry level of training.

Examples of piano improvisation are presented through recorded case study examples (Nordoff & Robbins, 1977, 2007; Lee 1996; Lee, 2010; Aigen, 2001), and instructional guidelines found in lectures (Robbins & Robbins, 1998) and texts (Nordoff & Robbins, 1977, 2007; Wigram, 2004; Lee, 2010). Examples of recorded guitar improvisation (Primadei, 2004), introduced into the Nordoff-Robbins method (Aigen, 2001; Soshensky, 2005) are available less frequently. Examples of vocal improvisation are described by Sokolov (1987) and Austin (1998, 2009).

Although both Priestley (1975) and Alvin (1975) used their instruments, the violin and the cello respectively, for improvisation, their methods are not detailed in their writing. There is no specific indication in the music therapy literature on how piano improvisation, vocal improvisation, guitar improvisation or rhythmic improvisation are taught at the university level, assuming they are included in undergraduate university curricula.

Having taught a course in clinical piano improvisation over the last two decades, I have noticed that it is primarily the piano majors who are afraid to go without music. Therefore, it has been helpful for me to review many resources (i.e., practicing rhythmic ideas, exploring melodic ideas within various modes, harmonic possibilities, blues progressions, concepts related to form) as reminders of what is available to draw from when creating one's own music. Further, it is important to practice improvising music in tandem with vocalizing (i.e., scat singing), to movement, with instrumental playing (i.e., drum/piano improvisation), and for listening purposes. It is difficult to say what comes first, the musical impulse, the image, or clinical purpose behind the musical impulse. For example, some students find it valuable to practice playing without music in order to generate an idea or feeling without having the pressure to relate this to a clinical purpose right away.

Gardstrom (2001) suggests that educators consider "growth in both functional and interactive musicianship as well as the development of complementary skill such as attending to, describing and processing the improvisational experience" (Gardstrom, 2001, p. 86). What I like about this approach is the general sensitization of the student to sound and the invitation for students to use their primary instrument to improvise with.

The publication of Gardstrom's more recent work (2007), with a focus on percussion activity, commonly used in group improvisation more so than other instruments, provides us with a beginning template for group music therapy.

The comprehensive writing regarding clinical improvisation (Bruscia, 1987c) serves as a theoretical backdrop for music therapy improvisation although much of this information suggests advanced competency and therefore will be discussed in Chapter 4.

Conducting Skills

10.1   Conduct basic patterns with technical accuracy.
10.2   Conduct small and large vocal and instrumental ensembles.

Discussion, Conducting Skills

There is limited literature on conducting skills as they pertain to music therapy. In his work, Clive Robbins demonstrates conducting children at eye level with simple broad motions, a technique that music therapists would not typically learn in any traditional conducting class.

In the earlier years of the profession, large-scale music ensembles (i.e., orchestra, chorus, musicals) were organized and conducted by music therapists in state institutions, such as Essex County Hospital, Cedar Grove, New Jersey, then known as Overbrook Hospital. This model is less often utilized since health care has changed over the decades. There is great therapeutic value in group ensemble work and where and when students have the opportunity to practice these skills in practicum or internship; they should take advantage of such opportunities.

VanWeelden and Whipple (2004) describe a one-hour-a-week field experience in leading a choir for senior citizens in conjunction with a two-hour-a-week undergraduate choral conducting course for music therapy students. The inclusion of technical skills of conducting, vocal pedagogy (i.e., including limitations of the voice as it ages) and choral literature paved the way for the field experience thereby creating a positive theory to practice model.

In the recent past, my students helped lead and conduct a choir at an adult psychiatric hospital and were able to track group music therapy goals within this context.

Movement Skills

11.1   Direct structured and improvisatory movement experiences.
11.2   Move in structural rhythmic and improvisatory manners for expressive purposes.
11.3   Move expressively and with interpretation to music within rhythmic structure.

Discussion, Movement Skills

Data suggesting that movement/dance received a less than average rating for breadth and depth (Maranto & Bruscia, 1988) as well as a paucity of literature on movement skills suggests that this subsection of the music-related competencies is not receiving the attention it deserves. Structured and improvisatory movement are typically presented in such courses as the formerly required NAMT social dance requirement, a substitute course in creative movement or modern dance and then, most importantly, practiced in methods courses, practicum or simulated role-playing for various populations. Adaptive music education approaches such as Orff-Schulwerk (Orff, 1980; Bitcon, 1976) and anthroposophical approaches to movement such as Eurthmy (Steiner, 1977, 1983) can also be introduced within the context of music therapy.

Beyond the obvious social importance of dance as an interactive and expressive tool, the role of movement as a curative neurological agent cannot be emphasized enough. The psychology of music and music therapy literature supports the activation of the brain through the combination of music and movement, citing, for example, protocols for improvement in gait training through the use of RAS, rhythmic auditory stimulation theory (Thaut et al., 1999; Thaut, 2005) for clients afflicted with stroke (Jeong & Kim, 2007).

Clinical Foundations: Areas of Study and Related Discussion

Exceptionality

12.1 Demonstrate basic knowledge of the potentials, limitations, and problems of exceptional individuals.

12.2 Demonstrate basic knowledge of the causes and symptoms of major exceptionalities, and basic terminology used in diagnosis and classification.

12.3 Demonstrate basic knowledge of typical and atypical human systems and development (e.g., anatomical, physiological, psychological, social).

Discussion, Exceptionality

In general, information regarding exceptionality is included in the curriculum within both psychology courses (i.e., Introduction to Psychology, Developmental Psychology, Child Psychology, Abnormal Psychology, Psychology of Children with Exceptionalities, etc.), and music therapy courses. If this is the case, it is important to require these psychology courses prior to the music therapy courses so that exceptionality is viewed from and integrated with the perspective of the music therapy session. It is probable that exceptionality, introduced in classes, is only really understood with the hands on learning of practicum and internship. I say this from the perspective of teaching The Psychology of Exceptional Children and Youth, Music Therapy with Children and Practicum that accompanies the latter course. It is truly within the practicum course that the information becomes alive. This would also explain educators, clinical supervisors and clinicians reporting that exceptionality has been taught primarily in class, in practicum/internship and on the job (Maranto & Bruscia, 1988).

Requiring relevant psychology courses prior to their related music therapy courses allows the student to understand information in a successively informed way. If music therapy courses requiring a background in exceptionality are presented without prerequisite psychology coursework, the instructor may feel overwhelmed in presenting too much information at once and, likewise, the student may feel overwhelmed in receiving and digesting too much information.

However, as music therapy literature proliferates and we work with populations and clinical scenarios not typically presented in undergraduate psychology courses (i.e., Neurorehabilitation, Medical, Alzheimer's, Hospice), we face the challenge of providing background information on exceptionality within music therapy courses.

Principles of Therapy

13.1   Demonstrate basic knowledge of the dynamics and processes of a therapist-client relationship.
13.2   Demonstrate basic knowledge of the dynamics and processes of therapy groups.
13.3   Demonstrate basic knowledge of accepted methods of major therapeutic approaches.

Discussion, Principles of Therapy

As with exceptionality, the principles of therapy regarding the therapist-client relationship, group psychodynamics and systems of psychotherapy have been taught in both psychology classes (34%) and music therapy classes (55%) (Maranto & Bruscia, 1988), only, I would suggest, to be realized through the analysis of case study material and with clinical experience. It is important to introduce examples of how principles of therapy function within the context of music therapy so that the student does not begin to compartmentalize these concepts. What is the possible nature of the therapist-client relationship? How does that relationship manifest in various case studies? In the clinical work you are observing? In the clinical work you are experiencing? What is the nature of group dynamics as you read about it, experience it in a music therapy-training group, observe it in your clinical setting and facilitate it in music therapy groups? What are the most prevalent methods of psychotherapy? How do you identify these within the context of music therapy (Scovel & Gardstrom, 2002)? In various case studies you read? In the clinical work you are doing? In the clinical work you are structuring and writing about? It is only with these successive levels of thinking and transferring information, that the music therapist will gain an appreciation for therapeutic principles.

The Therapeutic Relationship

14.1   Recognize the impact of one's own feelings, attitudes, and actions on the client and the therapy process.

14.2   Establish and maintain interpersonal relationships with clients that are conducive to therapy.

14.3   Use oneself effectively in the therapist role in both individual and group therapy, e.g., appropriate self-disclosure, authenticity, empathy, etc., toward affecting desired behavioral outcomes.

14.4   Utilize the dynamics and processes of groups to achieve therapeutic goals.

14.5   Demonstrate awareness of one's cultural heritage and socioeconomic background and how these influence the perception of the therapeutic process.

Discussion, Therapeutic Relationship

Whereas *Principles of Therapy* require the music therapist in training to learn basic knowledge, the competencies within *The Therapeutic Relationship* appear to transcend beginning knowledge and understanding in order to progress to a self-conscious understanding of beginning transferences in relationships with both individuals and groups. The implication here is that the therapist, in understanding self relative to others, will be professionally appropriate in both sensitivity and boundary setting with patients. This seems a great deal to ask of an undergraduate student, particularly if the student is studying primarily on the supportive level of music therapy.

As discussed extensively in Chapter 4 of this book, supervision proceeds on levels appropriate to developmental readiness. Pederson (2009) suggests that the first level of interpersonal awareness is simply awareness of oneself and the other; at this level the student is not yet ready to process their transference/countertransference issues and parallel processes. Yet I have also had the experience of supervising more mature undergraduates or equivalency students where they were at another level, focused on the patient in such a way that led to overidentification, followed by very strong countertransference reactions (Pederson, 2009). In such cases, it is necessary to process interpersonal reactions in such a way that helps the student problem-solve with the patient as well as the supervisor. Interpersonal issues can be discussed in the context of clinical supervision, experienced in a music therapy training group and journaled during clinical work (see Chapters 3 and 6).

Music Therapy: Areas of Study and Related Discussion

Foundations and Principles

15.1   Demonstrate basic knowledge of existing music therapy methods, techniques, materials, and equipment with their appropriate applications.

15.2 Demonstrate basic knowledge of principles, and methods of music therapy assessment and their appropriate application.

15.3 Demonstrate basic knowledge of the principles and methods for evaluating the effects of music therapy.

15.4 Demonstrate basic knowledge of the purpose, intent, and function of music therapy for various client populations.

15.5 Demonstrate basic knowledge of the psychological and physiological aspects of musical behavior and experience (i.e., music and affect; influence of music on behavior; physiological responses to music; perception and cognition of music; psychomotor components of music behavior; music learning and development; preference; creativity).

15.6 Demonstrate basic knowledge of philosophical, psychological, physiological, and sociological bases for the use of music as therapy.

15.7 Demonstrate basic knowledge of the use of current technologies in music therapy assessment, treatment, and evaluation.

Discussion, Foundations and Principles

Competencies 15.1–15.7 form an integral basis for those skills developed in the clinical realm. These competencies are the meat and potatoes of music therapy education. Notice that they all begin with the words, "Demonstrate basic knowledge," suggesting that there is a very real difference between these competencies and the practice competencies in music therapy that follow and are discussed in Chapter 3 under *clinical training*. However, *there is an overlap between competencies 15.1–15.7 and the practice competencies that follow since students are still in the process of demonstrating basic knowledge of the bases for music therapy at the same time they are entering practicum.*

I take the liberty of rewriting competencies 15.1–15.7, for purposes of discussion, in a different order:

1. Social and natural science perspectives on using music in therapy (15.6).
2. Influence of music on behavior related to what is generally identified with the psychology of music (15.5).
3. Assessment (15.2).
4. Purposes of music therapy (15.4).
5. Methods/techniques/materials/equipment (15.1).
6. Evaluation (15.3).

This order provides the student with a rationale for the use of music as a therapeutic tool before going on to discuss the procedural order of the intervention process (assessment, goals and objectives, methods and materials, evaluation). I regard the use of technology (15.7) as one that should have its own category since it relates to all aspects of the music therapy process.

In the initial presentation of these competencies, the student generally reads and discusses relevant concepts. However, in keeping with my *premise* regarding the educational challenge for the music therapy educator to extend, transfer and integrate all knowledge and skills, it is quite important for the instructor to do the following:

1. Demonstrate and invite simulation (i.e., role-playing) of the music therapy process (assessment, purposes of music therapy, methods/ techniques/materials/equipment, evaluation), including music technology applications in music therapy courses.
2. Contextualize and relate social and natural science perspectives (including all related to psychology of music) to music therapy.
3. Present research in such a way that demonstrates the relationships between clinical practice and the development of research hypotheses as well as research conclusions and their application to clinical intervention.

All instructor demonstration and experiential exercises serve to extend, contextualize and integrate the ongoing music foundations, clinical foundations and music therapy foundations skills. They provide a basis for entering preprofessional clinical training. For these reasons, it is helpful, in terms of curriculum design (see Chapter 6), to align music therapy foundations courses alongside practicum courses.

Social and Natural Science Perspectives on Using Music in Therapy (15.6)

The initial readings in music therapy written by both Sears (1968, 2007) and Gaston (1968) present a great deal of basic information about philosophical, physiological, psychological, and sociological bases for the use of music as therapy. It is valuable not only to introduce these writings, particularly the perhaps considered archaic "Processes in Music Therapy" (Gaston, 1968; Sears, 2007), in a beginning music therapy course, but, further, to emphasize them in context of the purposes and methods in using music with various populations. Seeking out writings on similar topics will be extremely instructive for students, helping them think out of the box in reference to our field.

While all music therapy application is related to social and natural science perspectives, the fairly recent growth of writing in the last decade (see Appendix B; see Chapter 6, "Reading"), for example the work of Stige (2002a, 2002b, 2010) nourishes these perspectives.

Psychology of Music (15.5)

The information in competency 15.5, generally considered under a course entitled Psychology of Music is, in my opinion, the fundamental basis of music therapy. The literature base for the psychology of music is extensive and it is best to focus on theoretical knowledge most applicable to music therapy, as alluded to or named in this competency: music and affect, influence of music on behavior, physiological responses to music, perception and cognition of music, psychomotor components of music behavior, music learning and development, preference and creativity.

I add to this list preliminary mention of references related to neurobiological processing of music and its application in music therapy (Thaut, 2005), and developmental psychology and its basis in understanding musical behavior (Goodman, 2007, Chapter 3). Beyond the readings associated with psychology of music, we must invite experiences and discussion in context of music therapy and the use of this information toward clinical intervention. The very real opportunity for students to relate this information to case study material is important. In discussing neurophysiologic processing of music, for example, Dr. Oliver Sacks' case studies help us speculate about how music therapy might be used with the patients described (Sacks, 2007).

Assessment (15.2)

The introduction to assessment includes its place within a process. We start with assessment, set goals and objectives, plan and provide intervention, evaluate the results of the intervention. When necessary, we return to assessment if the goals and objectives were unrealistically set.

Reasons for conducting assessment include the need to gather information about client strengths and weaknesses for the purposes of program planning (Cohen & Gericke, 1972), subsequent intervention and accountability and justification of services and professional credibility (Isenberg-Gzreda, 1988), all of which apply to both education and mental health (Wolery et al., 1994). In specific settings, assessment is required to establish medical reimbursement for services (Scalenghe & Murphy, 2000) as well as music therapy on the individual education plan (Coleman & Brunk, 1999).

In my writing (Goodman, 2007), I review at length several published assessments for children (Nordoff & Robbins, 2007; Goodman, 1989; Coleman & Brunk, 1999; Michel & Rohrbacher, 1982), and discuss the nature of the assessment tool in terms of purpose, client prerequisites, philosophy, time to administer, methodology and efficacy in the clinical setting. The same analysis is useful for other published assessments for children (Baxter et al., 2007; Libertore & Layman, 1999), adults (Cassity, 2006;

Botello & Krout, 2008) and seniors (Hintz, 2000; York, 1994; Adler, 2000).

In teaching assessment, it is appropriate for students on the undergraduate level to test their ability to observe and assess one component of behavior, gradually expanding their skills to do more. This information can be introduced in discussing various populations, then simulated in the classroom and ultimately be transferred into the clinical setting. Most educators (47%) and supervisors (67%) have agreed that client assessment is best learned in practicum or internships (Maranto & Bruscia, 1988). My experience with assessment is that observation skills and knowing what to look for are key determinants of success. Assessment can be a relatively sophisticated skill. Literature on music therapy assessment emphasizes assessment of the individual and this is an issue in a field where so many of us work with groups. Further detail on the link from theory to practice in practicing assessment is provided in Chapter 3.

Purposes of Music Therapy (15.4)

The purpose, intent and function of music therapy for various clients has been spelled out in literature covering populations in many contexts ((i.e., medical, special education, neurorehabilitation, psychiatry, gerontology. developmental disabilities, etc.) and diagnoses. As educators, we are hard-pressed to do adequate justice to the purpose, intent and function of music therapy in all these possible scenarios.

Therefore, it is important, in my opinion, to emphasize basic concepts that remind us of purpose from population to population. What are the issues the client faces in treatment? Why is this client being referred to music therapy? What can music, as a therapeutic intervention, provide that another intervention is not providing? How has the use of music as an intervention been used for similar purpose across populations? How can music be presented in a manner that fits the developmental and sensory profile of the client? These sorts of questions help us view purposes of music therapy from a more global perspective rather than compartmentalizing the use of music with certain populations.

In the undergraduate model of music therapy as adjunctive therapy, the purposes in therapy may be contextualized in a team treatment plan and it may be that this is the reason that most educators (51%) and supervisors (75%) (Maranto & Bruscia, 1988), have reported that treatment planning (which would include the identification of goals, objectives and methods and materials) is best learned in practicum and internship. In the graduate model of music therapy as a primary therapy, the purposes of therapy may be considered unique to the music therapist. It is important, however, to demonstrate both possibilities to the undergraduate music therapy student so there is a larger sense of music therapy as a discipline.

Further detail on the link from theory to practice in teaching treatment planning is provided in Chapter 3.

Methods/Techniques/Materials/Equipment (15.1)

Are we not talking about intervention here? Interventions are detailed across multiple texts, journal articles and case study accounts. These terms need to be defined clearly so students can, in reading and discussing books on methods as well as illustrative case studies, analyze and critically question the choice of these therapeutic components. They can be modeled by the educator and simulated by students.

Let us tease out the semantics of the words "methods" and "techniques." Bruscia considers methods as synonymous with procedures, "strategies, approaches, types of activity that may be accomplished through techniques" (Bruscia, 1987c) while Standley refers to techniques as "synonymous with strategies and procedures" (Standley, 1991).

For purposes of the competency, I define methods as the overarching decisions about how to format the session (Goodman, 2007) (i.e., songwriting, improvisation, verbal process, projective storytelling, composition, relaxation to music, movement, etc.) while techniques are the specifics in directing, facilitating or negotiating the methods (Goodman, 2007) (i.e., modeling, prompting, musical reflection, movement synchrony, verbal confrontation etc.). Therefore, there are two types of material to teach. Further, they go hand-in-hand with materials (i.e., music, instruments, etc.) and equipment (i.e., technology devices, augmentative, occupational therapy equipment, etc.).

The competency includes presentation of methods, techniques, material and equipment in context of different clinical purposes. It is obviously subjective judgment on the part of the educator to decide what information is to be prioritized and which methods and materials to cover in music therapy; so many exist based on theoretical orientation and the needs of the population. In the broadest sense, we can introduce receptive and active methods, which are referred to, for example, in the taxonomy of clinical techniques for adult psychiatry (Unkefer & Thaut, 1995) (this taxonomy could be considered relative to other ages and diagnoses as well) noting the delivery (techniques, materials, equipment) of methods depending upon client needs.

Since I created an appendix in this book (see Appendix B) of close to 300 books written on music therapy over the last six decades, I note that the bulk of subject matter (60 %) is devoted to music therapy methods. (*Note:* Inclusive of techniques and materials as well.). I am particularly struck by applications within the last ten years (2000–2009: 71 books) for/or involving the following: dementia, neurological disability, autism, group therapy, bereavement, trauma, GIM, songwriting, developmental disabilities, improvisation, palliative care, medical music therapy, vocal music therapy, adult learning disabilities, receptive methods, creative music therapy, music therapy for addictions and community music therapy. How does the educator pick and choose which methods to present to an undergraduate student?

Educators have reported (Maranto & Bruscia, 1988) that these areas of knowledge and skill are best learned in coursework (57%) as opposed to pre-professional clinical work (31%). In my experience, it is imperative to introduce methods and techniques through readings, critical analysis of case studies, simulated role-play, observation of real and filmed therapy sessions and, finally, transfer this information to preprofessional clinical work, using graduated expectations for the student to plan, conduct and evaluate the session.

I believe that it is important for the student to develop a critical but constructive mindset when reading, analyzing and evaluating the elements of intervention presented in literature. The educator can pose the questions:

- What is the therapist doing with the client(s) in response to the perceived needs of the client and the perceived or stated goals/objectives for the session?
- Are the methods, techniques and materials sufficiently detailed in the literature for you to understand them? If not, what other information are you seeking?
- What is the theoretical basis for the decisions the therapist is making in terms of methods, techniques and materials?
- Do these interventions match the needs of the client (s)? If yes, explain why. If not, explain why and propose alternative solutions.
- How would you evaluate the success of these interventions?
- How does this information help you in planning and/or proceeding with your own sessions?

As in treatment planning, it is incumbent upon the educator to identify overlapping uses of music also known as methods, etc., with varying theoretical premises, with varied populations, and for varied purposes. This will create a critical approach for the student to consider the value of various methods in a global context rather than feeling overwhelmed by compartmentalized knowledge. Ask basic questions.

For example, lets talk about improvisation: What is improvisation? What are various types of improvisation? What are various purposes of improvisation? What are ways to structure improvisation? How might this work with the following kinds of client situations? Case material demonstrating uses of an improvisation with different populations and in different ways may then invite a way to introduce possibility, providing comparative content for discussion followed with or preceded by experiential simulation. Within the detailed examples of how to utilize a particular music therapy approach on different levels, the educator can pose questions regarding techniques in delivery to a particular client group and techniques relative to the needs of the population. I think it is also important for a student to realize that not every single potential music therapy situation possible will be covered in the music therapy curriculum. We are helping students learn how to think critically about purposes and methods in therapy. It is only in this way that the student will avoid recipe-like sessions.

Standley (1991) suggests that students practice methods and techniques in a hierarchical manner whereby they move from level one through level five in order to develop the leadership skills necessary for music therapy. Graduated responsibilities in terms of the type of and number of objectives, the use of music, the varying needs and severity of needs in the given population, varying leader decisions and types of evaluation suggest a way of teaching that considers theory to practice in a thoughtful way and one which surely alleviates student anxiety as students master various levels of responsibility and self-assessment.

Further detail on the link from theory to practice in practicing methods and materials is provided in Chapter 3.

Evaluation (15.3)

The ability to evaluate progress or lack of progress in the music therapy sessions starts with the development of observation skills, observation skills that document both objectively and subjectively what the baseline behaviors of the client are. From this point, the student can treatment plan, intervene and evaluate if the client has made progress. This information can be introduced in music therapy class on successive levels but ultimately it is learned in fieldwork as an overwhelming majority, 61 percent of educators and 75 percent of supervisors, agreed (Maranto & Bruscia, 1988).

Objectively, evaluation involves keen observation, memory of what was observed and data collection. Subjectively, evaluation involves an ongoing sense of process. How do you personally perceive the behaviors of the client? Your own behavior? Do you have a theoretical basis for what you spontaneously do in the session? How do you learn from what happened in this session to plan for the next and/or expand your understanding of music therapy?

Sabbatella (1999) points out that evaluation includes assessment and evaluation of clients, evaluation of treatment procedures and techniques used, evaluation of treatment effectiveness and evaluation of interpersonal relationships in the therapeutic process, all of which should be written about and discussed in supervision.

Further detail on the link from theory to practice in practicing evaluation is provided in Chapter 3.

Technology (15.7)

Two decades ago, the use of computers was limited in music therapy training. Gregory (1987) noted the terms, computer-assisted instruction (CAI), computer-based instruction (CBI) and computer-based education (CBE), predicting that the future of CAI would be dependent upon administrative decisions and faculty involvement and suggesting the use of CAI for drill and practice, tutorials, games and simulations applicable to music therapy education. Wolfe (1987) recommended the use of AIMSTAR, a computer-based planning and management system to store, analyze and graph client data. Krout (1989) reported that 51 university professors responding to his survey were quite limited in the use of computers for university training. Only 31 percent reported using microcomputers for the purposes of general computer literacy, writing articles, preparing and maintaining client progress records, running statistics on music therapy data, computer-assisted instruction in music learning and using microcomputers to retrieve information. It would be interesting to replicate such a survey considering all the uses of computers that have surfaced since with reference to music therapy.

In their broad definition of technology, Crowe and Rio (2004) organize the relevant music therapy literature in terms of adapted musical instruments, recording technology, electric/electronic musical instruments, computer applications, medical technology, assistive technology for the disabled and technology-based music/sound healing practices. These all potentially play a part in assessment, intervention and evaluation. In terms of actual music therapy, assessment and/or intervention, adapted musical instruments, assistive technology for the disabled (i.e., Soundbeam, MidiCreater), electric instruments (i.e., Omnichord), sound healing practices (i.e., Somatron), and recording technology (i.e., for composition and arranging) are quite important. In terms of evaluation, it is important to be able to store and organize information on the computer.

As we move forward into this century, we look forward to more innovative uses of technology. Manzo (2010) has designed an electro-acoustic musical interactive room, EAMIR, which allows the client to create a musical expression through the use of sensors that can be triggered by stomping on the floor, bending the fingers or waving a hand in the air. Streeter (2010) is investigating the design of a computational tool, Music Therapy Logbook, that will help music therapists gather objective data from audio recordings of music therapy sessions. Undoubtedly, some of these technologies go beyond our subjective understanding of basic. While music therapists have expressed concern about whether or not music therapists are motivated to use newer technology, both in the United States (Crowe & Rio, 2004) and in Britain (Magee, 2006; Streeter, 2007), there is a recognized need for improved student training in this area.

Further detail on the link from theory to practice in practicing the use of technology is provided in Chapters 3 and 4.

Research Methods

25.1 Interpret information in the professional research literature.
25.2 Demonstrate basic knowledge of the purpose and methodology of historical, quantitative, and qualitative research.
25.3 Perform a database literature search.
25.4 Apply selected research findings to clinical practice.

Discussion, Research Methods

I take the liberty of moving the topic of *Research Methods* out of numerical order in order to introduce it as subject matter initiated in music therapy classes where 87 percent of educators (Maranto & Bruscia, 1988) agreed it should be taught. This is not to disclaim, however, the responsibility of educators and clinical supervisors to encourage students to initiate research based on ideas gleaned from clinical work.

The music therapy profession writes a great deal on the subject of research, as evidenced, for example, by a comprehensive reference text (Wheeler, 1995), a review of four decades of behavioral research (Gregory, 2008), and, in more recent decades, support for qualitative research (Aigen, 1998, 2008; Edwards, 1999, 2004; Bruscia, 1998b).

Concerns about training undergraduate and graduate students with differential expectations in research were initially suggested in the seventies and early eighties (Hanser & Madsen, 1972; Madsen & Furman, 1984; Madsen, 1986) when the difference between undergraduates and graduates in terms of research competencies was not found to be significant (Madsen & Furman, 1984). The issue of transfer, reviewing research information and applying it to clinical intervention was emphasized (Madsen, 1986) then and should be emphasized now as well.

We would probably all agree that research be introduced differently at the bachelor's, masters and doctoral level. In line with the stated AMTA competencies, Bruscia (1999) suggested that the Bachelor's level student understand the difference between quantitative and qualitative research and read and comprehend simple research. Beyond the AMTA competencies, however, he proposed that students design research-based clinical work at the adjunctive level. This, in my experience, makes eminent sense particularly if the student can design a simple meaningful piece of research. Madsen and Furman (1984) suggested that, although it is not stated in the competencies, it is helpful for the student to have a working background in statistics, a course that may also be used in many universities to satisfy a general education mathematics requirement. If the student does take statistics, it should be taken prior to a music therapy research course. If the student does not take statistics, that information should be folded into the music therapy research course. Some universities consolidate psychology of music and research into a two-semester sequence, in which case, the second semester of the course would be devoted to research.

In summary, the ability to understand basic research paradigms, critically review research literature and critically apply the results of research to intervention is essential in undergraduate training. Here again, we see theory to practice.

CONCLUSION

The goal of theory to practice begins with the core areas of music foundations and clinical foundations and the foundations and principles of music therapy. Extending student training as a musician and introducing information regarding exceptionality and interpersonal relationships may start in courses outside of music therapy but needs to be realized in music therapy courses.

Those who are ignorant about the profession of music therapy typically think that students study music, students study psychology and these two areas then constitute music therapy training. In fact, these two areas form a vital basis for the understanding and execution of music therapy as a specific discipline. Hence we arrive at *Foundations and Principles,* the music therapy courses prior to and/or concurrent with practicum, the initial supervised practice of music therapy. Music therapy courses then, bear the responsibility for extending and contextualizing knowledge and skills under music and clinical foundations, as they relate to music therapy foundations and principles.

As educators, we introduce the forest, larger guiding concepts about music therapy, and the trees, specific examples of how the music therapy process is accomplished. I have presented you with suggestions that, hopefully, will pave the way for this type of thinking.

As the students begin to leave the classroom and enter the clinical arena, another challenge is presented to both student and educator. How will the student translate their theory into practice? In our next chapter, Chapter 3, this question is explored.

Chapter 3

PREPROFESSIONAL CLINICAL TRAINING

The great aim of education is not knowledge but action.
Herbert Spencer (1820–1903)

INTRODUCTION

It is the first semester of a student practicum and I have advised students to initially observe at their clinical sites and then to start assisting and leading portions of a music therapy session. Some students balk. Others cannot wait to actively participate. What is it about getting one's feet wet that can sometimes be intimidating?

As educators in the field of music therapy, we juggle multiple roles. Of course we are educators, but we are also likely to serve as clinical supervisors, academic advisors, and mentors. Given these various roles as well as the need for the student to transition from the classroom to the clinical arena vis-à-vis short-term practicum assignments and, following, the longer-term internship, how do we help students make the transition from theory to practice? How can we translate knowledge into action per the Spencer quote?

This chapter discusses the entrance of the student into the clinical arena while also taking music therapy courses, both of which will lead to entry to the music therapy competencies that involve the actual practice of music therapy. The structure and supervision of both practicum and internship, requiring a minimum total of 1200 hours of training, including 900 of these in internship (AMTA, 2010), is presented in this chapter. It is in the theory to application arena of clinical work that the music therapy education finds meaning.

As we continue to emphasize *education as the initial introduction of skills and knowledge in the classroom* and *training as the application of skills and knowledge in the clinical realm,* preprofessional practica and internship, the following bear repeating.

62

1. How can we demonstrate and experience the components of the music therapy process in order to *transfer, extend* (in ways that may not be apparent from the stated competencies) *and therefore integrate the ongoing development of music foundation skills and clinical foundation skills with those of music therapy foundations and principles?* It is in this way that we create a new level of integration toward music therapy practice competencies. *This constitutes theory to practice and skills to practice.*

2. How can clinical practice refer back to theory in a way that is instructive?

OVERVIEW: PRACTICUM AND INTERNSHIP

Practicum: Structure, Support and Supervision

Prior to reviewing the competencies composed as training goals, it is helpful to review the structure, support and supervision involved in both practicum and internship

Structure

What is a practicum? Technically defined as a course or student exercise involving practical experience as well as theoretical study (Hawes & Hawes, 1962), it also constitutes a clinical/fieldwork experience in a healthcare setting under the supervision of a credentialed practitioner, practice carried out away from the institution and in direct contact with the people being studied. Practicum also has the potential of being defined as a service learning course since students are participating in organized service that meets identified community needs and promotes reflective practice regarding activity in order to gain further understanding of course content, a broader appreciation of the discipline and an enhanced sense of civic responsibility (Bringle & Hatcher, 1995). As a service-learning scholar at Montclair State University, I have structured practica in this manner.

The concurrent experience of practical experience as well as theoretical study, however, is a unique one and one not necessarily found in the internship. This is why the practicum, unlike other music therapy courses, poses such rich potential for theory to practice learning.

The structure of the practicum varies from university to university in terms of the number of semesters, the concurrent course of study and academic assignments that reinforce clinical work, the successive level of responsibilities on the part of the student and the involvement of on-site as well as faculty supervision. A university survey conducted a decade ago (Wheeler,

2000), found that the majority of university respondents conducted four semesters of practicum in conjunction with a once-a-week practice seminar. During these semesters, student responsibilities progressed to a leadership role (12 of 38 respondents) or involved leading only (14 of 38 respondents) under the guidance of an on-site supervisor (30 of 38 respondents). Concurrent assignments included assessment, session plans and documentation of progress. An earlier survey (Maranto & Bruscia, 1988) found that the average number of practica was five with the student spending time observing (26%), assisting (20%) or conducting group (46%) or individual (34%) sessions independently, subject to supervision (46%) from a music therapist (51%). Written assignments in conjunction with the practicum might include treatment planning, clinical logs, readings, and case studies.

Generally, each practicum involves periods of observation followed by partial or full clinical responsibility with varied populations under the guidance of an on-site supervisor affiliated with a university but not generally a paid faculty member. Practicum assignments constitute individual music therapy, group therapy or a combination of individual and group. Ideally, the student should receive both types of experience. Although there is merit to asking a student to focus on assessment, treatment planning, intervention and evaluation for one client versus the group, the need to meet the demands of group practice in the internship and eventual music therapy position is also a practical concern.

Students realize the value of the practicum experience and, according to McClain (1993) would appreciate more on-site supervisors, a greater possibility in choosing practicum placements, more orientation before beginning a practicum, a transition from less difficult to more difficult clients, from individuals or small groups to larger ones, an earlier start in practicum training and opportunities to assist, or co-lead before conducting sessions independently. Have your students shared their learning needs with you?

University programs may frequently have difficulties with less than ideal practicum situations, particularly when enrollments are high and placements are limited. Optimally, I suggest the following guidelines in order to maximize the clinical training prior to the internship:

- Minimum of four semesters of practicum starting in the junior year in order to dovetail the academic foundations and principles of therapy (15.1–15.7) with applied clinical work.
- Minimum of three different clinical populations in order for the student to gain a more global perspective on the use of music in therapy and the process of setting up and documenting treatment across a range of populations.

- Consistency in providing on-site music therapy supervision in order to provide a model for the student and a helpful level of structure and support.
- Consistency in providing faculty for supervision (observation visits and/or video-recorded review) in order to create a liaison between school and facility, sharing understanding of facility needs and university needs, two different clinical perspectives and link to evaluation of clinical competencies.
- Adequate opportunity for a student to progress from observation to partial assisting to leadership role in order to provide a developmental order that makes sense for a student within the course of a given rotation whether it be with an individual client and/or given music therapy group.
- Avoidance of more than one student placed in an assigned practicum situation (i.e., individual and/or group) at a time in order to have the supervisor provide adequate attention to the training needs of one student at a time and avoid two students co-leading a group when they may not be developmentally ready to do this.
- Addition of on-campus clinic, particularly in universities where rural university location and/or competitive urban center with a number of programs make access to desirable clinical placements inconsistent.
- Adequate academic support for practicum in order to create the theory to practice link and receive supportive theory and resources for practice with assigned client(s); cap of 7–10 optimal for practicum seminar.
- Ongoing communication between university and practicum site in order to problem-solve as necessary and create a smoother understanding of how the clinical placements and university seminars/classes support each other.

Hadsell and Jones (1988), emphasizing the levels of cooperative responsibility between the university educator and the on-site supervisor, provide a summary of suggestions that support and extend that which I have already stated above and will continue to elaborate upon. For example, it is important for the on-site music therapy supervisor to specify the level of student training that the practicum can provide, provide orientation about the program and clients, outline practicum expectations in writing, review specific procedures used with clients and observe on a regular basis and with specific feedback. Further, it is necessary to challenge students at their skill levels, attempt to resolve any problems with students openly, and, in completing evaluation forms, share these with the student whenever appropriate.

In turn, the educator should state the abilities and skills of the student(s) being placed at the practicum facility, clarify expectations, stay in regular communication with the on-site supervisors, stay informed, help when needed, provide evaluation forms stating expectations and deadlines and observe students as much as possible. If possible, it is helpful for supervisors to meet with faculty at the university setting to review guidelines for on-site supervision and structure a way of evaluating the student practicum experience, which includes benefitting from supervision. Unlike clinical training supervisors in internship, many on-site clinical supervisors do not necessarily have training in supervision and, if possible, a supervision workshop conducted once or twice a year is supportive and helpful for supervisors, students and the educational program.

At Montclair State University we have six practica, which begin in the sophomore year. Each sequence, two semesters long, exposes the student to a different population. Each fall semester involves observation, assisting and assuming portions of a group music therapy session as appropriate. Each spring semester involves responsibility for running groups and/or individual sessions independently while being supervised by an onsite supervisor in conjunction with two faculty visits. All practica are supported by weekly seminars as well as theoretical coursework related to the clinical populations students are actively observing or providing supervised intervention for. Technically practica are set up for undergraduates but graduate students fulfilling equivalency requirements are taking these courses as well.

The logical documentation of progress toward the applied clinical competencies, should be expedited with progressively more demanding standards as the student progresses through the undergraduate practicum and into the internship. It is helpful to take a written inventory of progress toward applied clinical competencies at the end of each practicum semester if the rotation is two semesters long and at the midpoint of each semester if the rotation is one semester long. Ideally a supervisor assessment and student-self assessment would be very useful for the sake of comparison and shared dialogue. It is suggested (Zigo, 2010) that students set sample objectives for themselves at the mid-point assessment for completion before the end of the clinical rotation.

Support

Moving into the clinical arena is always exciting but, at the same time, can be unnerving for students. According to an analysis of interviews conducted with eight students (Wheeler, 2002), challenges encountered by students may include generalized fear of a new experience, session planning (i.e., concern about what to include in session plans, how to handle unpredictability), needs of the clients (i.e., lack of experience with the population, lack of experience in handling clients at different developmental levels in a group), concerns about music skills and academic grading in a practicum for one credit but a great deal of academic work. However, many of these issues dissipate as practicum rotations continue (Kahler, 1998) since students develop skills in progressing from one practicum to another and, in so doing, develop more self-confidence along with the improvement of their musical and clinical skills.

Structure can be a comfort at this time and the need for graduated levels of structure has been suggested in the music therapy literature.

Hanser (1978, 1987, 2001) suggests a system analysis approach that assigns students to small supervision groups, provides weekly assignments in the context of seminar, and uses audio-recorded or videotaped sessions for supervision. Student tasks, crossing all population areas, include a facility tour, group activity observation form, initial assessment guidelines, setting of goals and objectives, response definition, proposed treatment plan outline and a music therapy treatment summary. Each assignment is formatted for the student, thereby clarifying successive expectations (Hanser, 1987). Although Hanser's model involves a student working with one client in a clinical rotation, I believe it can be modified for a student to work with a small group. General expectations relate to competency in creating appropriate activities, use of instructional methodology, pacing, preparation, and implementation and use of music, promptness, appearance and client-therapist interaction (Hanser, 1987). Feedback can be expedited with behavior checklists, video-recorded observations and observation forms (Hanser, 1987).

Wright (1992) suggests a levels system where the student has the opportunity to sequentially develop musical and clinical competencies. This begins with participation in an on-campus clinic for closest supervision and then moves into the community. The progressive designation of tasks helps the student develop specific clinical skills, with each new task building on previously learned skills. Students must acquire specific skills at each level before proceeding to the next level, which involves greater degrees of responsibility. In this way the student meets all expectations for four levels prior to graduation.

Perhaps similarly, Darrow and Gibbons (1987) identify three levels of practicum. At the first level, student strengths and weaknesses are identified and remedial work is outlined. At the second level, specific music therapy skills are to be developed. At the third level, student develops a client's music therapy program with little assistance from the supervisor at the university and is supervised by on-site personnel.

Whatever system of support the academic environment provides, it is important to be aware of the vulnerability of the student and the need for academic coursework that will define and reinforce the concurrent clinical work. In addition to specific assignments in the practicum along with supportive coursework, some students may benefit from a clinical training guide, which you can design, or purchase.

There is limited but valuable discussion in the music therapy literature relevant to preprofessional training techniques from the perspective of both educators and students with focus on the following:

1. Use of videotapes for student self-analysis of competencies (Alley, 1978) and/or feedback regarding competency skills (Hanser & Furman, 1980).
2. Differential evaluation of competencies between student and instructor (Greenfield, 1978).
3. Simulation and observation training (Ten Eyck, 1985).
4. Audio-cuing and immediate feedback (Adamek, 1994).
5. Simulated replication of problematic clinical moments as a means of supervision in the classroom (Summer, 2001).
6. Use of faculty supervisor modeling, verbal feedback and guided participation while observing clinical sessions (Anderson, 1982) versus less intensive feedback methods.
7. Faculty perceptions of the supervisory process with practicum students (Hadsell & Jones, 1988; Edwards & Daveson, 2004).
8. The use of subjective evaluation also referred to as reflective journaling skills (Goodman, 2007; Barry & O'Callaghan, 2008) in order to plan subsequent sessions and reflect on theory to practice.

I will elaborate upon these concepts in this chapter as they relate to the clinical competencies.

As noted in Chapter 2, the overlap between competencies 15.1–15.7 demonstrating basic knowledge of the bases for music therapy and the practice competencies that follow make it particularly important for us to remember that students are learning basic knowledge of the bases for music therapy, with respect to various populations, at the same time that they are entering the clinical arena.

Supervision

Students placed in practicum should be supervised both on-site by a professional music therapist and guided by the faculty supervisor in classes that support the ongoing clinical work.

Krout (1982) proposes a system of supervision that is entirely class-based and rests on student attendance and punctuality, data from fieldwork, class discussion contributions and discussion with the on-site therapist regarding student clinical skills. In cases where a faculty member is not able to observe clinical work, this is a useful scenario but ideally, another pair of eyes, those of the faculty supervisor, can be very useful. In cases where a faculty member does not directly observe students, the review of audio-recorded material has been found to be effective.

It bears repeating here that regular supervision sessions should be scheduled for practicum: weekly with the on-site supervisor, once or twice a semester with the faculty supervisor who visits, and weekly in the context of a practicum seminar. Further, the review of weekly log notes will help the faculty supervisor and/or faculty instructor of the practicum seminar become aware of any need to meet individually with a student. Supervision (based on in-person observation or review of video recordings) ideally takes place after the session in which the student is involved so that both student and supervisor profit from their detailed short-term memories of the session.

Levels of supervision will vary, moving from concrete feedback related to the session(s) to interpersonal issues related to the student's feeling about the client(s). Supervision can take place in a one-on-one meeting or within a group.

It is also possible to provide a sense of group supervision by sharing information in practicum seminar. First, it is important to recognize the therapeutic qualities of the student personality in each way of relating to clients. Summer (2001) suggests identifying the student's style and "accommodating it to their first client" (Summer, 2001, p. 70). I find this interesting and it reminds me of Daniel Stern's (1977, 1998) attunement theory between mother and child wherein the mother must acclimate to the temperament of the child in order to attune. How true this is in reference to bonding with any client as well.

Second, Summer (2001) calls for evoking the student's "musical character" (Summer, 2001, p. 70). What is the student's primary experience of music like and how can this be utilized as a meaning of understanding the importance of the client connecting through music? Third, it is useful to address preconceived notions about aspects of the music therapy process (Summer, 2001, p. 71). How many times have we, as faculty supervisors or clinical supervisors, heard ideas that we never expected to hear from students? Yet, it is important that these be voiced so they can be discussed.

The age and maturity of the student will affect the way in which supervision is received as well as helping inform the student about client needs. Edwards and McFerran (2004) write about the necessity to educate music therapy students about working with clients who have been sexually abused. Similarly, students need to be informed about the needs of any clients they are going to be working with. As an educational supervisor, it is normal to expect an emotional disconnect with students facing challenging client situations and, in these cases, it is helpful to discuss what emotional obstacles are providing difficulty for each student. This should be done in an individual meeting. There are many situations where confidential meetings with a student may lead to defended material in a person's past. I recall two situations of note. One situation involved a student who found working the elderly "disgusting" but could not readily identify why. We discussed what was offensive about it and her underlying fears about "dirty old men." She then free-associated to her grandfather having molested her as a young child, a situation she had never sought counseling for. Similarly, another student found working with adult psychiatric clients intimidating. We explored what was intimidating about the experience and she free-associated to her older brother molesting her as a young child, a situation she ultimately received counseling for.

In general, the more mature the student, the more willing he or she is to develop a sole identity in relation to the professional. The young student, on the other hand, may be looking for compartmentalized answers, which, as we know, do not exist. Initial practica should emphasize therapeutic presence, musical skills and carrying out the therapeutic process (Summer, 2001).

Depending upon the maturity of the student and the theoretical nature of the university content, preprofessional supervision may delve deeper into the life and motivations behind student conduct in the practicum and internship (Odell-Miller & Krueckeberg, 2009). Feiner (2001) recalls some situations where the supervisor might feel the compunction to "treat" the student. She (Feiner, 2001) suggests that personal issues that interfere with the intern's understanding of the treatment of the client, interfere with the intern's relationship with the supervisor or interfere with the intern's relationship with staff on-site should be explored by the faculty or on-site supervisor but only in order to refer the student to an outside therapist (Feiner, 2001).

The interest in supervisory issues has also been written about from the perspective of the graduate supervisee (Odell-Miller & Krueckeberg, 2009; Oldfield, 2009). I believe this possibility is appropriate for the entry-level student as well.

The student practicum experience may lead to a scenario where the faculty supervisor is in a position of providing supervision as well as assigning a grade. In situations of this nature, it is helpful to invite input in terms of a grade from the on-site supervisor as well and, depending upon the theoretical nature of the supervision, keep in mind the difficulty this overall situation may present for the student.

Internship: Structure, Support and Supervision

Structure

The structure of internship historically varied between the American Association for Music Therapy and the National Association for Music Therapy (Bruscia, 1987b). AAMT internships had traditionally been local, part-time (3 days a week over 9 months), and coincided with internship seminars and faculty supervision. NAMT internships were offered throughout the country, were customarily full-time (40 hours a week for 6 months) and did not include internship seminars or faculty supervision. It is for this reason that one still finds different structures for internship in place with former AAMT and former NAMT schools; the timeframe and university support system will vary from one university to another.

Boone (1989) cites several issues regarding the internship that are important for the educator. She emphasizes the importance of the educator getting more involved in approving, monitoring and selecting clinical sites that will complement the educational program the student is coming from (this can include identifying the treatment techniques and competencies an internship can best address), identifying areas of focus for the student to develop during the internship, and videotapes and conference calls as a means of continuing supervision between the academic institution and the internship,

During the unification phase (1996–1998) of the merger between AAMT and NAMT, it was necessary for NAMT schools to ask permission to create university affiliations with those internships not on the NAMT national roster. I recall going through this process with several major teaching hospitals in New York City in order to provide affiliation agreements for my students at Montclair State University. With the formation of AMTA in 1998, the national roster, subject to application and strict standards, remained but the ability for universities to create university affiliated internship no longer required permission from the national association. AMTA approved programs now routinely use internships on the national roster as well as university affiliated internships. In a relatively recent survey (Miller & Kahler, 2008), 42 academic program directors indicated that 83 percent of them were using university-affiliated internships. The great majority of academic program directors structured university affiliated internships by requiring mid-term and final exams, specified intern activity and hours, agreements approved by an attorney, and proposals.

In all cases, the entry into the internship should be conducted with care and the internship should be made aware of the prospective intern's progress to date in terms of the AMTA competencies. A legal contract between the university and the internship facility should safeguard the interests of the student, the university and the internship. This contract can outline methods, goals and expectations of the internship as well as anticipated collaboration between university director and internship facility, ethical guidelines, insurance responsibilities and documentation of services to be provided. There are some universities that will require a similar contract for practicum students.

Support

In selecting and applying for an internship, the student's need for support must be recognized. According to a 1999 survey (Madsen & Kaiser, 1999), music therapy students are most concerned with issues related to general preparation, fears about possible failure or not being cut out for therapy, and concerns about the supervisor and placement. While these fears will, most likely, dissipate as the student adjusts to the placement setting, it is helpful to set up a timetable for students to explore, discuss and apply to internships. Faculty are well-advised to meet with the student, discuss each possible placement at length and rationally process fears that a student may express. It is also important for the student to visit the internship prior to acceptance, observe clinical sessions, talk to other interns and meet with prospective clinical supervisors.

How is the average student doing in terms of mastering the competencies upon entrance into the internship? Relevant articles, although not necessarily able to answer this question, include discussion about the effectiveness of our ability to prepare students for clinical training (Gault, 1978), the prerequisite skills necessary for a student seeking clinical internship (Brookins, 1984), and a poll comparing student perception and clinical training supervisor perception about internship concerns (Knight, 2008).

In an informative study, Gault (1978) found that 60 percent of the 529 music therapists responding felt that their internship was satisfactory in terms of meeting professional training. What might be of concern to the educator is the fact that 56 percent of these respondents felt that training in application of specific music therapy procedures during academic work was insufficient. Gault suggests that this concern may indicate a need for academic program reevaluation in order to emphasize multiple treatment modalities, eclectic perspectives and exposure to a total therapeutic milieu during practicum experiences. These concerns are suggested today as well (Choi, 2008). I would add that, when we address these latter needs, we provide the student with a critical learning environment.

Prior to the formal development of the music therapy competencies, Brookins (1984) surveyed 25 clinical training directors in the Great Lakes region in order to determine what they looked for from an intern. The results were modest: piano skill, knowledge of psychology, emotional maturity and the ability to express needs and feelings. The results of this study mesh with the results of a much more recent poll (Knight, 2008) where 85 students report their greatest concern is clarity regarding internship supervisor expectations. Supervisors, in contrast, are concerned about interns being able to diagnose client needs as well as being able to present an appropriate level of musical skill.

Supervision

As previously explained, the varying structures of internship will find the student interning a few days a week in conjunction with an internship seminar at the university (replicating the former AAMT model) or, more commonly, interning full-time with supervision assumed by the facility. Bruscia suggests that graduate student apprentices can be trained to oversee internship supervision and related seminar experience (Bruscia, 2001). Discussion here focuses on the student being supervised by the on-site clinical music therapists at the internship. Various readings indicate different theoretical models in supervision. Those most pertinent to entry level training, predominantly product-oriented, are discussed in this chapter while supervision techniques most relevant to advanced competencies, predominantly process-oriented, are detailed in Chapter 4, "Advanced Competencies," under *Supervision*. On the undergraduate level, I personally suggest both product and process-oriented supervision, particularly for students who are, developmentally, ready to assimilate both.

Phase Development in Internship

As students enter and proceed through the internship, there is a phase development that has been recognized by various studies (Grant & McCarty, 1990; Madsen & Kaiser, 1999) and reported by Farnan (2001). It makes imminent sense that recognition of this phase development helps both the internship supervisor and the university educator better understand the emotional and learning needs of the student. I suggest that this information may also be considered in terms of the short-term practicum, particularly in cases when there is a successive two-semester assignment and the student may experience similar phase development in a less intensive manner.

Reportedly (AMTA, 2010), the stages of the internship are:

1. Dependency (first third of internship)
2. Autonomy (second third of internship)
3. Conditional Dependency

4. Fourth Month Blues Stage
5. Independence Stage

Indeed, the personal struggle revealed in the data of 63 interns (Grant & McCarty, 1990) suggests that the end of the fourth month can be a low point for the intern, well past the midterm evaluation, before growing independence, confidence and the beginning of a positive professional identity begin to emerge in months 5 and 6 of a six-month internship. Thomas (2001) provides us with sample vignettes demonstrating the progressive needs of the intern: to receive a greater degree of structure and orientation at the beginning of the internship, then sufficient time to observe, entrees into co-leading, assuming a leadership role, the vulnerable psychological possibility of comparing self with supervisor, and, functioning more independently toward the close of the internship.

Developmental stages of internship, each of which requires different supervision strategies on the part of the internship supervisor (I suggest these may be considered within the context of successive practica as well), may also be viewed within social work contexts (Fox, 1998):

- Stage One: Provide guidance, concrete assistance in clinical situations and opportunities for student to develop further knowledge (i.e., assignments) can lead to skills of self- appraisal and self-criticism.
- Stage Two: Opportunities for observation in the clinic and workplace allow student to imitate.
- Stage Three: Mutual reflection on dyadic exchange; discussion of interaction between supervisor and student may lead to verbal exploration of transferences.
- Stage Four: Supervisor becomes attuned to student experiences, anxieties, confusion as means of support for student to develop interest, empathy, tact, maturity and belief in the ability to help.
- Stage Five: Idealization and Mirroring in order for student to overcome self-doubt while experiencing a greater degree of self-confidence.
- Stage Six: Independence on the part of the intern which results in feelings of professional identity and personal individuation.

Problematic Phase Development

The departure from what is considered typical resistance to atypical resistance on the part of the intern may lead to problematic symptoms (Itzhaky & Ribner, 1998):

- A rigidity in responding to challenging clinical situations or supervisory suggestions particularly when change is required.
- Underdeveloped insight into one's behaviors and feelings.
- A lack of readiness or ability to integrate supervisory feedback into clinical practice.
- A hostile or aggressive response to supervisory feedback which includes efforts to try to engage the supervisor in arguments.
- Negative and illogical attacks on therapy work, supervision process, supervisor, clients, and/or other workplace peers.

These problematic symptoms as well as a phenomenon known as parallel processes (Edwards & Daveson, 2004, p. 76), where the dynamics in a supervision replicate those that occurred in the student music therapy session, can be unraveled and processed during the course of supervision. Should they become impossible to resolve, the student may, in the worst-case scenario, be dismissed from the internship. In such cases, it may be possible to recommence placement when the time is more conducive for learning and growth, or to commence a new placement when issues surrounding the failed placement have been adequately addressed. I maintain that it is important to refer the student to therapy in the hope that the student may work through interpersonal difficulties before going forward to another internship. It is important for academic music therapy faculty involved with the student to concur on a proper course of action (i.e., otherwise, where there are two faculty in the program, there is a great likelihood of the student "splitting").

> Resistance and parallel processes could be viewed as potential obstacles in the supervisory relationship in final placement, preventing the student from developing the skills for professional competence. . . . However, when appreciated more fully, they can be conceptualized as a useful contribution to improving the education of students undertaking clinical training. (Edwards & Daveson, 2004, p. 76)

Supervision Related to Phase Development

Farnan (2001) describes the internship in terms of three stages over a course of six months. Interestingly, the important practice elements of the music therapy competencies (assessment, treatment planning, implementation, evaluation and documentation) only begin to develop in stage two while the ongoing competencies of documentation, termination/discharge planning, professional role/ethics, interdisciplinary collaboration and supervision and administration as well as the earlier music foundations mentioned in chapter two solidify during the final stage of training (Farnan, 2001). Farnan suggests the identification of certain competencies in line with each segment of the internship in order to make the work manageable. This makes eminent sense, however, the compartmentalization of certain overlapping competencies, in my mind, also makes this problematic. What techniques in supervision are used with the student during this intensive period of study?

Techniques in Clinical Supervision, Internship

The literature concerning internship supervision is growing and most recently includes a survey (Tanguay, 2008) of national roster internship directors reporting on a variety of concerns. Incorporating responses from 85 female and 9 male internship supervisors throughout the United States with varying degrees of education (36% Bachelors level, 46% Masters level, 3% doctoral level) and clinical supervisory experience (3 months to 24 years) working with students from different university backgrounds at facilities serving clients with varying challenges, the survey reports a variety of techniques used for intern supervision, many of which can and have been used in practicum. Techniques mentioned by respondents in supervising students will sound familiar to us: co-leading (95%), live observation (95%), reviewing assignments/projects (95%), case presentation and discussion (73%), practicing/teaching music skills (72%), didactic instruction (70%), facilitating reflective process (66%), experiential music therapy processes (47%), audio/video record review (42%), and role-playing (30%). These are not detailed in terms of the competencies they specifically address. While 73 of the 95 clinical supervisors considered it their responsibility to help the student interns meet the AMTA competency areas, 19 respondents did not agree with this premise. The study does not include information regarding why the respondents disclaimed this responsibility.

Previous literature in our field cites the use of supervisors leading music therapy session and co-leading sessions (Braswell et al., 1985) with didactic supervision technique including reading, written case histories and research projects. Observation and feedback have been evaluated as the most successful method of supervision (Maranto & Bruscia, 1988) with case discussion, modeling and written evaluations considered less valuable. The most difficult aspects of intern supervision, according to the respondents in the Tanguay (2008) survey included giving criticism/negative feedback (38), making sure competencies are met (38), letting interns make mistakes (37), finding time for supervision/observation duties (34), individualizing the intern experience (27), addressing internship related issues with other staff (25), maintaining communication with the university (21), administrative duties (16), completing evaluations (12), being viewed as an authority figure (7) and co-leading sessions (4).

Only 21 of the reporting 93 reporting supervisors indicated they had received supervision training in graduate coursework. Considering that 49 percent of the respondents had received a graduate education in music therapy, the disparity in supervisory training is disturbing. These clinical supervisors indicated needs in experiential supervision techniques (55%), professional/ethical aspects of supervision (50%), methods for evaluation and goal setting (44%) and theoretical models of intern/therapist development (41%), many of which are detailed in this book in Chapter 4, "Advanced Competencies," under *Supervision.*

While current AMTA guidelines require clinical internship supervisors to complete a five-hour CMTE workshop or have other documented training (AMTA, 2010), a requirement the majority of clinical supervisors meet, over half of the respondents in the Tanguay (2008) survey felt more training in supervision was needed and more communication with academic institutions would be helpful. There is little specificity about which aspects of the competencies proved the most problematic while supervising. This would be helpful information for the educator in providing a smoother transition to internship. However, we, as educators, do recognize the internship as an intensive experience.

Within the two previously mentioned volumes on preprofessional supervision, internship supervision is detailed by Farnan (2001), Thomas, (2001), Feiner (2001,) Odell-Miller and Richards (2009,) Pederson (2009), Richards (2009) and Oldfield (2009), the further details of which are detailed in Chapter 4, under "Advanced Competencies," *Supervision.*

Probably most relevant to this chapter is the further commentary about a competency-based approach to internship supervision by Farnan (2001) who, starting in 1992 , wrote a column in *Music Therapy Perspectives,* offering her valuable advice on supervision and internship issues.

Additional perspectives on students benefitting from clinical supervision are discussed in this chapter as related to the competencies.

CONSIDERATIONS IN TEACHING
PREPROFESSIONAL CLINICAL COMPETENCIES

Premise

In this chapter, we continue our discussion of the entry-level professional music therapy competencies, 16–24, all of which refer to the actual *practice* of music therapy.

Educator and clinical supervisor goals in practicum and internship (the first two goals are carried over from the classroom competencies described in Chapter 2) include the following:

1. To transfer and integrate *music foundation skills* and *clinical foundation skills* with those of *music therapy foundations and principles,* thereby creating a new level of integrated *music therapy foundations and principles.*
2. To develop the integrated *music therapy foundations and principles* successively across varied clinical populations.
3. Introduce music therapy *practice* competencies in conjunction with *music therapy foundations and principles.*
4. During the process of supervision, support the student in reflecting practice back to theory.

The emphasis in my remarks here will be, as in Chapter 2, to reframe the competencies with suggestions toward a successive deepening of experience with the music therapy process. During the clinical requirement of 1200 hours for preprofessional training, the student typically accrues approximately 15 percent of the clinical hours (i.e., 200) during practica and 85 percent of clinical hours (i.e., 1000) during internship. This experience will help the student integrate *music foundations, clinical foundations* and *music therapy foundations and principles* through the *practice* music therapy competencies during the course of 4–6 practica, 4–6 practica seminars and, of course, the internship. Given that this book is primarily written for educators, emphasis will be given to the practicum experience and practicum seminar. Nevertheless, I trust that the clinical internship supervisor will find this chapter helpful as well.

Music Therapy: Areas of Study and Related Discussion

Client Assessment

16.1 Communicate assessment findings and recommendations in written and verbal forms.
16.2 Observe and record accurately the client's responses to assessment.
16.3 Identify the client's appropriate and inappropriate behaviors.
16.4 Select and implement effective culturally-based methods for assessing the client's assets, and problems through music.
16.5 Select and implement effective culturally based methods for assessing the client's musical preferences and level of musical functioning or development.
16.6 Identify the client's therapeutic needs through an analysis and interpretation of music therapy and related assessment data.

16.7 Demonstrate knowledge of professional Standards of Clinical Practice regarding assessment.

Discussion, Client Assessment

The assessment competencies boil down to a three step process of planning, implementing and evaluating the assessment process:

1. Selection and implementation of culturally based assessment methods to determine patient assets, needs, musical preferences and musical levels (16.4, 16.5)
2. Observation and recording of behavior during the assessment session (16.2, 16.3)
3. Identification and communication (written, verbal) of needs

As aforementioned (Chapter 2, 15.2, *Assessment*) it is important for the student to gain familiarity with different types of assessment, different purposes of assessment (Bruscia, 1988) and case studies demonstrating assessment with varied clinical populations. Given this larger picture, however, what type of assessment should the entry-level student conduct in practicum? It is logical that the entry-level student be comfortable conducting a prescriptive assessment as opposed to an interpretative or diagnostic assessment, which an advanced clinician would provide. In line with the concept of graduated expectations, the initial assignment should be simple and possibly limited to a portion of an assessment while successive assignments can require the student to observe more and ultimately provide a global assessment.

During the course of practicum, initial experience in client assessment can be provided for a client who is not yet receiving services, a client who is receiving services on an individual basis or a client who is receiving services within a group. In the latter situation, the assessment can take place while the client is either in or out of the group; both scenarios will provide a different dynamic.

Hanser (2001) suggests a series of initial assessment guidelines, a series that is straightforward and crosses all population areas. For these reasons, these guidelines are particularly useful for students in practicum. Hanser's assignment for initial assessment (Hanser, 2001) includes background information on the client (description, background, musical preferences, family history, skills and interest, culture, vocation) and then a narrative on non-musical functioning (social, perceptual-motor, language, cognitive, emotional) and musical functioning (enjoyment, creativity, abilities). I suggest that, as necessary to create a greater comfort level for the student, this process could be modified by asking the student to delimit the domains of functioning that are assessed. As the student progresses in practicum, the domains could all be assessed and, further, the assignment to conduct individual assessment could increase from one client to two to three, etc.

Educators may suggest that a student in practicum execute portions of or the entire use of a published assessment, but I would suggest that this process wait until the internship when there is sufficient time to plan, carry out, discuss and reflect on such an assignment. I teach a *graduate* course on assessment where the final project involves planning, conducting, evaluating and writing up a global assessment on a client with video-recorded presentation for the class. This assignment takes a great deal of thought, planning and work.

A format should be provided for assessment reporting, a format that gets progressively more detailed as the student assumes larger portions of assessment information. The format will include recommendations, essentially interpreting the information that has been observed and noted in order to provide treatment planning.

However, unless a student is delimited to conducting individual therapy in practica or has the time and place to assess each client in the group prior to treatment planning (see competency 17), the suggestion for each client to be assessed may not be possible. The importance of setting up realistic goals is critical.

The above assessment competencies do not detail preliminary information gathering or preliminary observation of a client prior to formal music therapy assessment, which I believe is an important part of the process.

Treatment Planning

17.1   Select or create music therapy experiences that meet the client's objectives.

17.2   Formulate goals and objectives for individuals and group therapy based upon assessment findings.

17.3   Identify the client's primary treatment needs in music therapy.

17.4   Provide preliminary estimates of frequency and duration of treatment.

17.5   Select and adapt music consistent with strengths and needs of the client.

17.6   Formulate music therapy strategies for individuals and groups based upon the goals and objectives adopted.

17.7   Select and adapt musical instruments and equipment consistent with strengths and needs of the client.

17.8   Organize and arrange the music therapy setting to facilitate the client's therapeutic involvement.

17.9   Plan and sequence music therapy sessions.
17.10   Determine the client's appropriate music therapy group and/or individual placement.
17.11   Coordinate treatment plan with other professionals.
17.12   Demonstrate knowledge of professional Standards of Clinical Practice regarding planning.

Discussion, Treatment Planning

In effect, the treatment planning competencies can be perceived as three areas of planning:

1. Determining individual or group placement.
2. Setting up goals and objectives for a client as a portion of a coordinated team treatment plan.
3. Planning methods and materials in accordance with the goals and objectives.

In reflecting on the link from theory to practice, it is important for the student to read about individual or group placement, setting up goals and objectives and planning methods and materials. In addition to a variety of readings on these subjects, this information can be teased out in the analysis of case study reading, applied through problem-based learning and then discussed in classes. These along with other teaching techniques, discussed in Chapter 6, provide interactive as well as collaborative and experiential means of active treatment planning in the context of the classroom.

The determination of individual or group placement is important and, in situations where this decision is dictated by the constraints of the facility, this type of discussion should still take place so the student is aware of theoretical guidelines (Goodman, 2007) for individual versus group placement in music therapy.

In situations where the student has assessed a client (17.2), the logical next step would be to see how information gleaned from the music therapy assessment does or does not fit into team treatment goals. However, in situations where the client has not assessed a client or every member of a group of clients, it is logical to have the student plan goals and objectives based on review of treatment team goals and objectives (i.e., Individual Education Plan, facility treatment team recommendations), particularly since the student is serving as an adjunctive therapist at the entry level of training. The student can be introduced to this process gradually by establishing goal(s) and objective(s) within one domain of treatment at a time. Wheeler (1987) suggests that levels of therapy can dictate the types of goals that students propose for the client(s). If we follow this line of thinking, then supportive therapy at the entry-level training for students would prioritize goals compatible with activity therapy and observable outcomes (Wheeler, 1987).

Setting goals and objectives for an individual is common in the literature, however, this kind of planning with a group is more problematic and will require consideration of how individual goals and objectives fit into group goals and objectives (Goodman, 2007). This can be accomplished by helping the student gather team-based goals and objectives as well as information gleaned from music therapy assessment, organizing the information into domains, prioritizing and selecting overlapping goals (Goodman, 2007). Again, this process can be done one step at a time so the student establishes group goals and objectives in one domain at a time and plans strategies in line with limited focus. Due to the more complex nature of treatment planning for a group, it is tempting for educators to propose broad generic goals. However, this type of approach, in my opinion, will not yield useful clinical documentation.

Planning methods and materials is multifaceted. I suggest that music therapists planning a session review basic considerations, formerly discussed with respect to music therapy groups for children (Goodman, 2007) but adapted here with respect to either individual or group work with clients of all ages:

- The space being used for music therapy.
- Physical arrangement between client (s) and therapist.
- Activity levels consistent with the functioning level (s) of the client(s).
- Methods/Techniques related to the primary strengths and weaknesses of the client(s).
- Methods/Techniques linked to goals and objectives for client(s) often resulting in adaptation of music materials.
- Incorporation of support and professional staff for interdisciplinary, multidisciplinary and transdisciplinary work.
- Methods/Techniques designed to invite a promote group process if the therapist is working with a group.
- Adaptive nature of the methodology/techniques.
- Therapist knowledge base and philosophy of helping that are suited to methodology/ techniques being used.

Over 30 years ago (Alley, 1978), the need for more practicum experiences, a broader overview of standard therapeutic methodology and more specific treatment techniques for each client population was expressed. While it remains important for us as educators to present specifics in regard to client population, it is just as important, in my mind, to see how these specifics are framed within the whole, the trees within the forest. I often think that students who claim, "I cannot think of what to do for a session" have missed the overall framework of how to design a session, how to take on the responsibility to build-up a population-appropriate repertoire and how to learn from each session in order to progressively build toward the next. The student, rather than viewing planning and conducting music therapy as an isolated series of activities, must be supported to see the ongoing process of therapy. I suggest this is constructed by the ongoing subjective evaluation of clinical work that encourages reflective thinking (see *evaluation* competencies in this chapter).

In designing methods to meet the goals of treatment, students should keep in mind the broad possibilities of listening, singing, making music, moving and composing while tailoring the methods and materials for delivering this information to clients with certain challenges. All the steps involved with actually providing intervention can be overwhelming for a student and it can be helpful for students in practicum to prepare weekly session plans that provide a beginning format. Even if the format is adapted during the session, as it often will be, the goal setting should remain foremost in the mind of the student during the session. Further, the steps described in the methods, although tedious for the student to write out, can provide a sense of consistency, which is often forgotten in the excitement of the session. I have students tell me that some clinicians never write session plans, choosing to use what they consider an exploratory approach. I would suggest that this type of approach can possibly be quite appropriate for a seasoned clinician and is the type of approach used in dynamic psychotherapy but may provoke more anxiety for the entry-level student experience.

As described in Chapter 2, it is helpful for students to practice hierarchical levels of leading activities (Standley, 1991) while in the practicum seminar class in order to gain a confidence level while in the session with clients. It is, of course, important for students to critically review case materials that lay the basis for music therapy techniques. However, in practicum seminar, simulating methods with peers is enjoyable and instructive while also holding the student responsible for active preparation and follow through.

Therapy Implementation

18.1   Recognize, interpret, and respond appropriately to significant events in music therapy sessions as they occur.
18.2   Provide music therapy experiences.
18.2.1   Change nonmusical behavior.
18.2.2   Assist the client's development of social skills.
18.2.3   Improve the client's sense of self and self with others.
18.2.4   Elicit social interactions from the client.

18.2.5   Promote client decision-making.
18.2.6   Assist the client in increasing on task behavior.
18.2.7   Elicit affective responses from the client.
18.2.8   Encourage creative responses from the client.
18.2.9   Improve the client's orientation to person, place, and time.
18.2.10   Enhance client's cognitive/intellectual development.
18.2.11   Develop or rehabilitate the client's motor skills.
18.2.12   Offer sensory stimulation that allows the client to use visual, auditory, or tactile cues.
18.2.13   Promote relaxation and/or stress reduction in the client.
18.3   Provide verbal and nonverbal directions and cues necessary for successful client participation.
18.4   Provide models for appropriate social behavior in group music therapy.
18.5   Utilize therapeutic verbal skills in music therapy sessions.
18.6   Communicate to the client's expectations of their behavior.
18.7   Provide feedback on, reflect, rephrase, and translate the client's communications.
18.8   Assist the client to communicate more effectively.
18.9   Sequence and pace music experiences within a session according to the client's needs and situational factors.
18.10   Conduct or facilitate group and individual music therapy.
18.11   Implement music therapy program according to treatment plan.
18.12   Promote a sense of group cohesiveness and/or a feeling of group membership.
18.13   Create a physical environment (e.g., arrangement of space, furniture, equipment, and instruments) that is conducive to effective therapy.
18.14   Develop and maintain a repertoire of music for age, culture, and stylistic differences.
18.15   Recognize and respond appropriately to effects of the client's medications.
18.16   Establish closure of music therapy sessions.
18.17   Establish closure of treatment issues.
18.18   Demonstrate knowledge of professional Standards of Clinical Practice regarding implementation.

Discussion, Therapy Implementation

This is the lengthiest list of competencies within the overall list of clinical responsibilities, noting a variety of therapeutic uses of music and the course of the music therapy session. These competencies could probably be extended even further if we consider everything that could conceivably happen in a music therapy session! However, in order to streamline, let us consider these competencies accordingly:

1. Methods and materials we have selected to lead to the desired results for the client(s) (18.13, 18.14, 18.2.1–18.2.13, 18.14)
2. Responding to the ongoing process of the session (18.1, 18.12, 18.15) with appropriate music and verbal (18.3, 18.5, 18.6, 18.7, 18.8, 18.9) techniques, pacing (18.9), beginning and end (18.13, 18.16, 18.17).

<u>Selected Methods and Materials</u>: In contemplating the link from theory to practice, it is helpful to remind the student of the ways in which music has been implemented as therapy throughout their readings, simulations, viewings of video-recorded materials, etc. What constructive criticisms have the students made while reviewing all these materials? Can the process of constructive criticism then be applied to one's own clinical work in the field?

<u>Feedback During the Session</u>: What can the supervisors do to make the clinical experience instructive? Supervisor instruction during the session can include supervisor modeling, supervisor prompting and cuing, supervisor audio-cuing with a checklist evaluation form (Furman, Adamek, & Furman, 1992) or the supervisor writing evaluative comments (preferably after the session rather than during) to be processed later. No matter what the level of feedback, assuming there is guidance during the session, it is very important that immediately after the session, for the on-site supervisor to provide feedback based on the session observed. This should be discussion-based, seeking initial feedback from the student regarding one's perception of the experience.

<u>Feedback in Practicum Seminar</u>: In order to create a link to the classroom seminar, it is helpful for the student to audiorecord the sessions, if possible, and then review it along with feedback of the faculty supervisor and classmates. This takes time as well as clearance from the facility and the client(s) and may only be possible once or twice during the semester. Earlier literature regarding the use of videorecorded playback of practicum sessions and evaluation of student effort shows much advantage to this method. According to Hanser and Furman (1980), there is no advantage to field-based observation compared to videorecorded analysis and I suggest that the videorecordings could then be shared in practicum seminar as well. Greenfield (1978) used video playback for student and instructor evaluations, finding that students rated themselves higher on giving direction, use of prompts/ cues, providing appropriate consequences for desired responses and praise

for client effort; it is useful to compare perceptions of the clinical work.

Alley (1982) used videotapes in classroom simulations as well as clinical practicum experiences in order to observe music therapy competencies while students were conducting various tasks: teaching a song, leading a group discussion and teaching a nonmusical objective. Forms were then used to evaluate student approval frequency and duration, delivery skills and sequencing and eliciting client responses. Results suggested that the student ability to perform certain music therapy competencies depended on the selected activity and that students with previous experience had more skills than naïve students. Interestingly though, the demonstration of the competencies during the simulation was representative of that shown in fieldwork.

In order to create a link to the practicum seminar, Summer (2001) suggests the simulation of portions of clinical sessions that proved problematic in order to problem-solve what the student therapist might have done differently.

Educators also find it helpful to videorecord sessions for instructor and student analysis of music and verbal skills (Wolfe, O'Connell, & Epps, 1998; Darrow et al., 2001) and co-relationships between student behaviors and clinical success (Darrow et al., 2001). Information may be notated using data collection computer programs (Darrow, et al., 2001) when observing varied behaviors including music behavior (singing, playing, listening), physical behavior (hand-over-hand assist, cuing, clapping), verbal behavior, (directives, feedback asking questions, explanations), music and verbal behavior, physical and verbal behavior, music and physical behavior, etc.

In short, evaluative comments in response to direct observation, videorecording and simulation of music therapy methods are all useful in developing clinical skills.

Verbal Skills: There is frequent mention of verbal skills (18.3, 18:5, 18:6, 18:7, 18:8), skills that have not been mentioned in the competencies prior to this point. The verbal skills that are most specifically indicated are particularly helpful. This is important because students are frequently confused about how to talk with clients; they need instruction, guidance and simulated role-play using these skills prior to entering clinical work.

During the course of clinical work, music therapy students in training may use verbal skills in several ways (Wolfe, O'Connell, & Epps, 1998):

1. Encouraging clients to continue talking.
2. Influencing, reinforcing, giving advice, asking questions or giving directives.
3. Providing instruction.
4. Providing explanation.

5. Expressing self-disclosure.
6. Greetings, closings.

A common characteristic of first semester practicum students is to ooverver-balize (Darrow, et al., 2010) and I suggest that this may reflect both the student's anxiety level as well as their need to focus on appropriate purposes of communication with different populations.

According to Wolfe, O'Connell, and Epps (1998), the greatest use of talking may occur in the category of questions, followed by a quantity of comments in influencing or reinforcing remarks in order to actively support ideas from group members. It has been observed that the percentage of time students spend making music is equal (Wolfe, O'Connell, & Epps, 1998) or less than (Darrow et al., 2001) the amount of time spent talking. Observation over a period of 11 weeks (Alley, 1980) led to the conclusion that the use of music was increased along with skills indicating increased clinical focus; perhaps this suggests that as students acclimate to their clinical assignments, they feel more confident using music as an intervention. Further, the finding that clinical success is not linked to the quantity of music-making but, importantly, to the quality of music-making and the rapport the student can build with clients (Darrow et al., 2001) supports the equal importance of music-making and interpersonal rapport. I believe that we need to emphasize the valued role of the music, as much if not more than talking, in creating this rapport.

There should be a clearer distinction between verbal skills used in entry level versus advanced level training. Amir (1999b) identifies the literature associated with three models of music therapy, the first two of which train at an advanced level, which identify the differentiated use of talking and/or verbal processing in music therapy sessions. First, models that are music centered recognize music as therapy and in these cases all interventions are musical and there is minimal talking during the session. Talking is not considered to be a psychotherapeutic intervention. The Nordoff and Robbins (2007) model is a prime example of this. Second, models that consider music as a primary agent of change also use talking in order to communicate ideas, share insights, make interpretations, etc. The Bonny Method of Guided Imagery, BMGIM, (Grocke & Bruscia, 2002) and Analytical Music Therapy (Priestley, 1975) approaches are good examples of this. Third, models that consider music therapy as music in therapy, giving equal importance to musical and verbal interventions, evidently show up in the limited number of studies analyzing entry-level clinical behavior. The question then arises: To what extent are we training students to judge when and how to talk? If we are training entry-level students as adjunctive therapists, for example, their primary role in talking may be delimited to the roles that Wolfe et al. (1998) describes.

The use of verbal processing, a means of gaining greater understanding and/or acceptance, is more commonly used in advanced training and, for that reason, will be discussed at greater length in Chapter 4, "Advanced Competencies."

Therapy Evaluation

19.1   Recognize and respond appropriately to situations in which there are clear and present dangers to the client and/or others.
19.2   Modify treatment approaches based on the client's response to therapy.
19.3   Recognize significant changes and patterns in the client's response to therapy.
19.4   Revise treatment plan as needed.
19.5   Establish and work within realistic time frames for evaluating the effects of therapy.
19.6   Review treatment plan periodically within guidelines set by agency.
19.7   Design and implement methods for evaluating and measuring client progress and the effectiveness of therapeutic strategies.
19.8   Demonstrate knowledge of professional Standards of Clinical Practice regarding evaluation.

Discussion, Therapy Evaluation

In considering the link from theory to practice, it is important to remind the student that the examination of music therapy outcomes is critical in order for the therapist to understand what went well, what did not go well and what this all means for the continuation of therapy. How many case studies reflect on outcomes? How are outcomes documented? What happens if we do not conduct evaluation?

Objective and Subjective Evaluation: Therapy evaluation includes both objective and subjective measures. Ideally, these should be done following every session and periodically reviewed to determine behavioral patterns (19.3), overall progress (19.5), and determine if it is necessary to amend the treatment plan (19.4), and/or strategies (19.7). Both objective and subjective evaluation serve towards these ends; they support each other.

Distinguishing Objective from Subjective Narrative: The documentation of clinical data, particularly in behavioral literature, is well defined. The documentation of subjective information, less so. I suggest that subjective evaluation serve in order to document the following (Goodman, 2007): (1) reaction of the therapist to client (s); (2) therapist interpretation of behavior; (3) issues that the therapist perceives in connection to the progress or lack of progress on the part of the client(s); (4) necessary modification made in the session that may be considered in subsequent session planning; (5) issues related to therapist-client and/or group dynamics; and (6) the realization of a link from theory to practice. These perspectives are reinforced by an account (Barry & O'Callaghan, 2008) of the usefulness of subjective evaluation, also known as reflexive journal writing, for a music therapy student in an oncologic clinical placement.

Data-collection based on clearly defined clinical objectives is typically included in music therapy education and training. However, the difference between objective and subjective narrative may not be discussed as extensively. It may be helpful for the student to write their account of what happened in the session based on instructor guidelines and then go back and italicize what is then perceived as inferential, interpretative, and so on, rather than observable behavior (Goodman, 2007).

<u>Selective Use of the Journal</u>: I point out (Goodman, 2007) that many students, encouraged by educators to focus on their feelings, will use the journal as a means of focusing on such sentiments as their doubts about their level of competence in making music and making clinical decisions, their anxiety, their need for positive feedback from the client(s), their reactions to the supervisor, their emotional attachment to the client (s), their difficulties with settings limits, etc. Much of this can be discussed in the context of transference-countertransference. However, while all of this is useful information and necessary for personal growth both during practicum and internship, it should not discount the importance of remembering other information about the session that allows the student to subjectively interpret what has happened, make inferences as to why, link theory to practice and, in short, learn as much as possible from the session. It is in the collection of both objective and subjective evaluation that the student, in practicum and internship, is able to master the competencies under evaluation.

Documentation

20.1   Produce documentation that accurately reflect client outcomes) and meet the requirements of internal and external legal, regulatory, and reimbursement bodies.

20.2   Document clinical data.

20.3   Write professional reports describing the client throughout all phases of the music therapy process in an accurate, concise, and objective manner.

20.4   Communicate orally with the client, parents, significant others, and team members regarding the client's progress and various aspects of the client's music therapy program.

20.5 Document and revise the treatment plan and document changes to the treatment plan.

20.6 Develop and use data-gathering techniques during all phases of the clinical process including assessment, treatment, and evaluation.

20.7 Demonstrate knowledge of professional Standards of Clinical Practice regarding documentation.

Discussion: Documentation

How do oral (20.4) and written (20.3, 20.5) documentation vary from evaluation? In terms of music therapy, we may consider documentation as evidence of what has transpired as a result of music therapy. This evidence can be collected in the course of evaluation (20.6, 20.2, 20.1) so there is a clear co-relationship between the two processes.

In short, documentation skills are keeping track of one's clinical work. Therefore, if the student is doing satisfactory work, all session planning and outcomes should be documented. It is helpful for the student to write at least one summary clinical report each semester of the practicum in order to develop objective, concise and complete writing skills. This should continue throughout the internship.

As professions become increasingly subject to pressure for evidence-based practice, the need for meticulous observation, enumeration and analysis will be emphasized versus anecdotal case description.

Termination/Discharge Planning

21.1 Inform and prepare the client for approaching termination from music therapy.

21.2 Establish closure of music therapy services by time of termination/discharge.

21.3 Determine termination of the client from music therapy.

21.4 Integrate music therapy termination plan with plans for the client's discharge from the facility.

21.5 Assess potential benefits/detriments of termination of music therapy.

21.6 Develop music therapy termination plan.

21.7 Demonstrate knowledge of professional Standards of Clinical Practice regarding termination.

Discussion, Termination/Discharge Planning

The need for discharge planning is most likely to happen in the course of an internship and involves forethought (21.5, 21.3), treatment planning (21.6,

21.2, 21.1), and teamwork (21.4). Beyond the strategic planning and paper-work involved, there is an emotional component regarding separation that should be discussed with the intern. This sense of attachment and separation anxiety will show up also in reflective journals during practicum and intern-ship and, ideally, should be processed.

Professional Role/Ethics

21.1   Interpret and adhere to the AMTA Code of Ethics.

22.2   Adhere to professional Standards of Clinical Practice.

22.3   Demonstrate dependability: follow through with all tasks regarding education and professional training.

22.4   Accept criticism/feedback with willingness and follow through in a productive manner.

22.5   Resolve conflicts in a positive and constructive manner.

22.6   Meet deadlines without prompting.

22.7   Express thoughts and personal feelings in a consistently constructive manner.

22.8   Demonstrate critical self-awareness of strengths and weaknesses.

22.9   Demonstrate knowledge of and respect for diverse cultural back-grounds.

22.10 Treat all persons with dignity and respect, regardless of differences in race, religion, ethnicity, sexual orientation, or gender.

22.11 Demonstrate skill in working with culturally diverse populations.

22.12 Apply laws and regulations regarding the human rights of the clients.

22.13 Respond to legislative issues affecting music therapy.

22.14 Demonstrate basic knowledge of professional music therapy organiza-tions and how these organizations influence clinical practice.

22.15 Demonstrate basic knowledge of music therapy service reimburse-ment and financing sources (e.g., Medicare, Medicaid, Private Health Insurance, State and Local Health and/or Education Agencies, Grants).

Discussion, Professional Role/Ethics

Music therapy ethics, generally taught as parts of other courses (Maranto & Wheeler, 1986) includes review and discussion of the AMTA Code of Ethics: http://www.musictherapy.org/ethics.html. and may include readings and books (Dileo, 2000) on the subject. In terms of practicum and internship, the area of confidentiality is particularly important.

These ethical guidelines are vital in both the school and work setting as students strive for good work habits (22.3, 22.6), benefit from constructive feedback (22.8, 22.4), resolve conflicts with clients, peers, staff, professors, supervisors, etc. (22.5, 22.7, 22.10, 22.11), respect the confidentiality of the client (22.12) and remain aware of issues effecting music therapy (22.13).

It is essential that the on-site supervisors and faculty supervisors involved with students emphasize that ethical development is important to overall personal growth. In situations where there are conflicts or could be potential conflicts, it is essential to confront these and discuss them. In the long run, the student is at a great disadvantage if ethical situations are not handled with candor.

Beyond the knowledge concerning patient rights, it is important for students to become knowledgeable about what is going on in the larger worlds of mental health and education in order to advocate for the rights of and facilities for clients and, of course, the furthering of our profession. This involves a daily reading of a reputable newspaper, following issues relevant to AMTA government relations and, most of all, the interest in and motivation to converse with peers, educators and supervisors about issues impacting our profession.

Interdisciplinary Collaboration

23.1   Demonstrate a basic understanding of the roles and develop working relationships with other disciplines in the client's treatment program.
23.2   Communicate to other departments and staff the rationale for music therapy services and the role of the music therapist.
23.3   Define the role of music therapy in the client's total treatment program.
23.4   Collaborate with team members in designing and implementing interdisciplinary treatment programs.

Discussion, Interdisciplinary Collaboration

A discussion of interdisciplinary collaboration is not only related to the ability to outreach as a music therapist, but, again, to problem-solve in situations where interdisciplinary collaboration is, for whatever reason, difficult. Examples of model interdisciplinary collaboration are important for the student to read about and, then, observe and experience while in preprofessional training.

While there may be limited interdisciplinary collaboration necessary in a short-term practicum, it is a great idea to expose the student to these possibilities in order to pave the way for the internship.

Supervision and Administration

24.1 Participate in and benefit from supervision.
24.2 Manage and maintain music therapy equipment and supplies.
24.3 Perform administrative duties usually required of clinicians (e.g., scheduling therapy, programmatic budgeting, maintaining record files).
24.4 Write proposals to create and/or establish new music therapy programs.

Discussion, Supervision and Administration

The ability to profit from supervision is related to the appropriate level and type of supervision given to the student as well as the individual ability to gain insight, reflect on theory as it relates to practice and profit from constructive feedback. Since there are differences in the supervision levels of the practicum experience versus the internship experience and supervision is such an important piece of clinical preprofessional work, my discussion on supervision was presented in the beginning of this chapter.

Administrative responsibilities are generally assigned during the internship but they can also be introduced in smaller ways (i.e., 24.2) during practicum, particularly at the field site. Farnan (2001) suggests that supervision in the internship teach competencies through "observation and feedback, assigned readings, modeling, written forms and well structured supervisory meetings" (Farnan, 2001, p. 132). She cites the third and final segment of the internship as a time where termination/discharge planning, supervision and administration and professional role/ethics are emphasized. The supervisor at this time might help prepare the intern for finishing by focusing on short-term goals for the remainder of the internship, how to separate from clients and staff and reflecting on accomplishments of the internship.

CONCLUSION

A number of studies as well as personal educator experiences make it clear that students entering preprofessional training require varying degrees of structure, support and supervision in acclimating to the phase development of clinical experiences. Structure can initially be realized in supportive coursework and sequentially challenging clinical assignments over the course of 4–6 successive semesters. Students are mastering the informational competencies of the music therapy process as they are learning to utilize the information in practice. Perspectives on how to introduce information related to assessment, treatment planning, intervention, evaluation, documentation, ability to benefit from supervision, etc. are all provided in this chapter. Since close to 85 percent of preprofessional hours are earned during the internship, the practica represent a limited but unique opportunity for the educator to combine theory and practice. Discussion in this chapter has included helpful information for clinical supervisors who bear the bulk of the responsibility for helping the student master the practice competencies.

Following the internship, the undergraduate student is, technically, no longer a student, presumably graduating and entering the world as a professional. This is another transition but, in a larger sense, a professional is still a student of music therapy in terms of needing to learn and grow, albeit independently and in the context of the professional environment.

Should the student continue in graduate studies, how are the possibilities of further learning defined? We move on to the next chapter, the consideration of "Advanced Competencies," with this question in mind.

Chapter 4

ADVANCED COMPETENCIES

The things taught in colleges and schools are not an education,
but the means of education.

Ralph Waldo Emerson

INTRODUCTION

W e meet in the corner of the Café Diem, an intimately lit corner of the
library. The class this semester is small, seven students, and the nature
of the learning experience is unique. Whether we are simulating supervision,
teaching each other a music therapy construct, presenting an original assessment tool or discussing our opinions about our class field trip to experience
a chanting workshop, we are mobilized. We are a graduate group and I rel-
ish the opportunity to share the ongoing sense of excitement about music
therapy. What is it that makes our learning experience different from those
of the undergraduates? I say this, not to demean the undergraduate experience, but to further define the difference between undergraduate and graduate education and training. The level of graduate education and training
allows us to further immerse ourselves in music therapy. My job is not to
teach music therapy, but rather to teach my students how to educate themselves about music therapy as Emerson so eloquently reminds us. It is in the
graduate school experience that we move from being generalists to delving
more deeply into music therapy.

As so many of us know, our colleagues in the related professions of art
therapy, dance therapy, speech therapy, occupational therapy, physical therapy, social work and psychology are professionally credentialed on the
Masters level. As the fledging profession in the creative arts therapies, we
have maintained the undergraduate degree as the entry-level training for the
field of music therapy in the United States. The growth of Masters programs
in music therapy (33% growth in masters level programs over the last two

decades) may eventually change this picture.

In this chapter, we discuss the delivery of graduate or advanced competency-based training, approved in 2007 and revised in 2009.

Consider the following:

1. What was the process that shaped the development of the *AMTA Advanced Competencies?*
2. How can we consider presentation of the *AMTA Advanced Competencies,* across a series of music therapy and related music therapy courses, as immersion experiences that allow us to focus on and refine selected areas within music therapy?
3. Unlike the undergraduate courses, which are more predictably presented based on the content of the *AMTA Professional Competencies,* how does the content of current graduate courses (reviewed and presented in this chapter) relate to the *AMTA Advanced Competencies?*
4. As with review of the *AMTA Professional Competencies,* how can discussion of the *AMTA Advanced Competencies* stimulate our thinking about their scope and the ways in which they can be integrated into the education and training of music therapy?

DEVELOPMENT OF AMTA ADVANCED COMPETENCIES

Historical Overview

The need for differentiated content in undergraduate and graduate programs was highlighted by Bruscia (1989) and Standley (1989) at the California Symposium on Music Therapy Education and Training. At that time Standley (1989) suggested the concept of specialization tracks: analytical psychotherapy, cognitive/behavioral therapies, medical treatment, special education and gerontology. Each specialty area would have a semester-long, 10-hour per week clinical requirement with a culminating independent project, exam or thesis in one of the specialty areas. Rather than specific program design, Bruscia referenced the advanced competencies he had composed (1986) and the need to incorporate these at the national level. He suggested that the purposes of the masters degree was to *integrate* undergraduate studies, to *extend* the undergraduate music therapy competency (i.e., to include psychotherapeutic, medical and holistic models), to *refine* entry level skills, to *build theoretical and research skills* and to *increase awareness* of supervisory, administrative and educational issues in music therapy (Brusica, 1989, p. 85). Bruscia suggested that the purpose of a doctoral degree was to provide specialization in music therapy which could lead to new clinical methods, new theory and research design, to advance the scope and depth of clinical competence in order to function as a primary therapist; and to prepare the person for becoming a supervisor, an educator, and/or an administrator (Bruscia, 1989, p. 85).

Prior to the approval of the *AMTA Advanced Competencies,* over two decades ago, directors of eight graduate programs indicated that their goals in providing masters level training (Maranto & Bruscia, 1988) were primarily research (32%), followed by advanced clinical skills (14%), clinical specialization (11%), supervision skills (11%), administrative skills (4%), refinement of undergraduate skills (4%), university teaching skills (4%) and ability to share professional knowledge. Reported goals (Maranto & Bruscia, 1988) of doctoral level programs were research skills (37%), university teaching skills (23%), advanced music therapy theory (14%), clinical specialization (7%), advanced clinical skills (5%) and music therapy supervision skills (5%). Areas reportedly receiving the most breadth in terms of coverage (Maranto & Bruscia, 1988) were, in order of priority, clinical music therapy skills, a knowledge of the literature, advanced theoretical knowledge, clinical supervision, individual/group psychotherapy, research skills, musicianship and the administration/teaching of music therapy. Due to the low number of respondents, this information is of limited value but outlines possible areas of emphasis in the past as well as teaching methods (i.e., lecture for teaching administration and advanced theoretical knowledge; experiential for individual and group psychotherapy skills, clinical music therapy skills and creative arts therapies; individual and group reports to teach knowledge of the literature; independent study to teach research skills and practicum to teach clinical supervision skills) and thesis and/or dissertation requirements (i.e., experimental studies required by 27% of respondents) at the time. Undoubtedly there have been shifts in the development of priorities with regard to masters' and doctoral level training.

My analysis, in this chapter, of coursework delivered in 32 masters level programs in the United States, indicates an equal priority given to both advanced clinical skills and research. According to Standley (2010), the doctoral level remaining highly specialized and therefore, holds the candidate responsible for becoming an expert in one area.

Following the 2005 adoption of the AMTA Advisory on Levels of Practice in Music Therapy, recognizing advanced levels of practice (see Chapter 1), AMTA appointed a Task Force on Advanced Competencies, which was charged with developing advanced competencies. Four domains for advanced practice were considered: Professional Growth, Musical Development, Personal Growth and Development, and Integrative Clinical Experience. These domains were subsequently reorganized and amended in order to constitute the original *AMTA Advanced Competencies* accepted in 2007 and

intended to serve as guidelines for Masters programs and for advanced practice. Further the Task Force realized that "the advanced therapist may not
demonstrate competence in each of these areas, but would instead demonstrate acquisition of the majority of these competencies, with most, if not all,
in the area(s) of his/her practice" (e.g., clinical, supervisory, academic and research) (AMTA, 2007). The *AMTA Advanced Competencies,* approved by the
Assembly of Delegates in November of 2007 and adopted as an official
AMTA document, acknowledge the work of Bruscia (1986), which served as
a basis for the competencies.

Current Status of Advanced Competencies Relative to Masters' Standards

The advanced competencies presented here, revised and approved as of
November 2009, represent a more abridged version of the previous efforts.
The current standards for masters study, stated in the *Standards for Education
and Clinical Training* (AMTA, 2009, pp. 7–9) expect students to acquire in-
depth knowledge and competence in *Music Therapy Theory* (e.g., principles,
foundations, current theories of music therapy practice, supervision, education, implications for research), *Advanced Clinical Skills* (e.g., in-depth understanding of the clinical and supervisory roles and responsibilities of a music
therapist acquired through a supervised clinical component), and knowledge
and competence in one or more of the following areas: *Research* (e.g., quantitative and qualitative research designs and their application to music therapy practice, supervision, administration, higher education), *Musical Development and Personal Growth* (e.g., leadership skills, self-awareness, music skills,
improvisation skills in various musical styles, music technology) and/or
Clinical Administration (e.g., laws and regulations governing the provision of
education and health services, the roles of a clinical administrator in institutions and clinical settings). These standards will be evaluated in conjunction
with Academic Approval Committee reviews (scheduled every decade)
(Sandness, 2010).

In suggesting different types of curricular structures for masters' degrees,
the *Standards for Education and Clinical Training* (AMTA, 2009) suggests emphasis in certain advanced competency areas, repeated here:

- *Practice oriented:* focus on advanced clinical practice.
- *Research oriented:* focus on "scholars and researchers in music therapy,
  preparing graduates for doctoral study" (AMTA, 2009).
- *Research and practice orientations:* simultaneous development of student
  ability to produce research "and utilize, combine or integrate these
  findings within the practice of music therapy" (AMTA, 2009).

CONSIDERATIONS IN TEACHING AMTA ADVANCED COMPETENCIES

Overview

The *Advanced Competencies* were originally approved in 2007 and recently revised and reapproved (AMTA, 2009). Revised standards for masters' degree programs were approved by the AMTA Assembly of Delegates in November, 2009 and, as such, are included in the current *Standards for Education and Clinical Training.* Commentary in this chapter reflects both revised standards for Masters degree and distance learning (AMTA, 2009). The competencies are broken down into the following core areas of study:

1. Professional Practice
   - Theory (1.1-1.6)
   - Clinical Practice
     - Clinical Supervision (2.1–2.9)
     - Clinical Administration (3.1–3.9)
     - Advanced Clinical Skills (4.1–4.20)
     - College/University Teaching (5.1–5.11)
     - Research (6.1–6.12)
2. Professional Development
   - Musical and Artistic Development (7.1–7.10)
   - Personal Development and Professional Role (8.1–8.11)

Whereas the AMTA standards for the bachelor's degree in music therapy (or its equivalent) are designed to impart entry-level competencies, as specified in the *AMTA Professional Competencies* for the entry-level clinician, the *AMTA Advanced Competencies* outline a broad range of possible content areas for inclusion in graduate curricular programming. As such, the *Advanced Competencies* are considered guidelines for the advanced level of professional practice and in setting standards for masters' programs. Universities have generally shaped graduate curricular content based on the expertise, theoretical orientations and interests of graduate faculty, as well as resources of the academic institution, possibly leaving some areas of the *Advanced Competencies* not addressed.

As aforementioned, with revised standards in place as of November 2008 (AMTA, 2009), masters' programs are advised to include coursework in *Music Therapy Theory* and *Advanced Clinical Skills* (i.e., along with an applied supervised clinical component) as well as one or more emphases in other competency areas, including *Research, Musical Development* and *Personal Growth,* and *Clinical Administration.* While the competency areas of *Supervision* and

College/University Teaching are not specifically included in these recommendations for the master's degree, they can be and are, as part of the *Advanced Competencies,* subsumed in graduate coursework. The "Preamble" of the *AMTA Advanced Competencies* states that the competencies also serve to guide the development of standards of the doctoral degree in music therapy, which "shall focus on advanced competence in research, theory development, clinical practice, supervision, college teaching and/or college administration" (AMTA, 2009). The fact that *Supervision* and *College/University Teaching* were not specifically included in the recent masters' degree standards but are included in *Advanced Competencies* may reflect the more general nature of the *Standards for Education and Clinical Training* versus the *Advanced Competencies* as well as the nature of these documents as evolving "works in progress" and the possible intention to consider supervision and college teaching at the doctoral level of training in the future (Sandness, 2010).

Review of Current Programs

In reviewing the online program content of 32 (two programs are in moratorium) of the current 34 masters programs in the United States, I find that content and program structure vary quite widely. Nine (28%) of the 32 programs I surveyed, programs in New York, Pennsylvania and Massachusetts, offer expanded content leading to creative arts therapy licensure or licensed professional counseling licensure. Five programs offer distance learning or hybrid format. The majority of programs require the entry-level music therapy coursework of undergraduate programs, which is frequently accommodated by combining the equivalency track and the master's track into one extended program. Two programs appear to subsume the entry-level music therapy training into the master's degree coursework. As a result of all these variables, the credits for completion of programs ranges from 30 to 60. Capstone requirements for completion of masters' degrees include one or a combination of the following: thesis, fieldwork project, and oral examination, written examination. Certain programs invite clinical specialization (i.e., Neurologic Music Therapy, Group Work in Music Therapy, Music Psychotherapy, Medical Music Therapy, Technology in Music Therapy) while others do not.

COURSE CONTENT OF CURRENT MASTERS'
PROGRAMS IN COMPETENCY AREAS

Based on course names, course catalogue description and email follow-up as necessary, I categorize all indicated coursework from the masters' level program in the United States in terms of the advanced competencies. Numbers of programs in relationship to the total number of programs surveyed (32) including coursework related to advanced competency areas are as follows:

- Theory: 29 of 32 (90.6%)
- Research: 30 of 32 (93.75%)
- Advanced clinical skills: 30 of 32 (93.75%)
- Musical and artistic development: 25 of 32 (78.1%)
- Clinical supervision: 14 of 32 (43.75%)
- Personal development and professional role (including multicultural content): 9 of 32 (28.1%)
- College/University Teaching: 6 of 32 (18.75%)
- Clinical Administration: 1 of 32 (3.1%)

From these numbers, we can see that, in terms of the number of programs that cover various competency areas, the highest priority is currently given in the areas of research and advanced clinical skills followed by theory. There is an above average interest in musical and artistic development and a below average interest in clinical supervision. At the bottom, in terms of priority, we see personal development and professional role, college/university teaching and, lastly, clinical administration.

When we calculate the total number of courses (as indicated throughout the curricula of 32 masters' programs) that appear to be devoted to the competencies as outlined below, we see that priority is given to theory, followed by advanced clinical skill and research and then a precipitous drop in the number of overall courses specifically devoted to musical/artistic development, personal development/professional role, clinical supervision, college/university teaching and clinical administration.

- Theory: 75 of 266 (28.2%)
- Research: 62 of 266 (23.3%)
- Advanced clinical skills: 64 of 266 (24%)
- Musical and artistic development: 32 of 266 (12%)
- Clinical supervision: 14 of 266 (5.26 %)
- Personal development and professional role (including multicultural content): 13 of 266 (4.9%)
- College/University Teaching: 8 of 266 (3 %)
- Clinical Administration: 1 of 266 (0.37%)

Considerations of Competencies in Current Training

Let us consider the relevance of the advanced competencies (AMTA, 2009) to current masters' level training. Wherever relevant in ongoing discussion, the numbers of various competencies are in parentheses. In programs where undergraduate competencies are folded into graduate level coursework, it is important for the prospective student to tease out which information is entry level and which information is considered advanced.

The forthcoming comments are intended not only to *track coursework related to areas of competence* but also, further, to *stimulate our thinking about the importance and scope of various competencies in graduate education and training.*

Theory

1.1   Apply comprehensive knowledge of the foundations and principles of music therapy practice.
1.2   Synchronize comprehensive knowledge of current treatment theories and deduce their implications for music therapy practice and/or research.
1.3   Differentiate the theoretical or treatment orientations of current models of music therapy.
1.4   Identify theoretical constructs underlying various clinical practices and research approaches.
1.5   Understand emerging models and trends in music therapy.
1.6   Apply current literature in music therapy and related fields relevant to one's area(s) of expertise.

Discussion, Theory

Current coursework in the 32 masters' programs in the United States that I consider potentially related to *theory,* as defined in the current competencies fall into two categories:

1. Counseling courses (18), psychology courses (including psychology of music and music learning theory) (31), and music education/therapy courses (5) which could potentially serve as knowledge of current treatment theory and therefore serve as a basis to deduce implications for music therapy practice and/or research (1.2), provide literature relevant to one's area of music therapy expertise (1.6), and/or serve as basis for theoretical constructs underlying clinical practices and research (1.4). Course names in these areas include the following:

- Theories/Techniques in Counseling (2)
- Group Dynamics and Counseling (2)
- Counseling and Personality Theory
- Family and Rehabilitation
- Group Processes/Counseling
- Studies in Counseling and Psychology
- Assessment for Counseling and Psychology: Children and Adolescents
- Assessment for Counseling and Psychology: Adults
- Theories of Counseling and Psychotherapy
- Family Therapy and Counseling
- Group Therapy Counseling
- Principles and Techniques of Counseling and Psychotherapy
- Interpersonal Relations (2)
- Group Process
- Group Dynamics
- Psychopathology (4)
- Theory and Process of Group Work
- Developmental Psychology (4)
- Advanced Survey of Developmental Psychology
- Abnormal Psychology
- Psychopathology of Childhood, Adolescence and Adulthood
- Social Processes
- Cognitive Processes
- Human Development (2)
- Exceptional Child
- Biopsychosocial Foundations
- Creative Imagination
- Neuroanatomy
- Cognitive Neuroscience
- Vocational Theory
- Examining Power, Privilege and Oppression in Clinical Practice
- Advanced Educational Psychology
- Psychology of Music (3)
- Psychological Foundations of Music I, II
- Theories of Learning Music
- Advanced Psychology of Music
- Foundations, Leadership and Communication in Music Education
- History and Philosophy of Music Education
- Methods, Materials and Pedagogy in Music Education
- Contemporary Issues in Music Education and Music Therapy
- Contemporary Foundations (Music Therapy)

Music therapists do not teach several of these courses and therefore I wonder about how the concepts in these courses will transfer to an integrated understanding of how this information can actually be applied in music therapy. The use of these courses in masters' curriculums is so widespread that I urge educators to help students make these connections in another venue of the educational process.

2. Music therapy courses (9) providing comprehensive knowledge of foundations and principles of music therapy practice (1.1) and/or differentiation of theoretical bases or treatment applications in diverse models of music therapy, emerging models and trends in music therapy (1.3; 1.5).

- Music Therapy Advanced Theory and Methods (overlap with advanced clinical)
- Basic Theories of Psychotherapy and their Relationship to Music Therapy
- Music Therapy Foundations
- Advanced Models of Treatment (Music Therapy)
- Advanced Music Therapy Models
- Theory Development in Music Therapy
- Theory and Practice of Music Therapy
- Theories of Music Psychotherapy
- Philosophy and Theory of Music Therapy
- Philosophies and Theories of Music Therapy
- History and Philosophy of Music Therapy
- Transcultural Issues in National and International Music Therapy
- Gender Issues in Music Therapy
- Current Trends in Music therapy
- Music Therapy Seminars
- Foundations of Music Therapy Groups
- Key concepts in Music Therapy
- Colloquy in Music Therapy
- Integrative Seminar
- Graduate Seminar
- Dynamics of Intervention

As we can all conjecture, theory, whether specific or inclusive, is the foundation for much of what develops in music therapy. The incorporation of current treatment theories and implications for music therapy has resulted in widespread publication and music therapy application for clinical work defined within or springing forth from behavioral, cognitive-behavioral, humanistic, and psychoanalytic traditions (Scovel & Gardstrom, 2002). Clinical work may be contextualized within a previously existing psychotherapeutic model, thereby constituting a transfer of information or, on the other hand, may emerge as a new entity, which has been influenced by a combination of previously existing psychotherapeutic models. Hence we have, to name just a few examples, clinical work which is conceptualized and discussed in context of the behavioral framework (Gooding, 2009), the cognitive behavioral framework (Hilliard, 2001; Botello & Krout, 2008), schema therapy (Aigen, 2009), transpersonal psychology (Rugenstein, 1996), grounded theory (Daveson & Grocke, 2008) and the psychoanalytic tradition (Turry, 1998; Austin, 1998, 2009) while newly-named models springing forth from various psychotherapeutic models include, for example, Analytical Music Therapy (Priestly, 1975; Eschen, 2002; Scheiby, 1998, 2005), Plurimodal (Benenzon, 1997) and Music Therapy Integrated Model (Perilli, 2004). Further, models deriving from related disciplines such as neurophysiology, Neurologic Music Therapy (Thaut, 2005) and arts aesthetics, Aesthetic Music Therapy (Lee, 2003) are exceedingly valuable in the music therapy profession.

Many of the previously mentioned courses in the category of *Theory* therefore are fertile ground for the birth of new theories that can then be applied in music therapy.

If the student is recontextualizing music therapy within a theoretical model, it is important to document previous efforts from the literature including literature that might have been packaged under different nomenclature.

Clinical Supervision

2.1 Establish and maintain effective supervisory relationships.

2.2 Promote the professional growth, self-awareness and musical development of the supervisee.

2.3 Apply theories of supervision and research findings to music therapy supervision.

2.4 Design and implement methods of observing and evaluating supervisees that have positive effects on music therapy students and professionals at various levels of advancement and at different stages in the supervisory process.

2.5 Analyze the supervisee's music therapy sessions in terms of both the effects of specific musical, verbal, and nonverbal interventions and the musical and interpersonal dynamics and processes of the client(s)-therapist relationship.

2.6 Use music to facilitate the supervisory process.

2.7 Apply knowledge of norms and practices of other cultures to the supervisory process.

2.8 Evaluate the effectiveness of various approaches and techniques of supervision.

2.9   Evaluate the effects of one's own personality, supervisory style, and limitations on the supervisee and the supervisory process and seek consultation when appropriate.

Discussion, Clinical Supervision

These competencies outline the need for graduate students to experience and reflect upon their own supervision, study models of music therapy supervision and be given the opportunity to provide supervision in tandem with self-assessment.

Current coursework in the 32 masters' programs in the United States that I consider potentially related to *clinical supervision,* as defined in the current competencies, falls into two categories:

1. Courses on how to supervise (6) (the majority of these included other course emphases as well):
   - Teaching, Administration and Supervision
   - College Teaching and Supervision in Music Therapy
   - Supervision
   - Supervision and Teaching
   - Advanced Clinical Supervision
   - Music Therapy Supervision
   - Clinical Supervision I: Introduction to Theory and Application
2. The experience of being supervised in advanced clinical practice (7):
   - Clinical Supervision I, II, III
   - Clinical Supervision
   - Clinical Supervision II: Applied Experience
   - Supervised Experience: Music Therapy Human Research
   - Music therapy graduate practicum

Needs in Supervision: The need to educate and train our graduate students to provide effective supervision is quite important, as this service will be necessary in many situations. Who needs to receive supervision?
   - On-site clinical supervisors for individual supervision, practicum
   - Faculty supervisors for individual and group supervision, practicum
   - On-site supervisors for individual supervision, internship
   - Faculty supervisors for individual and group internship
   - Clinical supervisors for entry level clinicians at a clinical facility
   - Private practice supervisors for entry level clinicians
   - Private practice supervisors for senior level clinicians
   - Peer supervision
   - Private practice supervisors *for* supervisors

Areas of specialty supervision can be developed depending upon the purposes of supervision, the theoretical contexts of the music therapy work and particular methodology which would be accomplished in post-graduate study such as Nordoff-Robbins (Turry, 1998; Turry, 2001), Analytical Music Therapy (Scheiby, 2001), GIM (Brooks, 2002; Ventre, 2001), and others.

Supervision needs for all students present on a continuum including concrete assistance in clinical situations and guidance as to related readings, opportunities for observation that allow for imitation, mutual reflection, exploration of transferences, support for anxiety and confusion, mirroring and separation from the supervisor. Exploration of transferences and countertransferences of the clinician can concurrently clarify the subsequent need for problem-solving options. For example, Jackson (2010) explores models of response to client anger in music therapy, a common phenomenon in music therapy. In working through a clinician's response to anger, contextualized as a transference and/or countertransference, not only can the supervisor helping the clinician recognize the seeds of the response but, further, the supervisor can help the clinician decide on a clinical response based on various models (i.e., Redirection, Validation, Containing, Working Through) that is compatible to the needs of the client, the theoretical orientation of the music therapy and the needs of the clinician.

In developing supervision strategies in music therapy, we first examine the supervision techniques used by verbal psychotherapists and their possible use in the context of music therapy (Memory, Unkefer, & Smeltekop, 1987). However, we need to move beyond recontextualizing other professional models and forward into developing and using models using music, our particular modality, as a supervisory venue.

The Use of Music in Supervision: Young and Aigen (2010) identify the following purposes of music in music therapy supervision: (1) To examine transference and countertransference; (2) Music for skill development; (3) To enhance supervisory relationships; (4) To facilitate the process of a supervision session; (5) For personal and professional development, self-care and maintaining a connection to music. Supervision techniques that employ music include some of the following scenarios:

- Clinical listening of the client/therapist musical expression for purposes of analysis and exploration of possible options (Lee & Khare, 2001).
- Supervisee and supervisor role-play client/therapist musical scenario in order to musically explore both roles in the relationship (Turry, 1998; Pederson, 2009).
- Verbal presentation of work leads to supervisee either playing the client or playing the feelings about the client (Austin & Dvorkin, 2001).

- Music making to support the relationship between supervisee and supervisor (Scheiby, 2001).
- The use of improvisation, reflection, holding, emphasis of qualities in the music, musical dialogue and imaging to music for peer supervision (Bird, et al,. 1999).
- Musical improvisation to reflect feelings about a session (Scheiby, 2001) followed by verbal process.
- Musical improvisation used to explore transference and countertransference feelings of a faculty practicum supervisor toward students (Young & Aigen, 2010).
- Supervisee simulates perceived musical qualities of the client and the client's music in order to more effectively identify with the client (Scheiby, 2001; Frohne-Hagemann, 2001).
- Music activity to simulate reconstruction of a portion of a session once the issues related to the session have been discussed (verbal to music), a simulation of a client's musical production in order to unearth discussion related to this material (music to verbal), simulation of a client's musical production in order to discover where the music could have led (music to music) and the music therapist's use of music to explore feelings about being a leader (Stephens, 1987).

The Supervision of Music: The topic of supervision of *music* in music therapy remains an area wide open for further exploration and overlaps into competencies for musical and artistic development. Lee (2001) places the supervision of music in music therapy in the context of his Aesthetic Music Therapy, "a process that views the core of musical dialogue as its explicit theoretical base. The form and architecture of the musical interplay and the clinical responses and understanding are determined and reflected in and of itself through the music" (Lee, 2001, p. 249). This type of supervision involves clinical listening for purposes of analysis. What is the nature of the client musical expression? How does the supervisee respond and what are other possible musical answers?

Transference/Countertransference: It is suggested in the music therapy literature that it is through individual or group supervision of one's own clinical work (Langdon, 2001; Frohne-Hagemann, 2001; Pederson, 2009), supervision of supervising others (Bruscia, 2001) as well as participation in experiential music therapy group (Stephens, 1987) that the student finds the opening for further awareness regarding transference and countertransferance issues (i.e., including resistance and parallel processes). Various case studies (Frohne-Hagemann, 2001) demonstrate how supervision regarding transference and countertransference issues result in greater consciousness of and problem solving about how these issues contribute to the management of the music therapy session.

Group Supervision: Group supervision of clinical work elucidates personal development at progressive stages of readiness. Pederson (2009) points out three possible levels of personal development in reference to a student's clinical work. These levels are based upon the Integrated Developmental Model (Stoltenberg, McNeill, & Delworth, 1998) delineated below:

1. *Level One (Awareness of oneself and the other):* Student not yet ready to process their transference/countertransference issues and parallel processes.
2. *Level Two (Motivation):* Newly qualified music therapists have moved from preoccupation with techniques to a focus on the patient. This may lead to a "risk of overidentification with the client, followed by very strong countertransference reactions" (Pederson, 2001, p. 49). Processing transference/countertransference patterns and parallel processes at this level must be carefully negotiated since the student needs to problem solve ways to move forward that incorporate understanding of interpersonal relationships with the patient(s) as well as the supervisor.
3. *Level Three (Autonomy):* After several years of clinical practice, supervisee has developed conscious awareness of countertransference mechanisms allowing both supervisor and supervisee to reflect on an equal basis.

Depending upon the professional experience of the student, I suggest that these levels may equate to supervision for the undergraduate student (Level One) and masters/doctoral level trainings (Levels Two/Three). Levels can prove helpful in understanding the developmental readiness of a student for either individual or group intensive personal work. Bruscia (2001), outlining responsibilities for the graduate student apprentice supervisor, suggests that there are also developmental stages of readiness in supervision, however, his stages of supervision (i.e., action-oriented, learning-oriented, client-oriented, experience-oriented, countertransference-oriented) presume readiness for countertransference discussion within the timeframe of the undergraduate internship.

Pederson suggests that students, particularly those with analytically informed theoretical background and self-experience in music therapy (Pederson, 2009, p. 49) can be appropriate candidates for group intensive supervision at either level two or three. Models for group intensive supervision in music therapy are analytically based (Pederson, 2009; Ahonen-Eerikainen,

2003; Frohne-Hagemann, 2001). For example, Frohne-Hagemann (2001) describes such theoretical bases lending to successive phases of perceiving and relating, working through and understanding, multiperspective reflection and integration and training (Frohne-Hagemann, 2001, p. 235).

Individual Supervision: Stages of personal readiness are also necessary, of course, to profit from individual supervision. The use of reflective journals (Goodman, 2007; Barry & Callaghan, 2008), in addition to elucidating the course of the therapy session, can become a commentary on the nature of transference and countertransference. With the proper supervisor, the transference and countertransference can be sorted out (Frohne-Hagemann, 2001; Jahn-Langenberg, 2001; Scheiby, 2001; Pedersen, 2009), hopefully to the personal and professional advantage of the student.

Faculty Supervision of Graduate Supervisor: The unique experience of a graduate student being supervised by a professor in supervising undergraduate interns (Bruscia, 2001) can be personally instructive for the graduate student as the student becomes aware of parallel processes and resistance. The graduate student may experience resistance from the undergraduate intern as a result of intervention at an ineffectual level, expectations at an inappropriate level, psychological issues on the part of the supervisee or the supervisor's own inability to be appropriately responsive to what the supervisee needs (Bruscia, 2001). According to Bruscia (2001), the problems and needs of the undergraduate intern may parallel those of the intern's clients; these in turn are projected onto the graduate student supervisor who projects them onto the professor.

Supervision Courses: How do we train students to supervise? As we have already discussed, it is best to experience supervision before considering how to become a supervisor. Therefore, students in training to become supervisors should have already profited and continue to profit from supervision. Additionally, I find the following strategies helpful:

1. Review of supervision techniques common to psychotherapy and their possible transfer into music therapy supervision.
2. Review of music therapy supervision techniques and a reflection on how these techniques have *transferred* psychotherapy techniques and/or developed techniques unique to the music therapy profession.
3. Progressively more demanding supervisory scenarios, written by the professor, of a varied nature (i.e., supervisees of varied backgrounds and experience working in varied clinical situations) for students to problem solve, simulate, and practice multiple supervisory approaches.
4. Group problem-based learning scenarios written by students themselves.

5. Applied assignments where students are supervising an undergraduate student and/or receiving supervision to supervise entry-level clinicians at their jobs.
6. Writing about what it is like to supervise and to be supervised in order to remain emotionally connected to both sides of this scenario.

Bruscia (2001) describes an apprenticeship program for graduate students to supervise and teach internship seminars for undergraduate students; presumably these students are placed in local internships that take place a few days a week in order to allow them to attend seminar at the University. It is possible that the Bruscia model can also be used for graduate students to supervise and teach practicum students and their seminars. The professor, through individual supervisory conferences, apprentice logs, telephone and email access and observations of the seminar class supervises the graduate student. Supervisor agendas with students generally fall into the following areas: (1) Action oriented; (2) Learning oriented; (3) Client oriented; (4) Experience oriented; and (5) Countertransference oriented. Each of these modes of supervision is developmental with the more advanced student eventually able to profit from the highest level of supervision (Bruscia, 2001, p. 286).

Teaching in a two-year graduate diploma program (analogous in Norway to a degree in between a bachelor and a masters degree in the American system), Stige (2001) proposes a fourth role for the supervisor. Not only does the supervisor serve as a teacher, therapist and gatekeeper (Watkins, 1997) but, further, the supervisor can serve as a listening coauthor, which is to be in "an uneasy role while negotiating the development of skills and knowledge, (i.e., teacher), personal development (therapist) and protecting the needs of the client, (gate-keeper)" (Stige, 2001, p. 164). Stige describes students role-playing improvisational music therapy, subsequent role playing of supervision with another student serving as supervisor and, finally discussion and reflection upon the role playing of supervision as well as discussion of the role-playing of music therapy.

<u>Summary Recommendations</u>: Currently there is a great deal of periodical literature on supervision in music therapy and two edited volumes (Forinish, 2001a; Odell-Miller & Richards, 2009). This literature will continue to develop. I emphasize three areas of concern in the training of supervisors:

1. The need to extend understanding about multicultural considerations in supervision is an important issue. Music therapists remain a someone homogenous group in terms of ethnicity and gender and, based on latest results of a survey (Young, 2009), their supervisors have not been exposing them to multicultural sensitivity.

2. Realizing that supervisees themselves can display aspects of resistance (Edwards & Daveson, 2004) and this may add yet another layer of need: the supervisor needing supervision in order to supervise.

3. Setting boundaries between supervisor and supervisee. There seems to be mixed opinion about this issue in the literature. Where transferences are explored, is the supervisor to act as therapist or avoid acting in the role of therapist (Brown, 2009)? "The supervisor is not a therapist and s/he works on personal problems of his supervisee only to the extent as is helpful for the supervisee's work as a therapy" (Pederson, 2009, pp. 233–234).

Clinical Administration

3.1 Adhere to laws and occupational regulations governing the provision of education and health services, particularly with regard to music therapy.

3.2 Adhere to accreditation requirements for clinical agencies, particularly with regard to music therapy.

3.3 Employ music therapy reimbursement and financing options.

3.4 Develop effective staffing patterns for the provision of music therapy services.

3.5 Develop effective recruiting and interviewing strategies for student and professional applicants.

3.6 Develop policies and procedures for staff evaluation and supervision.

3.7 Utilize management strategies to establish and maintain effective relationships and a high level of motivation among staff.

3.8 Integrate music therapy staff and programs into the agency's service delivery systems.

3.9 Design methods for evaluating music therapy programs and service delivery.

Discussion, Clinical Administration

These competencies focus on information regarding agency regulations and the *clinical* workplace as opposed to administrative competence in the *university* workplace educators are ultimately responsible for. Competency 3.5, which mentions students, is presumably in reference to clinical interns.

Coursework related to *clinical* administration is included in only one masters' curriculum reviewed; the course is called Administration and includes an overlap of clinical/higher education and grant writing information. There is another course, entitled Administration of Music Education/Music Therapy, which deals with higher education administration rather than clinical issues. There is clearly a need for coursework in clinical administration.

As we move into the era of health reform in the United States and the economy continues to fluctuate, it is vital that more research emerge on the role of music therapy in the United States healthcare system. These issues were discussed more than two decades ago (Clark & Ficken, 1988, pp. 23–25) and cited the following realities:

- The bulk of consumers needing healthcare continue to grow older.
- The cost of healthcare is increasing.
- There is a continuing effort to reduce expenditures.
- Health care technology continues to advance.
- Wellness lifestyles are more popular.
- Hospital stays are becoming shorter.
- Alternative setting for healthcare are evolving.
- Alternative financing systems are flourishing.
- Public ownership of healthcare is growing.
- The consolidations among providers is continuing.
- Changes are occurring in the physician marketplace.
- Our society continues to face medical and ethical decisions.

Clark and Ficken (1988) predicted that the above realities would lead to fewer jobs, leaner staff, more evening and weekend work, a demand for an increase in productivity and more managerial ability, decreased planning time, an emphasis on assessment and short-term treatment, documentation and treatment outcome, a shift to outpatient-nontraditional and wellness models, team building versus aggressive competing and an emphasis on the consumer. Related to these competencies, but not stated, is administrative awareness within the fields of health care and education about music therapy (Ropp et al., 2006). How is our education and training accommodating those shifts, which include the importance of cost-effectiveness (Dziwak & Gfeller, 1988) predicted over 20 years ago and happening today?

Although the administrative skills cited in the advanced competencies are all vital skills, they do not appear in the current curriculums of masters or doctoral level programs. This leads me to assume they are skills that are learned on the job, either the clinical setting, as a participant in music therapy advocacy or as an administrator within a program. Reimbursement issues are detailed by Simpson and Burns (2008).

There are a certain percentage of graduate programs that are designed for the entry level clinician, already working at a clinical position, to gain advanced competencies while going to graduate school during the evenings. The student in this kind of program has the ideal advantage of the theory to practice learning mode. The student can apply many aspects of graduate school education to on-the-job learning. Administration is just one example of this. Such a student can learn information that will be immediately relevant:

- Take a close look at his or her work facility in terms of related laws, legislative issues, accreditation requirements, and occupational regulations impacting the provision of music therapy services.
- Investigate funding opportunities for music therapy beyond the scope of already funded services.
- Consider the administrative functions one might, as a music therapist, undertake in the current facility, including a prospectus for expanded growth through advertising and interviewing for staffing throughout the facility, defining policies and procedures for anticipated personnel, (i.e., including job description and ethical responsibilities), integrating and evaluating programming, maintaining documentation of services.

Technically all of this information could conceivably be learned in a vacuum but what personal relevance would it then hold? In reviewing priorities within graduate education, it will be up to current and future educators to determine where these competencies belong.

Advanced Clinical Skills

4.1   Apply comprehensive knowledge of current methods of music therapy assessment, treatment, and evaluation.

4.2   Utilize comprehensive knowledge of human growth and development, musical development, diagnostic classifications, etiology, symptomatology and prognosis in formulating treatment plans.

4.3   Understand the contraindications of music therapy for client populations served.

4.4   Understand the dynamics and processes of therapy from a variety of theoretical perspectives.

4.5   Utilize the dynamics and processes of various theoretical models in individual, dyadic, family, and group music therapy.

4.6   Design or adapt assessment and evaluation procedures for various client populations.

4.7   Utilize advanced music therapy methods (e.g., listening, improvising, performing, composing) within one or more theoretical frameworks to assess and evaluate clients' strengths, needs, and progress.

4.8   Design treatment programs for emerging client populations.

4.9   Employ one or more models of music therapy requiring advanced training.

4.10 Utilize advanced verbal and nonverbal interpersonal skills within a music therapy context.

4.11 Assume the responsibilities of a primary therapist.

4.12 Relate clinical phenomena in music therapy to the broader treatment context.

4.13 Respond to the dynamics of musical and interpersonal relationships that emerge at different stages in the therapy process.

4.14 Fulfill the clinical roles and responsibilities of a music therapist within a total treatment milieu and in private practice.

4.15 Apply advanced skills in co-facilitating treatment with professionals from other disciplines.

4.16 Demonstrate comprehensive knowledge of client rights.

4.17 Understand the differential uses of the creative arts therapies and the roles of art, dance/movement, drama, psychodrama, and poetry therapy in relation to music therapy.

4.18 Apply creative processes within music therapy.

4.19 Employ imagery and ritual in music therapy.

4.20 Understand and respond to potential physical and psychological risks to client health and safety.

Discussion, Advanced Clinical Skills

The definition of advanced clinical skills may be open to some debate. AMTA (2009) uses the word "in-depth" to describe the level of advanced versus entry-level understanding and execution of the clinical role. In accordance with this word, the possible music therapy competencies include training as a primary therapist (4.11), able to apply advanced skills (4.10, 4.15) and use of advanced training in particular models of music therapy (4.9). However, advanced clinical skills have been associated with reeducative and/or reconstructive aims leading to greater insight (Wheeler, 1983; AMTA, 2009) within the psychotherapeutic model. This association could, I suggest, delimit the therapist from working at an advanced level with nonverbal clients or clients with limited abstracting ability.

In contrast to *theory,* the term *advanced clinical skills* implies clinical application as a result of understanding theory. I take this to mean that theory is the knowledge; clinical skills are the practice. Many of the competencies here imply a *level of advanced understanding* that is formulated prior to or during music therapy intervention. Adjectives such as comprehensive (4.1, 4.2, 4.16), variety (4.4), various (4.5, 4.6), advanced (4.7, 4.9, 4.10), emerging (4.8, 4.13), primary (4.11), broader (4.12), total (4.14), differential (4.17) tell us that we are responsible, on the advanced level, to train clinicians who are not only in critical thinking mode when conducting therapy but, further, inventive mode.

Note that the competencies require understanding (4.3, 4.4, 4.12, 4.17, 4.20) as well as broad active engagement of skills (4.1, 4.2, 4.5–4.11, 4.13–4.15, 4.18) relative to assessment (4.1, 4.6, 4.7), treatment planning (4.2, 4.3, 4.8), treatment (4.1, 4.5, 4.9, 4.13, 4.10, 4.18, 4.19), and evaluation (4.1, 4.6, 4.7), all in various contexts (4.14, 4.15).

Coursework potentially related to *advanced clinical skills,* as defined in the current competencies, several of which may also overlap in the *theory* competencies, falls into the following categories:

1. Music therapy courses introducing *treatment planning* in a manner that incorporates human growth or development, musical development, diagnostic classification, etiology, symtomatology and prognosis for current and emerging populations (4.2, 4.8) and incorporating comprehensive knowledge in understanding the rationale for *methods* of music therapy used in assessment, treatment and evaluation (4.1).

- Advanced Clinical Techniques in Music Therapy
- Music in Medicine (3)
- Music Therapy in Rehabilitation and Medicine
- Music Therapy in Medicine and Healthcare
- Music Psychotherapy (2)
- Special Studies in Music Therapy
- Music Therapy and Medicine
- Music, Imagery and Psychotherapy
- Psychiatric Music Therapy
- Medical Music Therapy
- Advanced Clinical Experience
- Seminar in Music Therapy
- Group Work in Music Therapy
- Music Therapy for Adults
- Music Therapy for the Elderly
- Music Therapy in Special Education (2)
- Advanced Topics in Music Therapy
- Music in Counseling (2)
- Advanced Music Therapy Course
- Advanced Methods and Materials In Music Therapy
- Special Applications in Music Therapy
- Music Psychotherapy
- Community and Therapeutic Applications of Drumming
- Advanced Clinical Practice
- Special Topics in Music Therapy
- Clinical Practice in Music Therapy
- Seminar in Music Therapy

2. Music therapy courses defining the *dynamics and processes of music therapy* models for individual, dyadic, family and group music therapy (4.5):
   - Individual Music Therapy: Advanced Theory and Techniques
   - Group Music Therapy: Advanced Theory and Techniques

3. Music therapy courses defining the design and adaptation of *assessment and evaluation procedures* (4.6) as well as the presentation of advanced music therapy methods within various theoretical frameworks in order to assess and evaluate (4.7):
   - Client Assessment
   - Assessment in Music Therapy
   - Music Therapy (in) Assessment (2)
   - Medical Music Therapy Assessment and Treatment
   - Clinical Appraisal and Assessment
   - Assessment and Evaluation
   - Assessment in Music Therapy

4. Music therapy courses using one or more *models of music therapy requiring advanced training* (4.9) (including *the use of imagery and ritual in music therapy,* 4.19):
   - Neurologic Music Therapy
   - Guided Imagery and Music (2)
   - Medical Music Therapy
   - Introduction to Guided Imagery
   - Bonny Method of GIM Level I Training

5. Music therapy courses providing training in *advanced verbal and nonverbal interpersonal skills* for music therapy (4.10) are not specifically identified but are implicit in subject matter being covered. The types of skills required to respond nonverbally and verbally vary depending upon clinical need and theoretical orientation. In Chapter 3, we discussed studies detailing the use of verbal skills with entry-level clinicians (Wolfe, O'Connell & Epps, 1998; Gardstrom, 2001; Darrow et al., 2001; Alley, 1980). Amir (1999b) identifies models of music therapy, which identify the differentiated use of talking and/or verbal processing in music therapy. Guided Imagery and Analytical Music Therapy are but two examples of this. Nolan (1995, 2005), teaching in a graduate program, emphasizes the importance of training music therapists in verbal skills, citing the use of verbal process with the client in order to "add form and clarification to affective states, imagery, symbolic and other phenomena" (Nolan, 2005, p. 27) from the shared musical experience. While verbal processing in this context can increase client awareness about internal and external events, the further use of verbal techniques, on the part of the therapist, to interpret or possibly employ confrontation is to be used judiciously and, I suggest, based upon ongoing clinical supervision. Our primary vehicle for change is music and the return to the music often provides clear resolu-

tion to issues (Grinnel, 1980). However, there is no question that the music therapist forming a primary alliance with the client, as was my experience during eight years of clinical experience at The Creative Arts Rehabilitation Center in New York City, needs to extend the alliance through verbal process.

6. Music therapy courses providing training for music therapy as a *primary treatment* as opposed to adjunctive (4.11) are not specifically identified but are implicit in subject matter being covered.

7. Music therapy courses *relating clinical phenomena to broader treatment context* (4.12) are not specifically identified but are implicit in subject matter being covered.

8. Music therapy courses that provide training in the ability to *respond to changing musical and interpersonal relationships during the course of therapy* (4.13) are not specifically identified but are implicit in subject matter being covered.

9. Music therapy courses that train the therapy for work within either a *total treatment milieu and/or private practice* (4.14) with co-treatment as necessary and desirable (4.15):
   • Interdisciplinary Studies

10. Music therapy courses that train the student with *regard to client rights* (4.16) are not specifically identified.

11. Music therapy courses that provide a careful understanding of the role of music therapy within the *context of creative arts therapies and creative process* (4.17, 4.18):
   • Orientation to Expressive Therapy

12. Music therapy courses that train the student in *contraindications of music therapy* (4.3) and, in doing so, how to understand and respond to physical/psychological risk to the client (4.20) are not specifically identified. Such a course would be overlapping with both psychology of music and a course on ethics.

The majority of courses identified as *advanced clinical skills* are theoretical, some with an applied component, others not. There are a number of programs that outline advanced clinical experience. The titles of these courses include the following:
   • Music Therapy Practicum (2)
   • Clinical Internship
   • Clinical Practicum
   • Advanced Music Therapy Practicum
   • Advanced Music Therapy Practicum
   • Advanced Music Therapy Internship
   • Music Therapy Internship
   • Advanced Practice
   • Advanced Practicum

- Practicum in Music Therapy
- Clinical Training
- Advanced Music Therapy Practice
- Graduate Practicum
- Advanced Music Therapy Practicum (2)
- Advanced Music Therapy Skills

The subcategory of *Advanced Clinical Skills,* in my opinion, rests on the realization of three compentency areas under Professional Practice and Professional Development: *Theory, Musical and Artistic Development, Personal Development/Professional Role.* I also believe that much of advanced clinical skills and practice can lead to research hypotheses. It is through doing that we learn.

The recent requirement for graduate students to go beyond the entry level requirement of 1200 clinical hours as a part of the graduate program recognizes clinical work and the supervision of clinical work as a high priority, presumably taking in all competencies addressed here under *Advanced Clinical* competencies. In order to make this experience as valuable as possible, it is important for us to link advanced practice opportunities to coursework, research, thesis, musical development, and personal development. In doing so, we integrate the identity of the music therapist.

College/University Teaching

5.1 Design academic curricula, courses, and clinical training programs in music therapy consistent with current theories, research, competencies, and standards, including those for national accreditation and program approval.

5.2 Utilize current educational resource in music therapy (e.g., equipment, audio-visual aids, materials, technology).

5.3 Draw from a breadth and depth of knowledge of clinical practice in teaching music therapy.

5.4 Establish and maintain effective student-teacher relationships.

5.5 Communicate with other faculty, departments, and administration regarding the music therapy program and its educational philosophy.

5.6 Develop standards and procedures for admission and retention that support educational objectives consistent with the policies of the institution.

5.7 Utilize various methods of teaching (e.g., lecture, demonstration, role-playing, group discussion, collaborative learning).

5.8 Supervise and mentor students in clinical training, supervision, teaching and research.

5.9 Advise and counsel students with regard to academic and professional matters.

5.10   Design and apply means of evaluating student competence, both internal (e.g., proficiency exams) and external (e.g., evaluation from clinical training supervisors).

5.11   Utilize internal, external and self-evaluations to monitor the effectiveness of academic courses and programs in meeting educational objectives.

Discussion, College/University Teaching

Current coursework in the 32 masters' programs in the United States directly or potentially related to *college/university teaching,* as defined in the current competencies, include the following:

- Teaching, Administration and Supervision
- College Teaching and Supervision in Music Therapy
- Supervision and Teaching in Music Therapy
- Supervision and Collegiate Teaching in Music Therapy
- College Teaching
- Music Therapy Education
- Curriculum Issues and Trends in Music Education
- Music Therapy College Teaching: Curriculum and Competencies

As previously noted, this is the first published book on music therapy education and training after a twenty-two-year lapse (Maranto & Bruscia, 1987, 1988). Fortunately, the periodical literature demonstrates a growing interest in teaching music therapy. However, with eight courses introduced at the masters' level of selected programs, attention to this important area remains extremely limited at this level.

Those of us who started teaching in the seventies did not have doctoral training in music therapy available. As a result of this, many pioneering educators pursued institute training, personal mentorships with those in related fields, or graduate coursework either independently or as a part of another doctoral degree such as music education or psychology. These were the educators who started today's doctoral programs in music therapy or in music education with music therapy specializations. As with many related professions (i.e., special education, social work, applied music, physical therapy, occupational therapy), the development of doctoral level training has led to a demand for colleges requiring doctoral level faculty. Although AMTA requires the masters to teach at university level, the trend to advertise for faculty with doctorates will, I predict, shift the demographics of the AMTA teaching roster, currently a mixed proportion of masters and doctoral level faculty, to all doctoral level faculty over the next two decades.

The presence of eight courses in college teaching indicates that 25 percent of the programs surveyed consider this training important at the masters' level. Doctoral programs may require a course in college teaching (note: most do not), the opportunity for students to become teaching assistants and/or develop courses; pedagogy is a byproduct rather than the goal of the degree. It is not clear what degree of teaching mentorship is provided. Doctoral applicants applying for faculty positions tend to study in the same areas of the country they seek employment in and this may make for some local uniformity in faculty education and outlook.

Some would argue that you cannot teach pedagogy but I believe that exposure to past practice and the sharing of ideas in pedagogy is important. Education and training advanced competencies are addressed in this book as follows:

Chapter 2: 5.1
Chapter 3: 5.1, 5.8
Chapter 4: 5.1, 5.8
Chapter 6: 5.2, 5.3, 5.4, 5.5, 5.6, 5.7; 5.9, 5.10, 5.11

Research

6.1   Perform comprehensive literature searches using various indices to identify gaps in knowledge.
6.2   Translate theories, issues, and problems in clinical practice, supervision, administration, and higher education into meaningful research hypotheses or guiding questions.
6.3   Apply quantitative and qualitative research designs according to their indicated uses.
6.4   Conduct advanced research using one or more research approaches (e.g., historical, philosophical, qualitative, quantitative).
6.5   Acknowledge one's biases and personal limitations related to research.
6.6   Write grant proposals for funding research.
6.7   Conduct research according to ethical principles for protection of human participants, including informed consent, assessment of risk and benefit, and participant selection.
6.8   Collect and analyze data using appropriate procedures to avoid or minimize potential confounds.
6.9   Collaborate with others in conducting research.
6.10   Use various methods of data analysis.
6.11   Interpret and disseminate research results consistent with established standards of inquiry.
6.12   Evaluate scholarly and student research regarding research questions

or problems, methods, procedures, data collection, analysis and conclusions.

Discussion, Research

Current coursework in the 32 masters' programs in the United States directly or potentially related to *research,* as defined in the current competencies, falls into four categories:

1. The use of bibliographic research is highlighted in Chapter 6 where I discuss literature resources and choices in reading for students. Although extensive literature review may very well be a part of standard research courses, and obviously the development of a master's thesis or doctoral dissertation, coursework specific to bibliographic research or extensive literature searches that identify gaps in information (6.1) is rarely identified among the 32 masters programs:

- Bibliography and Research
- Educational Research Bibliography

2. Although general and arts-related courses on research methods may be relevant to competency 6.2, coursework identified with the words "music therapy" alluded to *direct* formulation of research hypotheses related to the practice, supervision, administration and higher education of music therapy as well as the evaluation of music therapy scholarly and student research (6.12):

- Research in Music Therapy (2)
- Music Therapy Research and Program Evaluation
- Research on Music and Behavior
- Music Therapy Research
- Research in Music Education and Music Therapy
- Seminar in Research
- Research Methods and Rehabilitation

3. Although general courses in research methods and research courses in the related disciplines of music education and/or arts education, in all likelihood, include quantitative and qualitative research, courses directly focused on these topics (6.3) include the following:

- Qualitative Research Methods
- Qualitative Research in Arts Education
- Advanced Applications of Quantitative Research Methods
- Qualitative and Quantitative Research (2)
- Introduction to Behavioral Research

4. Presumably all comprehensive research courses subsume one or more research approaches (6.4), and review interpretation and dissemination of research results (6.11):

- Introduction to Research Methods
- Research Methods
- Research Methodology
- Introduction to Music Research
- Research Methods in Music and Multimedia
- Applied Research
- Systematic Research Methods
- Advanced Research in Music Education
- Research for Practitioners in Music Education
- Seminar in Research
- Research and Evaluation
- Research I
- Research II
- Arts-Based Research
- Introduction to Research
- Research in Music Behavior
- Advanced Statistics
- Assessment in Arts Education
- Research (2)
- Introduction to Descriptive and Experimental Research in Music
- Introduction to Research in Music
- Research Methods (3)
- Applied Research
- Systematic Research Methods
- Advanced Research in Music Education
- Introduction to Research Methods (3)
- Research Methods in Psychology (2)
- Methods and Research
- Research for Practitioners in Music Education
- Methods Research
- Introduction to Music Research
- Research Techniques
- Educational Research

5. Courses specifically dealing with methods of data analysis (6.8, 6.10) and understanding of possible confounding (6.8) as well as preparatory understanding of statistics include the following:

- Introduction to Statistical Analysis
- Lab-Introduction to Statistical Analysis
- Design and Data Analysis for Researchers
- Understanding Statistical Inference
- Nonparametric Statistics
- Statistics

- Analysis of Variance
- Research Design and Statistics

Opportunities to collaborate with others in conducting research (6.9) or write grant proposals for funding research (6.6) are not specified in my review of masters programs. What is clear to me is that the thesis process involves the student becoming aware of bias and limitations regarding research (6.5) as well as ethical responsibilities of research (6.7).

Those of us who teach at the graduate level know that, for many years, there was a great emphasis on research at the Masters level, possibly to the detriment of advanced musical and artistic development, advanced clinical skills and teaching pedagogy. Now I believe that we have tempered the importance of research in the context of other skill areas.

Bruscia (1999) considers the Masters level an intermediate level for research development, one that should include the ability to read and comprehend complex research (quantitative and qualitative), the acquisition of a greater breadth of knowledge of the research literature, the abilities to design simple quantitative or qualitative research at the intensive level of practice, understanding of quantitative methods of data analysis and interpretation (i.e., basic statistics) and the understanding of qualitative methods of data analysis and interpretation.

At a doctoral level, Bruscia (1999) suggests the student master the ability to critically evaluate both quantitative and qualitative research, have a comprehensive knowledge of the research literature, design complex quantitative and qualitative research studies for a primary level of practice, independently analyze and interpret data in both quantitative and qualitative paradigms and write comprehensive reports of research in appropriate style and format.

What has the course of published research been like in our field? The analysis of research literature from selected music therapy journals has been helpful in considering the development of the music therapy profession (Jellison, 1973; Gilbert, 1979), research topics related to specific clinical populations as a topic of greatest priority (Gilbert, 1979; Decuir, 1987; Codding, 1987; Wheeler, 1988), the relationship between theory, research and practice (Gfeller, 1987), the identification of gaps in the literature as well as research agendas (Gfeller, 1995; Gilbert, 1979; Wheeler, 1988; Dileo & Bradt, 2005; Standley, 1986) and the analysis of various types of quantitative (Gregory, 2008) and qualitative (Aigen, 2008) design. Bibliographic inquiry in music therapy (Brooks, 2003) includes the examination of article on specific topics appearing in one or more journals (meta-analysis), databases on graduate research and the content of various music therapy journals. This last area of concern, the content of various music therapy journals, comes to our most recent attention with a comparative look at the types of journal publication between the years 1964–2001. Using five journals previously or currently published in the United States (*Journal of Music Therapy, Music Therapy-Journal of the American Association for Music Therapy, Music Therapy Perspectives, The Arts in Psychotherapy, Journal of the Association for Music and Imagery*) and four international journals (*The Australian Journal of Music Therapy, The Nordic Journal of Music Therapy, The British Journal of Music Therapy* and *The New Zealand Society for Music Therapy Journal*), Brooks (2003) analyzed 1,521 articles, which included research as defined below:

- *Quantitative research:* numeric data statistically summarized or analyzed (includes experimental research, descriptive research, applied behavior analysis, writing about associated research methods and research protocols).
- *Qualitative research:* systematic collection and analysis of nonnumeric data to derive idiographic insights or meaning in relation to a phenomenon (research, individual or group, labeled as naturalistic, action based, participatory, hermeneutic, heuristic, phenomenological, constructive, critical or discursive, writing about associated research methods and research protocols).
- *Philosophical and Theoretical research:* philosophical inquiry or elaboration of theoretical constructs. Aimed at clarifying, evaluating, relating or arguing basic assumptions, beliefs, hypotheses, constructs, paradigms, principles or discovery guiding practice or research.
- *Historical research:* in order to gain knowledge or insight about the past through systematic study of past practice, materials, institutions, people, etc.

Results of bibliographic analysis (Brooks, 2003) reveal the following distribution relevant to research publication from 1521 articles in 10 journals in the years 1964–2001: Quantitative research (542), Qualitative research (98), Philosophical/theoretical research (136), Historical research (55). The journals publishing the greatest number of articles within a given research area were the *Journal of Music Therapy* with a quantitative research count of 426 out of 542 articles published, and the *Nordic Journal of Music Therapy* with a philosophical/theoretical research count of 32 our of 136 articles.

The predominance of published quantitative research is clear in journal articles; however there is a relative increase in qualitative research and this increase is also marked by the number of qualitative doctoral dissertations (1987–2006), 52, written in the English language (Aigen, 2008).

Beyond the classification of literature, it is instructive to consider how various types of research may complement each other (Gold, 2007), be used in combination (Hunt, 2010), be evaluated (Gold, 2010), play a role in furthering the profession (i.e., action research), be considered as evidence based

(Elyse & Wheeler, 2010), be little mentioned but of potential importance in the field (i.e., aesthetic research, bibliographic research), and/or pose research agendas in critical areas such as medical music therapy (Dileo & Bradt, 2005) and autism (Gold, Wigram, & Elefant, 2006). The fairly recent development of these latter Cochrane reviews completed by music therapists is a reflection of the level of scrutiny music therapy researchers are undertaking in considering literature (Elyse & Wheeler, 2010).

Irrespective of the type of research disposition the masters or doctoral student elects, it is critical to support a variety of agendas that will enhance our field. In so doing, it is particularly important to mentor the student (Wigram, 2009), offer supplementary-related coursework, small group seminars in the development of research agendas and rigorous training in research with emphasis on developing evidence-based practice.

Although evidence-based medicine, which led to the concept of evidence based practice, traditionally relies upon quantitative research (i.e., the randomized controlled trial, RCT, and the meta-analysis of RCT's relative to a specific topic are considered the gold standard for EBM), Edwards (2005) points out the possible difficulties in setting up strict protocol in music therapy studies and the responsibility of the educator in training the student:

> University teaching programs in music therapy and other creative arts therapies disciplines can be helpful in training students about the basics of research and its applications, including the applications of research evidence, as well as encouraging students to critique its principles through reading alternate views of evidence. (Edwards, 2005, p. 293)

Silverman (2010), in reviewing the psychiatric music therapy literature, concludes that the base is small and most studies are categorized into the lowest levels of evidence. Wigram, Pederson, and Bonde (2002), in providing a hierarchical structure for evidence based practice and its relationship to music therapy research and clinical records (Wigram, Pederson, & Bonde, 2002, p. 261) point out that case reports and case studies constitute the most common clinical evidence for music therapy. However, this would not represent any precedent for EBM. Hopefully, as we move forward in the field, we will find ways of presenting greater number of EBM studies or alternative means of presenting evidence in arts-based therapies.

Musical and Artistic Development

7.1   Reproducing, notate, and transcribe musical responses of clients.
7.2   Compose music, including songs, in various styles to meet specific therapeutic objectives.

7.3 Provide spontaneous musical support for client improvisation.

7.4 Improvise in a variety of musical styles.

7.5 Utilize a wide variety of improvisatory techniques for therapeutic purposes.

7.6 Design music listening programs for therapeutic purposes.

7.7 Use different methods of musical analysis for client assessment and evaluation.

7.8 Adapt and select musical material for different musical cultures and sub-cultures.

7.9 Apply advanced skills in the clinical use of at least two of the following: keyboard, voice, guitar and/or percussion.

7.10 Utilize extensive and varied repertoire of popular, folk, and traditional songs.

Discussion, Musical and Artistic Development

Music courses in Masters' program include the following three categories:
1. Designated or elective courses in performance, theory/composition, musicology and ensembles may impact the development of competencies 7.1, 7.2, 7.6, 7.8, 7.9, and 7.10, respectively related to notation, composition, music listening, world music and the development of song repertoire.
- Music of the Romantic Era
- Music since 1950
- Contemporary Issues in Music
- Topics in Music History and Literature
- Ensembles
- Music Theory: Analytical Techniques
- Music Structure and Style
- Advanced Music Skills
- Music History Period Course
- Form and Analysis
- Analytical Techniques (music theory)
- Styles in Music
- Survey in World Music
- Performance Pedagogy
- Music Theory, History, Composition (selected electives as part of program)

It is not clear how coursework in music theory, music history or ethnomusicology is appropriately contextualized into music therapy practice as suggested in the graduate competencies (7.1, 7.2, 7.6, 7.7, 7.8) and also discussed even as possibilities for entry level training (see Chapter 2). Therefore I suggest that music therapy educators offering these courses *ensure that they are linked to practice music therapy competencies.*

2. Music therapy courses designed to provide training in clinical improvisation (7.3, 7.4, 7.5).

- Advanced Improvisation and Composition in Music Therapy (2)
- Advanced Piano Improvisation
- Clinical Piano Improvisation
- Vocal Improvisation
- Voice and Music Therapy
- Clinical Improvisation
- Clinical Improvisation Methods
- Improvisation for Therapy
- Advanced Clinical Improvisation
- Advanced Practice of Improvisation in Music Therapy
- Theory and Application of Improvisation in Music Therapy

Beyond the theoretical foundations discussing improvisation, for example, the work of Bruscia (1987c), the study and practice of actual musical techniques for improvisation is essential, hopefully building on initial competencies in entry-level training (see Chapter 2). The use of improvisation has gained more momentum as the field has moved forward; its use is particularly pronounced in European music therapy training programs. For example, the use of analytic improvisation techniques can be experienced and processed with exploration of conscious, unconscious or ego mastery techniques (Priestley, 1975).

3. Music therapy courses for the development of advanced skill on the guitar (7.9), improvisatory experience (7.5) and a variety of clinical musicianship techniques.

- Advanced Guitar for Therapists and Educators
- Music Therapy Ensemble
- Clinical Musicianship

Coursework related to musical and artistic development amongst the 32 graduate programs in the United States is most clearly related to the competencies in terms of improvisation. Other skill development appears to require more attention. If students are actually practicing music therapy, either on the job, or in conjunction with a university placement, their skills in musical transcription, composition, improvisation, designing music listening, advanced applied music skill, continuing repertoire development and use of technology can be developed and evaluated. This is important. From my initial review of coursework in current graduate programs, I find no course that presents different methods of notation, such as graphic (Bergstrom-Nielson, 1993, 1998) or microtonal nor do I find coursework focusing on theoretical analysis of client-therapist improvisation (Lee, 2000) as suggested in competency 7.7 for assessment and evaluation. I recall studying microtonal and graphic notation on my own in the early eighties in order to guide a study on notation of infant/toddler vocal development with Dr. Judith Kestenberg, a clinical professor of psychiatry at the NYU Medical Center. This information should be taught at the graduate level.

Personal Development and Professional Role

8.1   Utilize self-awareness and insight to deepen the client's process in music therapy.
8.2   Identify and address one's own personal issues.
8.3   Apply the principles of effective leadership.
8.4   Use personal reflection (e.g., journaling, artistic involvement, meditation, other spiritual pursuits).
8.5   Recognize limitations in competence and seek consultation.
8.6   Practice strategies for self-care.
8.7   Selectively modify music therapy approaches based on knowledge of the roles and meanings of music in various cultures.
8.8   Work with culturally diverse populations, applying knowledge of how culture influences issues regarding identity formation, concepts of health and pathology, and understanding of the role of therapy.
8.9   Understand how music therapy is practiced in other cultures.
8.10 Apply current technology to music therapy practice.
8.11 Adhere to the AMTA code of Ethics and Standards of Clinical Practice using best professional judgment in all areas of professional conduct.

Discussion, Personal Development and Professional Role

This most recent reorganization of the *Advanced Competencies* reintegrates multicultural competencies (8.7, 8.8, 8.9), ethics (8.11) and technology (8.10) into the area of personal developmental and professional role. I appreciate the inclusion of multiculturalism and ethics under *personal/professional growth* because they speak to the extension of a personal sense of self and how we may or may not bias ourselves when working with clients and students from other cultures and making ethical decisions.

Discussion, Personal Development and Professional Role: Experiential Learning

Experiential music therapy group courses which build competencies toward self-awareness and insight (8.1), to identify and address personal issues (8.2), build leadership (8.3), utilize personal journaling (8.4) and increase awareness of need for self-care (8.5, 8.6) and ways in which to use music include:

- Music Therapy Training Group
- Music Therapy Group Experience

The personal development necessary to conduct effective clinical work has been an ongoing theme in music therapy education and training, particularly so in European models of music therapy education and training (see Chapter 7). More intensive personal development is particularly important on the graduate level, where students refine levels of insight in order to become primary therapists. The usefulness of the group music therapy experience in expressing and processing personal themes, transference/countertransference has been suggested in the literature (Bruscia, 1998c; Pederson, 2002b; Stephens, 1987) both as a means to create self-awareness for the prospective therapist and to link this self-awareness to clinical practice. Although there may be periods of silence or periods where it is difficult to make music, the opportunity to reflect upon previous as well as the here and now group experiences can pave the way to memorable musical moments that may resolve a difficult verbal issue (Streeter, 2002).

Review of pedagogy techniques for running music therapy training groups is detailed in Chapter 6.

Supervision groups for graduate students (see *Supervision* competencies in this chapter) are related to music therapy training groups insofar as they can reveal transference/countertransference but this is done in relationship to the therapist/client interaction. They hold different levels of structure, depending upon the nature of the training program, and the goals of the experiential group. Some may pose preplanned agendas while others may be completely open-ended. For example, Davies (2002), teaching in the UK, describes the experiential group as one that is unstructured in order to "trust the group to do its own work" (Davies & Greenland, 2002, p. 283), largely a template for free floating improvisation.

Discussion, Personal Development and Professional Role: Multicultural Consideration

Courses in multicultural awareness and its relationship to the practice of music Therapy (8.7, 8.8) include the following:

- Ethical and Multicultural Issues
- Multicultural Perspectives in Music Therapy
- Ethical/legal Issues in Music Therapy and Counseling

The literature on the use of music specific to *client culture and sensitivity to worldviews of culturally different clients* relative to assessment, treatment planning, intervention and evaluation, once sparse in the literature, despite the appearance of a regularly published column by Moreno (1990, 1992a, 1992b, 1993a, 1993b, 1994) and related articles (Moreno, 1988, 1995), is now growing (i.e., Darrow & Molley, 1998; Bright, 1993; Ruud, 1998; Kenny & Stige, 2002; Pavlicevic & Ansdell, 2004), as is the preliminary effort to supervise in terms of these issues (Estrella, 2001).

Stige (2002a) suggests that we consider culture in a broader and more flexible manner, from the vantage point of psychological, biological and social interactions from individual and group perspectives. These considerations invite culturally informed empathy that philosophically extends beyond our conventional definition of multiculturalism, more typically discussed in the music therapy literature as ethnic culturalism.

Although the intention to inculcate cultural awareness in music therapy is clear (Toppozada, 1995; Sloss, 1996) and the relationship between cross-cultural training and cross-cultural empathy has been demonstrated (Valentino, 2006), analysis of 25 randomly selected music therapy training programs (Darrow & Molley, 1998) indicated that education in multicultural awareness is presented through general education and elective coursework as opposed to integration within music therapy models and, further, that professionals, in general (Chase, 2003), and clinical training supervisors, specifically (Young, 2009), although motivated to amend practice in light of multiculturalism, have been ill prepared (Chase, 2003; Young, 2009). The information presented by Young (2009) is particularly interesting because percentages of 104 clinical training supervisor respondents had completed a course in multicultural issues (51%), a course in multicultural music therapy (28.7%) and/or ethnomusicology (42%). Yet they were not consistently addressing multicultural issues with interns.

The integration of multiculturalism and music therapy in university studies can, in part, be approached with practicum opportunities that entail diverse cultures (Dileo, 2000). Gaining the perspective of other cultural norms is critically important as is the use of cultural appropriate music (Brown, 2001). I would suggest that clinical supervision integrate aspects of this very important topic with graduate students.

Discussion, Personal Development and Professional Role: Technology

Evolving technology is prominent in music therapy and, as technology continues to advance, this importance of coursework in this area will become primary in music therapy training.

The application of *technology* in music therapy practice, includes coursework that provides preliminary knowledge that may be transferred to music therapy (8.10):

- Advanced Technology
- Technology, Foundations of Music Production,
- Principles of Multimedia
- Music Technology Methods
- Music Therapy Skills-Technological Applications

The use of *technology* in music therapy has already been briefly described under entry-level competencies in Chapter 2 of this book. Conference abstracts (as well as related references where available) from the Music Technology 2010 Conference Solutions to Challenges: The Interface between Music, Engineering, Special Needs and Neuroscience (June, 2010, London, UK) (http://www.rhn.org.uk/nec_001.asp#cn1) highlight emerging applications related to clinical practice and measurement and evaluation, a few of which I note below:

- Musically Assisted Rehabilitation Systems (MARS), musical instruments activated by movement which can be linked to computer MIDI systems in order to insure a quantitative record of progress (Ramsey, 2010).
- Tracking gestures in order to convert them to sound and further how the generation of that gesture leads to variable movement in the entire body (Lem, Paine, Drummond, 2010).
- Contingent music fitted into a medical pacifier for infants in the Neonatal Intensive Care Unit (Standley, 2010) already in commercial development in the United States.
- Use of "Touch Designer" used to program the interface of movement detection and mapping of movements to drum sounds. (Speth, Seifer, & Mainka, 2010).
- Conversion of EEG waves to music (Trevisan & Jones, 2010).
- Use of Jamboxx, a hardware and software application, allowing for hands-free interaction with a computer so those with disabilities can play hundreds of breath driven musical instructions (Di Cesare, 2010).
- Using a new approach, neurophenomenology (Varela, 1996) to integrate EEG and first person reports of the guided imagery experience (Hunt, 2010).
- Web-based interactive software for children with special needs to active developmentally gauged musical tasks (Vogiatzoglou, Himonides, Ockelford, & Welch, 2010).
- Web-based interactive software for music improvisation, created for children and adults with severe impairments (Oliveros, Miller, Polzin, Hazard, & Siddall, 2010).

Further, the possibility of electroacoustic musical environments (Manzo, 2010) and a computational tool to gather objective data from audio recordings of therapy sessions (Streeter, 2010) will advance clinical intervention and evaluation. There is a recognized need for encouraging and training music therapists in technology (Streeter, 2010; Magee, 2006).

Discussion, Personal Development and Professional Role: Ethics

Coursework related to ethics in music therapy (8.11):

- Music Therapy Ethics
- Professional Ethics in Music Therapy
- Standards and Ethics in Clinical Practice

The need for a Code of Ethics was identified in 1987 (Maranto, 1987). Interestingly, the *NAMT Code of Ethics* was completed in 1988; subsequently the *AMTA Code of Ethics* (http://www.musictherapy.org/ethics.html) was formulated. While all of it is certainly applicable to the profession, graduate students should be particularly cognizant of the following: not engaging outside of one's area of competence, protecting the rights of clients, confidentiality in the course of practice, supervision, teaching and/or research and rigor in ongoing research that has been approved, if subjects are involved, with the appropriate Institutional Review Boards. These matters should be discussed in coursework (Maranto, 1987, 2000) and in supervision.

CONCLUSION

With the growth of masters' degree programs in the United States, it is imperative that we consider how we can best train our advanced practitioners, researchers and prospective educators in the field. My current review of 32 masters level training programs and analysis of coursework reveals that the highest priority in coursework is given to advanced clinical skills and research, followed by lesser priorities in the areas of theory, musical and artistic development, clinical supervision, personal development and professional role and college/university teaching. Current guidelines (AMTA, 2009) suggest that students acquire in-depth knowledge and competence in music therapy *Theory* and *Advanced Clinical Skills* (e.g., through a supervised clinical component) and knowledge and competence in one or more of the following areas: *Research, Musical Development and Personal Growth* and/or *Clinical Administration.* This does not, of course, preclude the possibility of including coursework in supervision and college level teaching on the masters' level as a part of *Advanced Competencies.*

Suggestions about the need to integrate theory with theoretical and applied advanced clinical practice and the need to increase the number of courses which develop clinical music skills and supervisory training and experience have been discussed in this chapter. All discussion following each subcategory of the *Advanced Competencies* reflects on the scope and breadth possible in teaching these skill areas to graduate students.

As we consider the various ways in which we can teach the undergraduate and graduate competencies in the United States, it is important that music therapy pedagogy be viewed in the context of learning theories, our Chapter 5.

Chapter 5

THEORIES OF TEACHING AND LEARNING

The aim of education should be to teach us rather how to think, than what to think—rather to improve our minds, so as to enable us to think for ourselves, than to load the memory with thoughts of other men.

Bill Beattie

INTRODUCTION

Years ago, I had a student who became quite frustrated with my style of lecture and discussion. I have a tendency to ask leading questions in class, questions I feel will help students think critically and incorporate information in their own unique way. His response was: "Why are you always asking us questions? It is your job as the teacher to tell us what we need to know and you are not doing that!" My inner dialogue took off: "Is that really my job as a teacher? I thought my job was to teach a student how to think."

In this chapter, we take a step away from the practicalities of being in the classroom to reflect on teaching and learning theory. Or do we? Perhaps, it is only in the realization that perspectives on teaching embrace realities in the classroom that we can move forward. Which theoretical models of teaching are best suited to music therapy pedagogy and why? What is the developmental path of the college student? How do we teach students how to think? How do learning styles relate to teaching approaches?

In my own perspectives on teaching, I suggest many commonalities between teaching and conducting therapy:

- Students take a developmental path (Perry, 1999) in their capacity to learn. I suggest that this development can be nonlinear, especially in times of stress when students regress to earlier levels.

135

- Students learn in different ways, through different sensory modalities and varieties of instructional activities.
- Students form a group, which has its own dynamic and requires different levels of structure and facilitation from the instructor.
- Teaching may be considered as either linear, moving from one goal to another, and/or both nonlinear, working with the process that evolves in the often unpredictable path of learning.
- In structuring and facilitating a group, the educator has to appreciate different levels, which may be considered on a continuum. I suggest therefore that we are teaching on a continuum of teaching engagement, CTE, appreciating different levels of learning in any one instructional approach.
- Teaching involves methods which should vary based on the needs of the group and take into account the goals of teaching, the level of structure necessary for a particular group and learning through a variety of experiences.
- Teaching balances structured as well as spontaneous or improvisational experiences.
- Teaching may consciously or subconsciously suggest an underlying learning theory or combination of learning theories.
- Teaching involves assessment of how each student is doing.

The understanding of learning theory, learning styles and developmental stages of learning in higher education has been useful to me in understanding music therapy pedagogy. I offer these here in this chapter.

LEARNING THEORIES

Possible frameworks for teaching and learning are sparse in the music therapy literature. My opportunity to serve as a mentor in our Research Academy for University Learning (RAUL) at Montclair State University over the last two years led me to consider the ways in which students take in information and how these align to teaching methods.

With many different approaches to learning, three types of learning theory are discussed: behaviorist, cognitive constructivist and social constructivist. These theories are the basis for much of music therapy pedagogy although literature regarding their use in music therapy is extremely limited.

Behaviorist Theory

Behaviorist theory focuses on objectively observable, quantifiable events and behavior. This is true whether we apply behaviorism to therapy or teaching. Therefore, from the perspective of teaching and learning, the point of education is to present the student with an appropriate repertoire of behavioral responses to specific stimuli and reinforce these responses through effective reinforcement (Skinner, 1976, p. 161). Methods will include consistent repetition of material, small, progressive sequences of tasks, and continuous positive reinforcement. Behaviorist theory explains motivation in terms of positive and negative reinforcement. Instructional methods will rely on skill and drill necessary to reinforce response patterns, open a question and answer framework where questions are progressively more difficult, guide practice and review material. The most immediate reinforcement will be the grade. Exams are favored since they presumably have a "correct" response or easily memorized material.

Discussion, Behaviorist Theory

Behavioral teaching theory is implied in music therapy teaching strategies both in the classroom and out of the classroom. Strategies that implicate behavioral teaching theory are the following: efforts to provide positive or negative reinforcement in terms of feedback on music therapy competencies (Anderson, 1982); self-monitoring in the clinical arena based on positive comments from peers (Prickett, 1987); analysis of attending behavior in response to types of instructional strategies and related structure and reinforcements (Madson & Geringer, 1983); audio-cuing and immediate feedback for supervision purposes while conducting clinical work (Adamek, 1994), use and effect relationships between music and self-disclosure (Jensen, 2001); comparison of videotape-based feedback versus field-based feedback on developing clinical skills (Hanser & Furman, 1980); comparison of self and instructor rating of clinical videotapes (Greenfield, 1978); sequential levels of learning involved in leadership and simulated role-playing activity in class (Standley & Jones, 2008); sequential levels of learning involved in the structure of practicum (Wright,1992; Hanser, 1978) and behavioral contracting for completion of guitar competencies (Gooding, 2009). These strategies have been described in chapters two and three of this book in context of entry level competencies. I consider the break down of instructional information in lecture-discussion, experiential and collaborative learning assignments quite pertinent to behaviorist theory.

Typical strategies found in successful teaching can be related to behaviorism: the scaffolding of information in such a way as to present concepts sequentially, repeating and reinforcing main points and positive reinforcement of student responses.

Cognitive Constructivism

In contrast to behaviorists who consider knowledge as passively absorbed, cognitive constructivists view knowledge as actively constructed by learners. The most influential exponent of this perspective was Piaget who observed and then proposed learning as a dynamic process. As cognitive development (both intellectual and affective) moves towards increasingly complex and stable levels of organization, equilibration takes place through an adaptation process. The student assimilates new information and accommodates that information into existing cognitive structures (Piaget, 1968). Students therefore interpret experience and information in light of existing knowledge, their stage of cognitive development, their cultural background, their personal history, etc. All of these factors play a part in how the student organizes the learning experience and selects and takes in new information. As a means of active discovery, the educator providing appropriate resources and guidance facilitates learning in context of cognitive constructivism. When deciding how to present, sequence and structure new material, educators take into account current information the student already knows. Motivation is intrinsic and successful learning requires personal investment on the part of the student (Perry, 1999, p. 54). While "skill and drill" exercises may still be helpful in memorizing facts, formulae and lists, strategies that aid studies in actively assimilating and accommodating new material are used. This can include asking students to explain new material in their own words, providing study guide questions for structured readings and accommodating new material by providing a clear organizational structure. Many of these techniques are incorporated in lecture-discussion.

Since learning is self-motivated in the cognitivist framework, methods requiring students to self-monitor learning may be indicated. These can include ungraded tests and study questions, learning journals, self-analysis of study habits and guiding the reading of case studies by asking students to seek main themes (i.e., describe the client's challenges, describe the use of the music in remediating those challenges, point out strengths and weaknesses in the approach).

Discussion, Cognitive Constructivism

Active lecture-discussion techniques in small music therapy classes profit from building on what students already know (i.e., a schema) and introducing points of information in reference to learned information so that a student may generalize and transfer this information. In presenting, sequencing and structuring information, it is important to avoid cognitive overload.

Strategies associated with the active lecture-discussion include the appropriate use of questions, including the technique of asking students to rephrase what has already been presented in class lecture in their own words. At home, study guide questions, questions already included in a text or questions to aid reading comprehension and transition from one topic to the next are helpful as is the use of a journal. This can be a reflexive journal used for client, music therapy session and self-evaluative purposes (Goodman, 2007; Barry & O'Callaghan, 2008). It can also be a reading log, which I suggest as a means of monitoring one's comprehension of main ideas and related questions while reading.

Social Constructivism

Social constructivism is a variety of cognitive constructivism emphasizing collaborative learning. This theory was developed by Vygotsky (1978) who argued that learning is first between people (interpsychological) and then inside (intrapsychological) (Vygotsky, 1978, p. 57). While behavioral motivation is primarily extrinsic and cognitive motivation is essentially intrinsic, social constructivism views motivation as both extrinsic and intrinsic. While students are, to some extent, motivated by rewards from the knowledge community, the active construction of knowledge also depends on the student's internal drive to understand and promote learning.

Collaborative learning requires teamwork skills in an optimal group size of 4–5 people. However, more generally, collaborative learning is viewed as a process of peer interaction that is mediated and structured by the educator. Discussions can proceed by instructor presentation of specific concepts, problems or scenarios and be guided by effectively directed questions, introduction and clarification of concepts and information and references to previously learned material. Most teaching techniques subsumed under these perspectives are discussed in Chapter 6 under the category of collaborative discussion.

Discussion, Social Constructivism

Much of music therapy pedagogy relies on collaborative and experiential learning, which exists throughout music therapy classes in small group and dyad discussion formats. In a larger context, this is referred to as active learning, focusing the responsibility of learning on learners (Davis, 2009). Typical collaborative learning formats we use, although not necessarily presented by name, include problem-based learning (Baker, 2007), project-based learning, inquiry learning and case study discussion. Familiar experiential formats include role-playing, group music improvisation scenarios (Gardstrom, 2001), music therapy groups (Pederson, 2002b; Schieby & Pedersen, 1999; Stephens, 1987) and others (Murphy, 2007), all of which are detailed in Chapter 6 of this book.

With small class sizes and teaching dedicated to peer interaction and awareness of group dynamics, collaborative learning within the context of social constructivism is a perfect fit for music therapy pedagogy.

LEARNING TAXONOMIES

Bloom's Taxonomy

The grandfather of educational taxonomies, classification of forms and levels of learning, Bloom's Taxonomy originated in 1956 (Bloom et al., 1956) and has since been interpreted and modified by other theorists (Anderson & Krathwohl, 2001). It includes three domains of learning, cognitive, affective and psychomotor, each of which has its own respective levels or prerequisites. The cognitive domain, the most extensively used and developed is considered as linear, per the following order: Knowledge, Comprehension, Application, Analysis, Synthesis, and Evaluation. I include the taxonomy as a foundation and the possible steppingstone to other taxonomies that followed.

Discussion, Bloom Taxonomy

All of these cognitive processes seem entirely reasonable to us as music therapy educators and it is probable that we achieve them on both the undergraduate and graduate levels. The Bloom taxonomy, at the time it was written, was largely applied to grade school children. Since, it has been applied in other contexts. One example that is helpful for the educator is to consider the taxonomy in regard to the kinds of questions we ask of our students (Davis, 2009): Knowledge (definition questions), Comprehension (explaining concepts), Application (using information in new contexts in order to solve problems or perform tasks), Analysis (breaking concepts down and explaining interrelationships), Synthesis (putting parts together to form a new whole), and Evaluation (use of criteria to make a judgment).

Constructive Alignment

John Biggs, a psychologist, establishes a link between psychological theory and educational practice, by applying the SOLO (Structure of Observed Learning Outcome) taxonomy (Biggs & Collis, 1982), a theoretical succession of learning stages, to a process he calls Constructive Alignment (Biggs, 2003). Simply, Constructive Alignment defines the learning outcome and aligns teaching and assessment for the desired outcome. Biggs describes the following elements of Constructive Alignment:

- Outcome we intend students to learn.
- Align teaching and assessment to those outcomes.
- Outcome statement contains a learning activity, a verb, that students must perform to best achieve the outcome, such as "apply expectancy-value theory of motivation," or "explain the concept, etc."
- Learning is about what the student does.
- Assessment is about how well the student achieves the intended outcomes (note: therefore it is an example of outcomes-based education, OBE).
- The Solo Taxonomy delineates levels of understanding that can be built into the intended learning outcomes and, further, create the assessment criteria or rubrics.

Solo Taxonomy: Stages and Relationship to Constructive Alignment

The SOLO Taxonomy has been theoretically applied to teaching subjects such as history, mathematics, English, geography and modern language (Biggs & Collis, 1982) along with general suggestions for instructional design. Interestingly, Biggs and Collis (1982) suggests a link between the developmental theory of Piaget and learning theory in observing students of higher education.

The stages of SOLO are described below:

1. *Pre-structural Stage:* In this stage of the SOLO taxonomy, students are simply acquiring bits of unconnected information, which have no organization and make no sense. There is no understanding demonstrated and the student's approach involves acquiring disconnected bits of information. The student misses the point.
2. *Unistructural Stage:* In this stage of the SOLO Taxonomy, simple and obvious connections are made, but their significance is not grasped. The student shows concrete, reductive understanding of the topic. Simple and obvious connections are made but broader significance is not understood.
   - Verbs: identify, memorize, do simple procedure
3. *Multistructural Stage:* In this stage of the SOLO Taxonomy, a number of connections may be made, but the meta-connections between them

are missed, as is their significance for the whole. The student can understand several components but the understanding of each remains discreet. A number of connections are made but the significance of the whole is not determined. Ideas and concepts around an issue are disorganized and aren't related together.

- Verbs: enumerate, classify, describe, list, combine, do algorithms

4. *Relational Stage:* In this stage of the SOLO Taxonomy, the student is now able to appreciate the significance of the parts in relation to the whole. The student can indicate connection between facts and theory, action and purpose. The student shows understanding of several components, which are integrated conceptually showing understanding of how the parts contribute to the whole. The student can apply the concept to familiar problems or work situations.

- Verbs: Compare/contrast, explain causes, integrate, analyze, relate, and apply

5. *Extended Abstract Stage:* In this stage of the SOLO taxonomy, the student is making connections not only within the given subject area, but also beyond it, able to generalize and transfer the ideas underlying the specific instance. The student conceptualizes at a level extending beyond what has been dealt with in the actual teaching. Now the understanding is transferable and generalizable to different areas.

- Verbs: theorize, generalize, hypothesize, reflect, generate

Discussion: Constructive Alignment/ SOLO Taxonomy

I present Biggs' theory because of the importance of the *Relational Stage* and the *Extended Abstract Stage* in terms of teaching music therapy. Music therapy concepts are only infrequently linked to memorization skills (*Unistructural*) and while concepts may initially involve identification of behaviors in a case study or observed music therapy session that involves listing, classifying or mere description (*Multistructural*), these skills are primitive in comparison to what needs to follow. The abilities to compare/contrast, explain causes, integrate, analyze, relate, and apply (*Relational*) are integral to the field and the student who fails to achieve this level of thinking really cannot be successful with clinical practice. The *Extended Abstract Stage,* theorizing, generalizing, hypothesizing, reflecting, and generating original ideas, *allows* the novice therapist to adequately put skills to work, both in the clinical arena and, certainly, as a graduate student in writing a thesis or dissertation.

In order for Constructive Alignment to be applied to university learning, I suggest that the educator must be aware of the various levels at which students are taking in information (i.e., Solo Taxonomy) in order to set forth a continuum of outcomes statements and align teaching and assessment (i.e.,

Constructive Alignment) to those outcomes. In other words, be ready to teach at different levels within one instructional activity. Biggs certainly implies this concept by suggesting that the Solo Taxonomy delineate levels of understanding that can be built into the intended learning outcomes and, further, create the assessment criteria or rubrics.

I call this recognition of levels of understanding and aligned teaching and assessment, *Continuum of Teaching Engagement* (CTE). The underlying concept here is that in teaching, there is a range of response levels and the teaching activity must be structured in a way that accommodates all levels. Therefore, if a student has a concrete understanding of the material being discussed, there is an opportunity to begin at that point but move up the ladder to higher response levels so that all levels are modeled for students and eventually mastered. I suspect we all do this subconsciously if not consciously but it may be helpful to consistently start at the lowest level of student ability and work one's way up. At the very worst, this is a review for the student at the highest level of abstracting; at the very best, this is a comfort to the student who does not understand how to perform higher level skills and can watch those skills being modeled by other students.

In the below example, I suggest outcomes statements and my assessment of how various students at different levels of the SOLO taxonomy meet the outcomes statement.

Example, Outcome Statement

My outcome statement is the following: "Using the following case study, *relate* the goals and objectives of the therapist to the methods employed." These are the hypothetical responses of five students in my class:

- Michael tells us that the purpose of the music therapist is to help the client release anger though music; therefore it is necessary for the client to use the drum. I consider this a *unistructural* response since only one or few aspects of the learning outcome are identified. The issue of catharsis of anger constitutes a clinical purpose but it is not described in terms of a clinical goal and/or a specific musical objective. Further the "method" described is not really a method at all procedurally. It has no detail.
- Sharon tells us that the purpose of the music therapist is to decrease episodes of verbal aggression on the ward and, in order to do this, the client will engage in all musical interventions in the session without becoming verbally inappropriate toward other clients. If he wants to,

the client can play the drum to help himself. I consider this a *multi-structural* response because the student has come up with possible goal and objective but it is not appropriately related to the musical intervention and there is no method.

- James tells us that the purpose of the music therapist is to decrease episodes of verbal aggression on the ward. In order to do this, the client will engage in all musical interventions in the session without becoming verbally inappropriate. Methods will include songwriting with opportunity for projective lyrics, grounding role in group drum improvisation and closing yoga postures to music. The client is encouraged to verbally process emotional reactions to peers and leader and, in doing so; the therapist helps him integrate his actions with his feelings. I consider this response *relational* because all elements are integrated.
- Melinda provides information representing the afore-mentioned *relational* approach but she also explores the possibility that the client is projecting feelings through the music resulting in emotional reactions to peers and primary therapist. Although Melinda has not yet learned about transference, she is, perhaps unknowingly, picking up these possible concepts. This is a level I consider *extended abstract.*

Aligned Teaching and Assessment for Outcomes Based Education (OBE)

The aligned learning approach for music therapy here is initially based on cognitive constructivism, where students are charged with a guided reading/writing assignment in connection with a case study. Learning, however, then moves to a social constructivist framework because peer discussion is mediated and structured by the educator. The collaborative (i.e., see social constructivism) learning approach for the defined learning outcome in this example would be problem-based learning (Baker, 2007), a method of teaching whereby the educator serves to facilitate the learning process. A problematic situation (i.e., clinical scenario) is presented. The educator models inquiry and method in solving the problem, coaches and fades, thereby engaging in the process as a co-investigator of sorts and then assessing the learning abilities of the group members. A rubric (i.e., descriptive rating scale) outlining levels of response for the assignment can provide the assessment and be used as a means of self-evaluative learning and/or grading.

DEVELOPMENTAL LEVELS OF ACADEMIC ENGAGEMENT

William Perry: Ethical and Intellectual Development in the College Years

In contrast to the work of Biggs (2003), the studies carried out by Perry, a Professor of English and educational researcher at Harvard in the fifties and sixties, do not constitute theory. However, similar to Biggs, Perry's work suggests developmental levels of academic engagement. Perry conducted a 15-year study of 61 undergraduate college students (1958,1963) from Harvard and Radcliffe. The study is generalized to suggest post-adolescent development in terms of learning and attitude. Given the small, predominantly male and rather homogenous sample of students, there are limitations to the Perry study. However the narrative accounts of developmental transitions in his writing (Perry, 1999) are instructive in identifying adult learning stages. Similar to Biggs, Perry accepts the Piagetian concepts of assimilation and accommodation to transport new information into existing cognitive structure as well as a logical and hierarchical sequence of cognition. However, according to Biggs, gender, race, culture and socioeconomic class influence the approach to learning, ideas that he and Tang elaborate upon (Biggs & Tang, 2007).

According to Perry, whose book was first published in 1968, there are nine developmental positions identified by behavior from college students: (1) *duality* (i.e., *basic; full*), (2) *multiplicity (early; late)*, (3) *relativism (contextual, pre-commitment)*, and (4) *commitment (commitment, challenges to commitment, post-commitment)*. The path from one to the other is sometimes repeated and one can be at different stages at the same time given different subject areas.

In duality, things are right or wrong, true or false, good or bad and teachers, viewed as authority figures, impart right answers. Most students have passed beyond this stage by the time they arrive in the university. Those who have not quickly do so.

Full duality and early and late multiplicity are transitional as students being to develop and recognize the existence of a multiplicity of different points of view at the university but still look for the point of view that the "teachers wants us to learn" (Perry, 1999, p. 121).

Pre-commitment, commitment and challenges to commitment are also transitional as the student recognizes that relative knowledge depends upon a stable point of view in order to provide a feeling of continuity. Commitment to certain points of view, to relationships, to sorts of activities, etc., all compel the student to realize the necessity to find a point of view in a relativistic world. This is accomplished through questioning, reconsidering past beliefs and commitments and developing and expanding upon firm commitments regarding important areas of life and knowledge.

The final position is commitment. Commitment leads to the realization that each person determines his or her own fate and that commitments as well as identity are constantly evolving.

Analysis of the learner characteristics of critical periods within this scheme and degree of teaching structure implied by the Perry scheme (Cornfield &

Knefelkamp, 1979) are very helpful. The critical periods just introduced to you are now summarized below and discussed in regard to music therapy pedagogy.

Dualism (Position 2)

At this stage, the student appreciates a high degree of structure, which can include concrete examples, modeling, experiential learning, the chance to practice skills, and evaluation tasks. The educator should be careful with sequencing and timing of diverse information and create a safe learning environment.

The student is comfortable learning basic information, definitions of words and concepts, parts of the whole, beginning comparison and contrast and learning to explain their answers to questions. The view of the role of the instructor is to give the knowledge to the student as an absolute authority and knower of the truth.

Discussion, Dualism

Students presenting at this level are generally freshman. They may have come from a high school and/or home where learning was rote, where it is inappropriate to question authority, or where there is a high degree of dependency on an authority figures. This can result in feelings of resentment and confusion when they are asked, perhaps for the first time, to think for themselves. In order to help students like this transition to another level of learning development, I initially provide a greater degree of structure in the classroom and in homework.

Relative to music therapy pedagogy, de L'Etoile (2008) suggests that the *dualistic* student can be led toward critical learning skills through engagement in simple argument, solving a problem, making a decision, drawing conclusions from evidence, exploring different perspectives on a given topic and active learning (i.e., case studies, role-playing, self-evaluation projects and class presentations). She suggests that course comments she received as an instructor which focused on clear goals, assignments, expectations and efficient presentation of information might be indicative of *dualistic thinking:* "the students focused on elements of the class that they considered essential to finding the right answer" (de L'Etoile, 2008, p. 111).

Early Multiplicity (Position 3)

At this stage, the student will need structure while learning more diverse and possibly ambiguous information. The student will appreciate clear evaluation guidelines, procedures and assignment instructions although there is a sense of newfound freedom in learning. Peers are a big source of support and there is a comforting mentality insofar as the student thinks that someday we will know it all and the right answer and the right process is out there waiting to be found.

The student is comfortable doing compare-and-contrast tasks and can see multiple perspectives, parts, opinions and evaluations. Basic analytic tasks are possible with the use of supportive evidence. The instructor is viewed as a source of the right way to find knowledge or how to learn. The instructor's role is to model "the way" or process.

Discussion, Early Multiplicity

This seems to be a familiar level for those of us who teach at the undergraduate level. Students appreciate structure as well as freedom and it is our job as educators to balance the two. Since peers are a big source of support, students frequently turn to each other and are encouraged to study together, role-play together, work on assignments in small groups and musically support each other. Students who seem to be at this level are generally sophomores, juniors or first-year graduate students taking prerequisite courses and finding their comfort zone in a new environment, particularly when they are international students.

De L'Etoile suggests that comments she received from sophomore and junior music therapy majors such as "Sometimes it was difficult to know what (instructor) wanted from the assignment. That proved to be frustrating." "Grading should be based on what the student knows, not how the student writes" (de L'Etoile, 2008, p. 12) were characteristic of *multiplicity stage* statements since students were most focused on what was being asked of them as opposed to what and how they actually learned during their course

Late Multiplicity (Position 4)

At this stage, there is a clear enjoyment of diversity and a tendency to balk at structure. Students seek a classroom environment that is free and independent and are comfortable with different types of learning formats.

The student is good at analysis and can do some synthesis as well as critique with positives and negatives with supportive evidence well. The student can relate learning to other issues in other classes or to issues in real life. The student is learning to think in abstractions. The instructor is viewed as a source of the process of thinking. The instructor can model supportive evidence, i.e., good methods of scholarship. On the other hand, the instructor can also be completely discounted.

Discussion, Late Multiplicity

Students at this level are generally juniors, seniors or beginning graduate students. If the student is academically prepared to analyze and critique material in a solid type of fashion, teaching can be extremely enjoyable at this level. On the other hand, problem-based learning through solving clinical scenarios in small groups is suggested for the *multiplicity* student level in order to practice inductive reasoning skill and generalize information. Problem based learning in music therapy uses hypothetical clinical scenarios (Baker, 2007) in order to problem solve, justify and rationalize decisions for music therapy goals and intervention.

As a student transitions from multiplicity to contextual relativism, there is a growing awareness and ability to see that some arguments and opinions supersede others. This process promotes a more sophisticated level of logic and priority, which also paves the way to clinical decision-making.

Contextual Relativism (Positive 5)

At this stage, student enjoys diversity and options until they become a new form of the old Position 3 (*Early multiplicity*) confusion. There is a comfort level in moving across contexts and having the intellectual tools to feel a sense of mastery while seeking aid of the educator as necessary.

The student is able to relate learning in one context to learning in another with some ease and looks for relationships in the learning. Therefore, it is possible to evaluate, conclude, support one's own analysis, synthesize, adapt, modify and expand concepts. There is a fluidity of thought and analysis that also creates a comfort level with abstracting. The instructor is viewed as a source of expertise, an expert-guide-consultant in order to create mutuality of learning. One earns authority through having expertise.

Discussion: Contextual Relativism

Many students arrive at this level as seniors in an undergraduate program and certainly as graduate students. Classroom and clinical endeavors at this level are particularly rewarding as the student has, in effect, earned the ability to feel a sense of mastery and confidence and can truly impact one's perspectives in discussing case studies, reviewing research literature, providing original ways of using music in therapy, glean new connections in theory and practice, etc. This is, in effect, the reward level of college professors.

De L'Etoile considers comments she received from students in the junior and senior year such as "I liked the use of questions and discussion [because] they helped me pay closer attention to the material and challenged me to think" and "It [the repetition of techniques as part of in-class simulations] allows the students an opportunity to fully understand the goal of the techniques" (de L'Etoile, 2008, p. 113) to be at a *relativism* stage. These comments were interpreted as feedback indicating that students were "becoming active makers of meaning and were less concerned with finding the right answer (de L'Etoile, 2008, p. 113). De L'Etoile suggests that student assignments suited to the developmental phase of *commitment* can involve writing and discussion in order to examine more closely commitment and choices (de L'Etoile, 2008).

Developmental Learning Needs (Knefelkamp, 1981)

Concomitant with Perry's proposed levels of ethical and intellectual development is the contribution from Knefelkamp (1981) outlining four developmental instruction variables necessary to accommodate varying developmental learning needs: (1) Structure; (2) Experiential learning; (3) Diversity; and (4) Personalism.

Knefelkamp (1981) suggests a continuum moving from a high to a low degree of *structure,* including some of the following possibilities: explain how the course fits into the curriculum sequence, define terms used in the course, sequence information with tasks of increasing complexity, help student rehearse evaluation tasks, provide supplementary written materials (outlines, directions, assignments, evaluation procedures), provide guidelines for new learning tracks, process the learning, and use examples that relate to issues in student experience.

Along with the sense of structure, the need to provide opportunity for *experiential* learning is an avenue where all students benefit but some students may be more in need of this experience to reaffirm their learning. Experiential opportunities present both inside and outside of the classroom: case studies, role-playing, simulation exercises, interviewing projects, service learning, projects done in teams, design projects, data collection, recording events and reflecting on them, etc.

The need for *diversity* in the classroom can be provided through varied readings, points of view, assignments and learning methods; *diversity* also is a word in reference to the quantity and quality of differences in demands.

Structure, experiential learning and diversity may all contribute to a sense of *personalism* as one takes his/her place in a learning community where it is safe to learn, take risks, dialogue, listen to each other and evaluate ideas and concepts. Knefelkamp (1981) suggests that discussions, assignments that help students connect; instructor availability, feedback enthusiasm and objectivity contribute to fostering a sense of personalism in the class.

Structure, experiential learning, diversity and personalism are all familiar components of the music therapy teaching experience.

LEARNING STYLES

I have already mentioned the concept that, in both therapy and teaching, individuals have different sensory styles and learning styles, which makes it important for us to present different teaching approaches. Several educational models help sensitize us to this reality and, in so doing, supplement the information we have already reviewed on learning theory and developmental needs of the college student.

Types of Learners

Experiential Learning Styles

According to the experiential learning model (Kolb, 1984), student experience typically begins with exposure to a concrete experience (CE), observation of and reflection on that experience (RO) and forming abstract concepts (AC) based upon the reflection which serve as a springboard to testing new concepts also known as active experimentation (AE).

In a philosophical sense, these ideas are built upon the pragmatists, the best known of whom is John Dewey (1933). In a theoretical sense the work is built on field theory and learning (Lewin, 1951). In an applied psychological sense, the ideas are influenced by the work of Rogers, Jung and Piaget. Suffice it to say that experiential learning has a long and distinguished tradition.

Honey and Mumford (1982) describe different types of learners in terms of activist (prefers doing and experiencing, favors concrete experience), reflector (observes and reflects, favors reflective observation), theorist (wants to understand underlying reasons, concepts and relationships, favors abstract conceptualization) and pragmatist (likes to try things to see if they work, favors active experimentation).

Kolb's learning style inventory (Kolb, 1984) describes learners as follows:

- *Converger* (active experimentation- abstract conceptualization): Less concerned with interpersonal aspects of situations, converging learning style shows a preference for technical tasks as opposed to social or interpersonal issues and a strength in finding practical uses for ideas and theories.
- *Accommodator* (active experimentation–concrete experience): the accommodating learning style, "hands-on," appreciates intuition rather than logic. Learners with this style, according to Kolb, may rely on others for information rather than carry out independent analyses. A style that is prevalent where action and initiative is required, those

with accommodating learning style prefer to work in teams. They set targets and try different ways to achieve objectives.

• *Assimilator* (reflective observation-abstract conceptualization): this type of student is more concise and logical, more attracted to information and science careers and prefer to learn with readings, lectures, review of analytical models and having time to think things through.

• *Diverger* (reflective observation-concrete experience): this type of student watches in order to generate multiple perspectives in feeling and watching mode. According to Kolb, this learning style is attributed to people who are imaginative, emotional, like working in groups, listening with an open mind and are good recipients of feedback; they tend to be strong in the arts.

For example, the music therapy student exposure to concrete experience can initially involve observation of a music therapy technique modeled by the instructor of the course or modeled by the clinical supervisor. The resultant reflection and processing of those observations can form the basis for active experimentation on the part of the student, namely role-playing in class, assuming the leadership role in running a music therapy group, etc.

The learning styles described by Kolb (1984) are styles we can ascribe to students in different types of learning situations in music therapy. For our purposes, the model also helps us understand various approaches to learning on the part of students. In general, the style that appears to crop up most frequently is that of Diverger, where the student is deriving the maximum benefit from reflective practice which branches out to feed many possibilities in returning to the concrete experience to solve a problem. Kolb states, "Knowledge results from the combination of grasping experience and transforming it" (Kolb, 1984, p. 41).

While it is useful to keep these typologies in mind, it is probably more realistic for us to expect that we use different aspects of these learner profiles, depending upon the learning task at hand and the way in which the educator facilitates the learning experience. Knowing one's learning style can be helpful in undertaking activities that strengthen other styles.

Sensory Learning Styles

Fleming and Mills (1992), use the acronym VARK (Visual, Aural, Read/write, and Kinesthetic) to suggest four categories of sensory modalities used for learning:

1. *Visual:* information in charts, graphs, flow charts, diagrams, hierarchies (Note: does not include movies, videos or PowerPoint).

2. *Aural/Auditory:* heard or spoken lectures, tutorials, tapes, group discussion, email, cell phones, speaking web chat; in general—sorting things out by speaking as opposed to sorting things out and then speaking.
3. *Read/write:* information displayed as words which would include PowerPoint, the internet, lists, etc.
4. *Kinesthetic:* use of experience and practice through concrete personal experiences, examples, practice or simulation (Fleming & Mills, 1992, pp. 140–141); includes demonstrations, simulations, videos and movies of real things , as well as case studies, practice and applications.

The multimodal nature of life leads us to prefer many modes. There may be a *context specific* mode that I suggest is most relevant to music therapy pedagogy. In that case, I believe it would be kinesthetic. Although this word is associated with physical movement, Fleming and Mills (1992) present it in a broader context, suggesting experiential learning.

DETERMINING THE TYPES OF LEARNERS WE ARE TEACHING

I look around the classroom and students appear to be absorbed in discussion, in participating in role-play, in discussing overlapping clinical concerns, in suggesting readings and repertoire related to clinical work. Evaluative comments representative of different perspectives from both an undergraduate class and a graduate class provide additional information, which I share with you here to summarize thoughts on learning theory and learning styles.

First, I summarize the comments of juniors/seniors and beginning graduate students who appreciate hands-on work in their clinical sites and the opportunity to practice repertoire and technique: "[The strength of this course is] going to the clinical sites and working directly in the field"; "Hands-on experience very helpful in truly learning to do music therapy"; "Opportunities to role-play and learn about what other students are doing in practicum also very informative"; "Emphasis on student-directed activities encourages independent learning"; "We learned a great deal of useful/new repertoire this semester."

Yet other students express a need for more individual attention and talking: [Improvements that would enhance the effectiveness of this course include. . . .] "I wish that we had been encouraged to speak more about the issues that we were encountering on our practicum sites"; "Less role-playing—I felt we had little to no time to process sessions at our sites"; "Smaller class size—I understand money is an issue, but with such a huge class, it is nearly impossible to facilitate discussion in 50 minutes time and who can decide which student's experience is more important to process?" "Working in small groups helps but it would be more beneficial to have the instructor present during the discussions."

In a graduate course on music therapy assessment, comments seemed more homogenous: [Strengths of the course included the following]: "Students are encouraged to think independently and critically about assessment tools, while gaining hands-on experience with tools through role-play"; "There is a lot of independent work. The instructor encourages students to think critically about assessment and share concerns, criticisms or suggestions for improvement to the tools explored. She often asks the practicing clinicians among the students to share their perspectives and experiences, adding to the richness of the course for students whose only clinical experience so far has been practicum"; "Instructor offers constructive criticism focusing on the strengths and weaknesses of the assessment tools explored, creating an environment where students can feel safe role-playing the therapist to gain experience with the tools"; "Readings were very engaging. Role-playing the assessment tools was an excellent way to learn and really understand the course materials"; "Amazing resource for information. She knows everything about and everyone in music therapy and I have learned a great deal from her."

What I glean from these comments, both undergraduate and graduate, related to this chapter, is the following: (1) students are operating from the vantage point of different developmental levels, with some ready to reason and abstract on their own or with peers and others needing a greater degree of structure from the instructor in order to feel emotionally supported in their clinical work and verbal process; (2) students are operating from the vantage point of different learning styles. Some appreciate the hands-on role-play in class which is verbally processed by the instructor and peers and then related to the pre-existing clinical concerns of the students; others are more ego-centric and need to be present in much smaller learning environments than the university is currently supporting and invited, perhaps personally, to present their "story" on how clinical work is going; and (3) I can relate much of the material in this chapter to these two classes and find it helpful for myself as the instructor of the classes.

The learning theory most relevant to both of these classes was social constructivism, since I viewed learning as peer interaction, which I mediated and structured. The practicum seminar presented great challenge due to the size of the class (25), which I was not at liberty to change. The seminar was in tandem with another course, Music Therapy with Children, which presented theoretical material in concert with clinical assignments in practicum. Practicum weeks alternated free discussion (either facilitated by the professor or independently facilitated with each other in small peer supervision groups while I walked around the room to listen in and comment as appropriate) with assigned role-playing in order to insure that each student had the opportunity to share new repertoire and relevant music therapy approaches with the class three times during the semester.

The graduate music therapy assessment class included readings, which were discussed largely in context of role-playing activity of each assessment that had been studied outside of class. The final assignment required each student to conduct an assessment, videorecord it, and present it to the class with relevant discussion regarding related literature, use of the assessment tool, and how it served to provide necessary information about the client.

In terms of Bloom's taxonomy, satisfactory student preparation and ability to process what was done in class would utilize all cognitive skills from the bottom up. *Knowledge* about the clinical population area and *comprehension* of the observed clinical experience, demonstrated by the written log, were necessary in the practicum class in order for students to then *apply* their information through both discussion and/or role-playing. *Analysis* of information learned through discussion and/or role-playing lead to *synthesis* of information and *self-evaluation* of what skills needed to be learned by the student.

Similarly, in the graduate music therapy assessment class, *knowledge* of and *comprehension* of readings and assessment tools equipped students to write sample assessment activities they would *apply* for any given published assessment tool and, as assigned, role-play these assessment activities in the ten-member class. *Analysis* of the role-playing experience as well as related readings led to a *synthesis* of understanding about the ease of and appropriateness of each assessment tool. *Evaluation* of the learning experience was unique to each student's background, interest and capacity for higher-level learning.

Outcome statements for both courses were clearly stated in the syllabus and then broken down for assignments where teaching and assessment were aligned (Biggs, 2003). In terms of the SOLO taxonomy, student discussion appeared to indicate that the majority, in both classes, was at the *relational stage*. In the graduate course, student commentary indicated a consistently higher level, *extended abstract stage,* aided by the presence of practicing clinicians. In cases where students were confused at the *relational stage,* they would often come to office hours in order to discuss concepts they had a tentative understanding of. In many of these cases, the students were learning English as a second language.

Types of learners in these classes were diverse and, in many cases, recognizable from their questions and/or behaviors. Some students wanted to talk, abstract and philosophize more (Reflector); others wanted to be hands-on as soon as possible (Activist, Pragmatist); still others probed for underlying meanings and analytical commentary (Theorist).

Modes of inquiry presented were largely auditory (discussion) and kinesthetic (practice) although the at-home reading, of course, involved visual/reading and writing mode. Final presentations of video in the graduate class were important sources of visual information that everyone in the class found powerful and instructive.

In terms of the undergraduate practicum, developmental positions, based on class comments, appeared to deviate. Some students appeared more dependent on the instructor, implying a level of *early multiplicity*, not trusting their peer supervision unless I was present with their subgroup the entire time. Other students, whose behavior seemed to conform to *late multiplicity*, seemed to appreciate more freedom and independence in the learning environment and were comfortable with different learning formats presented.

In terms of the graduate course, developmental positions were more homogeneous, particularly with the members of the class who had already taken previous courses with me in the graduate program. Newer students deviated between *early multiplicity* and *contextual relativism* while more seasoned student behavior began at *contextual relativism*, able to easily relate learning in one context to learning in another. These students were able to contextualize various assessments relative to each other, consider assessments in contexts outside of the population they were written for and view the instructor as a guide. Since three of the ten students were actively working in the field of music therapy as seasoned clinicians, there was a clear sense of *commitment* on their part, which became contagious for the rest of the class and created a stimulating group dynamic.

CONCLUSION

In this chapter, we have explored various theories of learning (behavioral, social and cognitive constructivism), developmental taxonomies (Perry, 1999; Biggs, 2003) and experiential (Kolb, 1984) and sensory (Fleming & Mills, 1992) learning styles in order to consider how these ideas can help us in our teaching.

How can we apply the theory of this chapter in constructing lectures, collaborative learning, experiential learning, and means of assessment in music therapy pedagogy? We now move on to Chapter 6, "Music Therapy Pedagogy," in order to begin to answer this question.

Chapter 6

MUSIC THERAPY PEDAGOGY

*An education isn't how much you have committed to memory, or
even how much you know. It's being able to differentiate between
what you do know and what you don't.*

Anatole France (1844–1924)

INTRODUCTION

We have a guest speaker today in class, my colleague, Diane Kaufman,
a child psychiatrist who I had the good fortune to meet when I provided grand rounds at the University of Medicine and Dentistry–New Jersey.
She is coming to share the poetry workbook (Kaufman, 2007) she is using
with women at an outpatient substance abuse treatment center; it presents
themes that the women are able to identify with and, as a result of that, write
their own poetry. The students all follow along as Dr. Kaufman reads one of
the poems. I hear the potential music in the words as she reads. I ask the students if we can improvise to the poem. About eight of us quickly form a
musical ensemble: piano, percussion, vocals, and flute. Others listen as we
began to bring the poetry to life–rhythmically, harmonically, and melodi-
cally. It is such a successful experience that several students join Dr. Kaufman
and me for the rest of the semester in order to provide musical improvisation
that emotionally supports the poetry of the clients at the outpatient center.
The miraculous part is the spontaneity of the music, the connection to the
poetry and the transfer to therapy (Kaufman & Goodman, 2009).

As educators begin to organize the vast array of information necessary to
train students, it is ironic that none of us in higher education have ever been
required to study pedagogical technique. What do we know and what do we
have yet to learn? How can we most effectively teach music therapy?

In this chapter, we review selected teaching and evaluation techniques rel-

156

evant to music therapy: Lecture/discussion, collaborative learning, experiential learning and music-centered teaching, all of which relate to theories of learning and learning styles discussed in Chapter 5. Pedagogy approaches are supplemented with suggestions regarding the use of technology and guidelines for reading and writing assignments. Last but not least, we consider how to assess our own teaching, perhaps a fitting end and beginning to the chapter.

ADMISSIONS TO MUSIC THERAPY TRAINING PROGRAMS

Rationale for Choosing to Apply to Music Therapy Programs

Why do people enter the field of music therapy and how do they choose an institution?

AMTA suggests that personal qualifications for becoming a music therapist include "a genuine interest in people and a desire to help others empower themselves. Empathy, patience, creativity, openness to new ideas and understanding of one's self are also important attributes" (AMTA, 2010). Studies confirming these types of attributes as well as other attributes that may be related provide beginning profiles of students.

For example, use of the Myers-Brigg Type Indicator to compare 170 music education majors and 207 music therapy majors, found that both types of majors indicated an overall preference for Extrovert-Intuition-Feeling-Perception type of personality, a personality that is characteristically ingenuous, caring, imaginative, perceptive, supportive, assertive and able to improvise (Steele & Young, 2008). These results are consistent with earlier findings in smaller sample sizes indicating the greatest strength of the music therapist as an altruist (Oppenheim, 1984).

Data concerning the factors for choosing music therapy as a career and selecting an institution is delimited to the undergraduate student in the United States but may be considered in other contexts as well. Factors cited most frequently by 297 respondents (Clark & Kranz, 1996) for attending a given undergraduate academic program included the location (of highest concern); the quality of the music therapy program; the reputation of the faculty, program and institution; the size of the college; the quality of personal interactions; finances and the quality of the music program.

In order of priority, respondents chose music therapy as a career because of their interest in music, their desire to help others, the wish to combine music and helping, an interest in psychology, a personal experience in connection with music therapy and the opportunity for employment. The commitment to learning in music therapy courses has been demonstrated in preferential attitudes for these courses upon entry (Asmus, 1980). On a graduate level, survey responses (Wyatt & Furioso, 2000) of 103 professionals with Masters' degree in music therapy indicated that they sought this education for reasons of professional advancement, eligibility for undergraduate teaching, concurrent completion of equalivalency with master's degree and interests in learning research methods.

Academic Admissions

What types of academic and music admissions are we using to admit students most likely to succeed in music therapy?

Many undergraduate admissions offices in the United States will review both standardized testing scores, high school grade point averages, essays, record of extracurricular activity and recommendations submitted by prospective students. These components create a profile of the student; one aspect of the profile may complement a lesser aspect of the profile. To date, the common denominator has been the standardized aptitude testing score, the SAT, which appears to be lower relative to the grade point average. Clark and Kranz (1996) present data from 297 students from 33 colleges pursuing undergraduate music therapy education who reported a mean SAT of 1034 of 1600 (note: average reported in the United States that year was 902) while the mean high school grade point average, above average, was 3.42.

Further, the propensity for advanced placement courses as well as honors courses in high school and the tremendous variation in academic standards for entering and successfully participating in this type of teaching may provide a confusing picture of the student's actual ability. Hence, it is important for the college to receive advanced placement test scores, with a 4 or a 5 out of 5 indicating mastery of subject matter as opposed to the grade on the transcript.

Why am I discussing the academic admission as well as the admission to the music school? It is because the academic ability, the potential of the student to operate at a cognitively advanced level in terms of reading, writing, analyzing, abstracting, synthesizing, etc., is just as important as being a talented musician. This is the reason we should want to become more involved with the academic review of our students.

In terms of graduate school, some universities in the United States require the Graduate Record Exam as well as the undergraduate transcript and recommendations. Many, however, do not require the GRE. As the quality of the undergraduate experience will vary and, according to *The Chronicle of Higher Education* (Mansfield, 2001), grade inflation is rampant in this generation, the GRE, again, serves as a common denominator.

Auditions

Audition procedures for entrance to most schools of music include performance on one's primary instrument, basic ear-training and sight-singing tests and, on the graduate level, possible remedial placement if the student is not adequately prepared in other aspects of musical training (i.e., theory, history, secondary instruments). In recent years, various music therapy programs throughout the United States, particularly masters programs, have also been including evaluation of vocal, piano, and guitar and improvisation skills. This is valuable information since these skills are so intrinsic to music therapy practice. The audition schedule may also include an interview and include a written essay for review by the music therapy faculty prior to meeting with the prospective candidate. One advantage of reviewing the essay is for cursory, albeit valuable assessment of the prospective student's writing and reasoning ability.

What kinds of interpersonal skills and cognitive skills can we detect in the audition interview? I suggest that we can be aware of basic interpersonal skills: eye contact, staying on task in response to a question, maintaining interpersonal boundaries and appropriate facial expression. Cognitively, we can follow the prospective student's rationale for investigating the field of music therapy, related experience, related reading, and ability to abstract and problem solve questions regarding the potential of music as a therapeutic intervention. In the course of interviewing prospective students, I have found myself in conversations where a prospective student may, in the course of sharing a difficult time and/or struggle in their life related to their wish to become a music therapist, become very emotional. I have responded empathically but candidly, "I understand that must have been [or continues to be] very difficult for you. How do you see this playing a part in how you work with other clients who are engaged with emotional challenges?"

Rather than conducting an interview as a series of cut and dry questions and answers, I suggest that preliminary questions (i.e., What sparked your interest in music therapy? What have you read about music therapy? What background do you have that you feel is related to music therapy? Etc.) can form the basis of a process-oriented interview, which takes shape as the interview develops. A minimum of 20 minutes should be allocated for this type of approach. In order to evaluate nonverbal as well as verbal feedback, I suggest that those students interviewing from a distance be contacted through skype.

Considerations Unique to Music Therapy Admissions

Grocke (1999c), during the 10th World Music Therapy Congress, moderated discussion regarding entry for students with special needs that could potentially affect their ability to become therapists. She proposed the following question on the music therapy application form to the University of Melbourne:

> This course requires that students be accepted for clinical training placement by institutions external to the University. In this situation, the health and safety of patients must be put first, and students are required to declare any medical condition they have which may affect their acceptance for clinical work. Have you ever suffered from or received treatment for a physical or mental illness, which may impact on a clinical training placement? (Grocke, 1999c, p. 354)

This information, now disclosed, can be shared with clinical training supervisors, in order to create an awareness of the student's needs.

However, if the student is challenged with a psychiatric condition, the issues become more complicated: " If the condition is known and disclosed, a careful selection procedure needs to be in place to ensure Duty of Care. If the student has been successfully selected to the course, and subsequently develops a psychotic illness during the training, there needs to be provision for exclusion, or deferral, until the student's condition is not a danger to the Duty of Care provision" (Grocke, 1999c, p. 355). Similarly, faculty within the University of Aalborg program ask, "Have you received any intervention within the healthcare/psychiatric system that may influence your training?" (Grocke, 1999c, p. 355). Students applying to Nordoff-Robbins courses in the UK are required to have a physician's certificate: "This is a stringent and professional training. Do you know of any reason that this person may not be able to complete this training?" The same question is asked upon employment in the UK and in Israel. In Canada, they cannot ask about any illnesses or medication. Based on my understanding of the Americans with Disabilities Act, such questions, in the United States, could be construed as discriminatory. Should a student become emotionally unstable in such a manner that impacts on patient care while participating in a program, handling the situation is described under "advisement" in this chapter.

ADVISEMENT

Academic Advisement

The scope of academic advisement goes beyond helping a student track the course of study.

I still remember when students were lined up outside my door in order to review their schedules so I could sign off on their coursework and send them on their ways to wait in another line to register. With the advent of online registration, that is no longer necessary. Unfortunately, what may happen now is that the student will sign up for courses that are not relevant to the study program or for courses in semesters that are not sequential.

In order to best help a student, I suggest a scheduled meeting at least once during the semester to review the study program. Beyond clarification of and possible development of the educational plan, music therapy students benefit from different kinds of support during stages of their training: strengthening academic skills, comfort with organizational and decision-making skills, relating skill, clinical interests to academics and outside resources, etc. These meetings can become the evolving foundation for the selection of the internship and, subsequently, the search for employment. It is helpful to keep notes on your sessions with students for ethical, professional, legal and practical reasons. I find notes helpful in reminding myself of the content of discussion and helping students with a longer-range trajectory for personal and professional goals.

In addition to students who have declared "special needs" through the on-campus disability center, it is important to pay attention to students who show changes in terms of deteriorating quality of academic work, physical changes in appearance, mood changes, and other indications (i.e., isolation, dependency, direct statements indicating family problems, personal losses, etc.; concern about the student by peers; written notes indicating a sense of hopelessness, etc.).

Mentoring

Have you personally experienced the pleasure of having a mentor? Traditionally the recipient of the mentoring was referred to as the apprentice or protégé. That may still be the kind of relationship that develops between the practicing clinical supervisor and the student.

In terms of the student-faculty mentorship, mentorship refers to a personal relationship and a developmental relationship where a more experienced person helps guide a less experienced person, providing emotional support, assistance with professional development and role-modeling. There is wonderful potential in this type of relationship for the student because the faculty member is inviting professional dialogue that begins, continues through school and may continue beyond school when your former student is now a colleague. It is important, however, to define personal boundaries in this kind of a relationship while you are still teaching the student so that you retain the role of teacher rather than personal friend.

Retention

What makes students change their minds about continuing music therapy studies? What are the statistics of students entering programs versus graduating? If we consider the enrollment data from the AMTA office (Creagan, 2010) for the year AY 08–09, we have an average enrollment of 29 students in 72 programs (range of enrollment from low to high is 9 to 100) offering the 4.5-year undergraduate program. If the average number of students per year is 6.4 and the average number of degrees awarded in a year is 5, there is an attrition of 1.4, or realistically, 1–2 students per year leaving a program.

Graduate statistics indicate an average enrollment of 20 students in 32 programs (range of enrollment from low to high is 3 to 55) taking, on average, 3 years (assuming the majority of students need equivalency courses) to complete. If the average number of students per year is 6.6 and the average number of degrees awarded in a year is 5, there is an attrition of 1.6 or, again, 1–2 students a year leaving the program. So, to put aside all variables for the moment, of which there are many, the average attrition is surprisingly limited.

Education and training in a music therapy program can be emotionally and physically taxing due to demands of academic coursework, the concurrent clinical component and, of course, "challenges to the student's own conceptualization of their work" (Watson, 2005, p. 10). Despite this, students enter their training with realistic expectations and neutral skills self-attributes in evaluating their clinical skills (Gregory, 2009). However, if a student is uncomfortable in assimilating new ideas and feelings, it may be more difficult for an undergraduate student compared to a graduate student to express these feelings (Carter, 2005).

It is important and can be helpful for you as the educator to meet with students and try to sort out levels of discomfort. Sometimes you do not know there is self-doubt; at other times you do. There may also be a sense of contagion in a group of students. When one student leaves the major, others, who had harbored doubts all along, may feel a new sense of permission to now leave as well. In these cases, it might be well to initiate a group dialogue about what constitutes typical self-doubt about commitment to a field and what is atypical. Recalling the developmental stages of learning discussed in Chapter 5 is useful here. Both Biggs (2003) and Perry (1999) remind us that the student does not truly have a sense of integrated understanding and/or commitment until relatively late in the learning process. Therefore, it makes sense to me that if undergraduate students are going to leave a program, they typically do so by the end of the sophomore year, following the first year of practicum. Older, mature graduate students are less likely to leave and when they do so, it is frequently circumstantial (i.e., personal or financial reasons).

What means are necessary to counsel students out of a music therapy program? Discussion related to the issue of counseling students out of the music therapy major took place at the World Congress, 1999 (Grocke, 1999c). Suggestions from Congress participants responding to this issue included the following:

1. Provision of an external examiner halfway through the programs in the United Kingdom.
2. Provision of experiential training in Berlin, Germany in order to expose potential issues and refer the student to treatment.
3. Clinical practice, graded objectively and documented over a period of time, serving as a basis for staying in a program.
4. Continuous assessment of all phases of learning serving as a basis for staying in a program.
5. Specific objective summary of progress at the end of the first and second year for final acceptance into the therapy program.
6. Determining the level of practice that a student may or may not be effective at.

PROGRAM CURRICULUM DESIGN

Overview

As outlined in Chapter 1 of this book, certain percentages of coursework are devoted exclusively to music therapy, with a relatively higher percentage of these in the masters' curriculum. The overall curriculum design of a program is considered in relationship to the goals of the program, with more freedom at the graduate level since content is less defined by the competencies. Further, the nature of the curriculum in the graduate program, presumably building on entry-level competence, will be specific to its particular training emphases and theoretical foundation.

Therefore, while the nature of advanced music therapy courses on the masters' level appears to be quite focused on particular methods, theoretical orientations or clinical areas (see Chapter 4), the undergraduate coursework is responsible for providing foundations in music therapy. How is this best accomplished?

Undergraduate Curriculum Design

Frequently, courses are considered relative to the age of the client(s) (i.e., Music Therapy with Children, Music Therapy with Adults, etc.) or the clinical context (i.e., Music in Special Education, Music Therapy in Psychiatry). Less frequently, courses are considered relative to intervention methods (i.e., Receptive Approaches in Music Therapy, Song-writing in Music Therapy, Improvisation in Music Therapy) or phases of the music therapy process (i.e., Music Therapy Assessment, Music Therapy Treatment Planning, Music Therapy Methods, Music Therapy Evaluation, etc.). Presenting information related to intervention and/or phases of the music therapy process, as I frequently do, is quite instructive; in this way, the student can transfer information across a spectrum of clinical population areas. Folding in review of related clinical research also decreases compartmentalization of information.

The use of music is possible, of course, in any of these courses and is to be encouraged for self-inquiry, experiential exploration of assessment techniques and methods and evaluation.

TEACHING AND EVALUATION TECHNIQUES

Introduction

Throughout this book, we have been alluding to if not directly describing teaching techniques, understandably unable to compartmentalize this information. Therefore, in a sense, this chapter is developmentally progressive for the reader rather than redundant.

Format of Classes

Many music therapy courses are described as didactic and experiential. On the undergraduate level, courses are generally delivered within a 15-week semester format, meeting once or twice a week, 2–3 fifty-minute hours total. On the graduate level, courses are generally delivered once a week for two and a half hours. Some graduate programs provide didactic and experiential training in three-four day intensives; the educator organizing such courses should consider if the information can appropriately be digested in an intensive experience and if the class hours equate to the hours of the traditional weekly meeting time. Still other programs in graduate study deliver information in a hybrid format or a total online format; distance learning is discussed in Chapter 1.

There are no studies in music therapy defining learning outcomes between various learning formats.

Reported Use of Educational Methods in Teaching Music Therapy

Respondents to a survey regarding specific educational or training methods and materials (Maranto & Bruscia, 1988) have cited lecture, discussion, experiential, audiovisual and practicum as the most commonly used methods; readings, musical scores, computers, audiotapes, instruments, lab equipment, film or video were cited as common materials used.

As reviewed in Chapter 3, within the internship, techniques used to supervise students include (Tanguay, 2008), co-leading (95%), live observation (95%), reviewing assignments/projects (95%), case presentation and discussion (73%), practicing/teaching music skills (72%), didactic instruction (70%), facilitating reflective process (66%), experiential music therapy processes (47%), audio/video record review (42%), and role-playing (30%). I previously suggested that these could also be used in practicum and in methods classes.

Educational methods noted in the literature include the use of video recorded feedback to train competencies (Greenfield, 1978, 1980; Madsen, 1979; Alley, 1980, 1982; Hanser & Furman, 1980, Anderson, 1982), experiential methods (Stephens, 1984; Hesser, 1985; Tims, 1989; Scheiby & Pederson, 1999; Milgram-Luterman, 2000; Murphy, 2007), levels of clinical simulation (Standley, 1991), problem-based learning (Baker, 2007), and music-centered improvisation methods (Wigram, 2004; Lee, 2010; Nordoff & Robbins, 2007). In summary, the literature on music therapy pedagogy has been largely behavioral; experiential methods have focused on the music therapy training group experience.

Teaching methods relevant to music therapy, along with evaluative means, are reviewed in this chapter based on limited music therapy literature, pedagogy literature relevant to music therapy and my own suggestions and experiences. As with admissions and advisement, the goals, depth and theoretical orientation(s) of each program will create a context for appropriateness and variety of teaching methodology. However, it is useful to consider use of different styles of pedagogy within a given class in order to keep the attention of the student, avoid information overload and reinforce concepts in a variety of ways.

Teaching possibilities remain limited only by our imaginations and therefore those that do not appear in this chapter will hopefully, in the future, be represented in further writing. For a general text on teaching strategy, *Tools for Teaching* (Davis, 2009) can be useful.

Lecture and Discussion

Traditional teaching involves lecture and discussion and, in this respect, music therapy pedagogy is no exception. Although we associate the word didactic, intending to teach, with the word lecture, both of these words can evoke the image of a pompous instructor striding around the front of a lecture hall talking at the students rather than with them. There could be nothing further from the truth when we are discussing music therapy pedagogy and the concept of active learning.

Formats for Lecture

According to Bain (2004), who conducted a study interviewing over 100 popular professors and their students around the United States, outstanding lectures include five elements:

1. A question or problem.
2. Help for students in adopting the question or problem as their own.
3. Engagement of students in higher order thinking (i.e., applying, analyzing, synthesizing, evaluating).
4. Help for students in constructing a tentative answer or solution.
5. A new question or problem.

Different types of format are necessary depending upon the information you want to present in class. The expository lecture, used to present broad concepts and foundational information, comes closest to incorporating the elements Bain suggests since it treats a single question or problem with a hierarchical organization of major and minor points. The structured lecture begins with a short presentation and then, similarly to the expository lecture, poses a problem, task or questions. However, in this format, students may break into small groups to problem solve, followed by another short lecture before the end of the class to pull together themes or issues.

The format more likely to emerge in music therapy classes is the participatory lecture, in which the educator intersperses one or more activities, in order to shift the students from listeners into participants.

Structuring a Lecture

There is so much to teach in music therapy, many ways to go about presenting information and many interrelationships between concepts. In order to structure a lecture, keep two or three major points in mind, moving from general principles to specific examples, contextualizing new information in terms of what is already known, and providing clinical examples, preferably from your own practice, wherever possible.

Seated in a round so students can comfortably make eye contact with each other and with the instructor, students shape group dynamic through different levels of active engagement. It is important to involve students through-out the learning process by presenting basic points of information, putting this information in context of other information learned, asking questions to supplement basic points, helping students synthesize and posing hypotheti-cal situations so information can be applied. This is commonly referred to as *active learning* as opposed to the teacher doing most of the work and the stu-dents remaining passive (Meyers & Jones, 1993).

The Use of Questions

As a means of active learning, I have already mentioned the possibility of using the Bloom taxonomy (see Chapter 5) as a context for various kinds of questions presented for class. As a student who was given a low grade in deportment in fifth grade for "asking too many questions," I am the first one to ask questions of my students and encourage them to ask questions of each other and me. I have learned, however, that the answers to questions, even as they diverge (i.e., elaborate on a conclusion to reach further implications or synthesis with other ideas) from the subject matter at hand, must be brought back to converge (i.e., invite analysis and integration of existing data) in order to reach considered judgments. It is also important to make sure that students understand the foundational concepts that are involved in a lecture (generally based on assigned readings) before exploring and ex-tending subject matter. Further, it is important to pace classes accordingly so that the class is oriented, students explore and elaborate on concepts that are presented, there is sufficient time to present the information you planned on covering in a given class period and there is a sense of closure.

Davis (2009) suggests the following types of questions, all of which are appropriate for a music therapy lecture:

- *Challenge:* examine assumptions, conclusions and interpretations.
- *Relationships:* compare themes, ideas or issues.
- *Diagnostic:* probe motives.
- *Action:* call for conclusion or action.
- *Cause and effect:* relationships between ideas, actions or events.
- *Extension:* expand discussion.
- *Hypothetical:* pose change in facts or issues.
- *Priority:* identify the most important issue.
- *Summary:* identification of key themes in a given class.

Collaborative Learning

Definition/Rationale

Collaborative learning is an umbrella term for a variety of educational approaches involving joint intellectual effort by students, or students and teachers together (Goodsell, Mather, & Tinto, 1992). Terms generally used under this umbrella include *group work,* a generic term referring to learning accomplished with at least two or more people that involves discussion or problem solving and *cooperative learning,* learning that simultaneously includes interdependency, accountability to each other, interpersonal skills (communication, trust, leadership, decision making, and conflict resolution), face-to-face interaction, and processing (reflecting on how well the team is functioning and how to function even better).

If in music therapy so much of our work relies on strong interpersonal relationships with our clients as well as our colleagues, then what better way to cement this approach then to provide collaborative learning possibilities on a regular basis? Research shows that students often learn better from each other than they do from a teacher (Barkley et al., 2005, pp. 16–20). Group work promotes participation and interaction, fosters a deeper and more active learning process and exposes students to different approaches and ways of thinking, which help, in general, for students to mature, learn from and teach each other. The various purposes of collaborative work can include generating ideas, summarizing main points, assessing levels of skill and understanding, reexamining ideas presented before class meets, reviewing problems (i.e., for exams), processing what is learned at the end of class, generating comments to the instructor on class progress, comparing and contrasting concepts, solving problems and brainstorming. Groups can be formed randomly in order to avoid cliques and interactions with different peers throughout the semester or as selected groups in order to pair students with common interests or shared learning styles. The dyad formation can also be useful for very fast problem-solving assignments; similarly so for 3–4 students who take 10 minutes to discuss their reactions to a reading assignment. Formal group assignments, serving semester-long group projects, may profit from assignment of roles within the group (examples: recorder, reporter to the class, timekeeper, monitor, or facilitator), however, I would say the level of structure is relative to the maturity and degree level of the group. Beginning students profit from a greater degree of structure, structure that includes guidelines about the goal of the assignment, the expected product, and the time allotment before sharing results with the class. A mini-lecture from you that weaves in the comments, products, and ideas of the students in their small groups is also an effective way to close a group work activity.

Suggestions

Collaborative learning can take place both in and out of the classroom. A few suggestions, based on my own experience: (1) Consider if the assignments you are proposing both in and outside of class make sense developmentally for the students in terms of their academic background and their responsibilities in working together as a group; and (2) When using breakout groups in class, be careful to monitor the time necessary for groups to meet in class and complete their given assignments before reporting back to the class as a whole.

Overlap between Collaborative Learning and Experiential Learning

In music therapy pedagogy, there is an overlap between what is construed as collaborative learning and experiential learning, described next in this chapter. I refer to assignments that involve the active experience of doing in order to learn: the use of role-playing in classes, assigning students different case studies in small groups to read, review, discuss and present; dyads practicing improvisation; working together to put on a music therapy play; writing poetry and then accompanying each other, etc.

In addition to the types of learning strategies detailed below, I suggest other collaborative learning assignments in this chapter, which are directly related to reading and writing.

Problem-Based Learning

Probably one of the more familiar collaborative learning and active learning approaches in music therapy, problem-based learning is also described as action-based research. In developing clinical reasoning, Baker (2007) suggests that the integration of theory, evidence-based research (i.e., reading of published studies) and knowledge formed from prior experience are skills called into play. These skills, part and parcel of reflective thinking, critical thinking and problem-solving, therefore represent empirical, interpretive and critical perspectives on the part of the student.

Problem-based learning typically involves presentation of a set of clinical indicators which students use in order to hypothesize on diagnosis and then determine clinical treatment planning. It is pedagogically sound practice to work through an example of problem-based learning as well as present problems of successive difficulty in using this approach (Davis, 2009).

In her adaptation of this approach, Baker (2007) divided her students into small groups and provided them with a clinical case description. Students met for four one-hour time periods to analyze the cases and render music therapy plans (i.e., goals, program plan, interventions, materials, evaluation plan) as well as rationale for the program planning, discussion on the group process and rationale for contraindicating alternative approaches. One student in each group wrote about the areas that were discussed, the operation of the group and shared experiences. The instructor provided written feedback. In order to provide closure, students shared their therapy formulations with the class, role-played at least one intervention and discussed their rationale for their decision-making. Finally, students provided a written narrative about their learning experience (outcomes, group work). Although this particular assignment was used with first year students, it is generally better for students with additional background (Baker, 2007). Further, instructor modeling of problem-based inquiry will be helpful to students.

Jigsaw

In *Jigsaw* (Davis, 2009), each member of a group completes a specific part of an assignment; the group then joins the pieces to form a finished project. In music therapy, for example, each student in a given group presents one part of clinical inquiry, which takes shape as parts form the whole.

In a recent class assignment for the Music and Special Education class at Berklee College of Music, each student was asked to provide the developmental information relevant to various domains for his or her individual client. Working in small groups, students placed this information into a developmental grid (Goodman, 2007). Through this process, they were able to identify subsequent group formations and delineate goals, objectives and methods (Codding, 2010).

Think-Pair-Share

In this collaborative learning assignment, frequently referred to by Bain (2004) in the course of my experiences with the Research Academy for University Learning at Montclair State, the instructor poses a question. Students are given time (30 seconds or one minute) to think of a response. Each student then pairs with another and both discuss their responses to the question. The instructor invites pairs to share their responses with the class as a whole (Barkley et al., 2005; Meyers & Jones, 1993).

Think-pair-square is a variation where students report back to a team or class group of four to six.

Structured Controversy

Structured controversy starts by dividing the class into groups of four. The instructor identifies a controversial topic in the field and gathers material that gives information and background to support a different view of the controversy. Students work with one partner, forming two pairs within the group of four. Each pair takes a different side of the issue. Pairs work outside of class or in class to prepare to advocate and defend their position. The groups of four meet, and each pair takes a turn stating and arguing its position while the other pair listens and takes notes without interrupting. Each pair must have a chance both to listen and take notes and to argue their position. Then all four talk together as a group to learn all sides of the issue. Next, each pair must reverse its position and argue the opposite position from the one it argued before. Lastly the group of four as a whole discusses and synthesizes all the positions to come up with a group report. There may be a class presentation where each group presents its findings (Meyers & Jones, 1993).

Roundtable

In roundtable, students in small groups sit in a circle and respond in turn to a question or problem by stating their ideas aloud as they write them on paper. After the roundtable, students discuss and summarize the ideas generated, and report back to the class (Meyers & Jones, 1993; Bain, 2008).

Thinking-Aloud Paired Problem Solving

Using this exercise, students in pairs take turns thinking through the solution to a problem posed by the instructor. The student that is not the problem-solver takes notes, and then the two students switch roles so that each student gets a chance to be both solver and note-taker. Then they can go into larger teams or back to the class as a whole and report back about the solutions and the process (Barkley et al., 2005).

Experiential Methods

Definition

Experiential learning, the process of making meaning from direct experience (Itin, 1999), is the umbrella term subsuming a number of vital teaching approaches in music therapy training, both at undergraduate and graduate levels. Identified methods (Tims, 1989; Murphy, 2007; Bruscia, 1998c; Pederson, 2002a, 2002b) of experiential learning include demonstrations, laboratory experiences (i.e., practice and experience of music therapy methods presented in class), experiential exercises, and group models (i.e., Music therapy training groups).

Experiential training activities differ depending upon the level of training and the type of training. Tims (1989) suggests that, in teaching therapeutic skills, it is most effective to present the experiential component before the academic component. This makes eminent sense since we are, in effect, stimulating sensory processing on multiple levels when engaging in experiential instructional activity.

As a form of active learning, experiential learning is alluded to in the work of Rogers and discussed by Watson (2005). Watson (2005) emphasizes that learning involves change in self-perception, which is less likely to be resisted when it is safe to process experience, is facilitated when learning is achieved by doing and involves self-initiated learning.

Creating a safe space for learning, as in therapy, is paramount. The ways in which students resolve challenging feelings provoked by experiential learning could (Watson, 2005) include engaging, avoiding, temporizing (postponement of dealing with an issue) or retreating. Learning from mistakes and, as a result of this, questioning and modifying underlying ideas or beliefs, involves a personal learning shift (Watson, 2005), which is more difficult for some students, easier for others. The instructor leading any experiential exercise must be sensitive to and supportive of the emotional limitations of each student, as one would with a client.

Demonstration

The ability of the educator to lead experiential demonstration for students is one that plays a critical role in teaching. Demonstration can take place at any level of teaching and virtually for any subject. Sample demonstrations might include modeling of techniques used with various populations and/or in various theoretical contexts being studied while students role-play (see *role-playing*), The greater the scope and breadth of the educator's clinical experience, the more convincing the modeling of any demonstration will be.

Presentations from Others

It is valuable for students to share in the diverse experiences of visiting professionals. These visits may be, for example, from other music therapists, allied professionals or parents of children with developmental and/or psychiatric challenges profiting from music therapy. Here are two recent examples.

I was teaching a class on rehabilitative methods in music therapy and we were fortunate enough to have a speech language pathologist volunteer her time to share information regarding her Tomatis practice. This presentation was augmented with answers to the many questions posed by students. After the presentation, conversation continued with students engaged in linking these ideas to music therapy.

Every summer I teach Psychology of Exceptional Children and Youth. I host a panel of parents who come in to speak about their experiences in raising their children with special needs. I open with general questions and the parents are generally very effective about facilitating topics of mutual interest with the students. It is always instructive for the students and very real to hear firsthand about the difficulties as well as the pleasures of raising these children.

Role-Playing

Clinical Role-Play

The simulation of clinical situations is a technique that educators in music therapy frequently use. Typically this role-playing that can be authentic or empathic to types of client populations focuses on music therapy interventions. I notice that role-playing subconsciously lends to behaviors on the part of the student that demonstrate not only their own identification with clients but also their own projective feelings once in the "safe" guise of another personality; both of these phenomena can be explored if students are mature enough to consider these possibilities.

Role-playing can include but is not delimited to the following:

- Instructor models use of music therapy approach with peer(s) who act authentically.
- Instructor models use of music therapy approach with peer(s) who "empathize" (Murphy, 2007) or, in effect, role-play population (s) under study.
- Students model use of music therapy approach with peer(s) who act authentically.
- Students model use of music therapy approach with peer(s) who role-play population(s) under study.
- Students form pairs or groups to practice music therapy techniques with each other and report back to class for group discussion (Murphy, 2007). Teacher may or may not observe or participate.

One concept that is eminently useful with role-play is the use of graduated degrees of responsibility in student preparation, simulated intervention and evaluation within the classroom, previously detailed in chapter three of this book. Standley (1991) suggests five levels of responsibility, which present increasingly complex levels of attention to leadership attribute(s) (i.e., eye contact, posture, and facial expression), musical objective(s) with respect to disability label(s) and ability to preplan and plan extemporaneously. Levels four and five are repeated below:

- Multiple nonmusical objectives with groups of varying disability and severity of disability label, specify problems and procedures, select music, select techniques, prepare activities, select data collection (Level Five); evaluate music skills of leader, ability to physically lead group, group response, proportion of group objective achieved according to collected data, degree of individual objectives achieved according to collected data (Level Four).
- Spontaneous demonstration of all competencies learned in Levels one-four through spontaneous (five minutes) planning given session demographics (Level Five).

Further, these classroom simulations may be recorded (Alley, 1982) for the purposes of constructive feedback and closer analysis during playback.

Verbal Role-Play

In order to devote different kinds of focus to verbal skills necessary in music therapy training, it is helpful not only to keep track of how the student uses language with different kinds of "clients" in empathic role-play, but also, to set up experiential situations for this specific purpose. Below I describe supervisory role-play and team-meeting role-play as two examples.

In my graduate assessment class, we spend a portion of each meeting reviewing and discussing various supervision strategies from both counseling and music therapy. Following these discussions, I provide written supervisions scenarios for pairs of students to role-play. I initially model these techniques in order for students to discuss which strategies I utilized and why. Following, the students role-play with each other empathizing with the roles in the scenario.

Chadwick (2010) describes role-playing a team meeting where the music therapist is responsible for presenting information about a client and responding to questions from the rest of the team. These kinds of verbal skills require clear organization and articulation of thoughts as well as the ability to respond to questions in a manner that is affirmative without being defensive.

Experiential Exercises

Experiential learning need not be confined to the classroom. Students may profit from the demonstrations and self-inquiry exercises presented in class to practice on their own outside of class. Such practicing techniques, self-experiences and dyadic peer encounters are noted in the literature (Murphy, 2007). For example, students can practice various music therapy techniques, using self, dyad formation or others as subjects (i.e., relaxation, observation, verbal, music psychotherapy techniques taught in class), logging their experiences. Students can write songs, improvise and create an audio biography reflecting on their experience. Self-inquiry exercises presented by Bruscia (1998c) are presented here.

Experiential Self-Inquiry

Experiential self-inquiry has been conceptualized as a means of uncovering countertransference issues (Bruscia, 1998c). I suggest that these student therapist self-inquiries can also be considered for use on other levels in accordance with supportive and/or reeducative psychotherapy for clients with various needs for self-expression or developmental delays.

Musical Audio Biography

Musical audio biography, "a musical collage of your life" (Bruscia, 1998c, p. 108) is a tape of 5–60 second segments of "sounds and/or music that you associate with various events, periods, people, relationships, or feelings from your past" (Bruscia, 1998c, p. 108) that hold implications for one's work as a therapist.

The process has been modified. For example, Ruud (1997) asked a group of 20 students to record 12–15 pieces of music that were "significant" in their lives along with a ten-page commentary. These were subsequently analyzed based on grounded theory. Relevant dimensions that were related to the audio biographies included the following: (a) music and personal space; (b) music and social space; (c) space of time and place; and (d) transpersonal space.

Life Story Improvisation

Similar to the musical audio biography, Bruscia (1998c) proposes the life story improvisation which suggests that the student create an improvisation to describe each of at least six stages in one's life in which "you had a particular identity, exhibited a certain trait or behavior, lived under specific circumstances, had a particular goal or problem, and so on" (Bruscia, 1998c, p. 109). There are recorded and listened to first in entirety and then in segments; it can also be a vehicle to inspire dance movement. Sharing and processing the recording is recommended.

Family Improvisation

In a family improvisation, musical portraits of each person in the family of origin as well as "any other person who has played a significant role" (Bruscia, 1998c, p. 109) in one's life are recorded. After listening to this recording, the student therapist improvises musical portraits of self in order to demonstrate the nature of relationship with each particular family member. Improvisations can be separately titled and serve to describe the student therapist's "self and object introjects" for possible inclusion in future analysis.

Music Therapy Training Groups

Music therapy training groups are commonly conducted in programs throughout Europe and less commonly in programs throughout the United States. They have been the subject of discussion for many years now (Priestley, 1975; Stephens, 1984; Hesser, 1985; Scheiby & Pederson, 1999; Pederson, 2002b; Streeter, 2002) and may serve as a true music therapy group process for students or, as adapted, a group process that also involves didactic instruction. These various formats are described below.

Intertherap

The concept for a music therapy training group, "intertherap," IMT, originated through analytical music therapy training (Priestley, 1975), a psychoanalytically-based theoretical approach, as an opportunity for engaging in the process of music therapy before proceeding clinical work with clients who had complex psychological pathology. Rationale for IMT is sound if one considers the analytic model wherein "(he/she) has to learn to become more sensitive to and aware of what is going on inside himself (herself) in order to gain more knowledge of what is going on in and with his (her) patient" (Priestley, 1975, p. xi). IMT has been reported on by past participants, (Scheiby & Pederson, 1999; Eschen, 2002) who proceeded to design self-experience tracks at their respective universities in the late seventies and early eighties.

Experiential training in music therapy, ETMT at Aalborg University is incorporated into a five-year program (Pederson, 2002b) and proposes the following student goals:

- Become sensitive and flexible in the establishment of contact and communication through music.
- Explore traumatic blocks and, in so doing, develop insight.
- Develop musical techniques to process transference and countertransference issues.
- Develop musical techniques in order to establish and develop contact with clients at different levels.

In order to achieve these goals, the experiential assignments are as follows:

1. *Year one:* Students assume the client role in group music therapy.
2. *Year two:* Students assume the client role in individual music therapy for the first half of the second year. In the second half of the second year, students, in pairs, observe each other in individual music therapy.
3. *Year three:* Students participate in group therapy where they are role-playing various populations, alternating client and therapist role.
4. *Year four:* Students work with each other as psychodynamic group leaders under direct supervision and work with each other, in intertherapy, taking turns in being the client and the therapist. Students experience the first phase of GIM within an intensive time period.

The format for both group and individual music therapy is based on interactions and improvisation, which may be couched within, identified or not identified musical styles, based on associations and/or express interrelationship experiences and identity in music. Students reporting on the IMT experience at Aalborg, taking on both the client role and the therapist role (Scheiby & Pederson, 1999), profited from a greater sense of personal boundaries, increased ability to focus on and facilitate rather than direct client process, ability to differentiate between client/therapist alliance and friendship, mastery of music therapy approaches, and awareness of and response to transference and countertransference. Reportedly (see Chapter 7) many international programs, particularly those in Europe, incorporate the music therapy group training for students.

Tavistock Model of Experimental Improvisation

The Tavistock method, based on the early work of Bion (1974) at the Tavistock Institute of Human Relations, London, identifies group attributes of dependency, fight/flight and/or pairing and allows members of a group to experience issues of authority, responsibility, boundaries (input, roles, tasks, time), projection, organizational structure and large-group phenomena (Bion, 1974).

In presenting a Tavistock model of experimental improvisation (Murphy, 2007), the instructor can present principles of group improvisation therapy and then provide the class with a prompt to explore improvisationally. Group members elect their own leader and recorder and return to the large group for discussion following each improvisation. Discussion explores relevant principles related to the improvisation (Murphy, 2007).

Adaptive Models of Music Therapy Training Groups

Various adaptations of the music therapy group take place in different training programs abroad and in this country. Tims (1989) suggests that "the most effective pedagogical approach for achieving clinical competence is through experiential learning [where the] student experiences the effects of the music therapy process and has the opportunity to practice its implementation" (Tims, 1989, p. 91). Music therapy groups for students have been alternatively referred to as "music psychotherapy groups (Tims, 1989), with one of the goals being the understanding of transference and counter transference," "parallel groups" (Murphy, 2007), and "music therapy training group" (Goodman, 2010). Instructor practice varies at university with some universities employing fulltime faculty to lead the group while other universities assign an outside person to lead the group.

This process is, by and large, conducted with emphases in the here and now, as discussed by undergraduate (Milgram-Luterman, 2000) and graduate (Stephens, 1984; Tims, 1989) music therapy faculty. The logistics regarding instructional /therapeutic approaches for music therapy training groups have only been broadly described.

Stephens (1987,1983) describes an experiential training group that can be formed at the graduate level and commence throughout the course of one's education and training in conjunction with personal therapy. Various means of music making can be used to explore themes brought up by members of the group.

Murphy (2007) reports on training groups conducted at Temple University where students rotate their own leadership in a music therapy group, each student leading for 45 minutes of the three-hour session. The instructor is observing but not participating. Students log their experiences; student leaders log their experiences as well as self-evaluations, the instructor provides written feedback on all logs and meets with leaders before each session.

One format for training groups is presented at Montclair State University, at the undergraduate and graduate levels. Both full-time faculties, including myself, and visiting specialists, facilitate the training groups. Goals of both courses include the expression and exploration of feelings through use of creative media with particular attention to process so that experiences may be generalized and subsequently used with client groups. Groups meet for two and a half hours and may, on the graduate level, be repeated for credit. What may distinguish our format from other possible formats for training group is the combination of experiential and didactic approaches. When I lead the training group, I use both preplanned and spontaneous creative experiences, primarily using music (receptive and active) but also incorporating movement, art, poetry and drama. Here and now reactions to the creative experiences are processed and redirected into the music in order to extend the expression and provide new levels of insight for both individual and group. Themes that emerge in the group become the basis of ongoing planning for the group. Another possible format is for the instructor to facilitate the group for half the semester and then ask the participants in the group to co-lead a session, one at a time, for subsequent sessions. There are a total of 15 sessions in the semester.

Concurrent with the Montclair State experiential training group sessions is the assignment to read Yalom's text on group therapy (Yalom, 1995). This background reading, along with other suggested articles, make it possible for the student to review their weekly process journals in order to comment on the group dynamics and stages of group process depicted in the ongoing group. The "process journal" is multifaceted. The student is asked to reflect on and transfer experience within several levels:

- Personal experience and reactions in the group.
- Personal experience related to group process and dynamics.
- Understanding how personal experience of group process and dynamics may be transferred to leading a clinical group.

As the instructor, I read and comment on weekly logs as well as final analysis of the group experience. My comments are intended to facilitate awareness of transference and countertransference issues, the use of the music and transfer to overall awareness of group dynamic and implications for clinical work. Grading is based on completion of all assignments and a grade on the final paper.

What are the various interpersonal challenges in leading a music therapy group? Although some express concern that a university is not an appropriate place to be conducting music therapy groups, largely because of personal boundary issues, these concerns have been allayed by the explanation that here and now feelings, expressed verbally and through the music, need not necessarily include personal secrets or content (Tims, 1989) or that those in need of personal therapy can be redirected (Pederson, 2002). I would add some other thoughts concerning this issue. The primary issues, for me, in running the music therapy group are about defining the purpose of the group (i.e., is it therapy and/or educational process?), setting boundaries on the extent of self-disclosure, being sensitive to cliques within the group, and setting guidelines regarding confidentiality. It can also be useful to invite a visiting specialist to run the training group in order to reduce self-consciousness or anxiety on the part of the student in opening up in the group. The challenge for the instructor of this experiential training group, in my experience, is to guide students with various psychological challenges in such a way that they gain self-awareness from the group music therapy experience but are able to carry their various needs beyond the group for personal therapy as necessary. In this way, the training group is very important to one's personal development.

For the most part, students report that experiential training is challenging but rewarding and can lend to growth for self, relationship and spirituality (Milgram-Luterman, 2000). Possible contraindications could include confusion regarding boundaries, insufficient time to process experiences and strain on peer relationships as reported by Murphy (2007).

Psychology of Music Lab

Recent use of what might be referred to generically as psychology of music lab equipment has been notable in advancing self-awareness of one's physiological relationship to music (Miller, 1999) as well as our understanding of the relationship of physiological reactions to music, our understanding of neurological processing of music and, possible implications for clinical work. Some examples of this include the study of theta and alpha EEG synchronization, given a musical template, with respect to verbal learning (Thaut & Pederson, 2003), effects on musical training on the auditory cortex in children (Trainor, Shahin, & Roberts, 2003) and EEG tracking of subjects exposed to trance inducing sound work (Facher & Rittner, 2004). (*Note:* expedited in the Centre for Electropathology, University Witten/Herdecke.) Increasingly sophisticated means of imaging may be possible if universities can connect with medical centers for use of MRI or advanced EEG tracking.

Reading related to physiological reactions to music is noted in increasingly sophisticated publication devoted to psychology of music (Hallam, Cross, & Thaut, 2009) and rhythm, music and the brain (Thaut, 2005).

Our recent development of a psychology of music lab, David Ott Center for Music and Health, at Montclair State University will utilize interactive music sensors for physiological feedback during both active and receptive music experiences, computer hardware for recording and display of data, ipod for music storage and retrieval, somatron for vibroacoustic experiences and a variety of musical instruments for active music making. This lab can be used for both students and clients for clinical work, research and undergraduate and graduate classes such as Biofeedback and Music and Psychology of Music.

Videorecorded Feedback

Much has been written about videorecorded feedback in the practice seminar and during live observation in the clinical setting (Greenfield, 1978; Madsen, 1979; Alley, 1980; Hanser & Furman, 1980; Greenfield, 1980; Alley, 1982; Anderson, 1982) and it has been extensively detailed in Chapter 3 of this book. What about the use of video recordings for other purposes in teaching?

I have been teaching a graduate course on music therapy assessment. The final assignment is for the graduate student to present a videorecorded assessment session for purposes of analysis by both the presenting student and peers in the class. This has proved very worthwhile simply because the more one views the recording, the more information one observes, analyzes and discusses.

Performing Music Therapy Plays

Role-playing has been discussed with respect to brief presentations within the classroom. What about the performance of a music therapy play which is rehearsed over time? Whenever I teach the sophomore level class, I ask the students to organize their authentic roles in putting on Pif-Paf-Poultrie (Nordoff & Robbins, 1969). It is an instructive experience to follow the play with discussion about the therapeutic possibilities of musical drama for many children with challenges, and further, the possibilities of other types of musical drama for other populations.

Field Trips

Although field trips have not been mentioned in music therapy pedagogy, they constitute an opportunity for a small group of students to experience an event together and process it afterwards. Selected examples include student/faculty experiences attending Oliver Sacks' presentation at the New York Academy of Sciences on *Musicophilia: Tales of Music and the Brain* (2007), a chanting workshop with Silvia Nakkach at the Sound Health Studio in New York and "Music Therapy and Disorders of Consciousness: An International Perspective," a conference hosted by Elizabeth Seton Pediatric Center in New York.

There are two levels of process possible for such events. The first level of process is amongst students themselves; the second level of process is amongst students facilitated by the faculty member who has arranged the outing. I recall such a meeting with my students where we left our event to seek out a roadside diner and, while eating our dinner, were able to relate the events we had experienced to our own clinical work. What a lovely memory!

Music-Centered Experiential Approaches

In the Classroom

Ideally, we should be using music in every course we teach. After all, music is our tool. As educators, we serve as models for our students. What better way to help our students feel that music can create a context for any subject we teach in music therapy? This is particularly the case when modeling or role-playing various means of assessment and methods for any population of study or conducting music-based evaluation (Erkkilä, 2007). In this chapter, I focus on suggestions for teaching improvisation.

Improvisation

Within the field of music therapy, improvisation continues to be a key approach used with clients. In general, it is important for students to feel a sense of safety in improvising, understand their own sense of process in improvising and therefore begin to understand how clinical improvisation relates to therapeutic purpose. Both didactic, experiential and collaborative teachings are helpful in these regards. Didactic instruction includes reading, writing analyses and discussion/lecture on major approaches to improvisation within the music therapy literature, most of which are identified by Bruscia (1987c) and continue to be explored in other publications regarding group therapy improvisation (Gardstrom, 2001, 2007), piano improvisation (Lee, 2010; Wigram, 2004) and movement improvisation (Pederson, 2002a).

There are many types of improvisation and while they may be introduced through case materials, their actual exploration must be experiential, based on simulated or real experiences.

Referential and nonreferential examples of free-flowing individual improvisation models include creative music therapy, analytical musical therapy, paraverbal therapy, integrative improvisation therapy, and developmental therapeutic process (Bruscia, 1987c). Structured group models include experimental improvisation therapy, Orff, metaphoric improvisation and musical psychodrama. Practitioners are encouraged to write about how they train in these various improvisation models.

Suggested Guidelines for Learning Simple Improvisation

While the technicalities of advanced improvisation are described by Bruscia (1987c) and often introduced in graduate and post-graduate work, guidelines for learning simple improvisation are best introduced in entry level coursework.

Gardstrom (2001) finds that the ability to attend to sound and music, and use descriptive language in describing music and ability to help clients verbally process the improvisation experience are all key skills for music therapists.

In order to help students attend to sound and music, Gardstrom (2001) suggests listening exercises, starting with silence, to help students attend to environmental sounds and relate them to music. This can be followed by listening exercises where the aural goal is to follow an instrument or voice and then add a visual (i.e., graphic), physical (i.e., movement) component or verbal (i.e., telling a story or describing imagery) component evoked by the instrumental or vocal line.

In order to help students describe music, Gardstrom (2001) asks her students to focus on various elements of recorded or live pieces of music and then describe them; this can be followed by use of one musical element at a time to modify a live melody and discussion of how that change effects the whole.

Further, Gardstrom (2001, pp. 85–86; 2007) suggests open-ended questions, samples of which are related to cognitive, physical, emotional, or social/interpersonal experiences of the music:

1. *Cognitive:* What thoughts ran through your mind as you played music? As you listened?
2. *Physical:* How did your body feel as you played music? Listened?
3. Emotional: What feelings did you experience as you played music? Listened?
4. *Social: Interpersonal:* Which of the other players were you most aware of? Least aware of.

Students are asked to authentically role-play using the open-ended questions as well as other questions related to them in a process-oriented fashion.

I suggest other experiential approaches that have proved useful in teaching improvisation:

- Listening to improvisational sessions (Nordoff & Robbins, 2007; Lee, 1996; Aigen, 2005a) and videos with possible efforts to replicate these in role-playing and then discuss the rationale for the improvisation.

- Having students improvise—with voice, with voice/piano, with non-symphonic instruments, with symphonic instruments, with movement, etc.
- Using a personal journal to help the student keep track of the learning process, related feelings and ideas about theory to practice (Pehk, 1998).
- Attending nonmusic therapy events such as drum circles, chanting workshops, chamber music ensembles that improvise, etc.

I provide some particulars in reference to piano and vocal improvisation.

Piano Improvisation

When we think about teaching piano improvisation for music therapy, we typically associate this pedagogy with Nordoff-Robbins techniques (Nordoff & Robbins, 1977, 2007; Robbins & Robbins, 1998). However, Lee (2010) suggests components and forms related to many kinds of improvisation: baroque, classical, romantic, twentieth century, popular, blues, jazz and music elements unique to international genres (India, Korea, Argentina).

Overriding the importance of being comfortable with different kinds of components and forms of music is the necessity to help the student feel a comfort level at the keyboard, use the voice in conjunction with the piano improvisation and develop the clinical savvy to know which kind of piano improvisation suits clinical purpose. These purposes invite both experiential and collaborative teaching methods.

I suggest the following simple guidelines for teaching piano improvisation along with suggested resources (Lee, 2010; Wigram, 2004; Nordoff & Robbins, 2007, 2008; Ritholz, 2008):

- Establishing a comfort level at the keyboard: Initially, it is important for the student to feel "safe" improvising. Some suggestions for doing so include starting with simple constructions of melodies, rhythms and harmonies that are familiar. Expand to the use of intermediate chords, alternative scales and syncopated rhythms. It is also useful to introduce practice of bitonal scales in order to acclimate the ear to dissonance. Suggest collaborative techniques so students gain more of a comfort level by playing together, antiphonally and then, solo.
- Using the voice in conjunction with the piano improvisation: Get in the habit of modeling the use of the voice while playing the piano. Ask the students to do this as well, even if it means humming or chanting over a simple chord in order to get the self-conscious student to use the

voice. Expand to more demonstrative use of the voice (i.e., making up songs while improvising based on the clinical scenario you are role-playing).

- Develop the clinical savvy to know which kind of piano improvisation suits clinical purpose: Vary the purposes of piano improvisation and have the students keep a journal detailing how piano improvisation is used and their thoughts and feelings in conjunction with these experiences. This can include piano improvisation for movement, piano improvisation for instruments (as was the original momentum in using the drum and cymbal with the piano for Nordoff-Robbins methodology), piano improvisation for voice, piano improvisation for listening, piano improvisation for poetry (Kaufman & Goodman, 2009), piano improvisation in response to spoken imagery, etc.
- What comes first—the chicken or the egg? Do we explore different types of improvisation first and *then* consider them relative to various client needs or do we first consider client needs and then different types of improvisation? I say this depends upon the aptitude of the students. My experience is that the development of musical resources and the comfort level of students at the piano are primary. Thereafter, we explore different uses of improvisation and role-play.

At the graduate level, it is important to pursue the process in greater depth, a process which can include analysis of improvisations (Lee, 2000) in cooperation with a client or, if practicing in class, with a peer.

Vocal Improvisation

Those seeking food for thought in terms of vocal improvisation will do well to read the work of Austin (2009) where concepts regarding the breath, chanting, associative singing, vocal holding and the projective value of songs are discussed.

I recently interviewed Diane Austin on her teaching techniques (Austin, 2010) for vocal improvisation. Austin, who teaches from a developmental perspective, begins with nonsense sounds meant for play and self-enjoyment, rather than communication. This initial playing with sounds leads into games with sounds, the use of vocal holding, and, finally, the use of words, through such vehicles as free associative singing and improvised blues. Although we sometimes hear students, as well as clients, who appear to have trouble finding the pitch, Austin finds that those holding back emotionally will often sound out a pitch flat while those "pushing to be good" (Austin, 2010) will sound out a pitch sharp. To work with students as well as clients requires, as we all know, patience. For students, vocal improvisation "requires courage

... letting go of old frames of reference . . . to go into a place of not know-ing . . . allowing for a space of new ways of being" (Austin, 2010).

I teach vocal improvisation in the context of piano improvisation so stu-dents become comfortable doing both together. I model the ideas before ask-ing the students to try these with me and with each other in dyads. Some ideas I incorporate into my teaching include the use of breathing over sus-tained chords, breathing in response to my voice over relaxation induction (which includes sedative images and entrained use of voice), chanting over sustained chords, scat over moving chords, improvised backdrops to asso-ciative singing between members of the class and, of course, accompanying using a variety of styles while singing repertoire for different age groups, dif-ferent ethic backgrounds and different themes that may represent projective value for populations in clinical practice. All these experiences evoke differ-ent feelings in music therapy students as well as thoughts concerning clinical application. All feelings and ideas can be entered into student logs for process and feedback from the instructor.

Instructional Technology in Music Therapy Pedagogy

The use of technology in music therapy pedagogy is only as limited as the advances we make in the field. Much has been written in Chapters 2 and 4 related to technology and it is suggested that faculty demonstrate, within the context of methods classes and populations being studied, the use of adap-tive instruments, devices that are activated by movement to create sound, methods for transcribing and analyzing data from sessions, methods learned in music technology class (i.e., see Garage Band below as an example) and the opportunity for students to design their own technology for music thera-py purposes. Standard uses of video and audio playback as well as the use of power point is discussed below.

Video/Audio Playback, Music Therapy Documentaries

In reviewing any documentary in music therapy, it is important to help facilitate active viewing with sample questions prior to screening:

- What are the apparent needs of the client(s)?
- How is the music being used (*Note:* be as specific as possible)?
- What is the interpersonal stance between client(s) and therapist?
- What emotional reactions do you have to the footage?

These constitute just a sampling of the critical kinds of thinking that can be nurtured in the student. Similarly so for audio playback, with structural analysis of the music, if possible, on the part of the student. We are fortunate, in recent years, to have more audio playback included in publication and therefore easily available for analysis.

To Power Point or Not?

Power Point is a popular means of transmitting information in lecture/discussion, both in the classroom and in conference presentations. When preparing power point, one suggestion is to limit the number of key topic areas (i.e., five) and, rather than presenting and reading textual material on slides, to use the information as departure points for discussion and active learning. In short, the student should not feel that the power point represents all the notes in a given lecture/discussion but, rather, the elements (i.e., headings /subheadings) of the lecture/discussion. Each one of these elements can be presented visually one at a time in order to invite more focus from the student. Excessive graphics and sounds may detract from the presentation.

I find it useful to install an iMovie in Power Point presentations where clinical footage supports the presentation.

Garage Band et al.

Garage Band, user-friendly software, instructive for beginners and a valuable sketching tool for the more experienced, allows amateur recording artists (i.e., students, clients, faculty) to create and record multi-track audio recordings and/or speech and convert these to MP3 format for easy transmission online (Lautman, 2010). It may be an effective first step in motivating students to learn ProTools or Logic for professional quality recordings.

Participatory Culture

Students are networking amongst themselves and professionals given the popularity of webs and blogs on the Internet. Further encouragement for students as well as organizations of students, nationally and internationally, networking with each other in a way that invites academic purpose (as opposed to distractibility in the classroom) through blogging, skyping, and social networking sites is instructive. These cyber conversations can be centered on common areas of clinical interest and can either occur spontaneously or in context of student assignments.

I also suggest that faculty and clinicians throughout various countries make themselves available via Skype or webcast for interviews related to clinical expertise.

PURPOSES AND TYPES OF READING/WRITING/ PRESENTATION IN MUSIC THERAPY

Reading

Reading scholarly books and articles requires critical or analytical process: breaking down an argument into its constituent parts (premises, hypotheses, conclusions and corollaries, ramifications for other theories or arguments), retracing major stages and turns, evaluating strengths, weaknesses, and validity, and grasping implications (empirical, theoretical, moral, practical, and so forth). If this is what we expect from our students, we may need to provide guidance for readings that are particularly thorny.

Providing strategic questions beforehand is helpful as is the assignment of a reading log, which is turned in on a regular basis and reviewed by the instructor. I do both. Last semester, with a larger class than usual, I advised the students (note: who were working with study guide questions) that I was going to have short 10-minute quizzes just to evaluate their completion and comprehension of the reading. I was surprised that some of them literally begged me to reinstitute the reading log requirement. They actually had grown to enjoy it!

Reading log is simply an account of what the student learned during the reading: main ideas, questions related to reading and reading as connected to other material being covered in class.

Sample strategies for student collaborative work related to reading and writing include peer editing, paired annotations and reciprocal peer questioning (Davis, 2009), detailed below.

Collaborative Strategies

Peer Editing

In peer editing, students are asked to hand in a first draft of a writing assignment. These are photocopied and identified with a number instead of the student's name in order for another student in the class to edit an anonymous paper. It is helpful to give the students oral and written guidelines for editing criteria. After the students edit a paper, each student receives the anonymous feedback from his or her unknown peer editor. (*Note:* it is also possible for the instructor to expedite this process through word documents sent via email.) It is often useful to have a class discussion about how this process worked for everyone.

Paired Annotations

In paired annotations, the teacher or students identify a number of significant articles on a topic. Outside of class, each student individually writes a reflective commentary on one article. In class, students are randomly paired with another student who has written a commentary on the same article. The two partners then read each other's commentaries, comparing key points to their own commentary. Following this, the two students team-write a commentary based on a synthesis of both their papers (Barkley et al., 2005; Meyers & Jones, 1993).

Reciprocal Peer Questioning

In reciprocal peer questioning, the instructor assigns outside class reading on a topic. The instructor asks students to generate a list of two or three thought-provoking questions of their own on the reading. Students bring these lists of self-generated questions to class; they do not need to be able to answer the questions they generate. Students then break into teams of 3–4 where each student poses her questions to the team and the team discusses the reading using the student-generated questions as a guide. The questions of each student are discussed within the team. The team may then report back to the class on some key questions and answers generated.

Considerations in Selection of Course Reading Material

What do we consider when selecting periodical reading and books for courses we are teaching? Grocke (2003a) reminds us that our choice of literature for students is highly influential. In developing their own understanding of "the complexities and ambiguities in music therapy practice" (Grocke, 2003a), assigned readings impact the student and the way(s) in which they may come to practice music therapy. When programs focus on literature that reflects one model of practice, one theoretical orientation and/or literature published in only one country, are they limiting the student perspective? Wosch (2003c) suggests that they indeed may be. I suggest perhaps yes, perhaps no. What is the student seeking in choosing a particular program and how might the assigned reading further or delimit those purposes in training?

I have composed some basic guidelines for selection of reading assignments:

- *Course Objectives:* How does the reading specifically relate to the course objectives?

- *Scholarly:* Is the reading supported by theory and practice as well as related literature review in order to provide convincing information?
- *Multiple Perspectives:* How does the reading present multiple perspectives in order to challenge the student's ability to think critically?
- *Student Background:* How does the reading challenge but not overwhelm the student in terms of the current background information that most students in the class already have? Does the reading level suit the students in terms of vocabulary and clarity?
- *Methods:* If the publication is in the category of methods, does it offer theoretical rationale for the suggestions regarding client approaches? Or does it provide a series of recipe suggestions which do not help the student understand how the approaches or songs suggested were decided upon?
- *Level of Training, Undergraduate and Graduate:* How does the reading suit the beginning student at the undergraduate level versus the more advanced student in graduate coursework?
- *Timeframe:* How much time will you be able to devote to discussing these readings? Is the amount of reading assigned reasonable week-to-week and, overall, for the time period of the course? A good rule of thumb is to estimate 2.5 hours of work (reading, writing) for every hour of credit a student receives for a course (Bain, 2004). With music therapy students, we have to consider additional time spent in applied music students and practicum. If time does not allow the student to read the entire book, it is often reasonable to assign partial readings and consider the overall worth of the book to the student's ongoing library; books in music therapy frequently go in and out of print.
- *Edited Collections:* If the book is edited, do the contributions from different writers lend themselves to a collective voice that represents different perspectives on the themes of the collection? Do the essays avoid redundancy? (*Note:* 85 of the 287 books/monographs published since 1954 are edited, therefore representing 29% of total publication.)

Journal Literature

Key journals in the field, noted in Chapter 7, are published in the United States, Canada, Australia, United Kingdom, Norway, and New Zealand. I remember my reliance on interdisciplinary periodical literature (Eagle & Miniter, 1984) in the areas of psychology of music, neurology, special education, speech language pathology, occupational therapy, psychiatry, psychology, music education, social work and counseling in order to provide related reading for students when I started teaching. These areas and others still represent avenues for interdisciplinary periodical literature, which I suggest, continue to be accessed for our students in order to provide other perspectives on the use of music in therapy.

As we discussed in Chapter 4, bibliographic research provides a glimpse into the history and nature of this literature, most notably Brooks' account (Brooks, 2003) of music therapy journal articles published in the English language, spanning the years 1964–2001. Other useful bibliographic research includes, for example, comparative content analysis spanning defined periods from the *Journal of Music Therapy* (Codding, 1987; Decuir, 1987), *Music Therapy Perspectives, Music Therapy–Journal of the AAMT,* and *The Arts in Psychotherapy* (Wheeler, 1988), 40 years of case studies from *Music Therapy– Journal of the AAMT, Journal of Music Therapy,* and *Music Therapy Perspectives* (Silverman, 2006), four decades of behavioral research design from the *Journal of Music Therapy* (Gregory, 2008), and selected bibliographies on clinical topics such as assessment and evaluation (Sabbatella, 2004) and, now, historical commentary on communication disorders (Galloway, 1975).

Books Published Over the Decades

When I started teaching in 1978, I remember the excitement I shared with my colleagues every time a new book in our field was published. I had only 16 books to choose from in my teaching. Therefore, I relied on a great deal of periodical literature and interdisciplinary literature. Today, I have over 287 books to choose from as well as countless journal articles in the discipline of music therapy.

I have compiled a chronological listing of music therapy literature published in the English language over the last six decades (see Appendix B). This list was compiled by reviewing publisher websites and lists of music therapy holdings in universities here and abroad.

Table 6.1 details the number of books published over the decades as well as the general subject matter of books. I have organized all books into the following categories:

- *Comprehensive:* Books that provide an overview of the field of music therapy or an overview of a subject (i.e., education and training) in music therapy.
- *Assessment:* Books whose sole purpose is to present an assessment tool or provide explanation regarding a number of assessment tools.
- *Methods:* Books that describe music therapy methods, techniques and materials (primarily intended for a particular kind of population in music therapy and may also be based on a particular theoretical orientation).

- *Research:* Books whose sole purpose is to present research utilizing a particular method or methods.
- *Perspectives:* books where the focus is on providing a unique perspective on music therapy or an element of music as it relates to music therapy (i.e., feminist, multicultural, an element of music, etc.).
- *Pragmatic:* Books that provide information useful to writing, editing, fundraising, grant writing, orienting the student to practicum.
- *Supervision:* Books whose sole purpose is to present methods of music therapy assessment and case examples.

I have calculated percentages (rounded off to the hundredths) as follows:

1. Domain percentages relative to the total number of books (287)
2. Decade percentages relative to the total number of books (287).

Table 6.1

Decade	Comprehensive	Assessment	Methods	Research	Perspectives	Pragmatic	Supervision	Total
Total	31 (10.8%)	5 (1.74%)	175 60.97%	22 (7.66%)	41 (14.29%)	11 (3.83%)	2 (.67%)	287
2010–2011	1		4	1	1			7 (2.44%)
2000+	8	3*	71*	10*	26*	6*	2*	126 (43.9%)
1990+	12*	2	50	8	7	1		80 (27.87%)
1980+	7		35	2	6	3		53 (18.46%)
1970+	1		14	1	1			17 (5.92%)
1960+	1		1			1		3 (1.04%)
1950+	1							1 (.35%)

As a result of this preliminary analysis we can see that books published in music therapy have not merely peaked in the last decade but represent 44 percent of the entire publication record. Those numbers with the asterisk * represent the peak of literature in their particular domain. With the exception of comprehensive publications in the 1990s, all domains peaked in the last decade. Expanded publication may be linked to collaborative international networking, expansion of and accessibility to periodic literature, and the growth of publishing houses specializing in music therapy publications (Chadwick, 2010). It is also noted that nearly one-third of books (particularly in the last two decades) in music therapy are edited as opposed to one author voice.

Writing

The nature of writing assignments in music therapy is varied and demanding. Many types of skills are required in composing both expository and creative writing assignments. All of these skills will be important in becoming a successful professional. Beyond composing a specific rubric for evaluation of writing assignments (see *Evaluation of Student Assignments* below), it is helpful to meet with students to assist them with and provide feedback on their writing. If the final product is not satisfactory, an alternative to a low grade can be handing the work back to the student, suggesting a rewrite based on specific feedback and averaging the two grades together for a final grade. The important goal here is to help the student learn and master the art of writing.

Session Plans/Client Logs

The nature of session plans and client logs vary depending upon the requirements in a given practicum or internship as well as the theoretical orientation of the training. Instructors requiring undergraduate students to compose session plans generally suggest that the plan include the following: Goals, Objectives, Methods, Materials and Evaluations (Objective and Subjective), the latter of which may be folded into a student log. Where session plans are precomposed, the nature of the writing is specific and objective. I describe these extensively (Goodman, 2007) in reference to working with children of special needs. Similar formats can be used with other client populations.

Session plans constitute an effort to plan treatment interventions that dovetail with clinical goals. However, in the course of the actual music therapy session, the guiding principle is to follow the clinical needs of the client. This frequently necessitates adapting the session plan or even abandoning it in order to follow through with different methods or interventions that remain in line with client needs. Therefore, it is important to emphasize that session plans are a beginning rather than an end.

Whether or not the instructor requires session plans, client logs help the therapist remember and learn from what has happened in the session. As introduced under *Evaluation,* Chapters 2 and 3, client logs can include both objective and subjective evaluation notes (Goodman, 2007). Objective evaluation notes detail how the client performed relative to the goals that were originally set. The advantage of objective evaluation is in its supposed lack of bias, inference or interpretation. This can also be its disadvantage since the therapist can lose sight of additional anecdotal information that is invaluable in determining why the session went well or did not go well. Hence, we have the subjective evaluation which I have described (Goodman, 2007) as documenting the following:

- Reaction of the therapist to the client(s).
- Therapist interpretation of behavior.
- Issues that the therapist perceives in connection to the progress or lack of progress on the part of the client (s).
- Necessary modifications made in the session that may be considered in subsequent session planning.
- Issues related to client-therapist dynamic (i.e., transference/counter-transference) and/or group dynamics.
- The realization of a link from theory to practice. These factors provide a basis for reflective understanding of the therapeutic process (Goodman, 2007).

In the beginning, it is helpful for the student to write an account of the session and then, in reviewing this writing, italicize or underline those remarks, which form the subjective portion of the log.

It addition to reviewing the log from any given session, it is also helpful to review consecutive logs of individual therapy sessions logged with a single patient as well as logs of clients within group sessions over a period of time. The purpose here might be to "determine which responses are specific or unique to each client and which are characteristic of the therapist as related to clients in general" (Bruscia, 1998c, p. 110).

Case Study Summaries

We are fortunate in our field to have a variety and great number of case studies available for review. They are particularly instructive, when the student reading is guided by specific questions and subsequent written analysis. I typically ask students to track some or all of this information, bring their notes to class and engage in class discussion. Another alternative is to ask students to read and provide critical summaries of case studies and/or relevant music therapy articles. Other instructors I know assign case studies to students for presentation to the class and/or shared discussions with other peers in an assigned group.

I suggest sample questions:

1. What is the reason for referral and/or the apparent needs of the client?
2. How is the therapist using music to help the client with respect to the referral or apparent needs?
3. What is the nature of the interpersonal relationship between therapist and client?
4. What is the theoretical orientation underlying the intervention? Why?
5. How would you describe the process of the session(s) you are reading about?
6. How would you describe the outcomes?
7. What specific questions does this case study bring up for you?

Case Study Applications

In the context of different courses, I ask my students to read case studies that do not include music therapy applications. These include materials such as the case studies from *The Man Who Mistook His Wife for a Hat* (Sacks, 1985) and case studies published by the American Psychiatric Association in conjunction with the latest version of the DSM.

Given these case studies, the assignment is for the student to identify the needs of the client in the case study, speculate about how these needs can be met through music and design preliminary interventions with rationale. In some sense, this is related to problem-based learning, particularly if it is expedited in a group. Generally, the assignments are done independently and we then "compare notes" once back in class.

Papers, Research

Research papers are assigned in context of many types of music therapy classes: methods related to specific areas of practice or particular theoretical approaches, assessment, psychology of music, research, etc. This type of writing typically involves a literature review, an introduction, content, summary and closure. What becomes problematic for many students, particularly those on the undergraduate level, is the logical flow of information which may include comparative analyses, the integration of ideas necessary to form coherent opinions based on reading and summary statements.

It can be helpful for students to create a detailed outline and meet with the instructor to review this. Following, a draft of the paper can be reviewed together.

Clinical Summaries

Clinical summaries vary in format, again based on level of training and type of theoretical orientation. They provide the reader with a clear idea of why a client was referred for therapy, what goals were proposed or evolved, what interventions were used and how these interventions related to progress on the part of the client. Generalities should be avoided unless supported by specific examples from sessions.

Clinical Assessments

Clinical assessments, as with clinical summaries and session notes, deviate in format, based on level of training and theoretical orientation. Assessments typically indicate the reason for referral, the purpose of the assessment, the nature of the assessment tool and process for administering and, finally, the summary judgment and recommendation of the clinician, which is based on examples of what happened in the assessment session (Goodman, 2007).

Journals

The therapist journal is essentially a diary that allows the therapist to reflect on thoughts and feelings related to clinical work or factors affecting clinical work. Bruscia (1998c) suggests that the following material be included: personal reactions to clients, struggles in working with certain clients, feelings about one's approach or competence, events outside of therapy that may be affecting work and patterns in transference or countertransferences (Bruscia, 1998c, p. 111). The notes should be as detailed as possible in order to provide a clear account. However, I suggest that themes and patterns be identified.

I suggest that if the journal is separated from the clinical log, that it be used in conjunction with the log in order to consider how transference/countertransference reactions are impacting on the clinical work.

Literature Reviews

As a student, I actually have fond memories of sitting down in the musty aisles of various libraries and voraciously reading through various tables of contents in relevant journals and books in order to seek information related to my scholarly work. With the variety of databases and full print journal articles today, there is no need to do this in terms of journal literature. However, I have noticed a curious lack of exploration on the part of students and younger colleagues in searching the literature. Certainly, putting key words into search engines is a wonderful way of *beginning* to explore the literature.

But what about all the synonyms or possible words related to different perspectives on a topic we could be missing in entering key words? What about all the content in books that does not show up on the Internet searches? In my experience, students need to be reminded of the ethical and academic importance of conducting a thorough literature review as a part of a scholarly product, both unpublished and published.

In writing the literature review, it is important to read any information that is used in the review, process the information in a way that is personally meaningful and relate it to the primary topic underlying the reason for the literature review. As necessary, put the literature in a context that involves comparing and contrasting it with other sources of information. Delimiting the literature review is important.

Possible broad headings of literature review that might be applicable for a masters thesis or doctoral dissertation that is research based, for example, (Wigram, 2009) would include literature regarding the clinical population; treatment approaches for that population using disciplines most closely related to music therapy; and clinical reports, research studies and/or empirical studies in the therapy field relating to the population and/or the research question for student study.

Masters Thesis

In helping students develop masters thesis, I find it useful to provides guidelines for selecting a topic for development (i.e., quantitative, qualitative, historical, philosophical research; program development; development of music therapy model or theory; grant proposal; case study; original assessment tool, etc.) and executing the thesis and to conduct a thesis seminar. The thesis seminar incorporates review of music therapy theses related to student areas of interest and/or type of project, stimulates thinking regarding possible thesis topics and how these might be related to various formats, reviews effective use of searchable databases and, most importantly, provides a timetable for students to share the development of thesis proposals with each other as a collaborative endeavor. In addition to university thesis guidelines, it is helpful to design music therapy program thesis guidelines.

Ongoing thesis development necessitates regularly scheduled meetings with the student to ensure progress. Students frequently report feeling overwhelmed and in need of support for large scale writing projects of this nature. It is helpful to review portions of the work, use the editing device in Word to send back feedback to the student and support an ongoing conceptual framework for the thesis. In editing, one should be reminded that it is not necessary to correct multiple errors of the same type. The student should be held responsible for proofreading types of errors identified by the instructor.

Doctoral Dissertation

Wigram (2009) writes about mentoring the doctoral student in terms of helping the student understand that one of the primary purposes of writing the dissertation is to train as researcher as opposed to providing a ground-breaking piece of research. He provides more specific and helpful advice regarding the role of the dissertation sponsor also known, in his writing, as the supervisor (Wigram, 2009). The initial proposal includes the research statement and problem formulation, the theoretical framework and practical considerations (Wigram, 2009). Typically, a few drafts are needed in order to rectify problems related to the definition, delimitation and articulation of the research statement/question, a literature review that lacks foundation or is not sufficiently delimited, and/or appropriate methods related to the research question. In terms of your responsibilities as the educator supervising the dissertation, it is important to be realistic about your level of expertise, interest in the study, methodological expertise, time commitment and clinical perspectives (Wigram, 2009).

ASSESSMENT OF STUDENT LEARNING

Approaches in Assessment of Student Learning

Being an educator involves assessment of student learning and students earning grades. Where classes are small, we typically use *standards-referenced grading* where the grade represents the student level of achievement against a specified standard, independent of how other students in the class have performed (Davis, 2009). Standards-referenced grading commonly weights the value of each assignment in order to arrive at a final average. Other approaches can include grading according to achievement of course objectives, norm-referenced approaches (i.e., grading on a curve), self-grading (grade is accompanied by detailed justification based on extent and level of learning, performance on exams and assignments, perceived grasp of material, amount of time spent on course and amount of reading completed) or contract grading. (*Note:* student can choose from a menu of assignments and decide which to do and how much weight each will carry.)

I routinely read articles in *The Chronicle of Higher Education* (i.e., Barreca, 2010) where educators are concerned about grade inflation, for example, "To the B student who thinks he's not a B student" (Barreca, 2010). In order to avoid this scenario, let us try to keep the standards high and the means of evaluation as objective as possible.

Means of Assessment

Possible means of evaluation include quizzes, tests (i.e., written, oral, take-home, open-book, group), paired testing, papers, casework summaries, and portfolios. In terms of music improvisation courses, possible means of evaluation include weekly playing, applied exams, musical compositions, musical arrangements, etc.

Biggs (2003) suggests that aligned teaching demands assessment which is demonstrative of the teaching objectives of any particular course and the level of learning you, as the instructor, are trying to achieve.

Relative to music therapy, I suggest sample types of assessment and the kind of learning these tasks would assess (see Table 6.2). I also suggest that students receive ongoing assessment (assignments and grades which reflect written and verbal feedback and are kept track of through an online grading bulletin board) throughout their courses so there is no big surprise at the end of the class in terms of the grade. Most importantly, ongoing assessment makes it possible for the student, along with you, to identify learning needs and remedies.

Table 6.2 below describes sample assessment tasks and assignments in relationship to the kind(s) of learning being assessed. This is helpful in determining which kind of assessment is conducive to demonstrating levels of learning.

Table 6.2

Assessment Task	Learning Being Assessed
In class essay exam	Rote, question spotting, speed structuring
Take home paper topic	Read widely, interrelate, organize, and apply
Multiple choice or T/F quiz and/or exam	Recognition, strategy comprehension, coverage
Role-playing, Leading	Music skills, interpersonal skills, theory to practice
Class presentation	Communication skills, analysis, integration and synthesis
Problem-based learning	Group work skills, analysis, theory to practice
Reflective journal/summary	Reflection, application, sense of relevance
Client Logs	Reflection, interpretation, analysis, synthesis, theory to practice
Session Plans	Organization, relevance, co-relationships, theory to practice
Research Proposal	Definition of problem, relevance, organization, contextualize problem, defining interrelationships between problem, literature review, methods
Portfolio	Reflection, creativity, unintended outcomes

Use of a Rubric

Wherever and whenever you can provide a rubric and/or clear expectations for the basis of your evaluation, you will be helping yourself and the student in the evaluation process. A rubric outlines the components of an assignment and details definitions of performance levels for each component (Davis, 2009). I have used rubrics for music assignments as well as oral and written presentations. Within a table format, the components along with performance criteria (i.e., Developing, Competent, Exemplary) are indicated. It may be helpful for you to think of a rubric as a specific descriptive rating scale for each element you are looking for in the assessment. See Table 6.3, p. 201, as an example of selected and modified components of discussion performance in a undergraduate upper level or graduate seminar (Carnegie Mellon University, 2010).

The rubric and/or descriptive criteria for mastery of any assignment should be included in the syllabus, handed out separately or be posted to Blackboard. The syllabus should be as specific as possible in terms of requirements and policies (i.e., class attendance, late papers, assignments, grading policies and so forth) so as not to invite confusion.

INSTRUCTOR ASSESSMENT AND SELF-ASSESSMENT

The Role of Student Evaluations

Student evaluations are used in the evaluation of faculty applying for academic reappointment, tenure and promotion. The larger purpose of these, however, is to provide instructive feedback for you as the educator. Do they?

At Montclair State, we have an online system where students can anonymously fill out both objective and subjective forms that are eventually decoded and distributed, via email, back to faculty and chairs. It is helpful to look at the nature of the questions being asked to students and consider the answers on different levels:

1. What are the overall averages in response to rating scale numbers for each area of teaching focus?
2. How do these averages compare to related comments?
3. Are there any themes, positive, negative or neutral that you can identify in the remarks that are helpful to you as an educator?
4. What is the academic and developmental (Perry, 1999) level of the students and what relationship might this have to the evaluative feedback?

5. If you were filling out the questionnaire as a self-assessment, how would you rate yourself?

Table 6.3

Component	Exemplary	Competent	Developing	Not Acceptable
Reading	Oral contributions demonstrate reading and comprehension, familiarity with main ideas, supporting evidence and secondary points. Student is prepared with questions and critiques of readings.	Oral contributions demonstrate reading and comprehension, a grasp of main ideas and evidence but interpretations are questionable. Comes prepared with questions.	Comments often indicate that student did not read or think carefully about the readings, misunderstood or forgot many points. Contributions suggest inconsistent commitment to preparation.	Student is either unable to understand and interpret the reading or is unprepared, as demonstrated by obvious errors, inability to answer basic questions or contribute to discussion.
Listening	Active attending demonstrated by building on, clarifying or responding to class comments. Reminds the group of comments made by someone earlier that remain pertinent.	Takes steps to check comprehension by asking for clarification, questioning and making connections to earlier comments. Responsive to ideas and questions from peers.	Does not listen consistently as evidenced by repetition of comments or questions or non-sequitors.	Repetition of comments and questions, non-sequiturs, and off-task behaviors reflect failure to listen.
Reasoning	Reasonable arguments or positions are supported with evidence from readings and deepen inquiry by going beyond text, recognizing implications and extensions.	Arguments or positions are reasonable and generally are supported by evidence from readings. They contribute to group under-standing of material and concepts.	Contributions based on opinion or unclear views as opposed to reasoned arguments or positions based on reading.	Comments are illogical or without substantiation. Difficult to follow.

One issue with end-of-the-semester evaluations is that they arrive at the end of the semester. The university does not typically expedite intermediate evaluation; you would have to request this independently. If students want to provide feedback anonymously, you can set up a questionnaire on Survey Monkey or ask for typed feedback that is printed out and put in a suggestion box (Davis, 2009). Meaningful feedback for the instructor includes, for example, specific examples related to judgment calls, alternatives and preferences with rationale and positive and negative comments.

On the flip side, some educators (Dowling, 2000) consider student evaluations a popularity contest or a response from a student who is disappointed that they have not received the "product" they (or their parents) paid for. I find this to be the case in classes where the student is not a major as opposed to music therapy classes where students are, for the most part, truly invested in their learning.

Dowling (2000), a senior Professor of English at Rutgers University, writes:

> Anyone of my generation, educated before there were student evaluations, will remember one or two professors who changed our lives. Most often, they weren't "popular". They were the ones who pushed us, drove us, demanded more of us than we thought we had to give. In the age of teaching evaluation as an end-of-term popularity contest, that kind of teaching has all but disappeared. The results, such as dumbed-down instruction and runaway grade inflation, are visible everywhere in American higher education. . . . [There is] a still deeper problem about teaching evaluations. We live in an advertising-saturated society in which young people are invited to imagine everything in their lives in terms of a "consumer model": you pay your money, the university provides the product. . . . In reality, learning philosophy or physics or Greek is an *activity* (a process of inward development). It's much more like training for a marathon or learning to play the violin than buying a Chevrolet or going to the dentist. It's something you can only do yourself, with the guidance of the teacher and within the framework of the curriculum. (Dowling, 2000)

The sentiment in the last sentence conveys the spirit of industry and empowerment that we all encourage for our students.

Self-Evaluation

If you truly are interested in self-evaluation of your teaching, try video-recording one or more of your classes. You can view it by yourself, with a peer or with a member of your university's teaching support system (i.e., At Montclair State University we have a Research Academy for University Learning). Various faculties from research universities report (Davis, 2009) that the following categories of self-analysis (Davis, 2009, pp. 475–477) are instructive:

- Opening, Organization, Closing
- Voice, Pace and Eye Contact
- Clarity of Explanations and Student Understanding
- Questioning Skills
- Student Interest and Participation
- Classroom Dynamic
- Discussion
- Use of Physical Space

WHAT ABOUT GROUP PROCESS?

I can hardly close a chapter on music therapy pedagogy without mention of group process in our classes. We teach a subject which invites questioning, self-disclosure, shared music making and the development of self-insight. Typically, students may travel through several courses as a group and group dynamic may be unique and intensive. From my experience, students form a music therapy community within departments. I find that most aspects of the dynamic are positive: students are sharing, empathizing and supporting each other both in and out of class. However, the intense nature of the learning may also invite remarks or levels of self-disclosure that can be unsettling. Where there are heated remarks in class, you, as the instructor can defuse the remarks or make use of the group to problem solve by stopping the discussion, asking students to write about the incident and asking pairs to exchange their points of view before restarting discussion. Another alternative is to have students focus on group dynamics and how the group wants to work, giving students a chance to learn that they can handle difficult discussions on their own (Davis, 2009). It is instructive for students to be aware of their classes as groups with changing dynamics and roles.

CONCLUSION

The mix of lecture-discussion, experiential, collaborative and music-based instruction makes our discipline one that is challenging but quite enjoyable to teach. This chapter has provided many specific suggestions for the presentation of information as well as guidelines for reading, writing and music-based assignments. A unique analysis of six decades of music therapy books in the English language is presented as a resource for you.

In our efforts to share our academic experiences around the world and gain additional perspectives on teaching and learning music therapy, we now turn to our last chapter, "Around the Globe."

Chapter 7

AROUND THE GLOBE

The test and use of a man's education is that
he finds pleasure in the exercise of his mind.

Carl Barzun

INTRODUCTION

Oxford, UK, July 2001. The night has come. We gather together for our first dinner in the great hall at Keble College. Then we go out in the cool summer darkness under a white tent with small cloth-covered tables and chairs. Wine flows. Ivy climbs the walls of the ancient bricks. People stroll around and chat. It is all very congenial. I meet colleagues whose work I have read. They are from Italy, England, Scotland, Israel, Australia and my own country, the United States. Before tonight I had only met these international colleagues through written words. Yet somehow they seem familiar. We talk and I feel like we have met before. What is it?

Many of us chant in a large circle holding hands. Then, we feel even a greater sense of community. The next evening as the sun goes down, I go to my small dormitory room and hear the voices of Eventide in the chapel beneath me. They are the voices of my colleagues, joining together in song.

In this chapter, we take a look at international organizations and education and training models in each of 30 countries outside of the United States. Information has been organized from published historical notes, the most recent information available from VOICES, private email and university websites. As university information changes frequently, I suggest that those wishing to confirm information contact each program individually and also be aware that curriculum and degree structures in other countries vary from the United States, as further detailed in this chapter.

For each country cited, I include (wherever possible) the following:

- Brief historical overviews of music therapy in the country.
- National music therapy organizations and credentialing processes.
- Government regulation of music therapy.
- Economic concerns affecting the creation and stability of clinical practice.
- Regulation of higher education in the European Union.
- Trends in theoretical underpinnings and research.

Why is all of this related to education? The answer may be simple. Education is not created in a vacuum; it is created in conjunction with all the economic sociopolitical tumult of society here and abroad.

OVERVIEW TO INTERNATIONAL TRAINING

In 1987, clinical training was cited in nine countries (Bruscia, 1987). Today, we can cite thirty. We see music therapy practiced across all continents of the world. In 2003, the estimate of the number of practicing music therapists was 5,800 in Europe, 3,200 in South America, 930 in the Pacific and 4,600 in North America (Grocke, 2003b). Let's estimate 15,000 (Grocke, 2003b). Today, I expect that this number is similar or higher. As the profession of music therapy spreads internationally, we have become a global community, sharing the excitement of clinical training concepts with clinicians and educators from a plethora of cultural backgrounds and interests. My own opportunity to attend, participate and present at the last four world congresses has convinced me of this.

We are fortunate to have access to journals throughout the world, including the following: The *Journal of Music Therapy, Music Therapy Perspectives, The Nordic Journal, The Canadian Journal of Music Therapy, The Australian Journal of Music Therapy,* the *British Journal of Music Therapy, The New Zealand Journal of Music Therapy, International Latin-American Journal of Music Therapy, European Music Journal, Music Perception, Psychology of Music, International Journal of Arts Medicine,* the *Journal of Music Therapy, The Arts in Psychotherapy. International Journal of Arts in Psychotherapy,* and the *International Journal of Arts Medicine.* Further, we can share information from *related* research journals, proceedings of international congresses, links to music therapy organizations throughout the world, music therapy research sites, information regarding international study, the online forum of VOICES (http://www.voices.no/_), Music Therapy World (http://musictherapyworld.net/), World Federation of Music Therapy (http://www.wfmt.info/WFMT/Home.html_) and other related internet sites, joining each other in dialogue and experience, only to be continued through email, skype, and, of course, in person meeting opportunities.

International Organizations

From the first Music Therapy Congress held in 1974 to our thirteenth, scheduled for July 2011 in Seoul, Korea, we travel the world. This travel, as well as the wealth of Internet resources, has resulted in the formation of a strong international community.

Chief among organizations that have forged the way are the World Federation of Music Therapy, WFMT, and the European Music Therapy Confederation, EMTC. WFMT, founded in 1985 in Genoa, Italy, has officers, commissioners and regional liaisons in Africa, Argentina, Australia, Brazil, Canada, China, Finland, India, Ireland, Korea, Spain, UAE and the USA. Interestingly, the WFMT, within the constitution (revised 2005, http://www.musictherapyworld.de/modules/wfmt/od_const.htm), includes the following purpose: "To establish and maintain guidelines for the education and training of music therapists." Guidelines formulated in 1999 and included in this chapter are the most recent.

The European Music Therapy Confederation was founded in 1990. In May of 2004, the EMTC achieved status, according to Belgian law, as a nonprofit, international, professional organization with statutes, bylaws, and ethical code. Core boards as well as three vice presidents who represent south, middle and northern Europe currently manage it. Membership to date includes 26 countries: Austria, Belgium, Bulgaria, Denmark, Estonia, Finland, France, Germany, Greece, Hungary, Iceland, Italy, Latvia, Lithuania, Luxemburg, Netherlands, Norway, Poland, Portugal, San Marino, Spain, Sweden, Switzerland, UK, Yugoslavia, and Israel (nonvoting member). Conferences are held every three years.

The primary charge related to education and training in music therapy is for the EMTC to set up a European Music Therapy Register linked to the higher education standards of bachelor and master level qualification, as required by the European Congress, following the Bologna Treaty of 1999. The primary purpose of the Bologna Treaty which led to the creation of the European Higher Education Area is to make academic degree standards more comparable and compatible throughout Europe, thereby creating a common educational currency, while overseeing quality assurance standards. Currently, 46 countries are voluntarily participating in this initiative; 27 are members of the European Union. The decade-old installation of new standards suggests 180–240 ECTS (European Credit and Transfer Accumulation System) for the Bachelors degree (3 years) and 90–120 ECTS credits for a Masters degree (2 years). There is no range at this time recommended for a doctoral degree (typically 3 years). One academic year corresponds to 60 ECTS credits, equivalent to 1500-1800 hours of study, closer to North American and Japanese systems of education. One link that I suggest sum-

marizes this information. http://www.coe.int/t/dg4/highereducation/EHEA
2010/BolognaPedestrians_en.asp

Programmatic Guidelines from the
World Federation for Music Therapy

The 1999 guidelines include the following, to be applied within the context of the culture of the country:

- The practice of music therapy requires intensive study and supervised clinical training through an institution of higher education over an extended period of time.
- To include musical skills and knowledge, biological, psychology and social studies, music therapy knowledge and skills.
- Clinical training to include supervised field experience in various areas of music therapy.
- General or specialized program options.
- General program to cover active and receptive methods of music therapy, applications of music therapy with a wide variety of populations and in various settings, difference philosophical and theoretical orientation, ethical principles and research and existing models of music therapy practice.
- A specialized program may focus on one or more specific models or orientations.
- The program should promote student personal growth and professional development and may be basic or advanced depending upon depth and breadth of training, system of education, standards of practice and credential or qualification granted to the graduate. The most appropriate level may be determined, in part, by the educational system of the country.
- The program will have a set curriculum, include required reading, be offered on a regular basis, require the assessment and evaluation of student work, be recognized in the country by an appropriate professional organization or government agency and be periodically evaluated for quality of teaching.
- The program should stipulate criteria for selection of students, a selection based on assessment of music skill, academic qualification and suitable personal qualities.
- An appropriately educated and trained music therapist who has substantial clinical experience should teach the music therapy program. Similarly so for clinical training supervisors.

- The training institution should provide and maintain appropriate academic and technological resources.

These guidelines are generically sound and it may be a matter of debate as to whether or not WFMT should set forth more specific guidelines. Differences in the degree issued, the theoretical nature of coursework, the number of supervised clinical hours and entry requirements, for example, may rest on variables specific to history, culture and overarching government regulation. However, given the goal of a European Music Therapy Register and changes in programming as a result of the Bologna Treaty (1999), guidelines could conceivably become more specific, enabling more transfer possibilities in music therapy programs around the world. As we move forward in discussing education and training around the globe, it is incumbent upon us to engage in dialogue that continues to move the profession forward while preserving a sense of individualism in programming.

MUSIC THERAPY IN ARGENTINA

History

As one of the founding members of the World Federation of Music Therapy (Wagner, 2010), Argentina has played a major role in music therapy, not only in Latin America, but also throughout the world. As the home of both the second and the twelfth World Congress of Music Therapy, Buenos Aires, the capitol of Argentina, has achieved recognition as a city for well-established training programs open to students from all over the country as well as students from different parts of the world. Argentina, also a member of the Latin American Committee of Music Therapy (CLAM), organizes, along with other music therapy association in South American, music therapy courses, workshops, seminars, symposia and congresses (Wagner, 2010).

A celebrated music educator, Professor Nardelli, invited to join the interdisciplinary team of an important hospital for children with psychiatric and disabling conditions in Buenos Aires, started the first specialized training course for music educators in 1949 (Wagner, 2010). Psychiatrists and neurologists with musical training, stimulated by the possibilities of sound-musical interactions, the possibilities of accessing unconscious aspects of intrapsychic dynamics, overcoming defense mechanisms and achieving nonverbal and pre-verbal learning related to the patient's musical potential and communication challenges, joined Professor Nardelli and other music educators in promoting music therapy (Wagner, 2010).

The formation of the Argentinean Association of Music Therapy (ASAM), in 1966, served to actively support the development of training programs in Argentina (Wagner, 2010). The first of these was the training program at the Universidad del Salvador, Buenos Aires, which currently grants the bachelor degree as well as an intermediate diploma in preventive music therapy (Wagner, 2010). This program was founded in 1966 and directed until 1983 by Dr. Rolando Benenzon, the pioneering psychiatrist, musician and composer responsible for formulating music therapy theory, known as Plurimodal, in Argentina.

Dr. Benenzon went on to assume the role as supervisor of music therapists' training schools: Brazilian Conservatory of Music in Rio de Janeiro, Brazil; Marcelo Tupinamba Faculdade de Sao Paulo, Brazil; Atelier MBDX, Bordeaux, France; CRM, Napoli, Italy; CIM Bilbao, Spain; School Therapy of Neuchatel, Switzerland; and Associazione Anni Verdi, Rome, Italy His writing has been translated into English and remains available today (Benenzon, 1997).

Education and Training

At this time, all training programs in Argentina grant a bachelor degree (licenciatura) in music therapy following a minimum of 3600 hours of study, typically taking four to five years (Wagner, 2010). This includes a presentation and defense of a research thesis. Skills common to all programs include music, psychology, medical background and music therapy with various degrees of supervised practice (Hugo, 1999).

The following universities offer music therapy programs: Universidad del Salvador.School of Medicine; Universidad de Buenos Aires, School of Psychology; Universidad Maimonides, School of Health Science (Buenos Aires); and Universidad Abiera Interamericana, School of Psychology (Buenos Aires and Rosario) (Wagner, 2010). Specialization courses are organized through universities, hospitals, the Benenzon Foundation of Community Music Therapy, Grupo ADID, Assistance and Developments in Music Therapy, and ICMUS Research and Clinical Music Therapy. Recent agreements among universities have been made in order to permit a regular exchange of knowledge (Wagner, 2010).

Theoretical Frameworks

The primary theoretical framework underlying music therapy in Argentina is psychoanalytic (Barcellos, 2001), influenced by Benenzon (MBMT) the work of Priestley (Wagner, 2010) and related offspring of the psychoanalytical and humanistic movements such as Neo-Reichian, Lacanian, and

Transpersonal, Winnicott, Pearls, Bateson, Pichon-Riviere, Rogers, Maslow and Watzlawick. This is not surprising considering the emergence of Buenos Aires as a major center for psychoanalysis after World War II. Yet papers from Argentinean music therapists reflect a congruence of social science influences: neurophysiology, psychology, anthropology, ethnomusicology, social psychology and systems theory (Barcellos, 2001). Clinical practice is viewed from a holistic perspective (Wagner, 2010), in such a way that musical creativity is a system of an intersubjective constructive process within a culture and therefore open to a variety of methods in order to understand the complex relationships between music, sound, the human being and the uniqueness of the interpersonal music therapy interaction (Wagner, 2010). According to Ferraggina (2007) the survey results disseminated by Sabbatella indicate that active methods, based on client needs, revolve primarily around improvisation and expressive body movement.

Music Therapy Practice

Music therapy is practiced across all age ranges, individual and group, and in a variety of settings: in psychiatry (i.e., substance abuse, post-traumatic stress disorder), special education (i.e., autistic spectrum disorder, hearing or visual impairment), rehabilitation, medical (intensive care, burn patients, neonatal intensive care, AIDS, hospice) as well as prevention programs across mental health and social reintegration settings (Wagner, 2010).

Although continued financial concerns have reportedly prevented the growth of graduate study in Argentina, the country still prevails in the practice of foreword thinking music therapy.

At this time the music therapy degree is accepted as a prerequisite for employment; several provinces provide government legislations and licenses for music therapists as registered health professions. The need for national legislation remains (Wagner, 2010).

MUSIC THERAPY IN AUSTRALIA

History

The International Society for Musical Therapeutics, formed in the 1920s in Sydney, preceding the Australian Music Therapy Association, introduced music as a means of therapy and entertainment into the hospitals through the Red Cross following World War II. From the early 1960s, the pioneering work of Ruth Bright led to music therapy programs in psychiatric hospitals and programs for seniors.

The Australian Music Therapy Association, established in 1975, through the efforts of Denise Grocke and Ruth Bright, developed guidelines for establishing music therapy training programs in 1977, which included key areas of study: music, psychology, medical conditions, music therapy theory, and clinical practice. At that time, the guidelines also required lecturers to hold a minimum of two years of clinical experience (note: this had been the initial standard in the United States as well).

Education and Training

Denise Grocke, who completed her initial training in the United States at Michigan State, started music therapy in a Melbourne psychiatric hospital and established the first undergraduate music therapy-training program at The University of Melbourne in 1978. The University of Melbourne now offers masters and doctoral programs and is expanding research efforts through the National Music Therapy Research United. Two tracks toward the masters are available, either through the completion of coursework or through research. There is a certification program as well as a graduate diploma in GIM (Guided Imagery and Music) available.

The University of Queensland in Brisbane, conforming to the AMTA standards, started the undergraduate program in 1993 but, most recently, moved to a two-year Master of Music Therapy program as well as a research Ph.D. The masters includes music therapy methods, qualitative and quantitative research, music therapy theory and skills, clinical training, clinical improvisation and thesis.

Similarly, the University of Technology, Sydney, and Juring-gai campus offers a Masters of Arts in Music Therapy.

Nordoff Robbins training, leading to a Masters Degree in Creative Music Therapy, is conducted through a liaison with the Nordoff-Robbins Music Therapy Association and the University of Western Sydney at the Golden Stave Music Therapy Centre on the UWS campus. It offers Music Therapy Skills 1, Creative Music Therapy Practicum 1, Music Therapy Skills 2 and Creative Music Therapy Practicum 2 for registered music therapists who hold a Graduate Diploma in Music Therapy and who wish to refine their skills in clinical improvisation. This formal training was preceded by a Nordoff-Robbins Center established in Dural, NSW in 1977, as a result of a visit from Paul Nordoff and Clive Robbins in 1974. I had the personal opportunity to visit the programs in Melbourne, Sydney and Brisbane in July 2003 on my way to the 11th World Congress in Brisbane, Australia.

Music Therapy Practice

Currently, music therapists in Australia use a variety of music therapy approaches which include the use of pre-composed music, improvisation, song-writing and GIM (O'Callaghan, 2002). Research in music therapy papers from therapists in Australia reflects diversity in philosophical orientation. O'Callaghan (2002), reports the use of phenomenological, positivist, post-positivist and constructivist orientations as well as the use of grounded theory (Edwards, 1999). Many music therapists, particularly in the 1980s, completed clinical training placement in the UK, United States and Canada. I personally recall training Alison Davies, a native of Australia, at Montclair State University during her time in New Jersey.

Australian music therapists publish *The Australian Music Therapy Association Journal, The Bulletin—Newsletter of the Australian Music Therapy Association,* and *Network—A Forum for Discussion among Registered Music Therapists.* Three state branches are located in Victoria, New South Wales and Queensland with interest groups in the Northern Territory, South Australia, Western Australia and Tasmania.

MUSIC THERAPY IN AUSTRIA

History

Efforts to negotiate the legislation of music therapy reportedly started as early as 1959 by Edith Kiffer-Ullrich (Mössler, 2008), even though music therapy in Austria had, at that time, only been in existence for two years and, understandably, lacked theoretical background and a significant number of music therapists. The Austrian Music Therapy Law, influenced by laws for psychotherapists and clinical psychologists previously passed in 1992, is reportedly influenced by the "Viennese School of Music Therapy" (Mössler, 2008), resting on humanistic and psychodynamic concepts. The Austrian Association of Music Therapy was founded in 1984.

Education and Training

There are two music therapy training programs in Austria, one at the Institute of Ethno Music Therapy in Rosenau/Lower Austria and the other at the University of Music and Performing Arts, Vienna. The training at the University of Music and Performing Arts, Vienna, started in 1959 by Alfred Schmoelz who led this training until 1992, is most prominent (Gold, 2003) and offers a Master-equivalent degree with the possibility of a Ph.D. This training is unique in its requirement for 90 hours of individual therapy and 180 hours of group therapy. Designed as psychoanalytic and psychodynamic in nature, it now integrates other humanistic psychotherapy models (Gold, 2003).

All music therapists are required to continue their education with further training of at least 90 units every three years and, most interestingly, their work must be documented with such documentation kept for ten years.

The master's degree "must contain theoretical and practical subjects especially including clinical-psychological, medical and psychotherapeutic-scientific basics. . . . With at least 200 units of self-experience, 60 units relating to institutional settings, topics related to healthcare policy and psychosocial frameworks as well as 60 units concerning ethical issues" (Mössler, 2008).

The bachelor training requires content similar to the master training. However, units comprise only 30 units instead of 60.

Music Therapy Practice

The most recent information regarding the development of music therapy in Austria (Mössler, 2008) celebrates the passage of a law, through the Austrian Parliament, governing the practice of music therapy, which came into effect on July 1, 2009. This law affects about 200 music therapists working in Austria. Based on training, there are two different types of occupational qualification:

1. Music therapists with master's level training can work as freelance professionals and within an institution. If music therapy is indicated in order to treat an acute or chronic disease or for rehabilitation, a referral from a doctor, clinical psychologist, psychotherapist or dentist is necessary.
2. Those music therapists who have completed the bachelor degree are qualified to work as employees if recommended by a doctor, a clinical psychologist, an independent music therapist, a psychotherapist or a dentist. They are required to have ongoing supervision with another music therapist.

The Federal Ministry will maintain a list of music therapists and there are guidelines for those who have not studied in Austria. Natives from Austria who have completed their training abroad can practice music therapy in Austria after a positive evaluation of their equivalent background; music therapists from abroad who have completed training abroad can practice temporarily in Austria.

Clinical practice in Austria includes music therapy with learning disabilities, child, adolescent and adult psychiatric, neurological rehabilitation, substance abuse, forensic psychiatric, nursing homes and child oncology with emerging interests in at risk pregnancy, neonatology, preventive care and palliative care (Gold, 2003).

The announcement of a recently posted Mozart and Science 2010–Music in Medicine (http://www.mozart-science.at/) conference organized by the government of the province of lower Austria, may be indicative of the growing interest in interdisciplinary study of physical and neuropsychological foundations of music welcomed by music theorists, composers, psychologists, linguists, neuroscientists, and computer scientists in Austria.

MUSIC THERAPY IN BELGIUM

History

Historically, Belgium includes two communities that operate autonomously, Flanders (Dutch speaking) and Walloon (French speaking) each of which holds their own federal welfare, public health and educational system (DeBacker & Anke, 2006).

However, there is a concerted effort to bring all music therapists together through the efforts of the professional Association for Music Therapy, founded in 1998, and, as of 2006, numbering 48 members. Another organization, The Association for Research, Education and Application of Music Therapy, in Walloon, strives to provide and promote music therapy.

Education and Training/Music Therapy Practice

The College of Science and Arts, Lemmensinstituut, offers a Bachelors and Master's Degree in Music Therapy in cooperation with the University of Leuven and recognized by the government. The programs started in 1993.The Bachelors level of this program includes music training and entry level music therapy while master's training, theoretically based on psychoanalysis (DeBacker & Anke, 2006), provides a balance between music and psychotherapy with mandatory individual psychotherapy (two years) and group music therapy (two years). Preprofessional training is provided for 9 months in the fifth year of training at the University Dentre St-Jozef in Kortenberg and the program concludes with a thesis. The program includes theory of music therapy, methods, and clinical therapy, case material, literature research seminars, project learning, music studies and medical and related studies.

In addition to the program at Lemmensinstituut a program beginning in September 2010, through the Association for Research, Education and Application of Music Therapy-Brussels, is being offered. The new program is offered in collaboration with a college of psychology in Brussels and constitutes a two-year specialization for musicians and health professionals.

Therapists trained by Benenzon, Nordoff-Robbins and Edith Lecourt have influenced training here. Consequently, the information is presented as Psycho-musical Techniques (De Backer & Anke, 2006).

MUSIC THERAPY IN BRAZIL

History/Education and Training

The largest country in South America, Brazil, is composed of 26 states and one federal district. Music therapy education began in 1970 at Art Faculty of Parana and in 1972, the Conservatorio Brasileiro de Musica, Rio de Janeiro, started the first graduation course which was recognized by the government in 1978 (Smith, 2003). Other institutions followed, largely in the 1990s: Universidade Federal de Goiás, Universidad Federal de Pelotas, Escola Superior de Teologia, FEEVALE do Rio Grande do Sul, Faculdade de Artes do Paraná, Centro Universitário das Faculdades Metropolitanas Unidas, Faculdade Paulista de Artes, Universidad de Ribeirão Preto, Universidad do Sul de Santa Catarina and Universidad Católica de Salvador.

Music Therapy Practice

As of 2003, there were approximately 1,500 graduates of these programs (Smith, 2003). As in other Latin American countries, music therapy training has been very much influenced by the work of Benenzon and courses are taught in native language, which largely excludes texts in the English language (Smith, 2003).

The national organization, Uniao Brasileira das Associacoes de Musicoterapia, includes 12 music therapy associations, and regulates their activity.

MUSIC THERAPY IN CANADA

History

The Canadian Association for Music Therapy (CAMT), incorporated in 1977, now includes associations identified by separate provinces (Ontario,

Manitoba, Alberta, Saskatchewan) and eastern provinces (Music Therapy Association of the Atlantic). Prior to the incorporation of CAMT, music therapists were working in Canada: Fran Herman in Toronto, Norma Sharpe in St. Thomas and Therese Pageau in Montreal. The first music therapy program, starting in 1977, was at Capilano College in North Vancouver, British Columbia (Kirkland, 2007).

Education and Training

Canada offers six other university programs in addition to Capilano: Acadia University (Nova Scotia), Université du Québec à Montréal (Québec), Wilfrid Laurier University (Ontario), University of Windsor–Undergraduate and Graduate (Ontario) and Canadian Mennonite University (Manitoba). Concordia University in Quebec offers studies leading to eligibility for accreditation with CAMT (similar to the equivalency in the United States) and eligibility for admission to a Masters in Creative Arts Therapies (music therapy option). The University of Windsor is listed as an educational member of the American Music Therapy Association.

The program at Wilfred Laurier offers graduate study emphasizing Aesthetic Music Therapy, Group-Analytic Music Therapy, Clinical Supervision, Musical Resources, Analysis and Evaluation, Clinical Practice, Counseling, Inquiry and Research (emphasis on qualitative research).

Accredited music therapists, MTA, numbering 331 as of 2007 (Kirkland, 2007) complete the minimum of a four-year Bachelor degree in music therapy which includes study in music therapy research, music and psychology as well as supervised clinical fieldwork practica followed by 1000 hours of a supervised clinical internship (http://www.musictherapy.ca/musictherapists .htm#education). The MTA is granted through the Accreditation Review Board. This credential must be maintained through continued education on a five-year review cycle.

Music Therapy Practice

The enactment of a Health Professions Act in the nineties, in the province of British Columbia, motivated music therapists to become part of a movement toward the regulation of counselors with the suggested name, at this time, The College of Counseling Therapists. This opportunity would hold various professionals under a single umbrella, including marriage and family therapy, pastoral counselors, art therapists and clinical counselors.

In discussing this movement, Kirkland notes that the only other country that has achieved regulated status is the United Kingdom. The issue of regulation in the United States continues and thus far, various states have responded by either trying to get a state license for music therapy, becoming part of a creative arts therapy license (New York State) or adjusting educational structure in order to join another related license such as counseling (i.e., Pennsylvania, Massachusetts, Virginia).

Since several music therapy educators now teaching in Canada were trained in the United States, there appears to be an overlap in material and structure of training courses yet the character of each training course remains unique (Kirkland, 2007).

MUSIC THERAPY IN CHILE

Music Therapy Practice/Education and Training

Reportedly, the most important new development in Chile is the founding of a national association, Asociacion Chilena de Musicoterpia (ACHIM) in 2006 (Bauer, 2007). With a membership of 30 as of 2007, primarily graduates of the University of Chile (started in 1995), the association seeks to provide guidelines for regulation of music therapy in Chile. Emphasis in the postgraduate course at University of Chile includes the personal development of the music therapist explored in courses such as group improvisation, body music therapy, piano improvisation and clinical guitar playing (Bauer, 2007).

The Music Therapy Latin American Committee fosters growth in all Latin American countries and it is anticipated that further educational programs will develop in Chile.

MUSIC THERAPY IN CHINA

History

The primary information on music therapy in China is provided in this article by Tian Gao (2008). Music therapy in China began in 1984 as the Changsha Sanatorium began to use music in order to help their patients reduce stress and anxiety. The use of music at this time was based on efforts to develop a system of prescriptive music. More than a hundred hospitals set up music therapy departments in a few years although no employees had received formal training. The first music therapy-training program started in the China Conservatory of Music in 1989. In the same year the China Music Therapy Association (CMTA) was established.

The interest in music therapy practice declined in the 1990s as more and more hospitals closed their music therapy department within a relatively short period. As a result of this decline, there were very few music therapy departments by the end of the 1990s. The training program, which had started at the China conservatory in 1989, closed down in 1995.

Tian Gao, the director of the training program at the Central Conservatory of Music in Beijing, China, explains the declining interest in music therapy departments in terms of the shallow knowledge base (Gao, 2008). Those who called themselves music therapists did not have systemic training or education and were supportive of the notion that music prescriptions were based on the magical power of music and that a specific piece of music could cure a specific illness or health problem; hence, practice lacked evidence as well as scientific rationale. This may, in part, have been based on the five elements of music associated with traditional Chinese medical theory wherein the traditional Chinese musical scale (similar to the pentatonic) contains five pitches that can have healing power on five internal organs ("Do" related to spleen; "Re" related to lung; "Mi" related to liver; "So" related to heart; "La" related to kidney).

In 2007, a new music therapy organization was formed: China Professional Music Therapy Association (CPMTA) of which the membership is approximately 200. A certification system was established in 2008 and, at that time, credentialed 80 music therapists. It is the hope of CPMTA that the Chinese government will formally recognize this music therapy certification.

In order to bring together music therapists in Hong Kong, the Hong Kong Music Therapy Association (HMTA) was established in 2007.

In addition to mainland China, music therapy in Taiwan is addressed as a separate nation in this chapter.

Education and Training

Professor Tian Gao (2008), who received his undergraduate and master's level training in the United States, established a training program at Central Conservatory of Music in Beijing in 1999. The undergraduate (3 year) and graduate (5 year) curriculum is based on the model of the training in the United States. The program is similar in size to representative programs in the United States (i.e., 30 undergraduate students and 6 graduate students). Further music therapy training is offered through this program to physicians, nurses, musicians, music students and psychotherapists, approximately 700 of whom have been trained since 2004 (Gao, 2008).

As a result of the Central Conservatory of Music program, graduates have gone on to teach in other programs which, prior to their arrival in the years 2008 and 2009, did not have trained staff: Shanghai Conservatory of Music (2008), Undergraduate studies, Professor Ping Zhou; Sichuan Conservatory of Music (2004), Undergraduate studies, Professor Lujie Wang; and Jiangxi

University of Traditional Chinese Medicine (2006), Professor Lichun Liu.

Education and training remains problematic in China since only four of seven schools offering music therapy training have qualified instructors. Over 500 students on the undergraduate level are being trained in China at this time.

Music Therapy Practice

Music therapists work in facility settings such as hospitals, schools for special education, psychotherapy practices and prisons. Facilities within the city of Hong Kong employ approximately a dozen music therapists who received their training either from American, Britain or Australia. The primary clinical population being served is children with a variety of diagnoses.

MUSIC THERAPY IN COLUMBIA

History

As a country that combines the cultural and musical influences of Europeans, indigenous population and Africans, Columbia has an intriguing blend of influences. Similar to other countries, pioneers of music therapy in the 70s and beyond began to invite international lecturers to the country and became involved in international music therapy congresses. One example of this was the 1998 and 2001 symposia of music therapy that included therapists Clive Robbins, Diego Schapira, Monica Papalia and Suzanne Bauer. As natives of Columbia studied music therapy abroad and returned to Columbia, possibilities for further expansion started to come to fruition.

Education and Training

As part of the growing Latin-American constituency, Columbia started their first graduate program in music therapy at the Universidad Nacional de Columbia in 2004. Students from related disciplines (i.e., music education, medicine, physio and occupational therapy, psychology, sociology and social work) are enrolled in this program (Eslava, 2007) which is 4–5 semesters including practica and thesis. Practicum placements include hospitals, geriatric centers, child development center, neurorehabilitation center and schools. Since 2005, the program has also enjoyed an inter-institutional partnership with the music therapy program at Universidad de Chile. The program introduces European, American and Argentinean perspectives to students and, in so doing, is considered eclectic.

Juanita Eslava, who I had the pleasure of dining with in Buenos Aires, directs the sole program in Columbia and openly shares the trials and tribulations of music therapy education and training in the country: "As much as we have evolved I still feel there is a lot to do. We still have a long way to go to give music therapy the standing it should have in our society. We still have to educate people. This needs to be done so that people can have access to quality music therapy services. We have to help our society to understand what we do. I suspect the education process will never end" (Eslava, 2007).

Music Therapy Practice

The challenges, which will also affect education and training, include ongoing searches for appropriate practicum experiences, further communication between therapists from different cities, funding clinical projects, issues unique to Columbia (i.e., refugees living in cities or military personnel injured in the field) and the creation of culturally appropriate music therapy education.

One concrete goal is the creation of a Columbian Music Therapy Association to help "create standards of practice, mechanism of registration, solve legal issues, increase the number of educational programs," etc. (Eslava, 2007) and forge links with other national associations.

The cycle that Eslava (2007) predicts is probably one that is also operative in other countries—more employment and education will be fostered by the number of students currently being trained and graduating to then spawn both clinical positions and university positions in new training programs.

MUSIC THERAPY IN DENMARK

History

Music therapy in Denmark, from the 1950s to the early 1980s, involved independent practice within the clinical areas of special education, gerontology and psychiatry, resulting in the formation of the Dansk Forbund for Paedagogisk Musikterapi (DFMT) in 1969. Initially, Danish music therapy focused on music in special education and, then, subsequently a psychodynamic and psychotherapeutic orientation developed. Other influences on Danish music therapy included visits from Paul Nordoff and Clive Robbins in the seventies.

Education and Training

In Denmark, Aalborg University is well known as the only training program in the country as well as a program that has achieved international status. It is described in detail as a model for education and training (Wigram, Pedersen, & Bonde, 2002). In its initial phase, the four-year Masters training at Aalborg, started in 1982, was led by Inge Nygaard Pederson and then Benedikte Barth Scheiby, both of whom had trained in Herdecke, Germany in so-called "Mentor Training," a training with emphases on Analytical Music Therapy and Creative Music Therapy. In 1992, Tony Wigram started teaching at Aalborg and in 1993 a research network was initiated along with a Psychiatric Music Therapy Research Clinic. In 2006, a new curriculum overlapping the bachelors and the masters was created in order for music therapy to collaborate with courses in its new home, namely the Department of Communication and Psychology. Currently, Aalborg hosts a five-year Bachelor/Master's program that trains the music therapist to work both independently and as part of a team. The Bachelors component is technically three years, including theory, music and music therapy while the Masters is an additional two years and includes advanced music theory, music and music therapy (Bonde, 2007). As part of a psychodynamic tradition, self-experience, although different from traditional university curriculum and apart from the Danish system as well, is mandatory. Role-playing of different clinical populations is utilized in the context of clinical group music therapy skills and students learn to observe music therapists at work in an effort to gradually develop skills organizing and conducting clinical work with clients as a part of a psychiatric or special education setting. Entrance to the program now includes mastery of voice and a harmony instrument since it is no longer possible to provide individual musical instruction. The music therapy curriculum emphasizes improvisation skills, which begins in the second semester. The musical entrance criteria for Aalborg are considered akin to many other postgraduate European programs (Bonde, 2007).

The Ph.D. Program in music therapy, directed by Tony Wigram, began in 1999. In addition to the doctoral dissertation, students participate in six courses as approved by their course advisor, each of which also involves seminar presentation with peers.

Music Therapy Practice

In terms of theoretical orientation, a decade-long orientation toward the "German/Central European Music Therapy tradition, which is essentially psychodynamic and humanistic-existential" (Bonde, 2007) shifted over the nineties to include behaviorism and positivism as "current international practice of using multiple paradigms within the field of music therapy" (Bonde, 2007). Nevertheless the psychodynamic framework appears to be favored as is the emphasis on the client-music-therapist interrelationships. All kinds of research are invited as is meta-theoretical discussion (Bonde, 2007).

MUSIC THERAPY IN ESTONIA

History/Education and Training

The Estonian Society of Music Therapy, founded in 1990, (http://www .musictherapyworld.de/modules/emtc/estonia/emtclist.php) has a current membership of about 50. Talinn Pedagogical University, Department of Psychology, offers a one-year undergraduate course (225 contact hours) and a one-year advanced course (120 contact hours).

MUSIC THERAPY IN FINLAND

History/Education and Training

Finland, host to the 6th European Music Therapy Congress of June 2004, celebrates its status in terms of both Nordic affiliation, then European and, now, true international music therapy (Erkkilä, 2008). Two polytechnic schools, Prikanmaa Polytechnic and North Carelia Polytechniq, as well as one private school, Eino Roiha Institute, offer bachelor level training. University of Jyväskylä offers a master's program and also hosts a music therapy research and training clinic, which was established in 2004. Collaborative ventures with other training programs and local healthcare facilities have grown as a result of the clinic. One example of celebrated research is the development of a computational analysis tool for music therapy improvisation analysis (Erkkilä, 2007; Luck et al., 2006), which was a collaborative project between the Music Cognition Group at the University of Jyväskylä and the music therapy program. (http://www.braintuning.fi). Training in GIM (Levels I and II) are offered at Eino Roiha Institute.

Music Therapy Practice

At this time, there are about 200 music therapists working in Finland, largely linked to the healthcare system. One example of this is the Social Insurance Institution of Finland as an employer. Music therapists in Finland enjoy collaborative practice with other healthcare professionals in the care of clients with psychiatric, multiple disability, rehabilitation, chronic pain and learning disability challenges and a developing interest in music therapy group work. Although the profession has gained a great deal of momentum in the period of 1993–2008, Erkkilä (2008) reports that there are still "prejudices and obstacles to overcome." Music therapy is not on the official list of recognized healthcare professions and there are great pressures to conform to evidence-based medicine.

MUSIC THERAPY IN FRANCE

History

The creation of the first music therapy association in France dates to 1972, preceded by a center for music therapy in 1969, in Paris, through the efforts of Dr. J. Guilhot, a psychiatrist, Dr. M. A. Guilhot, a psychologist, Dr. J. Jost, an engineer, Dr. M. Gabai, a dentist, E. Estellet-Brun, a professional musician and Dr. E. Lecourt, a psychologist and psychoanalyst. At the time, individual and group receptive therapy were popular.

With the First World Congress of Music Therapy, held in Paris in 1974, where 40 countries were represented, Edith Lecourt became the powerhouse behind the World Congress. In 1980, another association was created in addition to the initial one. This was called *Association Française de Musicothérapie* with a core of psychiatrists and music therapists participating. The initial association was renamed *Centre International de Musicothérapie,* directed by Dr. Jost and his team (his daughter, S. Braun, is now at the head). As a consequence of this schism, two other world congresses in Paris were organized separately in conjunction with the two associations. Recently (Lecourt, 2004) the French Federation of Music Therapy (www.musicothera pie-federation francaise.com), recognized by the EMTC, has been formed to unify the profession and realize a register of trained music therapists. The initial association still exists but is not part of the Federation. Another organization, French Association for Music Therapy (www.musicotherapie-afm.com) has been formed at the University Paris V Rene Descartes. France hosts two journals, *The Journal of Music Therapy* (edited by the French Association for Music Therapy) and *MTC, Music Therapy Communication.*

Education and Training

The six universities (three new programs within the last few years) currently offering music therapy (Lecourt, 2010) are the following:

1. La Forge Formation, Adequatis (www.la-forge-adequatis-formation.fr).
2. University of Nantes–Institute of Music Therapy, Saint Sebastien sur Loire (musicotherapiet.nantes@wanadoo.fr).
3. Université Paul Valéry Montpellier III, Montpellier (musicotherapie @univ-montp3.fr).
4. Université René Descartes–Paris V, www.univ-paris5.fr (Two-year university diploma for professionals in other fields fulfilling basic music therapy requirements; Masters since 2006, new Creative Arts Therapy Masters, Master PRES Sorbonne Paris Cité of Arts Therapies, in conjunction with Universite Rene Descartes- Paris III and Paris V to begin October 2011).
5. Atelier de Musicotherapie de Bordeaux AMBx (www.ambx.net).
6. Atelier de Musicotherapie de Bourgogne (www.amb-musicotherapie .com).

In response to the new European Union standards for global academic currency in terms of interchangeable credits, programs are shifting to the Masters level. Those wishing to pursue the Ph.D. have done so either in psychology or in educational and social sciences.

Music Therapy Practice

French music therapists, generally professionals from related disciplines (medicine, psychology, education, nursing, special education, music education, music performance) receive postgraduate training in music therapy, which is offered by several universities as well as private institutes and association. Private practice is relatively undeveloped as the focus is on serving the welfare system and it is anticipated that the national health insurance will, in the near future, define categories of psychotherapy relative to music therapy in an effort to provide regulation.

Although rooted in Freudian psychoanalysis, the theoretical basis of music therapy practice in France has diverged to include biological and cognitive schools of thought. Lecourt (1993) notes various schools of practice, which include pedagogical, receptive and musical improvisation as a basis for psychoanalysis.

Currently Edith Lecourt, a Professor of Clinical and Pathological Psychology, is the Co-Director of the Institute of Psychology in Paris. Previously she started (1993) and directed the program at Universite Rene Descartes–Paris V, a program she continues to be affiliated with. Approximately 600 music therapists had been trained in France (Lecourt, 2004) as of five years ago but many are not in current practice; the current registry for the French Federation of Music Therapy lists 79 affiliate members.

MUSIC THERAPY IN GERMANY

History

Germany remains one of the European centers for training in music therapy. Toward the end of the 1950s, Schwabe, a music teacher, was beginning to develop music therapy in psychotherapy and psychiatry clinics at University Leipzig as a receptive music therapy that he referred to as regulative music therapy (Wosch, 2003a). In contrast, psychodrama, singing, Orff instrumental playing and an understanding of communication systems influenced the development of active group music therapy. These methods were modified with behavioral, interpersonal and humanistic interventions (Wosch, 2003a) and expanded by colleagues who used music therapy in child psychiatry and special education. At this point, during the 70s and 80s, music therapy was considered a further education for related professionals (i.e., nurses, physicians, psychologist, music education, music performers and musicologists), similar to what was happening, it seems, in France.

Other developing dimensions of music therapy in the 1970s included interest in Free Improvisation Therapy (Alvin, 1975), Nordoff-Robbins Creative Music Therapy and Analytical Music Therapy introduced by Priestley. Nordoff-Robbins approach had been the focus of the training at the University of Witten-Herdecke. Analytical music therapy is the focus in Hamburg (under the directorship of J. Eschen) and psychoanalytic schools/approaches have spawned Morphological Music Therapy (Tuepker, 2004) and Integrative Music Therapy (Frohne-Hagemann, 2010) as well as influencing the academic writing of countless other educators and clinicians in Germany.

The first German music therapy conference was held in Leipzig, 1969 with East and West German and Austrian participants. Music psychologists instrumental in the theoretical basis of music therapy at this time included the East German, Hermann F. Boettcher and the West German, Hans-Peter Reinicke (Wosch, 2003a). With the elimination of the wall dividing East and West Germany in 1989, the presence of many music therapy organizations became even more apparent and the situation between East and the different West-German music therapy organizations was problematic in the 1990s (Wosch, 2003a). However with the 8th World Music Therapy Congress in Hamburg and the Kassel Conference, the situation shifted.

Education and Training

With the signing of the Bologna Process in Bologna, Italy, 1999, ministers of education from 29 countries in the European Union joined the effort to standardize academic degree standards and quality assurance (http://ec

.europa.eu/education/higher-education/doc1290_en.htm), an ongoing effort. In Germany, there is now a standardized Diplom-Musiktherapeut/in (FH) and Diplom-Musiktherapeut/in equivalent to the European Bachelor and the European Master degrees. As a result of these changes, 50 percent of the former undergraduate training courses in Germany no longer exist and the movement appears to be towards masters and doctoral programs. There are two bachelors programs; eight masters programs and four doctoral level programs (Nocker-Ribaupierre, 2010; Wosch, 2010):

- University of Music Berlin (M.A.)
- University of Music and Drama Hamburg (M.A.; Ph.D.)
- University of Muenster (M.A.)
- University of Applied Sciences of Frankfurt (M.A.)
- University of Applied Sciences of Magdeburg (M.A.; Ph.D. in cooperation with Otto-von-Guericke-University of Magdeburg)
- University of Applied Sciences of Stendal (M.A.)
- University of Applied Sciences of Wuerzburg (B.A. in Social Work/Music Therapy; M.A., Ph.D. in cooperation with Julius-Maximilians–University of Wuerzburg or with University of Music of Wurzburg)
- University of Applied Sciences of Heidelberg (B.A., M.A., Ph.D. in cooperation with State University of Heidelberg)
- University of Augsberg (M.A.)

With over 450 books printed in German on the practice of music therapy, Germany is well-equipped to continue to move forward academically in the world of music therapy.

Music Therapy Practice

As described above (see History), music therapy practice has seen many influences.

Currently there are five music therapy associations with trained music therapists, each of who define their membership independently. Therefore there is no national standard.

- DMTG–Deutsche Musiktherapeutische Gesellschaft (German Music Therapy Association, 1,500 members)
- DMVS–Deutsche Musiktherapeutische Vereinigung zur Foerderung derKonzeption nach Schwabe (German Music Therapy Association of the Christoph-Schwabe-approach, 300 members)
- BVAKT–Berufsverband der anthroposophischen Kunsttherapeuten (Professional Association of Anthroposophic Art Therapy–"Art–

Kunst" is in German comprehensive for Music, the Fine Arts, Drama, etc., 150 music therapy members)
- Orff–Music Therapy (100 members)
- Nordoff-Robbins (100 members)

As a result of clinical advocacy and the presentation of evidence-based practice, music therapy has been accepted as a discipline for ten clinical disorders thus far (Wosch, 2010) through the national health organization in Germany.

MUSIC THERAPY IN HUNGARY

History

Hungary, a country with a rich tradition in folksong and music education training through Kodaly methods, joined the European Union in 2004. Two Hungarian music therapy associations were founded in the nineties, The Albert Schweitzer Music Therapy Association (1992), and the Hungarian Music Therapy Association (1994); the latter remains operative today.

Education and Training

The first training in music therapy began as a post-graduate course in 1992 at the Liszt Academy of Music in cooperation with the Medical School of Pécs and was converted in 2003 to a 2.5 post-graduate part-time arts therapies course. The first year lectures include psychiatry, psychotherapy and arts therapy lectures followed by a second year specializing in music therapy. Another post-graduate part-time music therapy training course is conducted at the Eötvös University in Budapest. As of 2008, approximately 70 music therapists had graduated from these programs (Forgács, 2008).

Although both university programs are psychodynamic in nature, a developmental focus is considered more applicable when working with clients who have special needs.

Music Therapy Practice

With a current economy that is not favorable to music therapy employment in the public health sector and the lack of state registration and regulation, music therapists face challenges in terms of professional identity and employment, challenges they are working to overcome.

MUSIC THERAPY IN IRELAND

History

The two jurisdictions of Ireland, Northern Ireland that remains part of the United Kingdom (6 counties in the Northeast), and the Republic of Ireland (26 counties), an independent sovereign, may administer health and education differently but the music therapists working throughout Ireland are united in their support of each other (Edwards, 2003). In the UK, music therapists are governed through the Health Professional Council with music therapists registered similarly to allied health professionals; in the Republic, the government, through the Department of Health and Children, proposes regulation of music therapy through a council named Complementary and Alternative Medicine. Therefore, at this time, only UK practitioners are regulated (Edwards, 2003). The Irish Association of Creative Arts Therapists remains the overarching organization for all arts therapists in Ireland.

Education and Training

The University of Limerick, started in 1998 and directed by Jane Edwards since 2001, offers a comprehensive two-year Masters program, which also includes a research component. Although a small group of students and practitioners are active in Ireland, regularly scheduled professional development inviting international speakers results in fruitful dialogue.

MUSIC THERAPY IN ISRAEL

Education and Training

Music therapists in Israel are trained to work with various populations including but not delimited to children in special education, psychiatry, general hospital, elderly, prisons, people in hostels and neurological rehabilitations.

There are three training programs in Israel:

- David Yellin College of Education, founded in 1980 by Chava Sekeles offers the three-year Masters degree in cooperation with The Hebrew University in Jerusalem. Training is based on theory, which is "eclectic, developmental-integrative model, psychodynamic" (Sekeles, 2004). Houses music therapy clinic.
- Bar Ilan University, founded in 1982 by Dorit Amir offers the Masters which includes the integration of the following subject areas: music

therapy, psychology, movement therapy, psychology of music, vocal improvisation, internship, supervision, three written projects and a final exam (Sekeles, 2004). Houses music therapy clinic.

- The Levinsky College, directed by Nehama Yehuda (note: who also teaches at Bar-Ilan) and Miriam Druks offers a post-graduate professional diploma in music and movement therapy which features combined music and movement therapy and a psychodynamic orientation.

I.C.E.T., the Ministry of Health, the Ministry of Education and/or the Committee of Higher Education accredit all three programs. Since 1988, the entry requirement for all training programs is the bachelor's degree as well as prerequisite studies in psychology.

Music Therapy Practice

Under the guidance of The Israeli Association of Creative and Expressive Therapies (I.E.C.T.), started in 1971 and, as of 2004 (Sekeles, 2004) including a membership of 260 music therapists, music therapy is recognized by the Ministry of Health in Israel. I.C.E.T. publishes *Therapy through the Arts.*

Music therapy research in Israel is growing and currently includes music in medicine, community music therapy, the ancient roots of music therapy and therapeutic music analysis. Although Israel remains impacted financially by ongoing social and political difficulties, which also emphasize the need for music therapy to acclimate to trauma and multiculturalism (Amir, 2005), the human aspects of all applications are prioritized over political issues. The association continues to help new immigrant and students help successfully develop their own districts. The attitude toward studies, clinical work, academic studies, supervision and the human attitude is one that Israelis can be proud of (Sekeles, 2010).

MUSIC THERAPY IN ITALY

Education and Training

In 2000, the Conservatory of Music in Pescara, organized a post-graduate diploma in music therapy open to students that hold a diploma in Didactic of Music. Subsequently in January of 2004, the degree level program in Italy began.

Music Therapy Practice

Theoretically, training in Italy covers all technical and practical approaches (i.e., Nordoff-Robbins, Benenzon, Tomatis, Orff, etc.); there is an emphasis on humanistic and psychodynamic frameworks (Zanchi & Suvini, 2004). At the beginning of the 90s, the regional associations joined together to form the Italian confederation of Music Therapy Association (Conf.IAM) in order to coordinate educational, clinical and research initiatives (Zanchi & Suvini, 2004). The Italian Professional Association of Music Therapy (AIM) was set up in June 2002 in order to recognize the professional efforts of music therapists and safeguard the practice of music therapy in Italy (Zanchi & Suvini, 2004). Specific criteria are spelled out for three registries: Music Therapists, Educators, Supervisors (Zanchi & Suvini, 2004). AIM provides advocacy for music therapy in the process of recognition at a legislative level within the National Council for Economy and Labour (CNEL).

In Italy, professions may be officially recognized from individual ministries or government department but lack specific legislation that would recognize their professional activity as defined by the national government (Ferrone, 2004). Such is the case with music therapy where the State Music Academy in Pescara, a three-year degree course and the University of Rome, a three-year degree course in art therapy (music therapy is a module within this degree) are recognized by the Department for Education and Research while the four-year course in music therapy at the European School of Music Therapy is recognized by the Department of Employment and Professional Training. However, lack of national recognition precludes a music therapist from taking part in a competitive state exam or being employed by a public organization with specific work contracts (Ferrone, 2004).

MUSIC THERAPY IN JAPAN

History

The formation of the Tokyo Association for Music Therapy in 1987 was preceded by several introductory efforts in the country of Japan to foster concepts regarding music therapy. From 1967–1977, various leaders interested in the work established several music therapy study groups. Juliette Alvin visited in 1969; Clive and Carol Robbins visited in the eighties and the concept of music therapy was often taught as an applied field within the psychology of music (Ikuno, 2005). In the 1990s, Japan had become a country where a number of specialists who had either self-trained or studied abroad were now practicing music therapy.

In an effort to mobilize these individuals, the Japanese Federation of Music Therapy (JFMT), established in 1995, started to certify music therapists although, similar to the United States, this was not a state certification and not applicable to health insurance. At the end of 2004, the JFMT, renamed the Japanese Music Therapy Association (JMTA) in 2001, had an astounding 6200 members. However, by 2003, only a relatively small number (943) of these members were certified. Certification in JMTA is achieved either through completion of JMTA approved schools, supervision, interview and paper exam or through cumulative points completed through participation in JMTA approved lectures as well as practical experience.

Education and Training

Nineteen four-year training programs in Japan are offered on the undergraduate level in universities and music colleges. However, many of the staff are self-taught clinicians and there is a noted shortage of teaching staff, clinical sites and supervisors (Okazaki-Sakaue, 2003). Interestingly, the Japanese culture does not support the need for psychiatric treatment since there is still stigma attached to the notion of psychotherapy. Therapeutic goals are more group or family oriented rather than individual and adults are expected to control their emotions rather than expressing them openly. It is expected that standards in practice and training will grow. Although some may feel the need to apply western music therapy learning to society and culture in Japan, I suggest that the therapeutic practice norms of a society be respected in and of their own right.

Music Therapy Practice

Music therapists in Japan have received the benefit of a variety of theoretical backgrounds and work primarily with children and adults in the context of developmental disabilities, gerontology, psychiatry, terminal care, and neurological settings (Ikuno, 2005). As opposed to the United States or European models, very few clinicians in Japan focus on psychodynamic or music-centered approaches. Funding is available in evidence-based medicine with a number of physicians working together with therapists in order to gain government recognition (Okazaki-Sakaue, 2003).

MUSIC THERAPY IN KOREA

History

Starting in the 1980s, music therapy was introduced by self-taught music therapists or faculty from the related disciplines of psychology or special education. Similar to this scenario in so many other countries, these pioneers began to stimulate interest in which would become a professional calling. Subsequently, music therapists trained in the United States, Europe and Australia returned to their homeland in order to contribute to growing expertise and practice (Chung, 2005).

Education and Training

It appears that many clinicians who studied elsewhere were trained in behavioral methodology in the United States as this is reportedly (Kim, 2006) the most popular clinical approach in Korea. Ewha Women's University has a Nordoff-Robbins Music Therapy Clinic led by two music therapists who were trained in New York. Although psychodynamic approaches are introduced to students, they are rarely applied in clinical practice. It would be interesting to understand how these approaches may clash with cultural traditions.

Since SookMyung Women's University established the first master's program in the 1997 and now has a doctoral program, there are six other universities offering graduate study (Masters study is generally five semesters, 45 credits and six-month internship):

- Ehwa Women's University: M.A.
- Sungshin Women's University: M.A.
- Hansei University: M.A., Ph.D.
- Myungji University: M.A.
- Sookmyung University: M.A., Ph.D.
- Wonk Wang University: M.A.

The Masters levels program in Korea generally require five semesters for 45 credit hours and a six-month full-time internship (Kim, 2006). There are also several nondegree programs not listed here.

Music Therapy Practice

There are several Korean music therapy associations: four in Seoul and others associated with SookMyung, Ewha and MyongJi Universities. The associations linked to universities are, respectively: Korean Music Therapy Association, Korea Music Therapy Education Association, and Korean Music Therapy Association for Clinical Practice and Applied Science. As a field that has experienced rapid expansion over the past 17 years, the goal for Korean music therapy is to establish a unified body for the profession (Kim, 2002).

MUSIC THERAPY IN LATVIA

History

The relatively recent independence of Latvia in 1991 has led to its membership in the United Nations, NATO and the European Union. During Soviet occupation, those with disabilities or mental health problems were shunned by society and now it is time to change this former mentality. Psychology has become a popular area of study and, along with this, the interest in creative arts therapies is beginning to take shape.

Education and Training

The first music therapy courses at the University Academy in Liepaja with sponsorship from Germany (Lagzdina, 2009) were offered in 1998 and accredited by the government in 2006. The Masters degree in Arts Therapies, at Rigas Stradina University under the auspices of the Faculty of Medicine (Lagzdina, 2009) was established in 2003 and accredited in 2008. Currently, there are professional associations for both music and art therapy in Latvia and international arts therapies conferences have been hosted there since 2003 along with European, Canadian and Australian faculty.

Music Therapy Practice

Music therapists provide services in integrated preschools, integrated primary schools, day centers for persons with disabilities and music therapy clinics. Professional recognition within school systems and funding within hospitals, rehabilitation, psychiatric hospitals and day centers remains difficult. Latvian is the national language and Russian is the second language, necessitating trilingual qualified supervisors and specialists. Nevertheless, there has been relatively quick progress given these difficulties and music therapists are considered highly motivated and dedicated (Lagzdina, 2009).

MUSIC THERAPY IN THE NETHERLANDS

History

Dr. Van der Drift, a psychiatrist in 1957, requested the very first music therapy position within a psychiatric hospital. From 1967 onward, professional meetings for pioneering music therapists began and national courses followed, organized by members of small music therapy organizations.

The Dutch Association for Creative Therapy, established in 1962, continues to promote the study, practice and development of creative arts therapies, including music therapy, while protecting the social interests of the members. Within the structure of this organization, the Dutch Association of Music Therapy (NVvMT) was formed in January 2006. This association is one of five independent associations for experiential therapies (music, drama, art, dance and psychomotor), which are united in a federation (FVB-Federation of Experiential Therapies) (Vink & Smeijsters, 2010). This Federation subsumes registration procedures, descriptions of the therapeutic and professional tasks of experiential therapists, a professional journal, task forces for the development and research of the profession and office facilities. Another organization, The Dutch Music Therapy Foundation (Stichting Muziektherapie), established in 1987, promotes research and treatment methodology through the organization of international congresses and workshops and the production of documentary films.

Education and Training

In 1999, the training institutions for creative arts therapists, Universities of Applied Sciences (UAS), agreed on basic competencies for the creative arts therapists at the bachelor level; these were specialized for music therapy. These training competencies were derived from the description of therapeutic and professional tasks as described by the FVB. In 2009, the job description by the FVB as well as the training competencies at the UAS were revised along with stated competencies for masters level training. All training programs are members of the European Consortium of Arts Therapies Education (E.C.ArT.E.). In the Netherlands the transformation to the bachelor-master structure has been made: the Universities of Applied Sciences (UAS), which host the arts therapies training program (as listed in the ECArTE directory), started or are developing master programs.

Within the regular educational system in the Netherlands, there are four full-time, four-year (at the bachelor level) courses for music therapy conforming to guidelines per the Bologna Process: Universities of Applied Sciences (UAS) of Utrecht, Arnheim-Nijmegen, Zuyd Heelen and ArtEZ School of Music, Enschede. The UASs are accredited, and are controlled and supervised by the government (Ministry of Education, Culture and Sciences).

At this time, there are two master level programs. The M.A. in Arts Therapies, offered through Zuyd UAS, was established by Smeijsters in 2004. It is affiliated with the Research Centre for the Arts Therapies, KenVaK, a joint venture of ZUYD UAS, Utrecht UAS and ArtEZ School of Music, Enschede. The KenVaK program focuses on competencies to develop and research the treatment methodology by means of evidence-based practice, practice-based evidence, qualitative and quantitative research. It is accredited by the Dutch Government.

The International M.A. of Arts Therapies, offered and accredited by both KGH Freiburg as well as Arnhem-Nijimegan UAS, focuses on theory, methods and research competence. Although master's degrees are in arts therapies, students majoring in music therapy focus on their discipline.

Research centers at the Universities of Applied Sciences have been established since 2003 for the purposes of creative arts therapies (drama, music, art, dance) research: Research Centre for the Arts Therapies, KenVaK, and the research center at Arnhem-Nijmegen UAS. These research centers also host doctoral research. Qualitative research is conducted, such as phenomenology, constructivistic inquiry and grounded theory, as well as quantitative multiple baseline designs and randomized controlled trials. Systematic reviews for the treatment of depression, ADHD, eating disorders, anxiety and mood disorders have been and will continue to be published.

Music Therapy Practice

Theoretically, several psychotherapeutic schools, have influenced music therapy education in the Netherlands: psychoanalysis, gestalt therapy, client centered therapy, behavior therapy and cognitive therapy. One example of creative arts theory that has influenced theoretical thinking is the Creative Process Theory, based on a combination of Freudian developmental stages and theories from art psychology. Another important model in music therapy, developed by Smeijsters, is the Analogue Process Model, based on the work of Stern and Damasio, which describes musical phrases as equal to felt vitality affects in the person's core self (Vink & Smeijsters, 2010).

The Professions in Individual Health Care and Cure Law (BIG-wet), protects the health professions in the Netherlands. At this time, there are negotiations within the Council for Postgraduate Training (CONO), the advisory board of the Dutch Ministry of Health Care, Cure and Well-Being, to accept arts therapists into the BIG law, thereby establishing arts therapies as a protected profession. This should aid towards the goal of stabilizing the pay scale and status of creative arts therapists in the Netherlands.

Currently, the Dutch health system requires that all treatments are described in so-called treatment products: a description of goals, indications, contraindications, interventions, rationales, resources, frequency and length of treatment connected to one particular problem of the client. The Dutch health system also requires the development of guidelines, based on research evidence, which show what sort of therapy is most successful with what sort of problem of the client. Evidence includes results from randomized controlled trials, professional tacit knowledge and client experiences. This is in line with Evidence Based Practice (EBP) expected in the European Union at this time (Hanser, 2005), as explicitly stated by Tony Wigram.

A professional register, Foundation for Registration of the Arts Therapists (SRVP), established in 1987, allows creative arts therapists meeting professional competencies to be registered as qualified professionals. In order to apply for registration, the music therapist must graduate from an approved training program at one of the UASs and have sufficient practical experience and further training as senior therapist.

MUSIC THERAPY IN NEW ZEALAND

History

Music therapists visiting New Zealand in the seventies, Paul Nordoff and Clive Robbins, Carol and Clive Robbins, Mary Lindgren (former student of Juliette Alvin), Maggie Pickett, then director of the Guildhall School training in London, and Auriel Warwick, stimulated sufficient interest in the work that the New Zealand Society for Music Therapy was formed. Several Australians, including Morva Croxson, went to Guildhall to study music therapy at that time.

Initial introduction to music therapy stressed humanistic approaches and tonal and atonal music improvisation. Australian music therapists, including Ruth Bright, Denise Grocke, Michael Atherton, and Robin Howat also lectured.

Subsequently, graduates from a New Zealand Society for Music Therapy (also known as Music Therapy New Zealand) accredited program took block courses while others went to the University of Melbourne to study and return to practice.

Education and Training

As of 2003, there were 14-16 qualified music therapists (Croxson, 2003); as of 2010, the membership numbered 54 (http://www.musictherapy.org

.nz/), obviously influenced by graduates of the Master of Music Therapy program in Wellington within the New Zealand School of Music established by Robert Krout (2003a) in 2002.

This program was formed by the merger of the music department of Massey University and Victoria University of Wellington and is directed by Sarah Hoskyns, former director of the music therapy course at the Guildhall School of Music and Drama, London. The two-year Masters program includes music therapy principles and methods, clinical training experiences (1200 hours of practicum and internship), selected topics, study of indigenous music of selected cultures, casework/research projects and thesis. The cultural mix of students in this program is extremely diverse as are musical traditions.

Successful graduates are eligible to apply to the Registration Board of Music Therapy New Zealand to become a Registered Music Therapist (RMTh). Opportunities for doctoral study are also available.

Music Therapy Practice

Student clinical practice and research are developing in a variety of settings: mainstream and special schools at all age levels, a deaf education center, two visual resource units in Wellington and Auckland, drug and alcohol rehabilitation services, adolescent and adult psychiatric services, a Rudolf Steiner school, music therapy within a play therapy context on pediatric hospital wards in Wellington and Auckland, child development centers, a center for adults with developmental delay, nursing homes, rehabilitation and two clinics in Christchurch and Auckland (Croxson, 2007). The *New Zealand Journal of Music Therapy* is published annually.

Music therapists hope to pay continuing attention to working with the healthcare and musical practice of both the Maori tangatawhenusa and Pacific Island populations. Millicent McIvor, in her interview with Kathryn Stevenson (2009), recalls her ten years living among the Maori people in Whakatane, listening to chants which were composed for specific areas and occasions: "Maori chant in traditional Maori life was *music therapy to them*" (Stevenson, 2009).

The fairly recent (Croxson, 2007) development of the Raukatauri Music Therapy Center in Auckland, headed by Yid-Ee Goh, a graduate of the Nordoff-Robbins Center in London, is busy with over 67 children a week treated by three full-time therapists. The center provides an excellent venue for the clinical and research opportunities for the Wellington training program. Likewise, a future McKenzie Music Therapy Center in Wellington will serve towards these ends.

MUSIC THERAPY IN NORWAY

History

The Norwegian Association of Music Therapy, established in 1971, held a membership of 250 members in 2004 (Aasgaard & Trondalen, 2004) and is an associate of the Norwegian Council of Music. With the title of Music Therapist approved by the government in 1992, many music therapists became member of the Norwegian Musicians Union under their working title. Although the first national conference was held in 1997 in Oslo, the first Nordic Conference in Music Therapy at Sandane preceded it in 1991. Norway has been a member of the European Music Therapy Conference since 1995.

Education and Training

The first training program in Norway, established in 1978 in Oslo by Even Ruud, was followed in 1988 by another branch of the program in Sandane, Sogn og Fjordane University College with Brynjulf Stige as Director. These programs were started as two-year post-baccalaureate programs accepting students with degrees in music, education, special education, nursing, psychology and occupational therapy. As of 2004, 340 students had been educated through these programs while another 30 students had completed their Master's degree in Music Therapy at the Norwegian Academy of Music/ University of Oslo (Aasgaard & Trondalen, 2004).

At this time, The Norwegian Academy of Music offers the B.A., M.A. and Ph.D. in music therapy; the former Sogn and Fjordane University College program moved to the University of Bergen in 2006 and now offers the Masters (five-year integrated program) and Ph.D., both in line with now standardized European educational practice.

Training in Norway includes theory and methods (theory of music therapy, improvisation, composition, clinical music therapy, practical projects and drama), pedagogical and psychological skills (neuropsychology, psychology and special education theory) and musical and personal development (music coursework, self-experience, GIM Level I, supervised clinical work) (Aasgaard & Trondalen, 2004). Research methodology is required in M.A. and Ph.D. programs.

The music therapy journal in Norway is called *Musikkterapi* and is published four times a year. The conversations at the first Nordic Conference in 1981 stimulated the formation of the *Nordic Journal of Music Therapy,* 1992, which is published twice a year, emphasizes qualitative research and has an international following.

Music Therapy Practice

Early music therapy practice in Norway focused on special educational systems with a strong influence from the Nordoff and Robbins approach, which had been introduced in the seventies. Improvisation remains important as a clinical approach. Olaf Skille developed vibro-acoustic therapy in 1980. Music therapists in the last decade have taken a greater interested in psychoanalytic and psychotherapeutic approaches (including the Bonny Method of Guided Imagery), developmentally informed theory and community-based work where music functions within the culture. Practice has extended to palliative care, pediatric oncology, HIV/AIDS, prison services, geriatric wards, private practice, childcare and community-based work.

The large-scale research project "Music and Health in Late Modernity: Resource-oriented Music Therapy and Community Therapy," initially funded at the Sogn og Fuordane University College and then relocated to GAMUT, Grieg Academy Music Therapy Research Centre (University of Bergen) (in collaboration with University of Pretoria and the Nordoff-Robbins Music Therapy Centre, London) was funded 2004–2008.

Throughout Norway, the hope exists that research into the relationships between music and medicine will come to fruition. There seems to be "an increased interest in relationships between music/the arts, health and spirituality" (Aasgaard & Trondalen, 2004), perhaps necessary to handle the high number of long-term ill, unemployed, psychiatric population and loss of traditional social networks.

MUSIC THERAPY IN SOUTH AFRICA

Education and Training

In 1999, the process of approving the two-year post-graduate Master's program through the Health Professions Council of South Africa was completed. The University of Pretoria is a small but vital program in South Africa and the only program on the African subcontinent (Pavlicevic, 2005). The training, 1000 hours of supervised clinical internships, includes coursework in music therapy theory, (music therapy theory, research studies, professional ethics and clinical pathology) clinical studies (clinical-musical resources, clinical improvisation techniques, clinical documentation, clinical internship), complementary studies (voice work, movement, medical psychology, neuropsychology, lectures on allied disciplines) and research. It was established by and is directed by Mercedes Pavlicevic who has expressed a strong interest in relating program studies to the culture of South Africa (Pavlicevic, 2005).

Music Therapy Practice

Small numbers make it difficult to gain autonomous national identity. The music therapists in South Africa, numbering 10 in the year 2005, are part of an arts therapists' standing committee under The Professional Board for Occupational Therapy (1996). This committee as well as The South African Network of Arts Therapies Organization (SANT0), formed in 1997, has helped foster collegial relationships amongst the creative arts professionals. With the approval of a competencies document in 2000, state registration examiners appointed by the Arts Therapies' subcommittee are in a position to provide formal registration for arts therapists in South Africa. Further, SANTO is represented on the Professional Board's Education Subcommittee and there is ongoing lobbying for an Arts Therapies portfolio on the Professional Board.

MUSIC THERAPY IN SPAIN

History/Music Therapy Practice

Educational agreement in Spain is complicated by the history of difficulties in forming a cohesive professional organization. The Spanish Association of Music Therapy was established in 1977 by the music therapy pioneer Serafina Poch and her colleagues in order to promote government recognition of music therapy in Spain establish professional standards and protect professional practice. During the eighties and nineties several music therapy associations were founded in different regions of Spain and despite the efforts to maintain a National Music Therapy Committee and/or proposed Spanish Music Therapy Federation, these efforts that began in 1992 have not come to fruition.

Music therapy in Spain is not recognized as a profession by the government. This makes it difficult to command effective employment, professional identity and consistency in academic background.

Education and Training

In 2004, it was noted (Sabbatella, 2004) that the country of Spain offered training, at Master or Post-Graduate level in both private institutions (since 1986) and universities (since 1992).

Private university settings (3) include: Universidad Catolica de San Antonio, Universidad Pontificia de Salamanca, Universitat Ramon Llull. Private Institutes (5) include Centro de Investigacion Musicoterapeuitica,

Instituto Musica, Arte y Proceso, Musitando, Fundacion Mayeusis. Public Universiteis (4) include Universidad Autonoma de Madrid, Univertsidad de Barcelona, and Universidad de Cadiz (in cooperation, Universidad Nacional de Educacion a Distancia.)

Reportedly (Sabbatella, 2005), there is no clear theoretical orientation; all programs give a broad picture of music therapy and its various approaches. There are no doctoral programs in music therapy in Spain.

Given the very large number of academic programs in the country of Spain, it is no wonder that finding common ground under new European educational guidelines is a matter of concern in Spain. This would necessitate an agreement amongst the Universities (7), the Music Therapy Associations and the Private Institutes (3) to establish criteria and standards for training leading to a Masters in Music Therapy according to the rules of the European Higher Education Area, EHEA (Sabbatella, 2004).

Mercadal-Brotons and Mateos Hernandez (2005) suggest some of the following reforms for European Music Therapy Confederation, EMTC, programs:

1. University training
2. Two hundred hours of personal process experience
3. Supervised clinical hours
4. Two years of full time clinical experience
5. Publication
6. Training programs consistent with European credit system
7. Well balanced curricular areas
8. Teaching methodology particular to music therapy
9. Means of evaluating the quality of training courses for submission to government accrediting agencies.

One model of following new European credit requirements may be the formation of the joint international training in music therapy covering the post-graduate diploma in music therapy (60 ECTS over three semesters) and the Master in Music Therapy (120 ECTS over four semesters), with the ECTS (European Credit Transfer System) as the common currency of academic institutions. This program, under the auspices of the University of Cadiz, Spain and the Instituto Politecnico do Porto, Portugal prepares students for doctoral study. As is the case with some of the training now in the United States, training takes place in intensive weekend seminars and distance learning. Research areas include assessment /evaluation in music therapy and music therapy in special education, psychiatry, neurological rehabilitation and medicine. The faculty is international and both cooperating institutions grant the degree. The course is open to those with an undergraduate degree in music, psychology, education, and medicine or health sciences and is coordinated by Patricia Sabbatella.

MUSIC THERAPY IN SWEDEN

History

Paul Nordoff and Clive Robbins introduced music therapy in Sweden with their eventful visit in 1974. Subsequently seminars and courses with an emphasis on music in special education were organized. Often these were co-operative ventures with music therapy associations in Norway and Denmark. Short courses at the Royal College of Music in Stockholm, starting in 1981, led to the development of the current masters program as interest in music therapy developed to include practice in child and adult psychiatry, neurological rehabilitation, oncology and geriatrics (Hammarlund, 2008).

Education and Training

Ingrid Hammarlund, trained in England, and Margareta Wärja, trained in the United States, established the Royal College of Music in Stockholm, home for music therapy training in Sweden, in 1991. The program is now a four-year part-time Masters degree "founded on a broad humanistic and psychodynamic basis with a focus on communicative musicality and the meaning of music for the patient and the therapist. It is designed to also include a basic psychotherapeutic training level and one's own personal psychotherapy experience" (Hammarlund, 2008). Entry requirements include a bachelor's level degree in music or music education, entrance exam and interview with musical activities and improvisation. Recently, a partnership between the University of Sarajevo Music Academy and the University of Stockholm Music Therapy Department led to the inclusion of four Bosnian students for subsequent music therapy training.

Music Therapy Practice

Music therapists in Sweden work primarily in multidisciplinary teams and therefore interdisciplinary information is integral to the program. Courses appear to overlap with current United States competencies, perhaps reflecting both the original training of faculty and influences from the homeland.

Reported influences in teaching music therapy in Sweden are Analytically Oriented Music Therapy, Guided Imagery and Music and Functionally Oriented Music Therapy (Paulander, 2008) with Music and Imagery (MAI) taught and practiced as a general short-term application (Körlin, 2008).

Functionally Oriented Music Therapy, developed by Lasse Hjelm, is described (Johansson, 2008) as nonverbal. Each session is structured with short-structured melodies, called codes, that have corresponding patterns of drums, and/or cymbals or wind instruments that can be used toward diagnosis and assessment. Changes in position of instruments, which necessitate varying postures as well as blocks of wood or drums under the feet and adapted drumsticks and wind instruments, can stimulate sensory and motor systems (Johansson, 2008).

The Association for Music Therapy in Sweden, FMS (Förbundet för musikterapi Sverige) began in 2000 in order to reconstitute the former SFM. The membership (Wallius, 2008) has varied between 150 and 230 and has mobilized members of several former associations for music therapists, which were related to three different kinds of training programs. Membership from the former AOM, Analytical-Oriented Music Therapy, moved to FMS in 2006; membership from the Functional Music Therapists moved to FMS in 2007. FMS hosted a Nordic conference in 2006, has initiated a cooperative with music therapists in Bolivia and is a member of EMTC.

MUSIC THERAPY IN SWITZERLAND

History

Switzerland, largely a German speaking country (64%) with another percentage of natives speaking French (20%), consists of 26 cantons and half-cantons, each of which holds a constitution that conforms to federal laws. The existence of two language groups has led to training in both languages within the country as well as a dual type of membership within the national organization. The Association Professionnelle Suisse de Musicotherapie, ASM, also known as the Schweizerischer Fachverband für Musiktherapie SFMT, was founded in 1961 and, as of 2010, held a professional membership of 150 (http://www.musictherapy.ch/) who utilize both active and receptive methods. The association accredits music therapists as MT SFMT and seeks national recognition of the music therapy professions (Munro-Porchet, Jacob & Fauch, 2006).

Education and Training

Schools accredited by the association and meeting guidelines for 1650 credit hours include the following: Ecole Romande de Musicothérapie (ERM) in Genève; Zurcher Hochschule der Kunste/Berufsbegleitendes Aufbaustudium Musiktherapie bam in Zurich (2007); Integrative Musiktherapie (SEAG) in Auskunft; Ausbildung Musiktherapie mit Instrumentenbau (FMWS) Forum in Dorfstrasse and Schwaderloch; and Orpheus Schule fur Muskitherapie.

The training at Berufsbegleitendes Aufbaustudium Musiktherapie bam in Zurich, conducted on a part-time basis over 3–4 years, leads to a post-graduate degree in Advanced Studies (comparable to a Masters) and is the only program under the auspices of a college. Music therapy curriculum in Switzerland includes theories and methods of music therapy, psychopathology, experiential music therapy (both individually and in group) and supervised clinical training.

MUSIC THERAPY IN TAIWAN

Education and Training

In 2004, Tainan National University of the Arts started the only comprehensive, degree-granting program in Taiwan. As an undergraduate program, it has adopted a four-year curriculum based on the format in the United States. Selected undergraduate courses in music therapy are available at the extension division of Fu-Jen Catholic University (2004) as are graduate courses through the Graduate Institute of Humanity in Medicine of Taipei Medical University (2003); neither of these schools offers a degree.

Music Therapy Practice

At this time, there is no certification system in Taiwan for music therapy. However, the Music Therapy Association of Taiwan remains active in advocacy for the profession of music therapy. As professionals are trained through Tainan National University of the Arts and more professionals from Taiwan return from their training in Australia, England, Germany, Japan and the United States, practice increases in Taiwan across a broad spectrum of needs. There is no clear distinction in Taiwan between the definition of medical treatment and therapy; this may lead to a conclusion that therapeutic intervention should be implemented by medical professionals (Lee, 2006). Music therapy, along with other creative arts therapists in Taiwan, have been asked to consider the creative arts therapies as examples of recreation therapy since the latter is listed within the scope of occupational therapy practice. Goals are to define music therapy competencies and regulate the practice of music therapy in Taiwan (Lee, 2006).

Despite these challenges, employment opportunities have increased in the last few years and practice is reported in schools, hospitals, gerontology, and hospice. Social welfare policy supports music therapy for the underprivileged and music therapy is listed as an eligible service in early intervention. National Health Insurance reimbursement is only available at select facilities since music therapy must be co-endorsed by other state regulated healthcare practitioners. Nevertheless, nonprofit organization does support music therapy workshops with government funding, such as the monies from the Department of Social Affairs. The overall ineligibility of music therapy for national Health Insurance reimbursement leads for-profit institutions to come up with private pay services (Lee, 2006). Ironically, treatment relying on National Health insurance would have to be delivered more frequently in order to prove financially competitive.

MUSIC THERAPY IN THE UNITED KINGDOM

History/Education and Training

The British Society of Music Therapy was founded in 1958 by Juliette Alvin, a pioneer in the field, who set up the first training course at the Guildhall School of Music and Drama in 1968. This was followed in 1974 by the first Nordoff-Robbins training, now at its present site in North London.

In line with a government issued initiative in the UK (Bunt, 2005), as of 2006 all professional training in the UK is now at the Masters level (two-year programs or 3 years part-time) and requires a three-year musical training leading to a diploma or graduation from a college of music or a degree from a university (or, similar to the United States, prerequisite training in music if the original degree is not in music). This requirement stands in stark contrast to the previously required post-graduate diploma required for state recognition of the music therapists in the UK (Bunt, 2005).

A review of websites indicates that programs include experiential training, supervised clinical practice, theoretical and research coursework, studies in musical improvisation and culminating project (Bunt, 2005) or thesis. A Ph.D. program is also available at Nordoff-Robbins. Interviews for training also consider if prospective students are personally suited to the work. The move some years ago to transfer training in music therapy from the department of music at the University of Bristol to the Faculty of Health and Social Sciences at the University of the West of England brings up the issue of acclimating to one's academic environment (Bunt, 2005). How do the overlaps between music, theory, relationship, practice and research fit into the specifications of university-based education in the UK (Bunt, 2005)?

Programs in the United Kingdom, accredited by the Health Professions Council and in accordance with European Standards include the following:

- Guildhall School of Music & Drama, London (validated by City University of London)
- Nordoff-Robbins Centre, London
- University of Surrey, Roehampton
- University of the West of England, Bristol, UK
- Anglia Polytechnic University, Cambridge
- Welsh College of Music and Drama, Cardiff
- Nordoff-Robbins, Scotland

Music Therapy Practice

Inspired by the work of Paul Nordoff and Clive Robbins, Juliette Alvin and Mary Priestley, music therapists in the United Kingdom continue to develop uniquely informed theories of practice and training.

The United Kingdom, long recognized as a center for music therapy, achieved state regulation in 1999, joining other professions considered supplementary to medicine. All of these professions are regulated under an act of parliament and each has their own professional association. Registration is compulsory in order to be employed thought the National Health Service and Social Services.

The Association of Professional Music Therapists, established in 1976, maintains a current registry and administers and monitors professional development, which includes supervision, study days and conferences. There are geographical subdivisions within the APMT (similar to the United States). At the end of 2009, there were 612 professional members.

The British Society of Music Therapy opens its membership to anyone interested in music therapy. BSMT promotes and helps develop music therapy throughout the United Kingdom, organizes conferences, workshops and meetings and serves as a center of information and a distributor of international publications. BSMT and APMT jointly publishes *The British Society of Music Therapy* twice a year, sponsor conferences together (i.e., such as the World Music Therapy Congress held in Oxford, 2002) and renew membership as a package. This is similar to the cooperative membership offered by CBMT and/or Registry and AMTA in the United States.

As the host to the 10th World Congress held in Oxford, UK, the welcome diversity of UK practice invited plenaries on community music (Ansdell, 2002) related to sociology, the relationship between music therapy and psychoanalysis and the evolution of music therapy and spiritual perspectives (Ansdell, Bunt, & Hartley, 2002).

COMMON THEMES ACROSS THE CONTINENTS

Introduction

What do we as music therapists share? As I review information country by country and correspond with colleagues, I can identify with patterns of change that we have gone through in the United States: pioneers in related disciplines introducing us to the possibilities of music therapy; the formation of different organizations based on theoretical orientations; geography and political climate; national accreditation identity that is initially confined to the music therapy membership but hopes to be linked to greater public possibilities through state and government licensing; the frustration of seeing others present themselves to the public as music therapists when they have no training; educational requirements which may be impacted by overarching government guidelines or related fields; institutional limitations in the way we present our educational programs; the tendency to present schools of music therapy rather than eclectic approaches necessary for different kinds of clinical scenarios and the identity crisis of music therapy as we try to translate what we have learned to homeland cultures and our role as musicians.

Beyond the common zeal to use music as a healing force, we all contend with changing economics and healthcare regulations within our countries of origin. In my review of information as well as information from world congresses (Bang, 2008; Wheeler, 2009) and international panels on education (Wheeler & Grocke, 2001; Wheeler, 2003a), common themes that affect education and training emerge.

I believe it is constructive for all of us to consider the following international issues and how they impact education and training.

Uniting Music Therapy Organizations within Countries

While there is no inherent problem in having several music therapy organizations, each of whom represents different interests and goals, there may be a problem in having several when it comes to developing a position of national strength for the profession in one's country of origin. This seems to be a theme that was mentioned in countries that continue to struggle with this issue or had a history of resolving this issue: Brazil (12 associations under one umbrella), France (2 associations recently united), Germany (5 associations), Korea (7 associations), Sweden (recently mobilized membership of 3 disparate groups), Switzerland (2 groups due to language differences) and the United States (2 associations united in 1998).

Standardization of University Training Throughout Europe

As detailed earlier in this chapter but worth summary here, the signing of The Bologna Declaration (1999) was the impetus in Europe and beyond (note: 46 countries have voluntarily agreed to standardize their educational requirements) to construct a European Higher Education Area (EHEA) by 2010 to make academic degree standards more comparable and compatible throughout Europe, thereby creating a common educational currency, while overseeing quality assurance standards. In accordance with these aims, the goal of the EMTC, European Music Therapy Confederation, is to set up a European Music Therapy Register linked to the new higher education standards of bachelor and master level qualification. The new standards suggest 180–240 ECTS (European Credit and Transfer Accumulation System) for the Bachelors degree (3 years) and 90–120 ECTS credits for a Masters degree (2 years). One academic year corresponds to 60 ECTS credits, equivalent to 1500–1800 hours of study, closer to North American and Japanese systems of education. One link that I suggest summarizes this information: http://www.coe.int/t/dg4/highereducation/EHEA2010/BolognaPedestrians_en.asp.

As a result of the European Higher Education Area oversight, many music therapy programs have changed their structure within the last five -ten years. This has not necessarily been easy; some of the growing pains are alluded to in accounts here. According to Mercadal-Brotons and Mateos Hernandez (2005) from Spain, ideally, the configuration of programming should follow guidelines of the EMTC (European Music Therapy Confederation), the WFMT (World Federation for Music Therapy) and the recommendations for European Convergence in the European Space for Higher Education (ESHE). Importantly, music therapy programs (also referred to as training courses) in Europe must recontexualize masters degrees within the guidelines of EHEA. Many have already done so. The overall goal here, however, would be "curriculum convergences and a set of professional competencies that facilitate European and national government recognition" (Sabbatella & Mota, 2007).

This has also led to interesting dialogue in terms of sequential training for music therapy. While some might consider the advantages of a music therapist holding the bachelors in music therapy going on to pursue the M.A. and the Ph.D. (Wosch, 2005), others might consider the possibility of the B.A. as an entry level knowledge of music therapy which could then lead to a credential following completion of the M.A. (Seidel, 2002). If we adopt this latter scheme, we might establish what some have already done: an "integrated master program" (Stige, 2005). Another intriguing possibility is to be more open to students of related disciplines finding value in the pursuit of the undergraduate music therapy degree in order to enrich our dialogue (Stige, 2005). Yet another possibility, proposed by Wosch at the European Music Therapy Congress (Wosch, 2010), is the concept of two levels of Masters training: The first Masters would provide an overview and different paradigms or approaches of music therapy while the second Masters would be specialized, in effect, creating five years of study for a student at graduate level study in Germany.

Determination of the Entry-level Degree for Registration in Europe

While the United States maintains the B.A. as the entry-level credential, Australia and the United Kingdom as well as many countries in Europe have now moved to the Masters level. It will be interesting to see how other countries, in light of changing economies and healthcare systems, proceed in the next decade. Seidel (2002) reminds us that since the beginning of 2001, efforts to launch acceptance of music therapy as a health profession in the European Union have advocated completion of a master's degree program in order to become registered as a music therapist.

Licensing

The issue of state and/or national licensing is one frequently discussed in the United States and also on the agendas of many countries discussed in this chapter. The United Kingdom, for example, has benefitted from national licensing, which the government sets. Although other countries, including the United States, have a national music therapy certification and/or registry, it is one that is not recognized by the government. This can impact upon employment. Some music therapy programs in the United States are linked to coursework that lead to related kinds of licensing and certifications (i.e., Licensed Professional Counselor, Licensed Creative Arts Therapist, etc., Special Education Teaching Certifications, Licenses in Psychology). How this defines education and training is a matter of perspective. Are we furthering the profession of music this way or selling ourselves short?

Various units of government called states, provinces, cantons, etc., may maintain their own licensing standards. In Brazil, the province of Buenos Aires granted government licensing for music therapy in 2005; in Canada, the province of British Columbia hopes to become regulated under a Health Professions Act; in the Republic of Ireland (part of the country), music therapy hopes to be regulated through a council of Complementary and Alternative Medicine. Italy may be recognized from individual ministries or government department but no legislation will recommend their activity on a national level and, therefore, certain employment opportunities are not available. In the Netherlands, there are ongoing negotiations within the Council for Postgraduate Training and the advisory board of the Dutch ministry of Healthcare, Cure and Well-Being to accept arts therapies into the Professions in Individual Health Care and Cure Law and establish arts therapies as a protected profession. In Norway, music therapy has become sanctioned under the Norwegian Musicians Union. Austria received national recognition of music therapy in 2009.

Inclusion of Music Therapy in National Healthcare Systems

Likewise, the inclusion of music therapy in a national healthcare system is an issue linked to national recognition and related insurance reimbursement. As a result of evidence-based practice and clinical advocacy, music therapy has been accepted as a discipline for 10 clinical disorders through the national health organization in Germany. To the contrary, Hungary is concerned that the economy is not favorable to music therapy employment in the public health sector due to lack of state registration and regulation. In Taiwan, ironically, the ineligibility of music therapy for national health insurance is thought to be a boon for music therapy employment.

Insurance reimbursement for music therapy remains a current issue of concern in the United States (Hanser, 2005). This may be linked to education and training if insurance reimbursement is linked to levels of education and training resulting in possible licensing requirements.

Guidelines for Levels of Practice

Guidelines for levels of practice in the United States have been linked to levels of education. With the master's degree as entry-level credential in Australia and throughout much of Europe, what are the guidelines, if any, for levels of practice and how do they compare to the United States in the scheme of things? In Austria, there are now differential levels of practice regulated by the government based on education.

The Nature of International Masters Level Training

In her research on ten masters programs in Europe that had achieved state recognition and professional acceptance (Belgium/Leuven, Denmark/ Aalborg, France/Paris, France/Nantes, Norway/Oslo, Norway/Sandane (since moved to Bergen), Sweden/Stockholm, Spain/Vittoria Gasteiz, UK/Cambridge, UK/London Nordoff-Robbins, Seidel (2002) found the following features in common:

1. Teaching in small groups.
2. Acceptance of the need for individual therapy as a part of training in addition to experiential music therapy, individual and group supervision.
3. Close teacher-student relationship where teacher is a role model (with a number of professors teaching and conducting clinical work).
4. Group-based structure of courses promotes collective learning (i.e., frequent use of improvisation as well as projects in groups or intertherapy).
5. Students are already working and attending school part-time: "This makes it possible to avoid creating a gap between professional practice and academic education, which often leads to tensions occurring in trying to put ideas into practice" (Seidel, 2002, p. 57).
6. Close interrelationship between theory and practice invites theory which is then based on practical experience (i.e., competency-based versus curriculum-based).

This very interesting analysis provides a perspective that directors of graduate programs in the United States may find instructive. I am particularly impressed with the requirement for individual therapy, the emphasis on clinical supervision and the role model of the teacher as a clinician-educator. I personally find these approaches very stimulating.

However, I do have a concern that I do not see cited in literature. How does training steeped in psychoanalytic traditions figure with the employment needs in various countries? In the United States, for example, I note that many jobs that are advertised are for positions that feature relatively short-term and outcomes-based therapeutic programming. What is the relationship, if any, between the training we are offering and the employment picture?

Concerns about Institutional Support

Many institutions cite concerns about financial support of their programs. We are, by nature, relatively small programs in terms of numbers and this is becoming more of a concern as economic woes prevail. How will we overcome these financial realities? I was disappointed to read, for example, that *Music Therapy Today,* the very fine online journal that started in November 2001 and was produced five times a year during the years 2002–2006 with three issues in 2007, had ended, apparently due to the concurrent closure of the Institute for Music Therapy at the University of Witten Herdecke. "The music and art therapy landscape is changing, as is the financing structure for training courses within Europe, and we have failed to convince the University that further support is necessary" (Aldridge, 2007). Another sign of financial exigency may be the merging of colleges, even across countries, to take in more students and grant degrees from two universities at a time as well as the movement of music therapy programs into other academic departments (Bunt, 2005; Stige, 2005). In Argentina, financial concerns are said to prevent the growth of graduate study. In the United States, the very first program in music therapy, at Michigan State, recently closed despite uproar from the music therapy community.

If we are compelled to grow our numbers and abbreviate the number of credits in programs in order to remain institutionally competitive, as has been suggested in my analysis of several programs in the United States, the nature of our training programs will change, not necessarily for the better.

Evidence Based Practice (EBP)

The issue of evidence-based practice has been cited in terms of research and practice (Edwards, 2005; Silverman, 2010; Wigram, Pederson & Bonde, 2002; Elyse & Wheeler, 2010), as discussed in Chapter 4 of this book. Wigram (Hanser, 2005) considers this issue one that affects all European countries. In Austria, music therapists must document their work and keep this documentation for ten years. In Finland where music therapy is not on the official list of recognized healthcare professions, the pressure to conform to evidence-based practice is clear. Similarly, in the Netherlands, EBP is expected.

Is it to be cited in education as well? Although the theme of the 2010 European Music Therapy Conference included education in its evidence-based practice agenda, there were no presentations relating to this topic. In the United States, there is an increasing trend for academic programs to conduct programmatic assessment; I recently completed a design for programmatic assessment of the graduate music therapy program at Montclair State University. How is this trend going to affect other training programs throughout the world?

Basic Musicianship as Entry Criteria

Many masters programs in music therapy, fortunately, continue to request the equivalent of the undergraduate music training as entry to their programs. This is important. We cannot, despite where we are housed within the institution, neglect the modality of our work. The role of music-centered music therapy appears to be alive and well.

Individual Therapy

Individual therapy is required in many programs throughout Europe, not so in the United States. Is this because of theoretical underpinnings in European programs? Is this imposing a financial burden on students or can we provide this experience within the context of individual or group music therapy within a given program? If so, how do we separate our roles as educators/therapists/supervisors?

Multicultural Awareness

Many educators (Ruud, 1997; Stige, 2002a; Amir, 1999a, Amir, 2005) consider the issue of multicultural awareness. Amir sums it up well:

> In a multicultural society, where there are many ethnic and cultural groups and continuous immigration, the identity of our clients can be shaken and even destroyed. Some of our clients suffer from cultural losses and radical changes in lifestyle, things that cause difficulties in interpreting cultural symbols and signs, thus interfering with their ability to give meaning to the world around them . . . we need to look at our clients from a cultural perspective instead of one that focuses only on the individual as a totally independent entity with external influences. (Amir, 2005)

In reviewing information about education and training around the globe, I noted that various cultural traditions may be more or less responsive to different theoretical models of music therapy education and training. I find this instructive and believe that it is a reminder to all of us that in addition to being cognizant of the multicultural needs of our clients, we need to, as educators teaching and designing programs, be open to the multicultural needs of our students.

CONCLUSION

Although we continue to have overarching concerns within all 30 countries where music therapy is taught, the growth of training appears to be relatively meteoric over the last two decades. In this closing chapter, we have considered the need for music therapy organizations within countries to unite, the standardization of university training throughout Europe, determination of the entry level degree for registration in music therapy, licensing, inclusion of music therapy in national healthcare systems and insurance reimbursement, guidelines for levels of practice, the nature of international masters level training, concerns about institutional support, basic musicianship as entry criteria, individual therapy and multicultural awareness. All of this provides food for thought, as we continue to strive for excellence in music therapy education and training, around the world, here and now.

With our first chapter as an overview of Music Therapy in the United States and subsequent chapters detailing the use of competencies in considering course content and the use of learning theory and pedagogy in guiding our teaching, our last chapter provides a larger perspective on education and training throughout the world and the challenges that we will all embrace.

Appendix A

MAJOR WEBSITES IN MUSIC THERAPY FOR EDUCATION AND TRAINING RESOURCES

A.M.T.A.: American Music Therapy Association, www.musictherapy.org
C.B.M.T. Certification Board for Music Therapy, _http://www.cbmt.org/-

World Federation of Music Therapy: http://www.wfmt.info/WFMT/Home.html

European Music Therapy Confederation:
http://www.musictherapyworld.de/modules/emtc/e_index1.php

VOICES: A world forum for music therapy, http://www.voices.no/

Appendix B

BOOKS/MONOGRAPHS PUBLISHED IN THE ENGLISH LANGUAGE IN MUSIC THERAPY

1954–2011*

Author	Title	Year of Publication	Publisher	Subject Matter
Goodman, K.	Music therapy education and training: Theory to practice	2011	Charles C Thomas	Comprehensive
Ruud, E.	Music therapy: A perspective from the humanities	2010	Barcelona	Perspectives
Lee, C.	Improvising in styles	2010	Barcelona	Methods
McFerran, K.	Adolescents, music and music therapy; Methods and techniques for clinicians, educators and students	2010	Jessica Kingsley	Methods
Hadley, S. (Ed.)	Qualitative inquiries in music therapy: Vol V	2010	Barcelona	Research
Aldridge, D. & Facher, J. (Eds.)	Music therapy and addictions	2010	Jessica Kingsley	Methods
Stige, B., Ansdell, G., Elefant, C. & Pavlicevic, M.	Where music helps: Community music therapy in action and reflection	2010	Ashgate	Methods
Rolvsjord, R.	Resource-oriented music therapy in mental healthcare	2009	Barcelona	Perspectives
Austin, D.	The theory and practice of vocal psychotherapy: Songs of the self	2009	Jessica Kingsley	Methods
Malloch, S. & Trevarthen, C. (Eds.)	Communicative musicality	2009	Oxford University Press	Perspectives

*This list reflects publication through June 2010 with the exception of this book.

Odell-Miller, H. & Richards, E. (Eds.)	Music therapy supervision	2009	Routledge	Supervision
Wolfe, D. & Waldon, E.	Music therapy and pediatric medicine	2009	AMTA	Methods
Kenny, C.	Music and life in the field of play: An anthology	2009	Barcelona	Perspectives
Salmon, S. (Ed.)	Hearing, feeling, playing: Music and movement for deaf and hard of hearing children	2009	Wiesbaden: Reichert Verlag	Methods
Hanson-Abromeit, D. & Colwell, C. (Eds.)	AMTA Monograph Series: Effective clinical practice in music therapy: Medical music therapy for pediatrics in hospital settings	2008	AMTA	Methods
Darrow, A. (Ed.)	Introduction to approaches in music therapy	2008	AMTA	Comprehensive
Schwartz, E.	Music therapy and early childhood: A developmental approach	2008	Barcelona	Methods
Hartley, N. & Payne, M. (Eds.)	The creative arts in palliative care	2008	Jessica Kingsley	Comprehensive
Gilbertson, S. & Aldridge, D.	Music therapy and traumatic brain injury	2008	Jessica Kingsley	Methods
Clair, A. & Memmott, J.	Therapeutic uses of music with older adults, 2nd edition	2008	AMTA	Methods
Gfeller, K., Thaut, M. & Davis, W.	An introduction to therapy: Theory and practice, 3rd edition	2008	AMTA	Comprehensive
Aldridge, G. & D.	Melody in music therapy: A therapeutic narrative analysis	2008	Jessica Kingsley	Perspectives

Oldfield, A. & Flower, C. (Eds.)	Music therapy with children and their families	2008	Jessica Kingsley	Methods
Twyford, K. & Watson, T. (Eds.)	Integrated team working: Music therapy as part of transdisciplinary and collaborative approaches	2008	Jessica Kingsley	Perspectives
Butterton, M.	Listening to music in psychotherapy	2008	Oxford: Radcliff Publishing	Methods
Thaut, M.	Rhythm, music and the brain	2008	Routledge	Perspectives
Sears, M. (Ed.)	Music, the therapeutic edge: Readings from Wm. Sears	2008	Barcelona	Perspectives
Hadley, S. (Ed.)	Qualitative inquiries in music therapy: Vol IV	2008	Barcelona	Research
Standley, J. & Jones, J.	Music techniques in therapy, counseling, and special education, 3rd edition	2007	AMTA	Methods
Meadows, A. (Ed.)	Qualitative inquiries in music therapy: Vol III	2007	Barcelona	Research
Sekeles, C.	Music therapy: Death and grief	2007	Barcelona	Methods
Reuer, B. L., Crowe, B., & Bernstein, B.	Group rhythm and drumming with older adults	2007	AMTA	Methods
Crowe, B. & Colwell, C. (Eds.)	AMTA Monograph Series: Effective clinical practice in music therapy: Music therapy for children, adolescents and adults with mental disorders	2007	AMTA	Methods
Wosch, T. & Wigram, T. (Eds.)	Microanalysis in music therapy	2007	Jessica Kingsley	Methods

Goodman, K. D.	Music therapy groupwork with special needs children: The evolving process	2007	Charles C Thomas	Methods
Robbins, C., & Nordoff, P.	Creative music therapy, 2nd edition	2007	Barcelona	Methods
Baxter, H. et al.	The individualized music therapy assessment profile	2007	Jessica Kingsley	Assessment
Ahonen-Eerikäinen, H.	Group analytic music therapy	2007	Barcelona	Methods
Grocke, D. & Wigram, T. (Eds.)	Receptive methods in music therapy: Techniques and clinical applications for music therapy clinicians, educators and students	2007	Jessica Kingsley	Methods
Gardstrom, S. C.	Music therapy improvisation for groups: Essential competencies	2007	Barcelona	Methods
Waton, T. (Ed.)	Music therapy with adults with learning difficulties	2007	Routledge	Methods
Simpson, F.	Every note counts: The story of Nordoff-Robbins music therapy	2007	James and James, Ltd.	Perspectives
Edwards, J. (Ed.)	Music: Promoting health and creating community in healthcare contexts	2007	Newcastle, UK: Cambridge Scholars Publishing	Methods
Garred, R.	Music as therapy: A dialogical perspective	2006	Barcelona	Perspectives
Humpal, M. & Colwell, C. (Eds.)	AMTA Monograph Series: Effective clinical practice in music therapy: Early childhood and school age educational settings	2006	AMTA	Methods

Cassity, M. & Cassity, J.	Multimodal psychiatric music therapy for adults, adolescents and children: A clinical manual, 3rd edition	2006	Jessica Kingsley	Methods
Batz, G.	Singing for life	2006	Routledge	Methods
Berger, J.	Music of the soul	2006	AMTA	Perspectives
Oldfield, A.	Interactive music therapy psychiatry: Clinical practice, research and teaching	2006	Jessica Kingsley	Methods
Hadley, S. (Ed.)	Feminist perspectives in music therapy	2006	Barcelona	Perspectives
Uhlig, S.	Authentic voices, authentic singing: A multicultural approach to vocal music therapy	2006	Barcelona	Methods
Baker, F. & Tamplin, J. (Eds.)	Music therapy methods in neurorehabilitation	2006	Jessica Kingsley	Methods
Schneck, D. & Berger, D.	The music effect	2006	Jessica Kingsley	Perspectives
Aldridge, D. & Facher, J. (Eds.)	Music and altered states	2006	Jessica Kingsley	Perspectives
Karras, B.	Down memory lane: Topics and ideas for reminiscence groups, 2nd edition	2005	Elder Song	Methods
Karras, B. & Hanson, S.	Journey through the 20th century: Activities for reminiscing and discussion	2005	Elder Song	Methods
Brunk, B. K.	Music therapy and augmentative/ alternative communication, 2nd edition	2005	Prelude	Methods
Smeijsters, H.	Sounding the self: Analogy in improvisational music therapy	2005	Barcelona	Perspectives

Galerstein, N., Martin, K. & Powe, D.	Age appropriate activities for adults with profound mental retardation, 2nd edition	2005	Barcelona	Methods
Meadows, A. (Ed.)	Qualitative inquiries in music therapy, Vol II	2005	Barcelona	Research
Robbins, C.	A journey into creative music therapy: Monograph 3	2005	Barcelona	Methods
Wheeler, B., Shultis, C., & Polen, D.	Clinical training guide for the student music therapist	2005	Barcelona	Pragmatic
Baker, F. & Wigram, T. (Eds.)	Songwriting	2005	Jessica Kingsley	Methods
Dileo, C. & Bradt, J.	Medical music therapy: A meta-analysis and agenda for future research	2005	Jeffrey Books	Research
Hilliard, R.	Hospice and palliative care music therapy	2005	Jeffrey Books	Methods
Adamek, M. & Darrow, A.	Music in special education	2005	AMTA	Methods
Standley, J.	Medical music therapy: A model program for clinical practice, education, training and research	2005	AMTA	Methods
Aldridge, D. (Ed.)	Music therapy and neurological rehabilitation	2005	Jessica Kingsley	Methods
Lorenzato, K.	Filling a need while making some noise: A music therapist's guide to pediatrics	2005	Jessica Kingsley	Methods
Pavlicevic, M. (Ed.)	Music therapy in children's hospices	2005	Jessica Kingsley	Methods
Perret, D.	Roots of musicality: Music therapy and personal development	2005	Jessica Kingsley	Perspectives

Michel, D. & Pinson, J.	Music therapy in principle and practice	2005	Charles C Thomas	Comprehensive
Thaut, M.	Rhythm, music and the brain	2005	Routledge	Perspectives
Dileo, C. & Loewy, J. (Eds.)	Music therapy at the end of life	2005	Jeffrey	Methods
Abrams, B. (Ed.)	Qualitative inquiries in music therapy: Vol 1 Monograph	2004	Barcelona	Research
Crowe, B.	Music and soul making	2004	Scarecrow Press	Perspectives
Borczon, R.	Music therapy: A fieldwork primer	2004	Barcelona	Pragmatic
Simpson, J. & Burns, A. (Eds.)	Music therapy reimbursement: Best practice and procedures	2004	AMTA	Pragmatic
Ansdell, G., Pavilcevic, M. & Procter, S.	Presenting the evidence: A guide for music therapists responding to the demands of clinical effectiveness and evidence-based practice	2004	London: Nordoff-Robbins Music Therapy Centre	Pragmatic
Darrow, A. (Ed.)	Introduction to approaches in music therapy	2004	AMTA	Methods
McGuire, M. (Ed.)	Psychiatric music therapy in the community: The legacy of Florence Tyson	2004	Barcelona	Perspectives
Wong, E.	Clinical guide to music therapy in adult physical rehabilitation settings	2004	AMTA	Methods
Wigram, T.	Improvisation: Methods and techniques for music therapy clinicians, educators and students	2004	Jessica Kingsley	Methods

Brunk, B. K.	Music therapy: Another path to learning and communication for children in the autistic spectrum	2004	Future Horizons	Methods
Skaggs, R. B.	Music: Keynote of the human spirit	2004	Publish America	Methods
Pavlicevic, M.	Community Music Therapy	2004	Jessica Kingsley	Methods
Aldridge, D. (Ed.)	Case study designs in music therapy	2004	Jessica Kingsley	Research
Knoll, C. & Henry, D.	Let's talk! Music therapy strategies to facilitate communication	2004	Music Works	Methods
Darnley-Smith, R. & Patey, H. M.	Music Therapy	2003	London: Sage	Comprehensive
Hadley, S. (Ed.)	Psychodynamic music therapy: Case studies	2003	Barcelona	Methods
Standley, J.	Music therapy with premature infants: Research and development	2003	AMTA	Research
Robb, S. (Ed.)	Music therapy in pediatric healthcare: Research and evidence based practice	2003	AMTA	Research
Pavlicevic, M. (Ed.)	Groups in music: Strategies from music therapy	2003	Jessica Kingsley	Methods
Lee, C.	The architecture of aesthetic music therapy	2003	Barcelona	Perspectives
Aigen, K.	A guide to writing and presenting in music therapy	2003	Barcelona	Pragmatic
Chase, K. M.	The multicultural music therapy handbook	2003	Southern Pen	Perspectives

Knoll, C.	Music therapy tool box: Developmental disabilities	2003	Music Works	Methods
Brunk, B. K.	Songwriting for music therapists	2003	Prelude	Methods
Chase, K. M.	The music therapy assessment handbook	2002	Southern Pen	Assessment
Summer, L. (Ed.)	Music and consciousness: The evolution of guided imagery and music: Helen Bonny	2002	Barcelona	Methods
Bunt, L. & Hoskyns, S. (Eds.)	The handbook of music therapy	2002	Brunner-Routledge	Comprehensive
Unkefer, R. & Thaut, M. (Eds.)	Music therapy in the treatment of adults with mental disorders: Theoretical bases and clinical interventions	2002	Barcelona	Methods
Grocke, D. & Bruscia, K. (Eds.)	Guided imagery and music: The Bonny method and beyond	2002	Barcelona	Methods
Wigram, Y. (Ed.)	A comprehensive guide to music therapy practice, research, and training	2002	Jessica Kingsley	Comprehensive
Loewy, J. & Hara, A. F. (Eds.)	Caring for the caregiver: The use of music and music therapy I grief and trauma	2002	AMTA	Methods
Eschen, J. (Ed.)	Analytical music therapy	2002	Jessica Kingsley	Methods
Kenny, C. & Stige, B. (Eds.)	Contemporary voices of music therapy: Communication, culture and community	2002	Oslo: Unipub Forlag	Perspectives
Wilson, B. (Ed.)	Models of music therapy interventions in school settings, 2nd edition	2002	AMTA	Methods

Standley, J.	Music techniques in therapy, counseling and special education	2002	MagnaMusic Baton	Methods
Aigen, K.	Playin' in the band: A qualitative study of popular music styles as clinical improvisation	2002	New York University	Research
Stige, B.	Culture-centered music therapy	2002	Barcelona	Perspectives
Lathom, W.	Pediatric music therapy	2002	Charles C Thomas	Methods
Davies, A. & Richards, E. (Eds.)	Music therapy and group work: Sound company	2002	Jessica Kingsley	Methods
Sutton, J. (Ed.)	Music, music therapy and trauma: International perspectives	2002	Jessica Kingsley	Perspectives
Berger, D.	Music therapy, sensory integration and the autistic child	2002	Jessica Kingsley	Perspectives
Montello, L.	Essential musical intelligence	2002	Quest	Methods
Bright, R.	Supportive eclectic music therapy for grief and loss: A practical handbook for professionals	2002	MagnaMusic Baton	Methods
Reuer, B. L.	Music therapy tool box: Medical settings	2002	Music Works	Methods
Knoll, C.	In harmony: Strategies for group music therapy	2002	Music Works	Methods
Karras, B.	Roses in December: Music sessions with older adults	2001	Elder Song	Methods
Knoll, C.	Music therapy tool box: Autism	2001	Music Works	Methods
Streeter, E.	Making music with the young child with special needs, revised editions	2001	Jessica Kingsley	Methods

Forinash, M. (Ed.)	Music therapy supervision	2001	Barcelona	Supervision
Lathom, W. & Eagle, C. (Eds.)	Music therapy for handicapped children, 2nd edition, Vols 1–3	2001	MagnaMusic Baton	Methods
Berger, D.	Music therapy, sensory integration and the autistic child	2001	Jessica Kingsley	Methods
Knoll, C., Henry, D. & Reuer, B.	You're the boss: Self-improvement strategies for music therapists	2000	Music Works	Pragmatic
AMTA	Effectiveness of music therapy procedures: Documentation of research and clinical practice, 3rd edition	2000	AMTA	Research
Aldridge, D. (Ed.)	Music therapy in dementia care: More new voices	2000	Jessica Kingsley	Methods
Dileo, C.	Ethical thinking in music therapy	2000	Jeffrey Books	Perspectives
Tillman, J.	Constructing musical healing: The wounds that heal	2000	Jessica Kingsley	Perspectives
Peters, J.	Music therapy: An introduction	2000	Charles C Thomas	Comprehensive
Thaut, M.	A scientific model of music in therapy and medicine	2000	IMR Press	Methods
Adler, R.	Musical assessment of gerontologic needs and treatment: The MAGNET survey	2000	MagnaMusic Baton	Assessment
Hibben, J. (Ed.)	Inside music therapy: Client experiences	1999	Barcelona	Perspectives
Knoll, C., Henry, D. & Reuer, B.	Music works: A professional notebook for music therapists	1999	Music Works	Methods
Davies, W. B., Thaut, M. H., & Gfeller, K.	An introduction to music therapy: Theory and practice, 2nd edition	1999	McGraw Hill	Comprehensive

Moreno, J.	Acting your inner music: Music therapy and psychodrama	1999	Barcelona	Methods
Dileo, C. (Ed.)	Music therapy and medicine: Theoretical and clinical applications	1999	AMTA	Methods
Hanser, S.	The new music therapist's handbook, 2nd edition	1999	Berklee Press	Comprehensive
Pavlicevic, M.	Intimate notes	1999	Jessica Kingsley	Comprehensive
Coleman, K. A. & Brunk, B. K.	SEMTAP: Special Education Music Therapy Assessment Process	1999	Prelude	Assessment
Libertore, A. & Layman, D.	The Cleveland music therapy assessment of infants and toddlers	1999	Cleveland Music School Settlement	Assessment
Wigram, T. (Ed.)	Clinical applications of music therapy in developmental disability, paediatrics and neurology	1999	Jessica Kingsley	Methods
Wigram, T. (Ed.)	Clinical applications of music therapy in psychiatry	1999	Jessica Kingsley	Methods
Aldridge, D. (Ed.)	Music therapy in palliative care: New voices	1999	Jessica Kingsley	Methods
Summer, L.	Guided imagery and music in the institutional setting	1999	Barcelona	Methods
Moreno, J.	Acting your inner music: Music therapy and psychodrama	1999	MagnaMusic Baton	Methods
Cassity, M. & J.	Multimodal psychiatric music therapy for adults, adolescents and children, 3rd edition	1998	MagnaMusic Baton	Methods
Aigen, K.	Paths of development in Nordoff-Robbins music therapy	1998	Barcelona	Methods

Robbins, Carol & Clive (Eds.)	Healing heritage	1998	Barcelona	Methods
Bruscia, K. (Ed.)	Dynamics of music psychotherapy	1998	Barcelona	Methods
Ruud, E.	Music Therapy: Improvisation, communication, and culture	1998	Barcelona	Comprehensive
Clarkson, G.	I dreamed I was normal: A music therapist's journey into the realms of autism	1998	MagnaMusic Baton	Perspectives
Tomaino, C. (Ed.)	Clinical applications of music in neurologic rehabilitation	1998	MagnaMusic Baton	Methods
Galerstein, N.	Age appropriate activities: For adults with profound mental retardation	1998	MagnaMusic Baton	Methods
Bruscia, K.	Defining music therapy, 2nd edition	1998	Barcelona	Comprehensive
Benenzon, R.	Music therapy theory and manual: Contributions to the knowledge of nonverbal contexts	1998	Charles C Thomas	Methods
Bright, R.	Wholeness in later life	1997	Jessica Kingsley	Methods
Borczon, R.	Music therapy: Group vignettes	1997	Barcelona	Methods
Bright, R.	Music therapy and the dementias: Improving the quality of life, 2nd edition	1997	MagnaMusic Baton	Methods
Skaggs, J.	Finishing strong: Treating chemical addictions with music and song	1997	Magna Music Baton	Methods
Loewy, J. (Ed.)	Music therapy and pediatric pain	1997	Jeffrey Books	Methods

Pavilicevic, M.	Music therapy in context: Music, meaning and relationship	1997	Jessica Kingsley	Perspectives
Boxill, E.	The miracle of music therapy	1997	Barcelona	Comprehensive
Smeijstsers, H.	Multiple perspectives: A guide to qualitative research in music therapy	1997	Barcelona	Research
Wigram, T. & Dileo, C. (Eds.)	Music vibration and health	1997	Jeffrey Books	Perspectives
Krout, R.	Music technology for music therapists	1997	West	Methods
Taylor, D.	Biomedical foundations of music as therapy	1997	MagnaMusic Baton	Perspectives
Clair, A.	Therapeutic uses of music with older adults	1996	Health	Methods
Shaw, J. & Manthey, C.	Musical bridges: Intergenerational music programs	1996	MagnaMusic Baton	Methods
Aigen, K.	Being in music: Foundations of Nordoff-Robbins music therapy	1996	Barcelona	Methods
Plach, T.	The creative use of music in group therapy, 2nd edition	1996	Charles C Thomas	Methods
Langenberg, M., Aigen, K., & Frommer, J. (Eds.)	Qualitative music therapy research: Beginning Dialogues	1996	Barcelona	Research
Wilson, B. (Ed.)	Models of music therapy interventions in schools, First edition	1996	AMTA	Methods
Furman, C. (Ed.)	Effectiveness of music therapy procedures, First edition	1996	AMTA	Research

Lee, C.	Music at the edge: The music therapy experience of a musician with AIDS	1996	Routledge	Methods
Froelich, M.	Music therapy with hospitalized children	1996	Jeffrey Books	Methods
Aldridge, D. (Ed.)	Music therapy research and practice in medicine: From out of the silence	1996	Jessica Kingsley	Research
Gfeller, K.	Music therapy programming for individuals with Alzheimer's diseases and related disorders	1995	Univ. of Iowa	Methods
Wigram, T., Saperston, B., & West, R. (Eds.)	The art and science of music therapy: A handbook	1995	Harwood Academic	Comprehensive
Bruscia, K. (Ed.)	Improvisational models of music therapy	1995	Charles C Thomas	Methods
Lecourt, E.	Music therapy	1995	MagnaMusic Baton	Comprehensive
Wheeler, B. L. (Ed.)	Music therapy research: Quantitative and qualitative perspectives	1995	Barcelona	Research
Gilroy, A.	Art and music: Therapy and research	1995	Routledge	Research
Kenny, C.	Listening, playing, creating: Essays on the power of sound	1995	State University of New York Press	Comprehensive
Gfeller, K. E. & Hanson, N. (Eds.)	Music therapy programming for individuals with Alzheimer's diseases and related disorders	1995	The University of Iowa	Methods
Coleman, K. A. & Brunk, B. K.	Learning through music: Music therapy strategies for special education	1994	Prelude	Methods

Krout, R.	Beginning rock guitar for music leaders: Skills for therapy, education, recreation and leisure	1994	MagnaMusic Baton	Methods
Prickett, C. & Standley, J. (Eds.)	Research in music therapy: A tradition of excellence: Outstanding reprints from the *Journal of Music Therapy,* 1964–1993	1994	National Association of Music Therapy	Research
Bunt, L. (Ed.)	Music therapy: An art beyond words	1994	Routledge	Comprehensive
Rykov, M.	Last songs: AIDS and the music therapist, 2nd edition	1994	Music Therapy Services of Metropolitan Toronto	Methods
Cordrey, C.	Hidden treasures: Music and memory activities for people with Alzheimers	1994	Elder Song	Methods
Priestley, M.	Essays on analytical music therapy	1994	Barcelona	Methods
Schalkwijk, R.	Music and people with developmental disabilities: Music therapy, remedial music making and musical activities	1994	Jessica Kingsley	Methods
Goll, H.	Special educational music therapy: With persons who have severe/profound retardation	1994	Peter Lang	Methods
Roskam, K.	Feeling the sound: The influence of music on behavior	1993	San Francisco Press	Perspectives
Shaw, J.	The joy of music in maturity	1993	MagnaMusic Baton	Methods
Birkenshaw-Fleming, L.	Music for all: Teaching music to people with special needs	1993	G.V. Thompson Music	Methods

Heal, M. & Wigram, T. (Eds.)	Music therapy in health and education	1993	Jessica Kingsley	Comprehensive
Bejjani, F. (Ed.)	Current research in arts medicine: A compendium of the Med Art International 1992 World Congress on Arts and Medicine	1993	A Cappella Books	Research
Maranto, C. (Ed.)	Music therapy: International perspectives	1993	Jeffrey Books	Perspectives
Michel, D. E. & Jones, J. L.	Music for developing speech and language skills: A guide for parents and therapists	1992	MagnaMusic Baton	Methods
Mills, P.	Helping the special learner through musical activities	1992	MagnaMusic Baton	Methods
Maranto, C. (Ed.)	Applications of music in medicine	1991	NAMT	Methods
Alvin, J.	Music therapy for the autistic child, 2nd edition	1991	Oxford University Press	Methods
Bright, R.	Music in geriatric care: A second look	1991	Music Therapy Enterprises (Wahroonga, Australia)	Methods
Chavin, M.	The lost chord: Reaching the person with dementia through the power of music	1991	Elder Song	Methods
Standley, J.	Music therapy techniques in therapy, counseling, and special education, 1st edition	1991	MagnaMusic Baton	Methods
Maranto, C. D. (Ed.)	Applications of music in medicine	1991	National Association for Music Therapy	Methods
Bruscia, K. (Ed.)	Case studies in music therapy	1991	Barcelona	Comprehensive

Scovel, M.	Reimbursement guide for music therapists	1990	National Association of Music Therapy	Pragmatic
Summer, L.	Guided imagery and music in the institutional setting, 2nd edition	1990	MagnaMusic Baton	Methods
Unkefer, R. (Ed.)	Music therapy in the treatment of adults with mental disorders: Theoretical bases and clinical interventions, 1st edition	1990	Schirmer Books	Methods
Kenny C.	The field of play: A guide for the theory and practice of music therapy	1989	Ridgeview Publishing Company	Perspectives
Scartelli, J. P.	Music and self-management models: A physiological model	1989	MagnaMusic Baton	Perspectives
Bitcon, C.	Risk it, express it: Expression in creative practice	1989	MagnaMusic Baton	Methods
Boxill, E.	Music therapy for living: The principle of normalization embodied in music therapy	1989	MagnaMusic Baton	Perspectives
Lee, M.	Rehabilitation, music and human well-being	1989	MagnaMusic Baton	Methods
Pratt, R. R. (Ed.)	Music therapy and music in special education: The international state of the art	1989	MagnaMusic Baton	Methods
Boyle, M. & Krout, R.	Music therapy clinical training manual	1988	MagnaMusic Baton	Pragmatic
Bright, R.	Music therapy and the dementias: Improvising the quality of life	1988	MagnaMusic Baton	Methods
Maranto, C. D. (Ed.)	Master's theses in music therapy: Index and abstracts	1988	Temple University	Pragmatic

Furman, C. (Ed.)	Effectiveness of music therapy procedures: Documentation of research and clinical practice	1988	National Association for Music Therapy	Research
Hodon, P. (Ed.)	Music as medicine: The history of music therapy	1988	Ashgate	Comprehensive
Maranto, C. D. & Bruscia, K.	Methods of teaching and training for music therapist	1988	Temple University	Comprehensive
Hanser, S.	Music therapist's handbook	1987	W. H. Green	Comprehensive
Bruscia, K. (Ed.)	Improvisational models of music therapy	1987	Charles C Thomas	Methods
Maranto, C. D. & Bruscia, K. E. (Eds.)	Perspectives on music therapy education and training	1987	Temple University	Comprehensive
Peters, J.	Music therapy: An introduction	1987	Charles C Thomas	Comprehensive
Henry, D.	Music works: A handbook of job skills for music therapists	1986	Music Works	Pragmatic
Bright, R.	Grieving: A handbook for those who care	1986	MagnaMusic Baton	Methods
Ruud, E.	Music and health	1986	Norsk musikforlag	Perspectives
Krout, R.	Music therapy in special education: Developing and maintaining social skills necessary for mainstreaming	1986	MagnaMusic Baton	Methods
Katsh, S. & Merle-Fishman, C.	The music within you	1985 (1999, 2nd ed., Barcelona)	Simon and Schuster	Comprehensive
Douglass, D.	Accent on rhythm: Music activities for the aged	1985	MagnaMusic Baton	Methods

Boxill, E.	Music therapy for the developmentally disabled	1985	Aspen	Methods
Karras, B.	Down memory lane: Topics and ideas for reminiscence groups	1985	Elder Song	Methods
Slabey, V.	Music involvement for nursing homes: For music therapists and other healthcare professionals	1985	Mt. Matthew Press	Methods
Priestley, M.	Music therapy in action, 2nd edition	1985	MagnaMusic Baton	Methods
Steele, A.	The music therapy levels system: A manual of principles and applications	1985	Women's Council of the Cleveland Music School Settlement	Methods
Michel, D.	Music therapy: An introduction, including music in special education, 2nd edition	1984	Charles C Thomas	Comprehensive
Lathom, W.	Music therapy for handicapped children, 2nd edition of the Project Music Monograph Series	1984	AMS Publications	Methods
Munro, S.	Music therapy in palliative/hospice care	1984	MagnaMusic Baton	Methods
Nordoff, P. & Robbins, C.	Music therapy in special education, 2nd edition	1983	MagnaMusic Baton	Methods
Krout, R.	Teaching basic guitar skills to special learners: A data-based approach	1983	MagnaMusic Baton	Methods
Elliott, B.	Guide to the selection of musical instruments with respect to physical ability and disability	1982	MagnaMusic Baton	Methods
Kenny, C.	The mystic artery: The magic of music therapy	1982	Ridgeview	Perspectives

Eagle, C.	Music therapy for handicapped individuals: An annotated and indexed bibliography	1982	National Association for Music Therapy	Research
Cormier, L.	Music therapy for handicapped children: Deaf-blind	1982	National Association for Music Therapy	Methods
Codding, P.	Music therapy for handicapped children: Mentally retarded	1982	National Association for Therapy	Methods
Buechler, J.	Music therapy for handicapped children: Hearing impaired	1982	National Association for Music Therapy	Methods
Schwankovsky, L.	Music therapy for handicapped children: Other health impaired	1982	National Association for	Methods
Rudenberg, M.	Music therapy for handicapped children: Orthopedically handicapped	1982	National Association for Music Therapy	Methods
Pfeifer, M. S.	Music therapy for handicapped children: Multi-handicapped	1982	National Association for Music Therapy	Methods
Paul, D.	Music therapy for handicapped children: Emotionally disturbed	1982	National Association for Music Therapy	Methods
Miller, S.	Music therapy for handicapped children Speech impaired	1982	National Association for Music Therapy	Methods
Adler, R.	Target on music	1982	Christ Church Music Center	Methods
Madsen, C.	Music therapy: A behavioral guide for the mentally retarded	1981	National Association for Music Therapy	Methods
Schulberg, C.	The music therapy sourcebook	1981	Human Sciences Press	Methods
Benenzon, R.	Music therapy manual	1981	Charles C Thomas	Methods
Tyson, F.	Psychiatric music therapy: Origins and and development	1981	Creative Arts Rehabilitation Center	Methods

Bonny, H.	The role of taped music programs in the GIM process	1980	ICM books	Methods
Ruud, E.	Music therapy and its relationship to current treatment theories	1980	MagnaMusic Baton	Perspectives
Robbins, C. M. & Robbins, C.	Music for the hearing impaired: A resource manual and curriculum guide	1980	MagnaMusic Baton	Methods
Plach, R.	The creative use of music in group therapy	1980	Charles C Thomas	Methods
Orff, G.	The Orff music therapy: Active furthering of the development of the child	1980	Schott	Methods
Clark, C. & Chadwick, D.	Clinically adapted instruments for the multiply handicapped	1979	Modulations Company	Methods
Bonny, H.	Facilitating guided imagery and music sessions	1978	ICM Books	Methods
Alvin, J.	Music therapy for the autistic child	1978	Oxford University Press	Methods
Trevisan, L. & Nowicki, A.	Beyond the sound: A technical and philosophical approach to music therapy, revised edition	1978	Self Published	Comprehensive
Eagle, C. (Ed.)	Music psychology index	1978	Institute for Therapeutics Research	Research
Nordoff, P. & Robbins, C.	Creative music therapy: Individualized treatment for the handicapped child	1977	John Day	Methods
Bitcon, C.	Alike and different: The clinical and educational use of Orff-Schulwerk	1976	Rosha Press	Methods

Alvin, J.	Music for the handicapped child, 2nd edition	1976	Oxford University Press	Methods
Purvis, J.	Music in developmental therapy: A curriculum guide	1976	University Park Press	Methods
Tomat, J.	Learning through music for special children and their teachers	1975	Merriam-Eddy	Methods
Priestley, M.	Music therapy in action	1975	Constable	Methods
Apprey, Z.	Applied music therapy: Collected papers on a technique and a point of view	1975	Institute of Music Therapy and Humanistic Psychology	Perspectives
Alvin, J.	Music therapy	1975	Basic Books	Methods
Bright, R.	Music in geriatric care	1973	St. Martins Press	Methods
Nordoff, P. & Robbins, C.	Therapy in music for handicapped children	1972	St. Martins Press	Methods
Bright, R.	Music in geriatric care	1972	St. Martins Press	Methods
Nordoff, P. & Robbins, C.	Music therapy in special education	1971	John Day	Methods
Gaston, E. T. (Ed.)	Music in therapy	1968	Macmillan	Comprehensive
Beggs, C.	Music therapy management and practice	1968	Rose Leigh Publications	Pragmatic
Nordoff, P. & Robbins, C.	Music therapy for handicapped children: Investigations and experiences	1965	Rudolf Steiner	Methods
Podolsky, E. (Ed.)	Music therapy	1954	Philosophical Library	Comprehensive

Note: This list does not include the following:

- Music published specifically for music therapy, available through Theodore Presser, Elder Song, Prelude Music Therapy, and Carl Fischer.
- Books in the subcategory of Psychology of Music
- Books in the subcategory of music education and special needs

BIBLIOGRAPHY

Aasgaard, T., & Trondalen, G. (2004). Music therapy in Norway. *Voices: A world forum for music therapy*. Retrieved from: http://www.voices.no/country/monthnorway_july2004.html

Abbott, E. (2006). The administration of music therapy training clinics: A descriptive study. *Journal of Music Therapy, 43*:1, 63–81.

Adler, R. (2000). *Musical assessment of gerontologic needs and treatment.* The MAGNET Survey, St. Louis, MO: MMB.

Adamek, M. S. (1994). Audio-cueing and immediate feedback to improve group leadership skills: A live supervision model. *Journal of Music Therapy, 31*:2, 135–164.

Ahonen-Eerikainen, H. (2003). Using group analytic supervision approach when supervising music therapists. *Nordic Journal of Music Therapy, 12*:2, 173–182.

Aigen, K. (1998). Creativity in qualitative music therapy research. *Journal of Music Therapy, 35*:3, 150–175.

Aigen, K. (2001). Popular musical styles in Nordoff-Robbins clinical improvisation. *Music Therapy Perspectives, 19*(1), 28–41.

Aigen, K. (2005a). *Music-centered music therapy.* Gilsum, NH: Barcelona Publishers.

Aigen, K. (2008). An analysis of qualitative music therapy research reports, 1987–2006: Doctoral studies. *The Arts in Psychotherapy, 35*:5, 251–261.

Aigen, K. (2009). Verticality and containment in song and improvisation: An application of schema theory to Nordoff-Robbins music therapy. *Journal of Music Therapy, 46*:3, 238–67.

Aldridge, D. (1993) Artists or psychotherapists? *The Arts in Psychotherapy, 20*:3, 199–277.

Aldridge, D. (2007) *Editorial Music Therapy Today:* Final issue. *Music Therapy Today.* Retrieved from: http://www.musictherapytoday.com/

Allen, M. L. (1996). Dimensions of educational satisfaction and academic achievement among music therapy majors. *Journal of Music Therapy, 33*:2, 147–160

Alley, J. M. (1978). Competency-based evaluation of a music therapy curriculum. *Journal of Music Therapy, 15*:1, 9–14.

Alley, J. M. (1980). The effect of self-analysis of videotapes on selected competencies of music therapy majors. *Journal of Music Therapy, 17,* 113–132.

Alley, J. M. (1982). The effect of videotape analysis on music therapy competencies: An observation of simulated and clinical activities. *Journal of Music Therapy, 193,* 141–160.

Alvin, J. (1975). *Music therapy.* London: Hutchinson & Co., Ltd.

Alvin, J. (1976). *Music for the handicapped child.* London: Oxford University Press.

American Association for Music Therapy (AAMT). (1978). *Manual for the approval of educational programs in music therapy.* Philadelphia, PA: AAMT.

American Music Therapy Association. (1999). *AMTA Professional Competencies.* Silver Spring, MD: AMTA. Retrieved from: http://www.musictherapy.org/competencies.html

American Music Therapy Association. (1998). *A manual for the approval of educational programs in music therapy under the AAMT model.* Silver Spring, MD: Author.

American Music Therapy Association. (1999). Final report and recommendations of the Commission on Education and Clinical Training of the American Music Therapy Association. Silver Spring, MD: Author.

American Music Therapy Association. (2002). *Standards of clinical practice.* Silver Spring, MD: AMTA. Retrieved from: http://www.musictherapy.org/standards.html

American Music Therapy Association. (2007). *AMTA Advanced Competencies.* Silver Spring, MD: AMTA.

American Music Therapy Association. (2009). *AMTA advanced competencies.* Silver Spring, MD: AMTA. Retrieved from: http://www.musictherapy.org/handbook/advancedcomp.html

American Music Therapy Association. (2009a). *Standards for education and clinical training.* Silver Spring, MD. Author.

American Music Therapy Association. (2009b). *Advanced competencies.* Silver Spring, MD: Author.

AMTA Education and Training Advisory Board. (2005). *Advisory on levels of practice in music therapy.* Retrieved from: http://www.musictherapy.org/handbook/advisory.html

Amir, D. (1999a). The role of music therapy in establishing cultural identity. 9th World Congress for Music Therapy, Washington, DC. Retrieved from E-Book of Articles, pp. 6–24.

Amir, D. (1999b). Musical and verbal interventions in music therapy: A qualitative study. *Journal of Music Therapy, 36:*2, 144–175.

Amir, D. (2003). Two congresses, two journeys. *Voices: A World Forum for Music Therapy.* Retrieved from: http://www.voices.no/columnist/colamir210403.html

Amir, D. (2005). Music therapy in Israel. *Voices: A World Forum for Music Therapy.* Retrieved from: http://www.voices.no/mainissues/mitext11amir.html

Anderson, L. (1982). The effect of feedback versus no feedback on music therapy competencies. *Journal of Music Therapy, 19:*3, 130–140.

Anderson, L. W., & Krathwohl, D. R. (Eds.). (2001). *A taxonomy for learning, teaching and assessing: A revision of Bloom's Taxonomy of educational objectives.* New York: Longman.

Ansdell, G. (2002). Community music therapy and the winds of change. *Voices: A World Forum for Music Therapy.* Retrieved from: http://www.voices.no/mainissues/Voices2(2)ansdell.html

Ansdell, G., Bunt, L., & Hartley, N. (2002). Music Therapy in the United Kingdom. *Voices: A World Forum for Music Therapy.* Retrieved from: http://www.voices.no/country/monthuk_april2002.html

Asmus, E. P. (1980) .Affective course entry perceptions of music therapy students in professional and preprofessional courses. *Journal of Music Therapy, 17:*2, 50–57.

Asmus, E. P., & Galloway, J. P. (1985). Relationship between music therapy students' contact with and attitude toward disabled persons. *Journal of Music Therapy, 22:*1, 12–21.

Austin, D. (1998). Vocal improvisation in analytically oriented music therapy with adults. In T. Wigram & J. De Backer (Eds.), *Clinical applications of music therapy in psychiatry.* London, UK: JKP.

Austin, D., & Dvorkin, J. (2001). Peer supervision in music therapy. In M. Forinash (Ed.), *Music therapy supervision,* pp. 219–229. Gilsum, NH: Barcelona Publishers.

Austin, D. (2009). *The theory and practice of vocal psychotherapy.* London, UK: JKP.

Austin, D. (2010). Personal communication.

Bain, K. (2004). *What the best college teachers do.* Cambridge, MA: Harvard University Press.

Bain, K. (2008). Personal communication.

Baker, F. (2007). Enhancing the clinical reasoning skills of music therapy students through problem based learning. *Nordic Journal of Music Therapy, 16*:1, 27–41.

Bang, C. (2008). Memories from the World Congress of Music Therapy 1974. *Voices: A World Forum for Music Therapy.* Retrieved from: http://www.voices.no/mainissues/mi40008000 290.php

Barcellos, L. R. M. (2001). Music therapy in South America. *Voices: A World Forum for Music Therapy.* Retrieved from: http://www.voices.no/mainissues/mitext11barcellos.html

Barkley, E., Cross, K. P., & Major, C. H. (2005). *Collaborative learning techniques: A handbook for college faculty.* San Francisco, CA: Jossey-Bass.

Barreca, G. (2010). To the B student who thinks he is not a B student. Commentary, *The Chronicle of Higher Education.* Retrieved from: http://chronicle.com/blogPost/To-the-B-Student-Who-Thinks/20792/

Barry, P., & O'Callaghan, C. (2008). Reflexive journal writing: A tool for music therapy student clinical practice development. *Nordic Journal of Music Therapy, 17*:1, 55–66.

Bauer, S. (2007). Update of Music Therapy in Chile. *Voices: A World Forum for Music Therapy.* Retrieved from: http://www.voices.no/country//monthchile_june2007.php

Baxter, H. T., Berghofer, J. A., MacEwan, L., Nelson, J.. Peters, K., & Roberts, P. (2007). *The individualized music therapy assessment profile.* London, UK: JKP.

Benenzon, R. O. (1997). *Music therapy theory and manual: Contributions to the knowledge of non-verbal contexts.* (2nd ed.). Springfield, IL: Charles C Thomas.

Bergstrom-Nielsen, C. (1993). Graphic notation as a tool in describing and analyzing music therapy improvisations. *Music Therapy, 12*:1, 40–58

Bergstrom- Nielson, C. (1998). Graphic notation: How to map the landscape of musical improvisations. 4th European Music Therapy Congress: Music & Therapy–A Dialogue. Leuven, Belgium. pp. 945–951. Retrieved from: http://www.musictherapyworld.de/

Biggs, J., & Collis, K. (1982). *Evaluating the quality of learning: The SOLO taxonomy.* New York: Academic Press.

Biggs, J. (2003). *Teaching for quality learning at university.* (2nd ed.). Buckingham, Australia: SRHE and Open University Press.

Biggs, J., & Tang, C. (2007). *Teaching for quality learning at university.* (3rd ed.). Buckingham, Australia: SRHE and Open University Press.

Bion, W. R. (1974). *Experiences in groups.* New York: Basic Books.

Bird, N., Merrill, T., Mohan, H., Summer, S., & Woodward, A. (1999). Staying alive In our work: A group's experience in peer supervision. *Canadian Journal of Music Therapy, 6*:2, 51–67.

Bitcon, C. (1976). *Alike and different: The clinical and educational use of Orff-Schulwerk.* San Diego, CA: Rosha Press.

Bittman, B., Berk, L., Felten, D., Westengard, J., Simonton, C., Pappas, J., & Ninehouser, M. (2001). Composite effects of group drumming music therapy on modulation of neuroendocrine-immune parameters in normal subjects. *Alternative Therapies, 7*:1, 38–47.

Bloom, B. S. (Ed.), Englehart, M. D., Furst, E. J., Hill, W. H., & Krathwohl, D. (1956). *The taxonomy of educational objectives, the classification of educational goals–Handbook I: Cognitive domain.* New York: McKay.

Bonde, L. (2007). Music therapy in Denmark [online]. *Voices: A World Forum for Music Therapy.* Retrieved from: http://www.voices.no/country/monthdenmark_january2007.html

Boone, P. C. (1989). Future trends and new models for clinical training. *Music Therapy Perspectives, 7,* 96–99.

Booth, S. (1997). On phenomenography, learning and teaching. *Higher Education Research & Development, 16*:2, 135–158.

Botello, K., & Krout, R. E. (2008). Music therapy assessment of automatic thoughts: Developing a cognitive behavioral application of improvisation to assess couple communication. *Music Therapy Perspectives, 26:*1, 51–55.

Boxberger, R. (1962). A historical study of the National Association for Music Therapy, Inc. *Music Therapy 1962,* 133–197.

Braswell, C., Maranto, C. D., & Decuir, A. (1979a). A survey of clinical practice in music therapy Part I: The institutions in which music therapists work and personal data. *Journal of Music Therapy, 16,* 2–16.

Braswell, C., Maranto, C. D., Decuir, A. (1979b). A survey of clinical practice in music therapy, Part II: Clinical practice, education, and clinical training. *Journal of Music Therapy, 16,* 50–69.

Braswell, C., Decuir, A., & Maranto, C. D. (1980). Ratings of entry level skills by music therapy clinicians, educators, and interns. *Journal of Music Therapy, 17,* 133–147.

Braswell, C., Decuir, A., & Brooks, D. M. (1985). A survey of clinical training in music therapy: Degree of compliance with NAMT Guidelines. *Journal of Music Therapy, 22,* 73–86.

Braswell, C., Decuir, A., Maranto, C. D. (1986). Advanced competencies in music therapy. *Music Therapy, 6A:*1, 57–67.

Braswell, C. (1987). Accountability in music therapy education. In C. D. Maranto & K.

Bright, R. (1993). Cultural aspects of music in therapy. In M. H. Heal & T. Wigram (Eds.), *Music therapy in health and education,* pp. 193–207. London: Jessica Kingsley.

Bringle, R. G., & Hatcher, J. A. (1995). A service-learning curriculum for faculty. *Michigan Journal of Community Service Learning, 2,* 112–122.

Brookins, L. M. (1984). The music therapy clinical intern: Performance skills, academic knowledge, personal qualities, and interpersonal skills necessary for a student seeking clinical training. *Journal of Music Therapy, 21,* 193–201

Brooks, D. (2002). Supervision strategies for the Bonny method of guided imagery and music. In K. E. Bruscia & D. Grocke (Eds.), *Guided imagery and music: The Bonny method and beyond,* pp. 519–532.

Brooks, D. (2003). A history of music therapy journal articles published in the English language. *Journal of Music Therapy, 40:*2, 151–168.

Brown, S. (2009). Supervision in context: A balancing act. In H. Odell-Miller & E. Richards, (Eds.), *Supervision of music therapy: A theoretical and practice handbook,* pp. 119–134. London: Routledge.

Brown, J. (2001). Towards a culturally centered music therapy practice. *Canadian Journal of Music Therapy, 8:*1, 10–23.

Brotons, M., Graham-Hurley, K., Hairston, M., Hawley, T., Michel, D., Moreno, J., Picard, D., & Taylor, D. (1997). A survey of international music therapy students in NAMT approved academic programs. *Music Therapy Perspectives, 15:*1, 45–49.

Bruscia, K. E., Hesser B., & Boxill, E. (1981). Essential competencies for the practice of music therapy. *Music Therapy, 1,* 43–49.

Bruscia, K. E. (1986). Advanced competencies in music therapy. *Music Therapy, 6A:*1, 57–67.

Bruscia, K. E. (1987a). Professional identity issues in music therapy education. In C. D. Maranto & K. E. Bruscia (Eds.), *Perspectives on music therapy education and training,* pp. 17–29. Philadelphia, PA: Temple University.

Bruscia, K. E. (1987b). Variations in clinical training: AAMT and NAMT models. In C. D. Maranto, C. D. & K. E. Bruscia (Eds.), *Perspectives on music therapy education and training,* pp. 97–106. Philadelphia, PA: Temple University.

Bruscia, K. E. (1987c). *Improvisational models of music therapy.* Springfield, IL: Charles C Thomas.

Bruscia, K. E. (1988). Standards for clinical assessment in the arts. *The Arts in Psychotherapy, 15:*5, 5–10.

Bruscia, K. E. (1989). The content of music therapy education at undergraduate and graduate levels. *Music Therapy Perspectives, 7,* 83–87.

Bruscia, K. E. (1998a). *Defining music therapy* (2nd ed.). Gilsum, NH: Barcelona Publishers.

Bruscia, K. E. (1998b). Standards of integrity for qualitative music therapy research. *Journal of Music Therapy, 35:*3, 176–200.

Bruscia, K. E. (1998c). Techniques for uncovering and working with countertransference. In K. E. Bruscia, *The dynamics of music psychotherapy,* pp. 93–120. Gilsum, NH: Barcelona Publishers.

Bruscia, K. E. (1999). Teaching research at three levels of education. 9th World Congress for Music Therapy, Washington, DC. Retrieved from E-Book of Articles, pp. 342–344.

Bruscia, K. E. (2001). A model of supervision derived from apprenticeship training. In M.Forinash (Ed.), *Music therapy supervision.* Gilsum, NH: Barcelona Publishers.

Bunt, L. (2004). Mary Priestley interviewed by Leslie Bunt. *Voices: A World Forum for Music Therapy.* Retrieved from: http://www.voices.no/mainissues/mi40003000155.html

Bunt, L. (2005). In which box does music therapy training fit? *Voices: A World Forum for Music Therapy.* Retrieved from: http://www.voices.no/columnist/colbunt141005.html

Camilleri, V. A. (2001). Therapist self-awareness: an essential tool in music therapy. *The Arts in Psychotherapy, 28:*1, 79–85.

Carnegie Mellon University. (2001). Everley Center for Teaching Excellence. Rubric to assess discussion performance in an upper-level undergraduate or graduate seminar. Everley Center for Teaching Excellence. Retrieved from: http://www.cmu.edu/teaching/design teach/teach/rubrics.html

Carter, S. (2005). And the question is? *British Journal of Music Therapy, 19:*1, 16–17.

Cassity, M. (1977). Nontraditional guitar techniques for the educable and trainable mentally retarded residents in music therapy activities. *Journal of Music Therapy, 19,* 39–42.

Cassity, M. (1987). Functional piano skills for music therapy interns. In C. D. Maranto & K. E. Bruscia (Eds.), *Perspectives on music therapy education and training.* Philadelphia: Temple University.

Cassity, M., & Cassity, J. (2006). *Multi-modal psychiatric music therapy for adults, adolescents and children* (3rd ed.). London, UK: JKP.

Certification Board for Music Therapists, Inc. (CBMT). (1983). *Job analysis: Knowledge, skill, and ability statements.* Philadelphia, PA: Assessment Systems Incorporated.

Certification Board for Music Therapists (CBMT). (1989). *Job reanalysis survey of music therapy knowledge and skills.* Author.

Certification Board for Music Therapists (CBMT). (1997). 1997 CBMT program survey results. *CBMT B.C. Status, 9*(2), 7–10.

Certification Board for Music Therapists (CBMT). (1999). CBMT looks to the future. *CBMT B.C. Status, 13*(1).

Cevasco, A. M., & Vanweelden, K. (2010). An analysis of songbook series for older adult populations. *Music Therapy Perspectives, 28:*1, 37–78.

Chadwick, D. M. (2010). Personal communication.

Chase, K. M. (2003). Multicultural music therapy. *Music Therapy Perspectives, 21:*2, 84–88.

Choi, B. (2008). Awareness of music therapy practices and factors influencing specific theoretical approaches. *Journal of Music Therapy, 41:*1, 93–109.

Chong, H. (2007). Music therapist's therapeutic relationship with music. *Voices: A World Forum for Music Therapy.* Retrieved from: http://www.voices.no/columnist/colchong240907.php

Chung, H. (2005). Some considerations for further development of music therapy in Korea.

Voices: A World Forum for Music Therapy. Retrieved from: http://www.voices.no/mainissues /mi40005000181.html

Clark, M. (1987). The institute for music ad imagery training program for guided imagery and music. In C. D. Maranto, C. D. & K. E. Bruscia (Eds.), *Perspectives on music therapy education and training,* pp. 191–194. Philadelphia, PA: Temple University.

Clark, M., & Ficken, C. (1988). Music therapy in the new healthcare environment. *Music Therapy Perspectives, 5,* 23–27.

Clark, M. E., & Kranz, P. (1996). A survey of backgrounds, attitudes and experiences of new music therapy students. *Journal of Music Therapy, 33:*2, 124–146.

Codding, P. A. (1987). A content analysis of the *Journal of Music Therapy,* 1977–85. *Journal of Music Therapy, 24:*4, 195–202.

Codding, P. A. (2010). Personal communication.

Cohen, G., & Gericke, O. (1972). Music therapy assessment: Prime requisite for determining patient objectives. *Journal of Music Therapy, 9,* 161–189.

Cohen, N., Hadsell, N., & Williams, S. (1997). The perceived applicability of applied music requirements in the vocational practices of professional music therapists. *Music Therapy Perspectives, 15:*2, 67–72.

Cohen, N. S., & Behrens, G. A. (2002). The relationship between type of degree and professional status in clinical music therapists. *Journal of Music Therapy, 39:*3, 188–208.

Coleman, K. A., & Brunk, B. K. (1999). *SEMTAP: Special Education Music Therapy Assessment Process.* Grapevine, TX: Prelude Music Therapy.

Colwell, C. M., & Thompson, L. K. (2000). "Inclusion" of information on mainstreaming in undergraduate music education curricula. *Journal of Music Therapy, 37:*3, 205–21.

Cornfield, J. L., & Knefelkamp, L. I. (1979). Analysis of the learner characteristics of students implied by the Perry scheme. Reprinted as Table 1.1 in Perry, W .G. (1999). *Forms of ethical and intellectual development in the college years.* San Francisco, CA: Jossey-Bass.

Cowan, D. S. (1996). Information sharing: Meeting whose needs? The personal needs of the therapist. *Music Therapy Perspectives, 14:*1, 50–52.

Creagan, J. (2010). Personal communication.

Crowe, B. J. (1986). Other perspectives: Developing a sense of vocation: Important step to professional acceptance. *Music Therapy Perspectives, 3,* 42–43.

Crowe, B., & Bruscia, K. E. (1999, Spring). Draft report of recommendations of the AMTA Commission on Education and Clinical Training: Subject to revision prior to adoption. *Music Therapy Matters, 2*(1), 8–9.

Crowe, B. J., & Rio, R. (2004). Implications of technology in music therapy practice and research for music therapy education: A review of literature. *Journal of Music Therapy, 41:*4, 282–320.

Croxson, M. (2003). Music therapy in New Zealand. *Voices: A World Forum for Music Therapy.* Retreived from: http://www.voices.no/country/monthnewzealand_february2003.html

Croxson, M. (2007). Music therapy in New Zealand. *Voices: A World Forum for Music Therapy.* Retreived from: http://www.voices.no/country/monthnewzealand_april2007.html

Curtis, S. L. Information sharing: A simulation game for students: The music therapy game. *Music Therapy Perspectives, 5,* 111–113.

Darrow, A., & Gibbons, A. C. (1987). Organization and administration of music therapy practice: A procedural guide. In C. D. Maranto & K. E. Bruscia (Eds.), *Perspectives on music therapy education and training,* pp. 107–126. Philadelphia, PA: Temple University.

Darrow, A., & Molloy, D. (1998). Multicultural perspectives in music therapy: An examination of the literature, educational curricula, and clinical practices in culturally diverse cities in the United States. *Music Therapy Perspectives, 16*(1), 27–32.

Darrow, A., Johnson, C., Ghetti, C., & Achey, C. (2001). An analysis of music therapy student practicum behaviors and their relationship to clinical effectiveness: An exploratory investigation. *Journal of Music Therapy, 38:*4, 307–320.

Darrow, A. (2004). *Introduction to approaches in music therapy.* Silver Spring, MD: American Music Therapy Association.

Daveson, B., & Grocke, D. (2008). Indigenous music therapy theory building through grounded theory research: The developing indigenous theory framework. *The Arts in Psychotherapy.*

Davies, A., & Greenland, S. (2002). A group analytic look at experiential training groups: How can music earn its keep? In E. Richards & A. Davies (Eds.), *Music therapy and group work: Sound company.* London, UK: JKP.

Davis, B. G. (2009). *Tools for teaching* (2nd ed.). San Francisco: Jossey-Bass.

Davis, W. B. (1987). Music therapy in 19th-century America. *Journal of Music Therapy, 24,* 76–87.

Davis, W. B. (1993). Keeping the dream alive: Profiles of three early twentieth-century music therapists. *Journal of Music Therapy, 30,* 34–45.

Davis, W. B. (1996). An instruction course in the use and practice of musical therapy: The first handbook of music therapy clinical practice. *Journal of Music Therapy, 33:*1, 34–46.

Davis, W. B. (1997). Music therapy practice in New York City: A report from a panel of experts, March 17, 1937. *Journal of Music Therapy, 34,* 68–81.

Davis, W. B. (1999). Information sharing: The American Music Therapy Association: An inventory of records. *Music Therapy Perspectives, 17:*2, 99–100.

De Backer, J., & Anke, C. (2006). Music therapy in Belgium. *Voices: A World Forum for Music Therapy.* Retrieved from: http://www.voices.no/country/monthbelgium_february2006 .html

Decuir, A. (1987). Readings for music therapy students: an analysis of clinical and research literature from the *Journal of Music Therapy.* In C. D. Maranto & K. E. Bruscia (Eds.), *Perspectives on music therapy education and training,* pp. 57–70. Philadelphia, PA: Temple University.

Decuir, A. A. (1989). Musicianship and music skills training for music therapists. *Music Therapy Perspectives, 7,* 88–90.

Decuir, A. A., & Jacobs, K. W. (1990). A comparison of clinical evaluations and studentself-evaluations of undergraduate practicum experiences in music therapy. *Music Therapy Perspectives, 8,* 20–22.

Decuir, A. A., & Vega, V. (2009). Career longevity: A survey of experienced professional music therapists. *The Arts in Psychotherapy, 37:*2, 135–142.

de L'Etoile, S. (2000). The history of the undergraduate curriculum in music therapy. *Journal of Music Therapy, 37:*1, 51–71.

de L'Etoile, S. (2008). Applying Perry's scheme of intellectual and ethical development in the college years to undergraduate music therapy education. *Music Therapy Perspectives, 26*(1), 110–116.

Dewey, J. (1933). *How we think.* New York: Heath.

Diaz de Chumaceiro, C. L. (1992). What song comes to mind? Induced song recall: Transference/countertransference in dyadic music associations in treatment and supervision. *The Arts in Psychotherapy, 19:*5, 313–408.

DiGiacomo, A., & Kirby, B. J. (2006). The effect of musical mode on emotional state. *The Canadian Journal of Music Therapy, 12:*1, 68–91.

D'Ulisse, M. E., & Palermo, M. T. (1999). The educational formation of the music therapist according to Benenzon's theory. 9th World Congress for Music Therapy, Washington, DC. Retrieved from E-Book of Articles, pp. 57–59.

D'Ulisse, M. E. (1999). For the training of music therapists according to the method of Prof. Benenzon. 9th World Congress for Music Therapy, Washington, DC. Retrieved from E-Book of Articles, pp. 60–62.

Di Cesare, M. (2010). Jamboxx: Giving those with disabilities the ability to play music and create art. Retrieved from: http://www.voices.no/mainissues/mi40008000295.php

Dileo, C. (2000). *Ethical thinking in music therapy.* Cherry Hill: Jeffrey Books.

Dileo, C., & Bradt, J. (2005). *Medical music therapy: A meta-analysis of the literature and an agenda for future research.* Cherry Hill, NJ: Jeffrey Books.

Dowling, W. C. (2000). *Why we should abolish teaching evaluations.* The Daily Targum: Rutgers University.

Dvorkin, J. (1999) Psychoanalytically oriented music therapy supervision. In T. Wigram & J. De Backer, *Clinical applications of music therapy in developmental disability, paediatrics and neurology.* London: JKP.

Dziwak, J., & Gfeller, K. (1988). Cost-effectiveness and music therapy practice. *Music Therapy Perspectives, 5,* 25–32.

Eagle, C. T., & Prewitt, S. A. (1974). A computer assisted information retrieval system in music therapy: A word and author index of published studies. *Journal of Music Therapy, 11,* 181–201.

Eagle, C. T., & Miniter, J. J. (Eds.). (1984). *Music psychology index: Volume Three.* Phoenix, AZ: Oryx Press.

Edwards, J. (1999). Considering the paradigmatic frame: Social science researchapproaches relevant to research in music therapy. *The Arts in Psychotherapy, 26:*2, 73–80.

Edwards, J., & Lesley, I. (2003). Music therapy in Ireland. *Voices: A World Forum for Music Therapy.* Retrieved from: http://www.voices.no/country/monthireland_january2003.html

Edwards, J., & Daveson, B. (2004). Music therapy student supervision: considering aspects of resistance and parallel processes in the supervisory relationship with students in final clinical placement. *The Arts in Psychotherapy, 31:*2, 67–76.

Edwards, J., & McFerran, K. (2004). Educating music therapy students about working with clients who have been sexually abused. *The Arts in Psychotherapy, 31:*5, 335–348.

Edwards, J. (2004). Report of the 5th International Symposium for Qualitative Music therapy Research. *Music Therapy Perspectives, 22:*2, 116–117.

Edwards, J. (2005). Possibilities and problems for evidence-based practice in music therapy. *The Arts in Psychotherapy, 32:*4, 293–301.

Ellis, M. V. (1991). Critical incidents in clinical supervision. *Journal of Counseling Psychology, 38,* 342–349.

Ellis, M. V., & Douce, L. A. (1994). Group supervision of novice clinical supervisors: Eight recurring issues. *Journal of Counseling and Development, 72,* 520–525.

Elyse, B., & Wheeler, B. (2010). Music therapy practice: Relative perspectives in evidence based reviews. *Nordic Journal of Music Therapy, 19:*1, 1–23.

Erkkilä, J. (2007). Music Therapy Toolbox (MTTB)–An improvisation analysis tool for clinicians and researchers. In T. Wosch & T. Wigram (Eds.), *Microanalysis in music therapy,* pp. 134–148. London and Philadelphia: Jessica Kingsley Publishers.

Erkkilä, J. (2008). The state of music therapy in Finland. *Voices: A World Forum for Music Therapy.* Retrieved from: http://www.voices.no/country/monthfinland_april2008.php

Eschen, J. Th. (2002). Analytical music therapy: An introduction. In J. Th. Eschen (Ed.), *Analytical music therapy,* pp. 17–33. London: Jessica Kingsley Publishers.

Eslava, J. (2007). Music therapy in Colombia. *Voices: A World Forum for Music Therapy.* Retrieved from: http://www.voices.no/country//monthcolombia_september2007.php

Estrella, K. (2001). Multicultural approach to music therapy supervision. In M. Forinash (Ed.),

Music therapy supervision, pp. 39–68. Gilsum, NH: Barcelona Publishers.

Fachner, J. (1999). The musical time-space, cannabis and the brain in an EEG-mapping investigation. 9th World Congress for Music Therapy, Washington, DC. Retrieved from E-Book of Articles, pp. 84–102.

Fachner, J., & Rittner, S. (2004). Sound and trance in a ritualistic setting visualised with EEG Brainmapping. *Music Therapy Today 5:*2 Retrieved from: http://musictherapyworld.net

Farnan, L. (1992). Issues in clinical training. *Music Therapy Perspectives, 10:*1, 11–12.

Farnan, L. (1994). Issues in clinical training. *Music Therapy Perspectives, 12:*1, 6–7.

Farnan, L. A. (1996). Issues in clinical training: The mystery of supervision. *Music Therapy Perspectives, 14*(2), 70–71.

Farnan, L. A. (1997). Issues in clinical training: What do interns think of their training? *Music Therapy Perspectives, 15:*1, 9–10.

Farnan, L. A. (1997). Issues in clinical training: Identifying and creating good interns. *Music Therapy Perspectives, 15:*2, 56.

Farnan, L. A. (1998). Issues in clinical training: Comparison of internship models. *Music Therapy Perspectives, 16:*1, 7–8.

Farnan, L. A. (2001). Competency -based approach to intern supervision. In M. Forinash (Ed.), *Music therapy supervision,* pp. 117–134. Gilsum, NH: Barcelona Publishers.

Feiner, S. (2001). A journey through internship supervision: Roles, dynamics and phases of the supervisory relationship. In M. Forinash (Ed.), *Music therapy supervision,* pp. 99–116. Gilsum, NH: Barcelona Publishers.

Ferraggina, A. (2007). La musicoterapia en la república Argentina: Music therapy in Argentina. *Voices: A World Forum for Music Therapy.* Retrieved from: http://www.voices.no /country//monthargentina_november2007.php

Ferrone, A. (2004). Music therapy in Italy. *Voices: A World Forum for Music Therapy.* Retrieved from: http://www.voices.no/country/monthitaly_june2004.html

Fleming, N. D., & Mills, C. (1992). Not another inventory, rather a catalyst for reflection. *To Improve the Academy, 11,* 137.

Forgács, E. (2008). Music therapy in Hungary. *Voices: A World Forum for Music Therapy.* Retrieved from: http://www.voices.no/country/monthhungary_august2008.php

Forinash, M. (1992). A phenomenological analysis of Nordoff-Robbins approach to music therapy: The lived experience of clinical improvisation. *Music Therapy, 11:*1.

Forinash, M. (Ed.). (2001a). *Music therapy supervision.* Gilsum, NH: Barcelona Publishers.

Forinash, M. (2001b). Music therapy in the United States. *Voices: A World Forum for Music Therapy.* Retrieved from: http://www.voices.no/mainissues/Voices1(2)Forinash.html

Fox, R. (1998). Essay on mutuality and parallel process in field instruction. *The Clinical Supervisor, 17:*2, 59–73.

Frohne-Hagemann, I. (1998). Integrative approaches to supervision for music therapists. 4th European Music Therapy Congress: Music & Therapy–A Dialogue, Leuven, Belgium, pp. 1039–1067. Retrieved from: http://www.musictherapyworld.de/modules/archive/stuff /papers/Euro2IVZ.pdf

Frohne-Hagemann, I. (2001). Integrative techniques in professional music therapy group supervision. In M. Forinash (Ed.), *Music therapy supervision,* pp. 231–245. Gilsum, NH: Barcelona Publishers.

Frohne-Hagemann, I. (2010). Working on and with dreams in Integrative Music Therapy: Keynote presentation, World Congress of Music Therapy, Rio de Janeiro, 1990. Retrieved from: http://voices.no/mainissues/mi359_keynote1990.pdf

Furman, C. E., Adamek, M. S., & Furman, A. G. (1992). The use of an auditory device to transmit feedback to student therapists. *Journal of Music Therapy, 29:*1, 40–53.

Furman, C. (Ed.). (1998). *Effectiveness of music therapy procedures: Documentation of research and clinical practice.* Silver Spring, MD: National Association for Music Therapy.

Galloway, H. F. (1975). A comprehensive bibliography of music referential to communicative development, processing, disorders and remediation. *Journal of Music Therapy, 12:*4, 175–196.

Gao, T. (2008). Music therapy in China. Address delivered at the Asian Music Therapy Symposium, March 8, 2009, Tokyo, Japan.

Gardstrom, S. (2001). Practical techniques for the development of complementary skills in musical improvisation. *Music Therapy Perspectives, 19:*2, 82–87.

Gardstrom, S. (2007). *Music therapy improvisation for groups: Essential leadership competencies.* Gilsum, NH: Barcelona Publishers.

Gaston, E. T. (1964a). The aesthetic experience and biological man. *Journal of Music Therapy, 1:*1, 1–6.

Gaston, E. T. (1964b). Developments in the training of music therapists. *Journal of Music Therapy, 1:*4, 148–50.

Gaston, E. T. (Ed.). (1968). *Music in therapy.* New York: Macmillan.

Gault, A. W. (1978). An assessment of the effectiveness of clinical training in collegiatemusic therapy curricula. *Journal of Music Therapy, 15:*1, 36–30.

Gfeller, K. (1987). Music therapy theory and practice as reflected in research literature. *Journal of Music Therapy, 24,* 178–194.

Gfeller, K. (1995). The status of music therapy research. In B. L. Wheeler (Ed.), *Music therapy research: Quantitative and qualitative perspectives,* pp. 22–64. Gilsum, NH: Barcelona Publishers.

Ghetti, C. M. (2001). An analysis of music therapy student practicum behaviors and their relationship to clinical effectiveness: An exploratory investigation. *Journal of Music Therapy, 38:*4, 307–320.

Gibbons, A. C., & Darrow, A. (1987). College university music therapy clinics: financial considerations. In C. D. Maranto & K. E. Bruscia (Eds.), *Perspectives on music therapy education and training,* pp. 126–136. Philadelphia, PA: Temple University.

Gibson. C. (1987). Music therapy in Japan: An 11-year update. *Journal of Music Therapy, 24*(1), 47–51.

Gilbert, J. P. (1979). Published research in music therapy, 1973–1978: Content, focus and implications for future research. *Journal of Music Therapy, 16,* 102–110.

Gilbertson, S. K., & Aldridge, D. Searching PubMed/MEDLINE, Ingenta, and the *Music Therapy World Journal Index* for articles published in the Journal of Music Therapy. *Journal of Music Therapy, 40:*4, 324–344.

Gilder, J. S. Trainee distress and burnout: Threats for music therapists? In C. D. Maranto & K. E. Bruscia (Eds.), *Perspectives on music therapy education and training,* pp. 195–207. Philadelphia, PA: Temple University.

Golboa, A., & Klein, A. (2007). The MAP: New software for describing, communicating, and analyzing music therapy sessions. European Music Therapy Congress, The Netherlands, 2007. Retrieved from: http://www.musictherapy2007.com/rooster/Idnumber/Id=212.asp

Gold, C. (2003). Music therapy in Austria. *Voices: A World Forum for Music Therapy.* Retrieved from: http://www.voices.no/country/monthaustria_december2003.html

Gold, C., Wigram, T., & Elefant, C. (2006). Music therapy for autistic spectrum disorder. Cochrane Database of Systematic Reviews, 2006, Issue 2. Art. No.: CD004381. DOI: 10.1002/14651858.CD004381.pub2. Retrieved from http://people.uib.no/cgo022/articles.htm

Gold, C. (2007). Beyond the "Qual versus Quant" debate. *Nordic Journal of Music Therapy, 16:*1,

2.

Gold, C. (2010). Evaluating the quality of qualitative research. *Nordic Journal of Music Therapy, 19*:1, 1–2.

Gooding, L. F. (2009). The effect of behavioral contracting on the acquisition of guitar performance skills in a college-level beginning guitar class. *Journal of Music Therapy, 46*:4, 323–338.

Goodman, K. D. (1981). Music therapy. In S. Arieti, M.D. (Ed.), *American handbook of psychiatry: New advances and directions, Vol VII,* pp. 564–585. New York: Basic Books.

Goodman, K. D. (1989). Music therapy assessment of emotionally disturbed children. *The Arts in Psychotherapy,* Vol. 16, No. 2, 179–192.

Goodman, K. D. (2001a). Review of Montclair State University undergraduate training program with respect to competencies: Faculty Sponsored Research. Unpublished.

Goodman, K. D. (2001b). National survey regarding prerequisites for graduate students applying to Masters without music therapy certification: Faculty Sponsored Research. Unpublished.

Goodman, K. D. (2005). The leap from theory to application: Undergraduate course content and therapy supervision. 11th World Congress, Brisbane, Australia.

Goodman, K. D. (2007). *Music therapy groupwork with special needs children: The evolving process.* Springfield, IL: Charles C Thomas.

Goodman, K. D. (2008). Critical and integrative thinking strategies for student growth and development in music therapy. 12th World Congress, Buenos Aires, Argentina.

Goodman, K. D. (2010). Unpublished syllabi, 1978–2010.

Goodsell, A., Mather, M., & Tinto, V. (Eds.). (1992). *Collaborative learning: A sourcebook for higher education.* University Park, PA: National Center on Postsecondary Teaching, Learning, and Assessment, Pennsylvania State University.

Graham, R. (1969). Practical research in music therapy. *Journal of Music Therapy, 6*:4, 94–97.

Graham, R. (1971). A new approach to student affiliations in music therapy. *Journal of Music Therapy, 8*:2, 43–52.

Grant, R. E., & McCarty, B. M. (1990). Emotional stages in the music therapy internship. *Journal of Music Therapy, 27*:3, 102–118.

Gray, L. A., Ladany, N., Walker, J. A., & Ancis, J. R. (2001). Psychotherapy trainees' experience of counterproductive events in supervision. *Journal of Counseling Psychology, 48,* 371–383.

Greenfield, D. G. (1978). Evaluation of music therapy practicum competencies: Comparisons of self and instructor ratings of videotapes. *Journal of Music Therapy, 15*:1, 15–20.

Greenfield, D. G. (1980). The use of visual feedback in training music therapy competencies. *Journal of Music Therapy, 17*:3, 94–102.

Greenfield, D. (1985). The evaluation of a computer system for behavioral observation training and research. *Journal of Music Therapy, 22*:2, 95–96.

Greer, R. D. (1974). Contributions of the psychology of music to music education and music therapy. *Journal of Music Therapy, 11*:4, 208–219.

Gregory, D. (1987). Applications of computers in music therapy education. In C. D. Maranto & K. E. Bruscia (Eds.), *Perspectives on music therapy education and training,* pp. 71–78. Philadelphia, PA: Temple University.

Gregory, D. (2008). Four decades of music therapy behavioral research designs: A content analysis of *Journal of Music Therapy* articles. *Journal of Music Therapy, 39*:1, 56–71.

Gregory, D. (2009). Using clinical video excerpts to prompt music therapy majors' recall of related experiences and self-attributions of comfort and skill. *The Journal of Music Therapy, 46*:4, 287–307.

Gregory, D. (2009b). Online video bridges gap between orientation and first session for arts in medicine volunteers. *Journal of Music Therapy, 46*:4, 308–322.

Gregory, D., & Belgrave, M. (2009). Identification of requisite skills for guitar accompaniment proficiency. *Music Therapy Perspectives, 2,* 97–102.

Grinnel, B. (1980). The developmental therapeutic process: A new theory of therapeutic intervention (Doctoral Thesis, Bryn Mawr College, PA).

Grocke, D. E. (1999a). Introductory comments - Setting the scene. 9th World Congress for Music Therapy, Washington, DC. Retrieved from E-Book of Articles, pp. 264–266.

Grocke, D. E. (1999b). Models of music therapy courses in Australia and New Zealand. 9th World Congress for Music Therapy, Washington, DC. Retrieved from E-Book of Articles, pp. 324–328.

Grocke, D. E. (1999c). Students who become unsuited to music therapy training. 9th World Congress for Music Therapy, Washington, DC. Retrieved from E-Book of articles, pp. 345–347.

Grocke, D. E., & Bruscia, K. E. (Eds.). (2002). *Guided imagery and music: The Bonny method and beyond.* Gilsum, NH: Barcelona Publishers.

Grocke, D. E. (2003a). The influence of recommended music therapy literature in the education of music therapists. *Voices: A World Forum for Music Therapy.* Retrieved from: http://www.voices.no/columnist/colgrocke300603.html

Grocke, D. E. (2003b). Thoughts on the Global Community of Music Therapy. *Voices: A World Forum for Music Therapy.* Retrieved from: http://www.voices.no/columnist/colgrocke130103.html

Grocke, D. E. (2005). The role of the therapist in the Bonny methods of guided imagery and music (BMGIM). *Music Therapy Perspectives, 23*:1, 45–52.

Groene, R., & Pembrook, R. (2000). Curricular issues in music therapy: A collegiate faculty. *Music Therapy Perspectives, 18*:2, 92–99.

Groene, R. (2001). The effect of presentation and accompaniment styles on attentional and responsive behaviors of participants with dementia diagnoses. *Journal of Music Therapy, 38*:1, 36–50.

Groene, R. (2003). Wanted: Music therapists: A study of the need for music therapists in the coming decade. *Music Therapy Perspectives, 21*:1, 4–13.

Hadsell, N. A., & Jones, J. L. (1988). Music therapy practicum: A cooperative effort. *Music Therapy Perspectives, 5,* 52–56.

Hadsell, N. A. (1993). Levels of external structure in music therapy. *Music Therapy Perspectives, 11*:2, 61–65.

Hallam, S., Cross, I., & Thaut, M. (2009). *Oxford handbook of music psychology.* London: Oxford University Press.

Hammarlund, I. (2008). The music therapy programme at the Royal College of Music in Stockholm. In A. Paulander (Ed.), Music therapy in Sweden. *Voices: A World Forum for Music Therapy.* Retrieved from: http://www.voices.no/country/monthsweden_june2008.php

Hanser, S. B., & Madsen, C. K. (1972). Comparisons of graduate and undergraduate research in music therapy. *Journal of Music Therapy, 9*:2, 86–93.

Hanser, S. B. (1978). A systems analysis model for teaching practicum skills. *Journal of Music Therapy, 15*:1, 21–36.

Hanser, S. B., & Furman, C. E. (1980). The effect of videotape-based feedback vs. field-based feedback on the development of applied clinical skills. *Journal of Music Therapy, 17*:3, 103–112.

Hanser, S. B. (1987). Observation and feedback techniques for student practica. In C. D. Maranto & K. E. Bruscia (Eds.), *Perspectives on music therapy education and training.*

Philadelphia, PA: Temple University.

Hanser, S. B. (2001). A systems analysis approach to music therapy practica. In M. Forinash (Ed.), *Music therapy supervision,* pp. 87–98. Gilsum, NH: Barcelona Publishers.

Hanser, S. B. (2005). Challenges to music therapy in a world of need. *The Arts in Psychotherapy, 32:*3, 217–224.

Hart, G. (1982). *The process of clinical supervision.* Baltimore, MD: University Park Press.

Hasselbring, T. S., & Duffus, N. A. (1981). Using microcomputer technology in music therapy for analyzing therapist and client behavior. *Journal of Music Therapy, 18:*4, 156–165.

Hasselgren, B., & Beach, D. (1997). Phenomenography a good-for-nothing brother of phenomenology? Outline of an analysis. *Higher Education Research & Development, 16:*2.

Hawes, G. R., & Hawes, L.,S. (1962). *The concise dictionary of education.* New York: Van Nostrand Reinhold Company.

Hesser, B. (1985). Advanced clinical training in music therapy. *Music Therapy, 5:*1, 66–73.

Hesser, B. (1999). New developments in music therapy. 9th World Congress for Music Therapy, Washington, DC. Retrieved from E-Book of Articles, pp. 281–286.

Hesser, B. (2002). Supervision of music therapy students in a music therapy graduate training programme, chapter 10 in J. Eschen (Ed.), *Analytical music therapy,* pp. 157–167. London: JKP.

Hilliard, R. E. (2001). The use of cognitive-behavioral music therapy in the treatment of women with eating disorders. *Music Therapy Perspectives, 19:*2, 109–113.

Hintz, M. (2000). Geriatric music therapy clinical assessment: Assessment of music skills and related behaviors. *Music Therapy Perspectives, 1,* 31–40.

Holloway, E. L. (1987). Developmental models of supervision: Is it development? *Professional Psychology: Research and Practice, 18,* 209–216.

Honey, P., & Mumford, A. (1982). *Manual of learning styles.* London: P. Honey.

Howard, M. (2009). An interview with two pioneers of Canadian music therapy: Carolyn Kenny and Nancy McMaster. V*oices: A World Forum for Music Therapy.* Retrieved from: http://www.voices.no/mainissues/mi40009000329.php

Hugo, M. (1999). South American models of training. 9th World Congress for Music Therapy, Washington, DC. Retrieved from E-Book of Articles, pp. 298–304.

Hunt, A. M. (2010). Integrating EEG and first -person reports: Examining the Guided Imagery Music experience. Conference Abstracts: Music Technology: Solutions to Challenges. Royal Hospital for Neuro-Disability, London, UK.

Hwang, E., & Park, S. (2006). A decade of music therapy in Korea: An analysis of Korean graduate research from 1997 to 2005. *Voices: A World Forum for Music Therapy.* Retrieved from: http://www.voices.no/mainissues/mi40006000207.html

Ikazaki-Sakaue, K. (2003). Music therapy in Japan. *Voices: A World Forum for Music Therapy.* Retrieved from: http://www.voices.no/country/monthjapan_may2003.html

Ikuno, R. (2005). Fact sheet of music therapy in Japan. *Voices: A World Forum for Music Therapy.* Retrieved from: http://www.voices.no/mainissues/mi40005000167.html

Intveen, A. (2007). Musical instruments in anthroposophical music therapy with reference to Rudolf Steiner's model of the threefold human being. *Voices: A World Forum for Music Therapy.* Retrieved from: http://www.voices.no/mainissues/mi40007000245.php

Irwin, E. C. (1986). On being and becoming a therapist. *The Arts in Psychotherapy, 13:*3, 191–195.

Isenberg-Grzeda, C. (1988). Music therapy assessment: A reflection of professional identity. *Journal of Music Therapy, 23*(3), 166–173.

Isenberg-Grzeda, C. (1999a). Music therapy training in Canada. 9th World Congress for Music Therapy, Washington, DC. Retrieved from E-Book of Articles, pp. 305–310.

Isenberg-Grzeda, C. (1999b). Qualifications of music therapy educators of the Canadian Association for Music Therapy. 9th World Congress for Music Therapy, Washington, DC. Retrieved from E-Book of Articles, p. 351.

Itin, C. M. (1999). Reasserting the Philosophy of Experiential Education as a Vehicle for Change in the 21st Century. *The Journal of Experiential Education, 22*:2, 91–98.

Itzhaky, H., & Ribner, D. (1998). Resistance as a phenomenon in clinical and student social work supervision. *Australian Social Work, 51*:3, 25–29.

Jackson, N. A. (2010). Models of response to client anger in music therapy. *The Arts in Psychotherapy, 37*:1, 46–55.

Jahn-Langenberg, M. (1999). German models of training. 9th World Congress for Music Therapy, Washington, DC. Retrieved from E-Book of Articles, pp. 293–297.

Jahn-Langenberg, M. (2001). Psychodynamic perspectives in professional supervision. In M. Forinash, *Music therapy supervision*, pp. 271–280. Gilsum, NH: Barcelona Publishers.

Jellison, J. A. (1973). The frequency and general mode of inquiry of research in music therapy, 1952, 1972. *Journal of Music Therapy, 22*, 79–94.

Jensen, K. L., & McKinney, C. H. (1990). Undergraduate music therapy education and training: Current status and proposals for the future. *Journal of Music Therapy, 18*, 158–178.

Jensen, K. L. (2001). The effects of selected music on self-disclosure. *Journal of Music Therapy, 33*:1, 2–27.

Jeong, S., & Kim, M. T. (2007). Effects of a theory-driven music and movement program for stroke survivors in a community setting. *Complementary Therapies in Medicine, 17*:4, 125–131.

Johansson, H. O. (2008). The FMT method- Functionally oriented music therapy. In A. Paulander (Ed.), Music Therapy in Sweden. *Voices: A World Forum for Music Therapy.* Retrieved from: http://www.voices.no/country/monthsweden_june2008.php

Johnson, R. E. (1981). E.Thayer Gaston: Leader in scientific thought on music in therapy and education. *Journal of Research in Music Education, 29*:4, 279–286.

Jones, C., Baker, F., & Day, T. (2004). From healing rituals to music therapy: Bridging the cultural divide between therapist and young Sudanese refugees. *The Arts in Psychotherapy, 31*:2, 89–100.

Joyce, B., & Weil, M. (1996). *Models of teaching.* Boston, MA: Allyn and Bacon.

Kahler, E. P. II (1998). A comparison of selected factors with music therapy students performance on clinical skills. Ph.D. dissertation, University of Kansas, United States–Kansas. Retrieved March 25, 2010, from Dissertations & Theses: Full Text. (Publication No. AAT 9833838).

Kaufman, D. (2007). *Cracking up and back again: Transformation through poetry.* Calgary, Alberta, Canada: Palabras Press.

Kaufman, D., & Goodman, K. D. (2009). Cracking Up and Back Again: Transformation Through Music and Poetry. 8th Global Conference: Making Sense of Health, Illness and Disease: Inter-Disciplinary.Net: A Global Network for Dynamic Research and Publication. Mansfield College, Oxford, UK.

Kennedy, R. (2001). A survey of guitar course offerings in degree programs. *Music Therapy Perspectives, 19*:2, 128–133.

Kennedy, R. (2003). Guitar skills for music therapy majors. *Music Therapy Today, 4*:2. Retrieved from: http://musictherapyworld.net

Kenny, C. B. (1998). Embracing complexity: The creation of a comprehensive research culture in music therapy. *Journal of Music Therapy, 35*:3, 201–217.

Kenny, C., & Stige, B. (Eds.). (2002). *Contemporary voices of music therapy: Communication, culture and community.* Oslo: Unipub Forlag.

Kim, J. (2002). Music therapy in the republic of Korea. *Voices: A World Forum for Music Therapy.*

Retrieved from: http://www.voices.no/country/monthkorea_october2002.html

Kim, J. (2006). Music therapy in the republic of Korea. *Voices: A World Forum for Music Therapy.* Retrieved from: http://www.voices.no/country/monthkorea_october2002.html

Kim, S. H. (1990). Competency rations in applications to the American Association for Music Therapy for certification 1981–1987. *Music Therapy, 9:*1, 82–109.

Kim, S. (2008). The supervisee's experience in cross-cultural music therapy supervision. In S. Hadley (Ed.), *Qualitative inquiries in music therapy: A monograph series,* pp. 1–44. Gilsum, NH: Barcelona Publishers.

Kirkland, K. (2007). Music therapy in Canada. *Voices: A World Forum for Music Therapy.* Retrieved from: http://www.voices.no/country//monthcanada_may2007a.html

Knefelkamp, L. (1981). The four developmental instruction variables. Reprinted as Table 1.2 in W. J. Perry, *Forms of ethical and intellectual development in the college years: A scheme.* San Francisco, CA: Jossey-Bass.

Knight, A. J. (2008). Music therapy internship supervisors and preinternship students: A comparative analysis of questionnaires. *Journal of Music Therapy, 41:*4, 75–92.

Kolb, D. (1984). *Experiential learning.* Englewood Cliffs, NJ: Prentice Hall.

Körlin, D. GIM in Sweden–Training, practice and research. In A. Paulander (Ed.), Music Therapy in Sweden. *Voices: A World Forum for Music Therapy.* Retrieved from: http://www .voices.no/country/monthsweden_june2008.php

Krout, R. (1982). Supervision of music therapy practicum within the classroom setting. *Music Therapy Perspectives, 1:*1, 21–26.

Krout, R. (1989). Microcomputer use in college music therapy programs. *Journal of Music Therapy, 26:*2, 88–94.

Krout, R. (1990). Integrating technology. *Music Therapy Perspectives, 8,* 8–9.

Krout, R. (1993). Integrating technology. *Music Therapy Perspectives, 11:*2, 50–52.

Krout, R. (1994). Integrating technology. *Music Therapy Perspective. 12:*1, 4–5.

Krout, R. (1994). Integrating technology. *Music Therapy Perspectives, 12:*2, 59–60.

Krout, R. (1995). Contemporary guitar applications. *Music Therapy Perspectives, 13,* 68–69.

Krout, R. (1997). Contemporary guitar applications. *Music Therapy Perspectives, 15,* 13–15.

Krout, R. (2003a). A kiwi odyssey. *Voices: A World Forum for Music Therapy.* Retrieved from: http://www.voices.no/mainissues/mi40003000114.html

Krout, R. (2003b). Essential guitar skill development: Considerations for the contemporary music therapist. *Music Therapy Today, 4:*2, retrieved from: http://musictherapyworld.ne

Lagzdina, V. (2009). Music therapy–One of the newest professions in Latvia. *Voices: A World Forum for Music Therapy.* Retrieved from: http://www.voices.no/country/monthlatvia _january2009.php

Langan, D., & Athanasou, J. (2005). Testing a model of domain learning in music therapy. *Journal of Music Therapy, 42:*4, 296–312.

Langdon, G. S. (2001). Experiential music therapy group as a method of professional supervision. In M. Forinash (Ed.), *Music therapy supervision,* pp. 211–218. Gilsum, NH: Barcelona Publishers.

Langenberg, M., Frommer, J., & Tress, W. (1993). A qualitative research approach to analytical music therapy. *Music Therapy, 12:*1, 59–84.

Lathom, W. B. (1982). Survey of current functions of a music therapist. *Journal of Music Therapy, 19:*1, 2–27.

Lautman, S. (2010). Personal communication.

Leblanc, A. (1978). A study of psychology of music instruction. *Journal of Music Therapy, 15:*4, 185–198.

Lecourt, E. (1993). Music therapy in France. In C. D. Maranto (Ed.), *Music therapy–Interna-*

tional perspectives. Piperville, PA: Jeffrey Books.

Lecourt, E. (2004). Music therapy in France. *Voices: A World Forum for Music Therapy.* Retrieved from: http://www.voices.no/country/monthfrance_april2004.html

Lecourt, E. (2010). Personal communication.

Lee, C. (1996). *Music at the edge.* London: Routledge.

Lee, C. (2000). A method of analyzing improvisations in music therapy. *Journal of Music Therapy, 37:*2, 147–167.

Lee, C. (2003). *The architecture of aesthetic music therapy.* Gilsum, NH: Barcelona Publishers.

Lee, C. (2010). *Improvising in styles.* Gilsum, NH: Barcelona Publishers.

Lee. C., & Khare, K. (2001). The supervision of clinical improvisation in aesthetic music therapy: A music-centered approach. In M. Forinash (Ed.), *Music therapy supervision,* pp. 247–270. Gilsum, NH: Barcelona Publishers.

Lee, C. S. (2003). Music therapy in Taiwan. *Voices: A World Forum for Music Therapy.* Retrieved from: http://www.voices.no/country/monthtaiwan_june2003.html

Lee, C. S. (2006). Music therapy in Taiwan, 2003-2006. *Voices: A World Forum for Music Therapy.* Retrieved from: http://www.voices.no/country/monthtaiwan_november2006.html

Leite, T. (2002). Music therapy in Portugal. *Voices: A World Forum for Music Therapy.* Retrieved from: http://www.voices.no/country/monthportugal_sept2002.html

Lem, A., Paine, G., & Drummond, J. (2010). A dynamic sonification device in improvisational music therapy. Retrieved from: http://www.rhn.org.uk/nec_001.asp#cn1

Lett, W. R. (1993). Therapist creativity: The arts of supervision. *The Arts in Psychotherapy, 20:*5, 371–386.

Levin, H. (1998). *Learning through music.* Gilsum, NH: Barcelona Publishers.

Lewin, K. (1951). Field Theory and Learning. In D. Cartwright (Ed.), *Field theory in social science: Selected theoretical papers.* London: Social Science Paperbacks.

Lewis, D. (1964). Chamber music–Proposed as a therapeutic medium. *Journal of Music Therapy, 1:*1, 19–20.

Libertore, A., & Layman, D. (1999). *The Cleveland music therapy assessment of infants and toddlers: A practical guide to assessing and developing intervention.* Cleveland, OH: Cleveland Music School Settlement.

Loganbill, C., Hardy, E., & Delworth, U. (1983). Supervision: A conceptual model. *The Counseling Psychologist, 10,* 3–42.

Loth, H. (2006). How gamelan music has influenced me as a music therapist–A personal account. *Voices: A World Forum for Music Therapy.* Retrieved from: http://www.voices.no/mainissues/mi40006000201.html

Luce, D. W. (2008). Epistemological development and collaborative learning: A hermeneutic analysis of music therapy student experience. *Journal of Music Therapy, 41:*1, 21–51.

Luck, G., Riikkilä, K., Lartillot, O., Erkkilä, J., Toiviainen, P., Mäkelä, A., et al. (2006). Exploring relationships between level of mental retardation and features of music therapy improvisations: A computational approach. *Nordic Journal of Music Therapy, 15*(1), 30–48.

Lusebrink, V. B. (1989). Education in creative arts therapies: Accomplishments and challenges. *The Arts in Psychotherapy, 17:*1, 5–10.

Madsen, C. (1965). A new music therapy curriculum. *Journal of Music Therapy, 2:*1, 83–85.

Madsen, C. K. (1978). Theory versus practice: A psychology of music survey. *Journal of Music Therapy, 15:*1, 2–8.

Madsen, C. K., & Alley, J. M. (1979). The effect of reinforcement on attentiveness: A comparison of behaviorally trained music therapists and other professionals with implications for competency-based academic preparation. *Journal of Music Therapy, 16:*2, 70–82.

Madsen, C. K., & Geringer, J. M. (1983). Attending behavior as a function of in-class activity in university music classes. *Journal of Music Therapy, 20:*1, 30–38.

Madsen, C. K., & Furman, C. E. (1984). Graduate versus undergraduate scholarship: Research acquisition and dissemination. *Journal of Music Therapy, 21:*4, 170–176.

Madsen, C. K. (1986). Research and music therapy: The necessity for transfer. *Journal of Music Therapy, 23:*2, 50–65.

Madsen, C. K., & Kaiser, K. A. (1999). Pre-internship fears of music therapists. *Journal of Music Therapy.*

Magee, W. L. (2006). Electronic technologies in clinical music therapy: A survey of practice and attitudes. *Technology and Disability, 18,* 1–8.

Magee, W., & Burland, K. (2008). An exploratory study of the use of electronic music technologies in clinical music therapy. *Nordic Journal of Music Therapy, 17:*2, 124–141.

Mansfield, H. (2001). Grade inflation: It's time to face the facts. *The Chronicle of Higher Education.* April 6, 2001. Retrieved from: http://chronicle.com/article/Grade-Inflation-It-s-Time-to/9332

Manzo, V. J. (2010). *V. J. Manzo: Projects and Technology.* Retrieved from: http://vjmanzo.com/clients/vjmanzo/projects.htm

Maranto, C. D., & Wheeler, B. L. (1986). Teaching ethics in music therapy. *Music Therapy Perspectives, 3,* 17–19.

Maranto, C. D. (1987). Continuing concerns in music therapy ethics. *Music Therapy, 6:*2, 59–63.

Maranto, C. D. (1987). Ethical issues in music therapy education and training. In C. D. Maranto & K. E. Bruscia (Eds.), *Perspectives on music therapy education and training,* pp. 45–49. Philadelphia, PA: Esther Boyer College of Music, Temple University.

Maranto, C. D. (1987b). Continuing themes in the literature on music therapy education and training. In C. D. Maranto & K. E. Bruscia (Eds.), *Perspectives on music therapy education and training,* pp. 1–15. Philadelphia, PA: Temple University.

Maranto, C. D. (1987). Ethical issues in music therapy education and training. In C. D. Maranto & K. E. Bruscia (Eds.), *Perspectives on music therapy education and training.* Philadelphia, PA: Esther Boyer College of Music, Temple University.

Maranto, C. D., & Bruscia, K. E. (Eds.). (1987). *Perspectives on music therapy education and training.* Philadelphia, PA: Temple University.

Maranto, C. D., & Bruscia, K. E. (1988). *Methods of teaching and training the music therapist.* Philadelphia: PA: Temple University.

Maranto, C. D., & Bruscia, K. E. (1989). The status of music therapy education and training. *The Arts in Psychotherapy, 16:*1, 15–19.

Maranto, C. D. (1989a). California symposium on music therapy education and training: Summary and recommendations. *Music Therapy Perspectives, 7,* 108–109.

Maranto, C. D. (1989b). Future trends, issues of accountability and new models for music therapy education and training. *Music Therapy Perspectives, 7,* 100–102.

Maranto, C. D. (1993a). *Music therapy: International perspectives.* Pipersville, PA: Jeffery Books.

Maranto, C. D. (1993b). An historic chronology of 20th century international music therapy developments. In C. D. Maranto (Ed.), *Music therapy: International perspectives,* pp. 707–717. Pipersville, PA: Jeffrey Books.

Maranto. C. D. (1993c). Music therapy in the United States of America. In C. D. Maranto (Ed.), *Music therapy international perspectives,* pp. 605–662. Pipersville, PA: Jeffrey Books.

Marton, F. (1981). Phenomenography- describing conceptions of the world around us. *Instructional Science, 10,* 177–00.

McClain, F. J. (1993). Student evaluations of practicum training in music therapy. Ph.D. dissertation, Temple University, United States–Pennsylvania. Retrieved March 25, 2010, from

Dissertations & Theses: Full Text. (Publication No. AAT 9332828).

McGinty, J. K. (1980). Survey of duties and responsibilities of current music therapy positions. *Journal of Music Therapy, 17:*3, 148–166.

Memory, B. C., Unkefer, R., & Smeltekop, R. (1987). Supervision in music therapy: Theoretical models. In C. D. Maranto & K. E. Bruscia (Eds.), *Perspectives on music therapy education and training.* Philadelphia, PA: Temple University.

Mercadal-Brotons, M., & Mateos Hernández, L. A. (2005). Contributions towards the consolidation of music therapy in Spain within the European Space For Higher Education (ESHE). *Music Therapy Today 6:* 4 (November). Retrieved from: file:///Users/goodmank /Desktop/Musictherapytoday,%20guitar%20skills%20for%20mt%20majors.webarchive

Meyers, C., & Jones, T. B. (1993). *Promoting active learning: Strategies for the college classroom.* San Francisco: Jossey-Bass.

Michel, D., & Madsen, C. (1969). Examples of research in music therapy as a function of undergraduate education. *Journal of Music Therapy, 6:*1, 22–25.

Michel, D. (1971). Music therapy: An idea whose time has arrived around the world. *Journal of Music Therapy, 8*(3), 90–95.

Michel, D., & Rohrbacher, M. (Eds.). (1982). *The music therapy assessment profile for severely/profoundly handicapped persons.* Silver Spring, MD: National Association for Music Therapy.

Milgram-Luterman, J. A. (2000). A phenomenological study of a music therapy peer support group for senior music therapy students (Doctoral dissertation, Michigan Dissertation Abstracts International, AAT 3009149.

Miller, E. (1999). Rachel Describes Learning about her Physiological Response. In J. Hibben (Ed.), *Inside music therapy: Client experiences,* pp. 130–134. Gilsum, NH: Barcelona Publishers.

Miller, K. E., & Kahler, E. P. (2008). The current use of the university-affiliated internship option by universities/colleges approved by the AMTA. *Music Therapy Perspectives, 26*(2), 117–123.

Mills, B. J., & Cottrell Jr., P. G., (1998). *Cooperative learning for higher education faculty.* Phoenix, AZ: American Council on Education/Oryx Press.

Moore, R. S., Staum, M. J., & Brotons, M. (1992). Music preferences of the elderly: Repertoire, vocal ranges, tempos, and accompaniments for singing. *Journal of Music Therapy, 29,* 236–252.

Moreno, J. (1969). The identity of the music therapist. *Journal of Music Therapy, 6:*1, 19–21.

Moreno, J. (1988). Multicultural music therapy: The world music connection. *Journal of Music Therapy, 25:*1, 17–27.

Moreno, J., Brotons, M, Hairston, M., Hawley, T., Kiel, H., Michel, D., & Rohrbacher, M. (1990). International music therapy: A global perspective. *Music Therapy Perspectives, 8,* 41–46.

Moreno, J. (1990). International perspectives. *Music Therapy Perspectives, 8,* 14.

Moreno, J. (1992a). International perspectives. *Music Therapy Perspectives, 10:*1, 10.

Moreno, J. (1992b). International perspectives. *Music Therapy Perspectives, 10:*2, 86–88.

Moreno, J. (1993a). International perspectives. *Music Therapy Perspectives, 11:*1, 12–13

Moreno, J. (1993b). International perspectives. *Music Therapy Perspectives, 11:*2, 53–54.

Moreno, J. (1994). International perspectives, Music therapy 2001. *Music Therapy Perspectives, 12:*2, 57–60.

Moreno, J. (1995). Ethnomusic therapy: An interdisciplinary approach to music and healing. *The Arts in Psychotherapy, 22:*4, 329–338.

Moreno, J. (1999). International perspectives. *Music Therapy Perspectives, 17:*2, 63–64.

Mössler, K. (2008). Update on music therapy in Austria: Celebrating an officially recognized profession. *Voices: A World Forum for Music Therapy*. Retrieved from: http://www.voices.no /country/monthaustria_october2008.php

Munro-Porchet, S. Jacob, B., & Fauch, H. (2006). Music therapy in Switzerland. *Voices: A World Forum for Music Therapy*. Retrieved from: http://www.voices.no/country/monthswitzer land_January2006.html

Murphy, K. (2007). Experiential learning in music therapy: Faculty and student perspectives. In A. Meadows (Ed.), *Qualitative inquiries in music therapy: A monograph series*. Volume Three. Gilsum, NH: Barcelona Publishers.

Murphy, K., & Wheeler, B. L. (2005). Symposium on experiential learning in music therapy: Report of the symposium sponsored by the World Federation of Music Therapy-Commission on Education, Training and Accreditation. *Music Therapy Perspectives, 23*.2, 138–143.

Musumeci, J. S., Fedelibus, J. F., & Sorel, S. N. (2005). Software tools for music therapy qualitative research. In B. Wheeler (Ed.), *Music therapy research* (2nd ed.), pp. 187–196. Gilsum, NH: Barcelona Publishers.

National Association for Music Therapy. (1983). NAMT Standards of Clinical Practice. *Music Therapy Perspectives, 1*.2, 13–27.

National Association for Music Therapy. (1986). *Standards and procedures for academic program approval and approval renewal* (revised.). Silver Spring, MD: Author.

National Association for Music Therapy. (1988). Code of ethics. *Music Therapy Perspectives, 5,* 5–8.

National Association for Music Therapy. (1997). *Standards and procedures for academic program approval* (revised). Silver Spring, MD: Author.

National Association of Schools of Music. (1985). *NASM Handbook: 1985–86*. Reston, VA: Author.

Nocker-Ribaupierre, M. (2010). Personal communication.

Nolan, P. (1995). The integration of mental health science concepts in the education of the music therapist. In T. Wigram, B. Saperston, & R. West (Eds.), *The art and science of music therapy: A handbook,* pp. 433–441. Switzerland: Harwood.

Nolan, P. (2005). Verbal Processing within the music therapy relationship. *Music Therapy Perspectives, 23*:1, 18–28.

Nordoff, P., & Robbins, C. (1964a). *The three bears: A musical adventure for an orchestra and chorus of young children, storyteller and piano*. Bryn Mawr, PA: Theodore Presser.

Nordoff, P., & Robbins, C. (1964b). *The story of Artaban, the other wise man*. Bryn Mawr, PA: Theodore Presser.

Nordoff, P., & Robbins, C. (1969). *Pif-paf-poultrie*. Bryn Mawr, PA: Theodore Presser.

Nordoff, P. (1972). *Spirituals for children to sing and play, Vol. I and II*. Bryn Mawr, PA: Theodore Presser.

Nordoff, P. (1977). *Folk songs for children to sing and play*. Bryn Mawr, PA: Theodore Presser.

Nordoff, P. (1979). *Fanfares and dances*. Bryn Mawr, PA: Theodore Presser.

Nordoff, P. & Robbins, C. (1983) *Music therapy in special education*. Gilsum, NH: Barcelona Publishers.

Nordoff, P., & Robbins C. (1977). *Creative music therapy*. New York: Harper & Row.

Nordoff, P., & Robbins, C. (2007). *Creative music therapy: A guide to fostering clinical musicianship*. Gilsum, NH: Barcelona Publishers.

O'Callaghan, C. (2002). Music therapy in Australia. *Voices: A World Forum for Music Therapy*. Retrieved from: http://www.voices.no/country/monthaustralia_may2002.html

Odell-Miller, H. (1999). Music therapy training in the United Kingdom. 9th World Congress for Music Therapy, Washington, DC. Retrieved from E-Book of Articles, pp. 311–317.

Odell-Miller, H., & Richards, E. (Eds.). (2009). *Supervision of music therapy: A theoretical and practical handbook.* London, UK: Routledge.

Odell- Miller, H. (2008). The history and background of supervision in music therapy. In H. Odell-Miller & E. Richards. (Eds.), *Supervision of music therapy: Atheoretical and practical handbook,* pp. 5–22. London, UK: Routledge.

Odell- Miller, H., & Krueckeberg, N. (2009). Music therapy supervision with trainees in adult psychiatry. In H. Odell-Miller & E. Richards (Eds.), *Supervision of music therapy: A theoretical and practical handbook,* pp. 101–118. London, UK: Routledge.

Okazaki-Sakaue, K. (2003). Music therapy in Japan. *Voices: A World Forum for Music Therapy.* Retrieved from: http://www.voices.no/country/monthjapan_may2003.html

Oldfield, A. (2009). Supervision of music therapists working with children in schools. In H. Odell-Miller & E. Richards (Eds.), *Supervision of music therapy: A theoretical and practical handbook,* pp. 135–152. London, UK: Routledge.

Oliveros, P., Miller, L., Polzin, Z., Hazard, S., & Siddall, G. (2010). Music improvisation software: An interface for severely impaired children and adults. Retrieved from: http://www.voices.no/mainissues/mi40008000295.php

O'Morrow, G. (1967). Clinical training in music therapy. *Journal of Music Therapy, 4:4,* 128–131.

Oppenheim, L. (1984). A work values profile of university music therapy and performance majors. *Journal of Music Therapy, 21:2,* 89–94.

Orff, G. (1980). *The Orff music therapy: Active furthering of the development of the child.* New York: Schott.

Paulander, A. (Ed.). (2008). Music therapy in Sweden. *Voices: A World Forum for Music Therapy.* Retrieved from: http://www.voices.no/country/monthsweden_june2008.php

Pavlicevic, M., & Ansdell, G. (Eds.). (2004). *Community music therapy.* London: Jessica Kingsley.

Pavlicevic, M. (2005). Music therapy in South Africa: Compromise or synthesis? *Voices: A World Forum for Music Therapy.* Retrieved from: http://www.voices.no/mainissues/mitext11 pavlicevic.html

Pederson, I. N. (2002). Psychodynamic movement: A basic training methodology for music therapists. In J. T. Eschen (Ed.), *Analytical music therapy,* pp. 190–215. London: JKP.

Pederson, I. N. (2002b). Self-experience for music therapy students–experiential training In music therapy as a methodology–a mandatory part of the music therapy program at Aalborg University, pp. 168–189. In J. T. Eschen (Ed.) (2002), *Analytical music therapy.* London: JKP.

Pedersen, I. N. (2009). Music therapy supervision with students and professionals: The use of music and analysis of countertransference in the triadic field. In H. Odell-Miller & E. Richards (Eds.), *Supervision of music therapy: A theoretical and practical handbook,* pp. 45–66. New York: Routledge.

Pehk, A. (1998). Improvisation teaching within music therapy training. *Nordic Journal of Music Therapy,* 179–180.

Perilli, G. G. (2004). The emotional and therapeutic value of the music by the Music Therapy Integrated model–MIM. In D. Aldridge, J. Fachner, & J. Erkkilä (Eds.) (2004), Many faces of music therapy: Proceedings of the 6th European Music Therapy Congress, June 16-20,2004 Jyväskylä, Finland (pp. 1252–1272). E-Book (PDF) available at MusicTherapy Today.com Vol. 6. Issue 4 (November 2005) Retrieved from: http://www.musictherapy world.de/modules/mmmagazine/issues/downloads/Proce

Perilli, G. (2008). Comparing notes on music therapy culture. *Voices: A World Forum for Music Therapy.* Retrieved from: http://www.voices.no/columnist/colPerilli291208.php

Perry, W. G. (1999). *Forms of ethical and intellectual development in the college years: A scheme.* San

Francisco, CA: Jossey Bass.

Petrie, G. E. (1989). The identification of a contemporary hierarchy of intended learning outcomes for music therapy students entering internships. *Journal of Music Therapy, 26,* 125–139.

Petrie, G. E. (1993). An evaluation of the National Association for Music Therapy undergraduate academic curriculum: Part II. *Journal of Music Therapy, 30:*3, 158–173.

Piaget, J. (1968). *Six psychological studies.* New York: Vintage Books.

Préfontaine, J. (2006). On becoming a music therapist. *Voices: A World Forum for Music Therapy.* Retrieved from: http://www.voices.no/mainissues/mi40006000213.html

Prickett, C. A. (1987). The effect of self-monitoring on positive comments given by music therapy students' coaching peers. *Journal of Music Therapy, 24:*2, 54–75.

Priestley, M. (1975). *Music therapy in action.* London: Constable.

Primadei, A. (2004). The use of the guitar in clinical improvisation. *Music Therapy Today* (online) Vol. V, Issue 4 (August), available at http://musictherapyworld.net

Ramsey, D. (2010). Musically assisted rehabilitation systems: Utilizing music technology to enhance therapy. Conference Abstracts: Music Technology: Solutions to Challenges. Royal Hospital for Neuro-Disability, London, UK.

Register, D. (2002). Collaboration and consultation: A survey of board certified music therapists. *Journal of Music Therapy, 39:*4, 305–321.

Reuer, B., & Gfeller, K. (1989). An investigation of the influence of external criteria on music therapy practice. *The Arts in Psychotherapy, 16:*1, 49–56.

Reuer, B., Crowe, B., & Bernstein, B. (2007). *Group rhythm and drumming with older adults: Music therapy techniques and multimedia training guide.* Silver Spring, MD: American Music Therapy Association.

Richards, E. (2009). Whose handicap? Issues arising in the supervision of trainee music therapists in their first experience of working with adults with learning disabilities. In H. Odell-Miller & E. Richards (Eds.), *Supervision of music therapy: A theoretical and practical handbook,* pp. 5–22. London, UK: Routledge.

Rickson, D. (2009). Researching ones own clinical practice: Managing multiple roles in an action research project. *Voices: A World Forum for Music Therapy.* Retrieved from: http://www.voices.no/mainissues/mi40009000307.php

Ritholz, M. (Ed.). (2008). *Clinical improvisation: Expanding musical resources.* New York: The Nordoff Robbins Center for Music Therapy at New York University.

Robbins, A. (1988). A psychoaesthetic perspective on creative arts therapy and training. *The Arts in Psychotherapy, 15:*2, 95–100.

Robbins, C., & Robbins, C. M. (Eds.). (1998). *Healing heritage: Paul Nordoff exploring the tonal language of music.* Gilsum, NH: Barcelona Publishers.

Ropp, C., Caldwell, J., Dixon, A., Angell, M., & Vogt, W. P. (2006). Special education administrators' perceptions of therapy in special education programs. *Music Therapy Perspectives, 24:*2, 87–93.

Ruud, E. (1997). Music and identity. *Nordic Journal of Music Therapy, 6:*1, 3–13.

Ruud. E. (1998). *Music therapy: Improvisation, communication and culture.* Gilsum, NH: Barcelona Publishers.

Rugenstein, L. (1996). Wilber's spectrum model of transpersonal psychology and its application to music therapy. *Journal of Music Therapy, 14,* 9–28.

Ruutel, E., & Tamm, S. (1995). Information sharing: Thoughts about music therapy possibilities in Estonia. *Music Therapy Perspectives, 13:*1, 51–52.

Sabbatella, P. (1999). The process of evaluation in music therapy clinical practice. 9th World Congress for Music Therapy, Washington, DC. Retrieved from E-Book of Articles, pp.

176–193.

Sabbatella, P. E. (2004). Assessment and clinical evaluation in music therapy: An overview from literature and Clinical practice. *Music Therapy Today* (online) Vol. V, Issue 1, available http://musictherapyworld.net

Sabbatella, P. (2004). Music therapy in Spain. *Voices: A World Forum for Music Therapy.* Retrieved March 31 2004, from: http://www.voices.no/country/monthspain_march2004 .html

Sabbatella, P. (2005). Music therapy training within the European higher education system: A survey on music therapy training courses in Spain. Proceedings of the 6th EMTC 2004 Conference, University of Jyyaskyla, Finland. *Music Therapy Today, 6*:4.

Sabbatella, P., & Mota, G. (2007). A model for music therapy training in Spain and Portugal according to the European higher education area. In 7th European Music Therapy Congress: Dialogues in Music Therapy, Veldhoeven, the Netherlands. Retrieved from: www.musictherapy2007.com

Sacks, O. (1985). *The man who mistook his wife for a hat and other clinical tales.* New York: Summit Books.

Sacks, O. (2007). *Musicophilia: Tales of music and the brain.* New York: Knopf.

Sandness, M. (1994). NAMT Standards and Procedures for Academic Program Approval. *Music Therapy Perspectives, 12*:1, 39–50.

Sandness, M. (2010). Personal communication.

San Vicente, P., Maranto. C. D., & Vodegel, F. (1993). The World Federation of Music Therapy and other international initiatives. In C. D. Maranto (Ed.), *Music therapy international perspectives,* pp. 677–680. Pipersville, PA: Jeffrey Books.

Scalenghe, R., & Murphy, K. (2000). Music therapy assessment in the managed care environment. *Music Therapy Perspectives,* 123–30.

Scartelli, J. (1989). A rationale for levels of certification in music therapy. *Music Therapy Perspectives, 7,* 93–95.

Scheiby, B. B. (1998). The role of music countertransference in analytical music therapy. In K. E. Bruscia (Ed.), *The dynamics of music psychotherapy,* pp. 213–248. Gilsum, NH: Barcelona Publishers.

Scheiby, B. B., & Pedersen, I. (1999). Intermusic therapy in the training of music therapy Students. *Nordic Journal of Music Therapy, 8*:1, 59–72.

Scheiby, B. B. (2001). Forming an identity as a music psychotherapist through analytical music therapy supervision. In M. Forinash (Ed.), *Music therapy supervision,* pp. 299–333. Gilsum, NH: Barcelona Publishers.

Scheiby, B. B. (2005). An intersubjective approach to music therapy: Identification and processing of musical countertransference in music psychotherapeutic context. *Music Therapy Perspectives, 23*:1, 8–17.

Scovel, M., & Gardstrom, S. (2002). Music therapy within the context of psychotherapeutic models. In R. Unkefer & M. Thaut (Eds.), *Music therapy in the treatment of adults with mental disorders: Theoretical bases and clinical information* (2nd ed.), pp. 117–132. Gilsum, NH: Barcelona Publishers.

Sears. W. W. (1968). Processes in music therapy. In E. T. Gaston (Ed.), *Music in therapy,* pp. 30–44. New York: Macmillan.

Sears, M. (Ed.). (2007). *Music: The therapeutic edge: Readings from William W. Sears.* Gilsum, NH: Barcelona Publishers.

Seidel, A. (2002). Heading towards internalisation. European comparison of state-approved studies of music therapy at master level. *Nordic Journal of Music Therapy, 11*:1, 54–60.

Sekeles, C. (1999). Music therapy training programs–Europe. 9th World Congress for Music

Therapy, Washington, DC. Retrieved from E-Book of Articles.

Sekeles, C. (2004). Music therapy in Israel. *Voices: A World Forum for Music Therapy*. Retrieved from: http://www.voices.no/country/monthisrael_November2004.html

Sekeles, C. (2005). Report from the European Music Therapy Confederation (EMTC). *The Arts in Psychotherapy*.

Sekeles, C. (2010). Personal communication.

Shatin, L., Kotter, W., & Longmore, G. (1968). Personality traits of music therapists. *Psychological Reports, 23:*2, 573–574.

Skinner, B. F. (1976). *About behaviorism*. New York: Vintage Books.

Silverman, M. J. (2006). Forty years of case studies: A history of clinical case studies in the *Journal of Music Therapy, Music Therapy* and *Music Therapy Perspectives. Music Therapy Perspectives, 24:*1, 4–12.

Silverman, M. J. (2010). Applying levels of evidence to the psychiatric music therapy literature base. *The Arts in Psychotherapy, 36:*1, 1–7.

Simpson, J., & Burns, D. (2008). *Music therapy reimbursement: Best practices and procedures*. Silver Spring, MD: AMTA.

Sloss, C. M. (1996). Cross-cultural music therapy in Canada. *Canadian Journal of Music Therapy, 4:*1, 1–18.

Smeijsters, H. (2003). Music therapy in the Netherlands. *Voices: A World Forum for Music Therapy*. Retrieved from: http://www.voices.no/country/monthnetherlands_september 2003.html

Smeijsters, H., & Vink, A. (2006). Research in practice. *Music Therapy Today*. Retrieved from: http://www.musictherapyworld.de/modules/mmmagazine/showarticle.php?articlet Oshow, 191

Smith, M. (2003). Music therapy in Brazil. *Voices: A World Forum for Music Therapy*. Retrieved from: http://www.voices.no/country/monthbrazil_april2003.html

Sokolov, L. (1987). Vocal improvisation therapy. In K. E. Bruscia (Ed.), *Improvisational models of music therapy*, pp. 353–359. Springfield, IL: Charles C Thomas.

Solomon, A., & Heller, G. (1982). Historical research in music: An important avenue for studying the profession. *Journal of Music Therapy, 19:*3, 161–178.

Solomon, A. (1993). A history of the *Journal of Music Therapy:* The first decade (1964–1973). *Journal of Music Therapy 30,* 3–33.

Soshensky, R. (2005). Developing a guitar-based approach in Nordoff-Robbins music therapy. *Music Therapy Perspectives, 23:*2, 11–117.

Southard, S. (1973). The process of student supervision. *Journal of Music Therapy, 10:*1, 27–35, 328–330.

Speth, F., Seifer, U., & Mainka, S. (2010). Repetitive sensorimotorical hand-function training for paretic upper extremities with multimodal feedback. Retrieved from: http://www .voices.no/mainissues/mi40008000295.php

Standley, J. M. (1985). An investigation of the relationship between selected characteristics, educational values, and teaching competencies of freshman music therapy majors. *Journal of Music Therapy, 22:*1, 2–11.

Standley, J. M. (1986). Music research in medical/dental treatment: Meta-analysis and clinical applications. *Journal of Music Therapy, 23,* 56–122.

Standley, J. M. (1989). A prospectus for the future of music therapy: Education standards, requirements, and professional designations. *Music Therapy Perspectives, 7,* 103–107.

Standley, J. (1991). *Music techniques in therapy, counseling and special education*. St. Louis, MO: MMB.

Standley, J., & Jones, J. (2007). *Music techniques in therapy, counseling and special education*. Silver

Spring, MD: American Music Therapy Association.

Standley, J. (2010). Verbal communication.

Standley, J. M. (2010b). Technology for contingent music to improve feeding of premature infants. Retrieved from: http://www.rhn.org.uk/nec_001.asp#cn1

Steele, A. L., & Young, S. (2008). A comparison of music education and music therapy majors: Personality types as described by the Myers-Briggs type indicator and demographic profiles. *Journal of Music Therapy,* Spring 2008, 2–21.

Steiner, R. (1977). *Eurhythmy as visible music.* London: Rudolf Steiner Press.

Steiner, R. (1983). *The inner nature of music and the experience of tone.* London: Rudolf Steiner Press.

Stephens, G. (1983). The use of improvisation in developing relatedness in the adult client. *Music Therapy: Journal of the American Association for Music Therapy, 3:*1, 29–42.

Stephens, G. (1984). Group supervision in music therapy. *Music Therapy, 4,* 29–38.

Stephens, G. (1987). The experiential music therapy group as a method of training and supervision. In C. D. Maranto & K. E. Bruscia (Eds.), *Perspectives on music therapy education and training,* pp. 169–176. Philadelphia: Temple University.

Stern, D. (1998). The process of therapeutic change involving implicit knowledge: Some implications of developmental observations for adult psychotherapy. *Infant Mental Health Journal. 10:*3, 300–308.

Stern, D. (1977). *The first relationship.* Cambridge, MA: Harvard University Press.

Stevenson, K. (2009). Millicent McIvor interviewed by Kathryn Stevenson. *Voices: A World Forum for Music Therapy.* Retrieved from: http://www.voices.no/mainissues/mi40009000 317.php

Stige, B. (2001). The fostering of not-knowing barefoot supervisors. In M. Forinash, *Music therapy supervision* (161–180). Gilsum, NH: Publishers.

Stige, B. (2002a). *Culture-centered music therapy.* Gilsum, NJ: Barcelona Publishers.

Stige, B. (2002b). The relentless roots of community music therapy. *Voices: A World Forum for Music Therapy.* Retrieved from: http://www.voices.no/mainissues/Voices2(3)Stige.html

Stige, B. (2005). Which academic education? *Voices: A World Forum for Music Therapy.* Retrieved from: http://www.voices.no/columnist/colstige040705.html

Stige, B., Ansdell, G., Elefant, C., & Pavlicevic, M. (2010). *Where music helps: Community music therapy in action and reflection.* Farnham, UK: Ashgate.

Stoltenberg C. D., McNeill B., & Delworth U. (1998). *IDM supervision: An integrated developmental model for supervising counselors and therapists.* San Francisco: Jossey-Bass Publishers.

Streeter, E. (2002). Some observations on music therapy training groups. In A. Davies & E. Richards (Eds.), *Music therapy and group work,* pp. 262–273. London, Jessica Kingsley Publishers.

Streeter, E. (2007). Reactions and responses from the music therapy community to the growth of computers and technology–Some preliminary thoughts. *Voices: A World Forum for Music Therapy.* Retrieved from: http://www.voices.no/mainissues/mi40007000227.php

Streeter, E. (2010). Do music therapists want to use computational music analysis for evaluating sessions? Proceedings, 8th European Music Therapy Congress. Cadiz, Spain.

Summers, L. (2001). Group supervision in first-time music therapy practicum. In M. Forinash (Ed.), *Music therapy supervision,* pp. 69–86. Gilsum: NH: Barcelona Publishers.

Sundar, S. (2006). How to introduce standards for competent music therapy, Education and training in countries where music therapy is in an early stage of development. *Voices: A World Forum for Music Therapy.* Retrieved from: http://www.voices.no/mainissues/mi4000 6000212.html

Tanguay, C. L. Supervising music therapy interns: A survey of AMTA national roster internship directors. *Journal of Music Therapy,* Spring 2008, 52–74.

Taylor, D. B. (1987). A survey of professional music therapists concerning entry level competencies. *Journal of Music Therapy, 24:*3, 114–145.

Ten Eyck, S. G. (1985). The effect of simulation and observation training on the music teaching behaviors of undergraduate music therapy/music education majors in a field teaching experience. *Journal of Music Therapy, 22:*4, 168–182.

Tennant, M. (1997). *Psychology and adult learning* (2nd ed.) London: Routledge.

Thaut, M., Kenyon, G., Schauer, M., & McIntosh, G. (1999). The connection between rhythmicity and brain function. *IIEE Engineering in Medicine and Biology,* 101–108.

Thaut, M. H., & Pederson, D. A. (2003). The role of theta and alpha EEG synchronizations in verbal learning with a musical template. *Proceedings of the Society for Neuroscience, 194,* 21.

Thaut, M. (2005). *Rhythm, music and the brain: Scientific foundations and clinical applications.* New York: Routledge.

Thomas, C. (2001). Student-centered internship supervision. In M. Forinash (Ed.), *Music therapy supervision,* 135–148.

Thompson, A. B., & Arnold, J. C. (1990). Music therapy assessment of the cerebrovascular accident patient. *Music Therapy Perspectives, 8,* 23–29.

Tims, F. (1989). Experiential learning in the music therapy curriculum. *Music Therapy Perspectives, 7,* 91–92.

Toppozda, M. R. (1995). Multicultural training for music therapists: An examination of current issues based on a national survey of professional music therapists. *Journal of Music Therapy, 32:*2, 65–90.

Trainor, L. J., Shahim, A., & Roberts, L. A. (2003). Effects of musical training on the auditory cortex in children. *Annals of the New York Academy of Sciences, 999,* 506–513.

Trevisan, A., & Jones, L. (2010). A low-end device to convert EEG waves to music. Retrieved from: http://www.voices.no/mainissues/mi40008000295.php

Tuepker, R. M. (2004). Morphological Music Therapy. In *Nordic Journal of Music Therapy, 13*(1) pp. 82–92.

Turry, A. (1998). Transference and countertransference in Nordoff-Robbins music therapy. In K. E. Bruscia (Ed.), *The dynamics of music psychotherapy,* pp. 161–212. Gilsum, NH: Barcelona Publishers.

Turry, A. (2001). Supervision in Nordoff-Robbins music therapy training program. In M. Forinash (Ed.), *Music therapy supervision,* 299–334.

Turry, A., & Marcus, D. (2005). Teamwork: Therapist and co -therapist in the Nordoff-Robbins approach to music therapy. *Music Therapy Perspectives, 23:*1, 53–69.

Tyler, H. (1999). Nordoff-Robbins training worldwide. 9th World Congress for Music Therapy, Washington, DC. Retrieved from E-Book of Articles, pp. 287–292.

Unkefer, R. F., & Thaut, M. H. (Eds.). (1995). *Music therapy in the treatment of adults with mental disorders: Theoretical bases and clinical information* (1st ed.). St. Louis: MMB Music, Inc.

Valentino, R. E. (2006). Attitudes toward cross-cultural empathy in music therapy. *Music Therapy Perspectives, 24:*2, 108–114.

VanWeelden, K., Juchniewicz, J., & Cevasco, A. M. (2004). Music therapy students' recognition of popular song repertoire for geriatric clients. *Journal of Music Therapy, 41:*1, 443–456.

VanWeelden, K., & Whipple, J. (2004). Effect of field experiences on music therapy students' perceptions of choral music for geriatric wellness programs. *Journal of Music Therapy, 41:*4, 340–352.

VanWeelden, K., & Cevasco, A. (2007). Repertoire recommendations by music therapists for geriatric clients during singing activities. *Music Therapy Perspectives, 25:*1, 4–12.

Varela, F. J. (1996). Neurophenomenology: A methodological remedy for the hard problem.

*Journal of Consciousness Studies, 3:(20)*4, 330–349.

Ventre, M. (2001). Supervision in the Bonny methods of guided imagery and music. In M. Forinash (Ed.), *Music therapy supervision,* pp. 335–350. Gilsum, NH: Barcelona Publishers.

Vink, A., & Smeijsters, H.. (2010). Personal communication.

Vogiatzoglou, A., Himonides, E., Ockelford, A., & Welch, G. (2010). *Sounds of intent: Software to gauge musical development in complex children.* Retrieved from: http://www.voices.no /mainissues/mi40008000295.php

Voyajolu, A. (2009). *The use of the music therapist's principal instrument in clinical practice.* Montclair State University, Unpublished Masters Thesis.

Vygotsky, L. (1978). *Mind in society.* London: Harvard University Press.

Wagner, G. P. (2010). Personal communication.

Watkins Jr., C. R. (Ed.). (1997). *Handbook of psychotherapy supervision.* New York: J. Wiley.

Watson, R. (2005). Steering a path through change: Observations on the process of training. *British Journal of Music Therapy, 19:*1, 9–15.

Watts, T. D. (1984). Information services and the music therapy curriculum. *Music Therapy Perspectives, 1:*3, 18–20.

Wallius, R. (2008). The association for music therapy in Sweden. In A. Paulander (Ed.), *Music therapy in Sweden. Voices: A World Forum for Music Therapy.* Retrieved from: http://www .voices.no/country/monthsweden_june2008.php

Webster, J. (2005). Music therapy training: A personal experience. *British Journal of Music Therapy, 19:*1, 18–19.

Wetherick, D., & Brand, G. (2010). The musical training of music therapists–is it fit for purpose? Anglia Ruskin University–The Music of Music Therapy Conference, Cambridge, UK.

Wheeler, B. L. (1983). A psychotherapeutic classification of music therapy practices: A continuum of procedures. *Music Therapy Perspectives, 1*(2), 8–16.

Wheeler, B. L. (1987). Levels of therapy: The classification of music therapy goals. *Music Therapy–The Journal of the AAMT, 6:*2, 39–49.

Wheeler, B. L. (1988). An analysis of literature from selected music therapy journals. *Music Therapy Perspectives, 5,* 94–101.

Wheeler, B. L. (Ed.). (1995). *Music therapy research: Quantitative and qualitative perspectives.* Gilsum, NH: Barcelona Publishers.

Wheeler, B. L. (1999). WMFT Proceedings of the education symposium. 9th World Congress for Music Therapy, Washington, DC. Retrieved from E-Book of Articles.

Wheeler, B. L. (2000). Music therapy practicum practices: A survey of music therapy educators. *Journal of Music Therapy, 4,* 286–311.

Wheeler, B. L., & Grocke, D. E. (2001). Report from the World Federation of Music Therapy Commission on Education, Training, and Accreditation Education. *Music Therapy Perspectives, 19:*1, 63–67.

Wheeler, B. L. (2002). Experiences and concerns of students during music therapy practica. *Journal of Music Therapy, 39:*4, 274–304.

Wheeler, B. L. (2003a). First international symposium on music therapy training: A retrospective examination. *Nordic Journal of Music Therapy, 12:*1, 54–66.

Wheeler, B. L., Shultis, C. L., & Polen, D. W. (2005). *Clinical training guide for the student music therapist.* Gilsum, NH: Barcelona Publishers.

Wheeler, B. L. (Ed.). (2009). Memories from the World Congress of Music Therapy, July 1983. *Voices: A World Forum for Music Therapy.* Retrieved from: http://www.voices.no /mainissues/mi40009990339.php

Wigram, T. (1999). Qualifications of music therapy educators. 9th World Congress for Music

Therapy, Washington, DC. Retrieved from E-Book of Articles, pp. 323–348.

Wigram, T., Pedersen, I. N., & Bonde, L. O. (2002). *A comprehensive guide to music therapy– Theory, clinical practice, research and training.* London: JKP.

Wigram, T. (2004). *Improvisation: Methods and techniques for music therapy clinicians.* London: JKP.

Wigram, T. (2009). Supervision of PhD doctoral research. In H. Odell-Miller & E. Richards (Eds.), *Supervision of music therapy: A theoretical and practical handbook,* pp. 173–192. London, UK: Routledge.

Wolberg, L. (1977). *The technique of psychotherapy* (3rd ed.). Oxford: Grune & Stratton.

Wolery, M., Gessler Werts, M., & Holcombe, A. (1994). Current practices with young children who have disabilities: Placement, assessment, and instruction issues. *Focus on Exceptional Children, 26*(6), 1–12.

Wolfe, D. (1987). Computer based decision making: contemporary tasks for practicum students and professionals. In C. D. Maranto & K. E. Bruscia (Eds.), *Perspectives on music therapy education and training,* pp. 137–148. Philadelphia, PA: Temple University.

Wolfe, D., O'Connell, A., & Epps, K. (1998). A content analysis of therapist's verbalizations during group music therapy: Implications for the training of music therapists. *Music Therapy Perspectives, 16*:1, 13–20.

World Federation of Music Therapy–WFMT. (1999). Guidelines for Music Therapy Education and Training. 9th World Congress for Music Therapy, Washington, DC. Retrieved from E-Book of Articles, p. 355.

Wosch, T. (2003a). Music therapy in Germany. *Voices: A World Forum for Music Therapy.* Retrieved from http://www.voices.no/country/monthgermany_march2003.html

Wosch, T. (2003b). The same procedure as every year–Musicality and music therapy. *Voices: A World Forum for Music Therapy.* Retrieved from: http://www.voices.no/columnist/col wosch270103.html

Wosch, T. (2003c). Are ten books enough?–Pluralism and tempo in music therapy education. *Voices: A World Forum for Music Therapy.* Retrieved from: http://www.voices.no/columnist /colwosch180703.html

Wosch, T. (2005). Which academic education in music therapy do we need? *Voices: A World Forum for Music Therapy.* Retrieved from: http://www.voices.no/columnist/colwosch 060605.htm

Wosch, T. (2010). Personal communication.

Wright, L. M. (1992). A levels system approach to structuring and sequencing prepractica musical and clinical competencies in a university music therapy clinic. *Music Therapy Perspectives, 10,* 36–44.

Wyatt, J. G., & Furioso, M. (2000). Music therapy education and training: A survey of master's level music therapists. *Music Therapy Perspectives, 18*:2, 103–109.

Yalom, I. (1995). *The theory and practice of group psychotherapy* (4th ed.). New York: Basic.

York, E. (1994). The development of a quantitative music skills tests for patients with Alzheimer's disease. *The Journal of Music Therapy, 31*(4), 280–296.

Young, L. (2009). Multicultural issues encountered in the supervision of music therapy internships in the United States and Canada. *The Arts in Psychotherapy, 36,* 191–201.

Young, L., & Aigen, K. (2009). Supervising the supervisor: The use of live music and identification of parallel processes. *The Arts in Psychotherapy, 37*:1, 125–134.

Zanchi, B., & Suvini, F. (2004). Perspective of music therapy in Italy: Past, present and future: A search for a national identity. In D. Aldridge, J. Fachner & J. Erkkilä (Eds.), Many faces of music therapy, Proceedings of the 6th European Music Therapy Congress, June 16–20, 2004 Jyväskylä, Finland (p. 1686–1695). EBook (PDF available at MusicTherapy

Today.com Vol. 6. Issue 4 (November 2005) Retrieved from: http://www.musictherapy world.de/modules/mmmagazine/issues/downloads/Proceedings_eBook.pdf

Zigo, J. B. (2010). Personal communication.

NAME INDEX

SUBJECT INDEX

ABOUT THE AUTHOR

Karen D. Goodman, Professor of Music Therapy at the John J. Cali School of Music, Montclair State University, is credentialed as a music therapist, a creative arts therapist, and a special education teacher. She has served as the Director of Music Therapy Programs at Montclair State for over two decades.

She received her Bachelors in English Literature from the University of Wisconsin–Madison, her music therapy certification from Montclair State University, her full fellowship Master of Science in Special Education from Hunter College–City University of New York, and her post-graduate training in neurology, child psychology, and music from New York University. She is trained as a pianist and vocalist and was drawn to music therapy through her introductory training in the Nordoff-Robbins approach.

Professor Goodman, the recipient of 22 research awards related to her ongoing clinical work, research and teaching, presents and publishes on a range of topics

323

including the following: projective music therapy assessment, developmental theory relative to music therapy, considerations in group music therapy, sensory integration, the use of poetry and music in treatment and the reflective model of teaching music therapy students.

Professor Goodman has published an original assessment based on her work with emotionally disturbed children, served as editor of *Music Therapy–The Journal of the A.A.M.T.* and written the seminal chapter on music therapy in *The American Handbook of Psychiatry*. She represented the music therapy discipline on the Advisory Board of The Creativity Foundation founded by Dr. Silvano Arieti as well as the Advisory Board of The Center for Parents and Children founded by Dr. Judith Kestenberg.

In addition to her national and international presentations at music therapy conferences, Professor Goodman serves as senior clinician to the music therapy clinic at the John J. Cali School of Music, provides music therapy assessment to multiple school districts in New Jersey, consults to The University of Medicine and Dentistry–New Jersey, and provides internal book review services for Oxford University Press and Pearson Higher Eduction.

Prior to this book, she published *Music Therapy Groupwork with Special Needs Children: The Evolving Process,* which garnered international praise.

In writing this book, *Music Therapy Education and Training: From Theory to Practice,* Professor Goodman draws from teaching 31 courses throughout the undergraduate and graduate music therapy curriculum as well as coursework in psychology, creative arts therapy and music.